W9-AXO-726

Business in American Life

A History

BUSINESS IN AMERICAN LIFE: A History

by

THOMAS C. COCHRAN

Benjamin Franklin Professor Emeritus of History
University of Pennsylvania

McGraw-Hill Book Company

New York • St. Louis • San Francisco • Paris • Düsseldorf
Tokyo • Mexico • Montreal • Panama • São Paulo • Toronto

Copyright © 1972 by McGraw-Hill, Inc. All Rights Reserved.
Printed in the United States of America. No part of this publication
may be reproduced, stored in a retrieval system, or transmitted, in any
form or by any means, electronic, mechanical, photocopying, recording,
or otherwise, without prior written permission of the publisher.

Library of Congress Cataloging in Publication Data

Cochran, Thomas Childs, 1902-
    Business in American Life.

    Includes bibliographical references.
    1. U.S.–Commerce–History. I. Title.
HF3021.C55   917.3'03   78-38740
ISBN 0-07-011525-7

123456789 MUMU 7987654

First McGraw-Hill Paperback Edition, 1974

To my wife,
Rosamond B. Cochran

Contents

Part III

INDUSTRIALISM, 1850 - 1915

Part IV

AFFLUENCE, 1915 - 1970

Preface

This book was in preparation for many years and, during that time, benefitted from the aid and cooperation of numerous institutions and many scholars, experts, and authorities on diverse specialized aspects of the development of American business. The manuscript was initially undertaken as the natural extension of the Walgreen Lectures delivered at the University of Chicago in 1957. Subsequent work was assisted and encouraged by conferences supported by McGraw-Hill Book Company: these conferences ultimately led to the plan for a three-volume series including, as well as the present work, volumes by Alfred D. Chandler, Jr. on the development of management, and by Arthur H. Cole and Irene D. Neu on the structure of the business system in our society. *Business in American Life* is the first of the three volumes to appear. My work has also benefited from research assistance provided by the American Philosophical Society and the University of Pennsylvania.

I want to acknowledge my appreciation and indebtedness not only to my three colleagues mentioned above, but also to Louis Galambos, William Miller, James T. Patterson, and Charles E. Rosenberg for reading the manuscript and making many valuable suggestions; to Lee Benson, Richard S. Dunn, Mary Maples Dunn, Arnold M. Paul, Carol Smith Rosenberg, Robert Zemsky, and Michael Zuckerman, who have all been helpful in commenting on various chapters; and to my wife, Rosamond B. Cochran, who as always has been a continuous research assistant and constructive critic.

Research for the book was completed in 1969, and because of the wide scope of the synthesis, no extensive effort has been made to include references to each of the relevant books that has appeared in the interim. In no case would these cause one to significantly alter the factual exposition or modify the generalizations presented in this volume.

THOMAS C. COCHRAN

Radnor, Pennsylvania

Business in American Life

Introduction:
A New Focus on American History

Commenting on American society around the end of the nineteenth century, foreign and domestic pundits were impressed by the uniquely important position of business. Herbert Spencer spoke of Americans' "sole interest—the interest in business."[1] Lord Bryce saw preoccupation with business as the result of extraordinary material development. "It is natural," he wrote, "that in the United States, business . . . should have come more and more to overshadow and dwarf all other interests, all other occupations . . . Business is king."[2] A few years later Woodrow Wilson said, "Business underlies everything in our national life."[3] Yet, historical tradition, as illustrated in Wilson's own writing, led to an interpretation not built around this sole, underlying or regnant theme, but rather one centered on national politics.

While it is true that in earlier periods of American history the preoccupation with business, as conventionally interpreted, was less extensive, there were still longer periods in which national government was either nonexistent or relatively unimportant.[4] In the nearly four hundred years of American history, business would seem to have been as continuously present and important as any social institution other than the family and its social or religious rituals.

Dictionaries apply the word "business" to any type of occupation, activity, or serious concern. This makes the meaning too broad to designate a particular kind of social force. Business historians and economists confine the term to "decision making by individuals seeking private profit through production of goods and services."[5] Some of those speaking of "business" before the nineteenth century undoubtedly had in mind the classic or dictionary breadth of meaning, although almost always the specialized latter-day activity for profit was included. The limited definition of "activity for private profit" will be used in this book, but it will be applied to all operations where pecuniary gain is the principal motive. Thus a nearly self-sufficient farmer buying and selling land was a part-time businessman, as was the Southern planter managing slaves to produce a staple crop for foreign markets. These agrarians, to be sure, tended to be "hedonistic" entrepreneurs, anxious to make money but not giving their full attention to its pursuit, in contrast to the more "rational" capitalism of merchants who gave most of their attention to plans for monetary gain.

A DIFFERENT SYNTHESIS

In considering the elements in past social change, there are some positive advantages in focusing attention on the institutions of business. Democratic government, for instance, is an institution with a rigidly defined hierarchy of power and with periodic rhythms; these characteristics readily lead to the writing of a coherent internal narrative that may have little reference to underlying or gradual social change. In contrast, the institutions of business are inextricably intertwined with their social environment and can be satisfactorily interpreted only in relation to other institutions.

This book, therefore, is presented not as a comprehensive interpretation of our history, but rather as one synthesized around a single institution, in this case business rather than politics. Inasmuch as the political narratives have conventionally been regarded as general in scope, the same may be claimed for the present synthesis. There are, however, some major historiographical difficulties in making this shift in emphasis. Political development and many of its relations with institutional change have been the subjects of countless monographs and general histories. Only occasionally can any interpretation either aspire to being really new or risk being wholly erroneous. History of the relation of business to its environment, however, has only recently attracted scholars. Monographic literature is sparse at best and completely lacking in many important areas.

For this reason an initial attempt at an overall synthesis must be suggestive rather than comprehensive; the institutions dealt with have to be limited to those generally regarded as basic to social change; and much descriptive background has to be supplied. Because of these difficulties, this account deals only with business influences on family life, education, religion, law, politics, conditions of employment, and the general social structure. Even within these limitations, little illustrative detail or narrative can be included in a one-volume study of such long and complicated processes.

In each of the four periods into which the book is divided, the major developments within business will be shown in relation to the social and physical environment. These chapters will be followed by others, systematically suggesting some of the influences of business on the various selected institutions. In making such analyses for different periods, it is helpful to use a consistent theoretical framework, which will be described briefly in the remainder of this chapter. But in the rest of the book, theory is always kept in the background; the reader who prefers to skip this analytical section will not be at a disadvantage in understanding subsequent chapters.

A PARADIGM FOR SOCIAL CHANGE

A broadly acceptable descriptive paradigm is possible because all of the basic forces, such as demographic or technological change, operate in society by altering the behavior or policies of individuals, and also because the behavioral sciences, at least, all use role theory to describe such activity.[6] The explanatory system, therefore, is focused on role playing as the central process involved in social change, and relates other social elements to roles in a systematic way. Business activities are a type of role behavior, and hence such theory goes immediately to the core of change related to business practices.[7] The paradigm has proved highly useful, therefore, in organizing the data of business history.

To state the theory in simple terms, each person is assumed to behave in the job or status he occupies in ways normal or conventional in that society.* Each such pattern of behavior is a social role. Both normal playing of the role or any change in it will depend on the personality of the player or actor, the resources in knowledge and social institutions available to him, and the pressures upon him from other people involved in the activity. In applying the paradigm to business in American life, the focus will be on how existing business roles were altered by new social environments and innovations and how business institutions reacted upon American society.

The conventional way to play roles such as carpentering, for example, is passed on from generation to generation, and constitutes habits or institutions (recognized, repetitive patterns of behavior) that are accepted without question by most men plying the trade. Perception of how the role of carpenter should be carried out is limited by common education, values, and aims. But once in a while some new element in the role-playing situation will cause a change. The disturbing force may be some unusual knowledge that leads the carpenter to perceive that lighter material will satisfy the needs of the structure, or it may be a desire to get the work done faster with different joining of members which impels him to break with the anticipated or institutional practice. The cause of deviation may also be an external change, such as having to build in a new area with wood instead of stone. If the role player is in a professional field, such as law, he may have been conditioned to see certain new aspects of cases more clearly than his colleagues and be able to convince judges and his legal peers of the importance of his view. If he wins, it is usually because the environment favors his innovation; modification of the English land law in the colonies was such an instance.[8]

Roles tend to change from many inward differences in individuals and outward causes, and if they were not held in place to some extent by men wanting to perpetuate habitual social institutions, it would be impossible to anticipate results from one performance of an operation to the next. The most immediate guardians of stability are those that have directly to accept or reject the performance of the role. In the first example above, these groups would be fellow carpenters, the builder for whom the innovator works, and the client who

---

* Some sociologists define value as an idea of rightness applicable to any situation, while a "norm" refers to the conception of the right way within the general value context to perform a particular action. "Learning" means the stock of ideas applicable to problems.

is paying for the building. These people are collectively called the actor's role-set. While the different members vary in their power to reject the innovation (their sanctioning force), most men try to please as many of them as possible, in the order of their sanctioning power.

Thus roles and role-sets constitute the institutionalized patterns of behavior that make up the relatively stable social structure. But since, ultimately, almost all institutions bear upon each other—business on the school, the school on the family, the family on the church, and so on—change at some rate is continuous. From the mere eccentricities of nature transmitted through the genes, and the uniqueness of each individual's conditioning, somebody is always deviating from a role, changing the ideas of some part of his role-set, and thus altering, however slightly, the institutional behavior.

The social mechanism of change is not a one-way process. A new idea spread quickly and widely, as by a generally read newspaper, may alter the desires of role-sets, who will then ask certain role players to do things differently. Presumably the role player has also read the paper and perhaps readily agrees. History is a record of changing fads, fashions, and convictions, often of obscure origin, that alter social institutions.

Efforts to adjust to *zeitgeists* are, of course, in themselves a source of further change, but in addition a physically developing society presents novel situations; for example, in a new town or industry the expectations of both the role player and the role-set are relatively undefined or opportunistic. While all parties will proceed on the basis of past knowledge and former roles, innovation is likely. It will, however, be conditioned by the norms, values, and learning the people bring with them and not be merely random. Throughout American history the highest rate of migration of any modern nation, both westward and from country to city, has been a continual cause of such uncertainties and innovations.[9] The same reasoning accounts for the greater likelihood of innovation in young rather than old societies and explains why stability breeds stability and change induces change.

Some of the institutional relationships within the business system help to explain the character of its influence on social change. To begin with, in trying to create economically valuable goods or services, entrepreneurs can only employ the physical resources available to them, and to this extent business practices depend on technology. This seemingly simple statement, however, has complex corollaries. The entrepreneur innovating in his role, for example, may alter existing technology in either physical or procedural ways, while a new technology, introduced by a few innovators, may leave other businessmen struggling frantically to adjust their roles to the new conditions.

The history of entrepreneurship in America and elsewhere suggests that relatively static technology tends to develop firmly defined, noninnovative social roles for its entrepreneurs. In such situations there may be strong sanctions by the role-set against any important change. This stagnation may be reenforced if the entrepreneurs carrying on the business are dependent for financing on other men who are neither stimulated nor challenged by any changes in the immediate situation. Thus conservative Eastern bankers were unsympathetic to the innovative needs of the early automotive entrepreneurs, and in an earlier day, London merchants opposed risky innovations on the part of their colonial correspondents.

A similar situation has often characterized a declining industry. It declines because its particular technology and procedures no longer properly satisfy economic needs; this results, in turn, in declining profits, general attitudes of caution and pessimism on the part of entrepreneurs, and difficulty in recruiting new men of ability. Hence there is likely to be a speeding-up of the rate of decline, as with railroads in the twentieth century, beyond that made necessary by the best employment of existing resources. On the other hand, a rapidly changing technology is generally accompanied by the reverse of these symptoms. New and able entrepreneurs are attracted, and technological innovation suggests to such men the possibilities of new ways of playing their managerial roles.

Regardless of whether technology is dynamic or static in a particular activity, entrepreneurs are inclined to be wary of external political or social change. Unless such change is essential to their success, they would sooner make their plans on some other basis, nonbusiness matters "being equal." This does not mean that the entrepreneurs of a rapidly growing and changing type of business are as likely to be conservative regarding external problems as those in a declining one; the latter are usually less used to thinking along any new lines and have less confidence about meeting new challenges. But although either group may be major initiators of social change, both would prefer a stable social environment.

A further consideration is that type and scale of activity also have affected entrepreneurs' relations with their environment. A man whose commitments are short term does not have to fear the effects of the long-run possibility of adverse conditions as much as one whose investment has to be amortized over many years. Hence, unpredictable or irresponsible governments retard the growth of manufacturing more than trade, and men in trade are more likely to be indifferent to gradual politico-social change.

Business institutions affect the rest of society in a seemingly infinite number of ways. Since the function of business is the control of productive technology, it may alter the physical conditions of life by market-oriented decisions that take no account of social effects. In a developing nation such as the United States, business decisions, usually in an unplanned way, have been the most important source of physical Change. During much of American history, such change was accepted as both desirable and inevitable, as part of the working of the laws of nature. Only with the exhaustion of resources toward the end of the nineteenth century was there serious discussion of a reversal of the process.

Another continuing social impact of business has been its usefulness as the chief avenue to success and social prestige. This meant that many parents wanted to make their children businesslike, and that many young men wanted to acquire the information and habits that would aid them in the pursuit of business. Since culture is most deeply imbibed in youth, making material success a goal may have been the most important influence of business.

But in addition to reshaping the physical environment and inspiring youth, businessmen were citizens and neighbors whose ideas and ways of doing things spread by the usual social mechanisms: the influence of institutions (based on social roles) upon each other, largely through interpersonal relationships. While businessmen, to be sure, had unusual ability to influence society through the use of newspapers, advertising, and later mass media, as well as by manipulating politics, innovating business influences probably spread through much the same personal and institutional channels as other social change.

THE SERIES AS A CHALLENGE

While the effects of innovation and the environment on the nature of business roles will be discussed briefly in the first one or two chapters of each chronological division, or part, the main emphasis of this book will be on the effects of business roles and their institutional forms on change in the rest of society. Two companion volumes, one written by Arthur H. Cole and Irene Neu on the structure of the system, and one by Alfred D. Chandler, Jr., on the development of management will give more details on the internal history of business. These two volumes will add greatly to our specialized knowledge; the present one is a more general brief for a new emphasis.

Behind the planning of the series is the supposition that if a relatively free enterprise capitalism, or even a "mixed system," is to be the economic mode of the future, it needs to be guided, more than it has been, by knowledge of the mistakes and successes of the past, and of the interrelations of the parts of society to each other. The better informed leaders of the future should be able to assess the part that business has played in American society with a greater degree of objectivity and understanding and be aware of the intricacy of the causes of social change.

Part I

HERITAGE, 1607-1775

CHAPTER 1

Business in a New Environment

By the early seventeenth century London had produced wealthy merchants with capital ready for investment in large ventures. Intermarrying with the gentry, these men had been favorably recognized and partly absorbed in those governing circles that in the twentieth century came to be referred to as the Establishment. Having seen some unpleasant experiences with the problems of colonization, such as those of Sir Walter Raleigh and his "lost colony," men like Sir John Popham, lord chief justice of the King's Bench, Sir Thomas Smith, head of the East India Company, and Sir Ferdinando Gorges, governor of the fort at Plymouth on the English coast, saw that individual ventures would continue to be inadequate. Colonization, wrote the latter, had been "founde fatall to all interprices hitherto undertaken by reason of delaies, jeloces and unwillingness to back that project that succeeded not on the first attempt."[1]

COLONIZATION AS BUSINESS

Consequently these men with experience and government influence sought the aid of substantial merchants who were also anxious to exploit the opportunities of the Western world through the relatively new device of the chartered stock company. This combination of aristocratic landed politicians and urban capitalists sought to harness some of the new ventures in various types of overseas trade into a focused attempt at permanent colonial development. "America could hardly have been settled at this time," wrote Charles Andrews, "had not the period of occupation coincided with the era of capitalism in the first full flush of its power, an era, the origin of which dates from Elizabeth's reign and of which we of the twentieth century may be witnessing the transformation or the end."[2]

Guided by the views of the new capitalists, as well as by lack of pressure for any other course, the British government adopted a favorable, but disinterested, attitude toward colonial settlement. Instead of protective military posts, royal administrators, and state-financed exploration and colonization, the crown turned the job of colony building over to the corporate entrepreneurs. The latter set up chartered stock companies whose shareholders hoped for a reasonably quick profit from the operation. The government left them alone to succeed or fail on the capitalist basis of producing goods and finding a profitable market.

In their search for profit the chartered companies turned to the unoccupied coast of North America, where they settled Virginia and parts of New England in the early seventeenth century. The initial costs of colonization and the hazards of early development proved far greater than estimated, and in no instance did companies pay dividends to their English investors. Within a generation, colonization companies had lost favor as business investments.

The crown continued to depend on private acquisitive enterprise, however, rather than government-financed settlement. The latter royal policy was to grant large tracts of land, such as Maine or New Jersey, to individuals or small groups of proprietors who had the right to govern and exploit, subject to certain restrictions. Each of the proprietors hoped to profit from the sale of the land to settlers, but it was also highly prestigious to be such a great landlord. In addition, the Calverts of Maryland and the Penns in Pennsylvania and Delaware were interested in aiding their coreligionists.

Like the stockholders of the chartered colonization companies, most of the initial proprietors made no profit from their land, and for much the same reasons. They were unwilling or unable to invest the large amounts of capital and energy necessary for founding a new settlement, to wait a generation for returns, and to administer their efforts personally in America rather than from London. As a result, in all cases save Maryland, Pennsylvania, and Delaware, the unsuccessful ventures were surrendered to the crown.

The other important seventeenth-century colonizing efforts on the Eastern seaboard were Dutch and Swedish business ventures. Largely inspired by hopes of profit from the fur trade, the Dutch settled in the Hudson Valley, and the Swedes established trading posts on the Delaware. Both ventures were taken over by an English military expedition in 1664.

Despite the general failure of private enterprise to profit from seventeenth-century ventures in colonial settlement, the effect of such origins on American institutions should not be overlooked. The great majority of colonists came for neither the glory of God nor the British Empire, but to benefit themselves. They came also on the basis of contracts for land or indentures for labor drawn up with various types of colonial promoters, and when they arrived, they became parts of societies whose leaders, save for an occasional early-day religious enthusiast, were thinking in terms of expansion and material advancement. Even in Puritan Massachusetts a Marblehead fisherman reproved a too strongly exhorting preacher with the remark "Our ancestors came not here for religion. Their main end was to catch fish!"[3] Regardless of why they came to America, all settlers had one trait in common—they were migrants.

THE COLONIAL SITUATION

A high rate of migration, both into and within the country was a major element in creating an American culture different from that of any of the older

Western nations in ways favorable to the needs of business. While the proportions of the two types of movement have altered from time to time, by the mid-twentieth century the total rate of migration was still higher in the United States than in the British Isles, Europe, or Latin America.

New colonies inevitably have the economic and social characteristics of areas of rapid in-migration. Because migration, particularly long-range movement, appeals chiefly to the young male, the people in the new area are more physically vigorous and less burdened by family obligations than in areas which the migrants are leaving. Recent tests have indicated the probability that migrants have a higher average intelligence than people of the same status left behind. Whether this is invariably true or not, the very fact of migration indicates a certain degree of discontent with the familiar environment and enough vigor and imagination to seek a way out. Alienation from the home environment might indicate nothing more than a neurotic personality, but probably social groups discontented because of religious beliefs or some other set of values differing from those held by the majority are particularly likely to be agents of social change.[4] Such migrants were driven to ask questions that other men had no need to raise.[5]

Thus, migration to a new, unsettled country produced many of the effects on the individual that social scientists have associated with "modern" rather than "traditional" societies. The settler was forced to modify his previously conditioned patterns of action when he found that they worked improperly in the new situation. Thrown in with strangers, he was not sure what their responses would be to his customary behavior. In addition, he might also occupy a social status with which he was unfamiliar. Thus these factors, which in the usual studies of social change are attributed to technological advance and contact with people from other national cultures, were present to some extent throughout the colonial period, even though there was little change in technology, and the local population remained largely British.

The cultivation of pragmatic or businesslike values was another social characteristic engendered by colonial conditions. The early hardships of colonial life in a wilderness populated only by savages made inexorable demands on settlers. Regardless of social backgrounds or religious beliefs, men had to meet the problems of the world in a somewhat practical way in order to survive. Hence, the initial rigors of migration and settlement emphasized successful economic behavior at the expense of ceremonies and traditions, an attitude that, in America at least, came to be regarded by future generations as businesslike. Similarly, initial lack of local historic traditions, hereditary aristocracy, or other privileged orders removed some of the most powerful obstacles to economic and social change.

One should not, however, picture a society open to any type of change. All societies are in some respects traditional, and in the early colonies, family relations, religious rites, occupations, technology, and social ethics were all deeply affected by the habits carried from England or Europe. The difference was in the strength of the challenge to traditions that had developed in other environments. On occasion, powerful American forces "broke the cake of custom" by frontal attack, as in the case of seventeenth-century laws dealing with the sale of land (Chapter 3); probably more often, however, social customs were subtly changed in spite of the belief that the old ways were being preserved, as in child rearing (Chapter 2).

Furthermore, against the forces encouraging innovation, economic development, and social change in the colonies, there were retarding factors peculiar to America, as well as others shared with Western Europe. By later standards, economic development, even in the most favored areas of the world, was slow. The colonial home market, particularly in the seventeenth century, was small and relatively poor. The English and European markets were larger, but too distant, too competitive, and too regulated for the Americans to invade except with raw materials and food products. English and European industrialization still depended largely on the poorly paid labor of skilled craftsmen which America lacked. People in remote provincial societies, weak in intellectual and political leadership, were inclined to treasure, as far as possible, some of the customs of their former life, and to fear that some social changes would lead away from civilization; this tendency worked against ready innovation. Many writers have noted that as the colonists acquired financial means, they sought to imitate European practices, particularly those of the upper class, and that colonial businessmen conformed, only partly from necessity, to established English practice. Carl Bridenbaugh remarks "With the possible exception of Philadelphia's eighteenth century prison," there was "hardly a single example of the development by one town of a unique institution."[6]

From 1651 on, successive British navigation acts laid restrictions on certain manufactures, exports, and directions of trade, while other acts provided bounties for cultivation of desired raw materials such as indigo and supplies for shipbuilding. The restrictive laws, not regularly enforced before 1763, probably retarded colonial business development more in theory than in fact. While domestic manufacturing may have been hindered, export trade, particularly in timber, naval supplies, tobacco, rice, and indigo, probably benefitted. The relatively low level of industrialization in colonial America was less the result of English regulations than of lack of capital, small markets, opportunities in farming, scarcity of skilled handicraft labor, and lack of machines.

THE MIGRANTS

While economic opportunities in America attracted ambitious young men, developments in the Old World made such men willing to leave. Population and wealth were gradually increasing in England, and farming land was even harder to acquire than in earlier times.[7] With successful artisans and merchants bidding for land in order to gain social status, the impecunious younger sons of yeoman farmers had little chance of securing a workable tract. Even farmers on long leaseholds were likely to be squeezed out by higher rents when leases expired. Hence, a large proportion of early emigrants appear to have been farmers of the "middling classes."[8] A somewhat similar squeeze was operating in the skilled crafts. Associations of craftsmen in the major British towns limited their membership, largely on an hereditary basis, leaving little chance for younger sons or outsiders to become masters.

For either farmers or artisans, migration to the colonies under forms of indenture offered a way to new opportunity. While the general form of such an agreement was indentured servitude, one must not be misled into thinking of this as demeaning. Almost all craftsmen and many farmers bound their children out as apprentices, often for seven-year terms. It was the usual way of learning how to do things—even housekeeping. Consequently, rather than adventure to America on their own, the unattached men or women chose what was, by eighteenth-century standards, the conservative, reasonable course; they bound themselves for a four- or five-year term in return for passage to the colonies and a terminal payment in land or money. A majority of the colonial immigrants appear to have come as single men or women, perhaps three-quarters being men, from eighteen to twenty-four years of age under terms of indenture.[9] That it was not unusual in the seventeenth century for both English males and females to still be unmarried at twenty-four is indicated by Peter Laslett's analysis of parish records. Probably many of these migrants had already served one apprenticeship.[10] Some indentured servants were children, and some were convicts accepting "transportation" in place of punishment, but these two groups were a small percentage of the total.[11]

The minority who paid for their passage were probably older farmers or shopkeepers who had sold property and often brought servants as well as capital with them. In all, migrants appear to have represented middle-income, skilled portions of the British population, the strata from which businessmen were probably drawn, while common laborers were a minority. It is not surprising in view of the terrific rigors of the ocean trip, which often killed the weak or sickly, that one merely looking for menial work would not be tempted. In other words, migrants were generally ambitious young people seeking to better themselves, rather than those squeezed out by sheer lack of the necessities of life. This pattern also conforms with present studies of migration showing that, up to relatively high levels, the tendency to move increases with income.[12]

The tendency to have careers dependent upon family connections is strong in stable agricultural and trading societies. Benjamin Franklin noted that his "family has lived in the same village for three hundred years, and how much longer he knew not . . . on a freehold of about thirty acres, aided by the smith's business . . . the eldest son being always bred to that business."[13] Such institutionalized nepotism inevitably interferes with rational fitting of men to jobs. Entire families seldom moved, and migration almost always broke the pattern of local kinship.* With each succeeding generation in the colonies,

---

* Relatives living near each other should not be confused with an extended family living in one house (see Laslett, *World*, 90-94).

further migrations inland tended to limit to a few older areas the reemergence of extensive kinship systems. Without such neighboring family support and guidance, self-help and individual initiative became more necessary. Since the European aristocracies were built on family connections, the lack of these connections in most of the new settlements automatically started American society on a more democratic base. Most colonial immigrants brought little with them and initially favored equality. Also, since in many areas they came from different churches, they were usually led to support a degree of religious toleration.

Thus in the colonies business and other social institutions were all influenced, initially at least, by the usual characteristics of areas of in-migration. Seen in this way, the important element was not sparcity of population in the colonies or on the colonial frontier, but rather the large number of new in-migrants in relation to the more settled population.

BUSINESS AND AGRICULTURE IN THE NORTH

The flow of migrants into the colonies continually raised the price of good land. To most men with money, land seemed by far the safest investment, and they all, whether farmers, artisans, or merchants, became dealers in back-country tracts, farms, or town lots. In modern terms, real estate was the ubiquitous business of America, and it remained so far into the industrial age.

The ease with which land could be bought and sold was reflected in the methods and attitudes of American farmers, making a greater contrast between farm life than between city life in Europe and America. Consequently, colonial farmers steadily making up over four-fifths of the labor force, may collectively have been more important agents in the development of a businesslike culture than the relatively few artisans or merchants.

A major difference from either England or continental Europe appears to have been that in America the farmer had no sentimental, hereditary attachment to the particular plot of land that he initially acquired and had no fear of difficulty in buying more in a new locality. Hence, acreage bought cheaply in fee simple might be sold within a few years at a higher price. Although this ready means of acquiring more capital did not always work as well as the optimistic farmer anticipated, it tended to give the farm operator the calculating attitudes and imagery in terms of profit associated with businessmen. "The colonial farmer," writes Everett E. Edwards, "was dominated by a generous optimism. Neither his non-descript past nor his humdrum present provided a basis for boasting.... Accordingly he always looked to the future, which was unhampered by realities and let his imagination have full sway."[14]

In the middle colonies, land was initially disposed of by proprietary grants or sales in both large and small acreages. A history of farming in Hunterdon County, New Jersey, by Hubert G. Schmidt, gives a detailed picture of the business aspects of land operations.[15] In the late seventeenth century, the western part of the colony passed from two royal proprietors to a joint-stock association known as the Proprietors of West Jersey. Quakers from the Philadelphia area owned most of the 100 shares of stock, or "proprietories," and dividends were to be paid in land. As was customary in the eighteenth century, the shares were divided into fractions, and a lively market in these securities developed in both England and America.

The history of these investors was much like that of the royal proprietors of early settlements: those who occupied or personally supervised their land made money; absentee owners, such as those of the West Jersey Society of London, lost. Professor Schmidt writes of the active purchasers, "close behind the surveyors came the speculators who flourished for a century by subdividing and selling land . . . . Lands often went through the hands of several speculators before getting into the possession of actual dirt farmers."[16] Until well into the nineteenth century, much land was traded for increases in value, while the farming was done by tenants.

By easy stages a man, lacking any initial capital, could become a land operator. The first step was to occupy some desirable land without regard to title, to become a "squatter." Proprietors were not opposed to a small number of squatters who served to open up the country and raise the value of surrounding land. The squatters could generally negotiate reasonable long-run terms of purchase from the owners. Now possessing a certificate of ownership, the potential capitalists "extended their boundaries at the expense of the absentee owners."[17] Soon the erstwhile squatter was ready to sell some of "his" land. Eventually he would probably sell all of it, and either repeat the process elsewhere on a larger scale or invest his capital in some other activity. Thus clever, thrifty dirt farmers, rising to be owners of excess acreage, were able to join in the operation of buying and selling land at increasing prices.

In New England, land had originally been granted freely to voluntary associations prepared to settle towns. But by the second quarter of the eighteenth century, free distribution had virtually ended, and land was being sold by the provincial governments as it had been by proprietors and royal governors in the middle colonies. By this time, the desirable land near water transportation had already passed to at least one set of private owners, many of whom were primarily real estate operators. Forrest McDonald writes of the original settlers of the town of Kent in western Connecticut, "They could scarcely have been poor or even 'common' for they paid £150 to £200 each for their shares. Some of them sold parts of their lands at a profit to settlers of similar backgrounds (what people did for a living in Connecticut was sell land to one another)."[18]

Robert E. Brown emphasizes the extent to which landowning was combined with small business in eighteenth-century Massachusetts. It would appear that only the unlucky or improvident artisan failed to acquire some stake in land, and only the unambitious small farmer failed to develop a business specialty such as a skilled craft to make money during the off-season for agriculture. In Lynn, for example, a man who was listed as a "Heelmaker, glazier, and joiner, also had a house and thirty-nine acres of land, and a half interest in another house and barn." In Dorchester a "cordwainer, had a house and barn and 102 acres of land."[19] Brown cites other examples of the combined activities of the businessmen-farmers in Massachusetts towns. These nearly universal business activities must have greatly increased the level of productivity in the community by utilizing the "concealed" unemployment of agriculture.

Brown's examples suggest how much land may have been held for future sale; or, looked at another way, they indicate the tendency to invest business profits in additional acreage. Often only a small part of a man's land would actually be in use. For example, in Northampton, one man had but 5 of his 80 acres improved, and in Westhampton the ratio for another man was 27 out of 187 acres.[20] It would appear that even the average landholding was probably in excess of the forty or so acres that one man and his family could cultivate with eighteenth-century equipment. "The vast majority of the population," writes Brown, were "farmers whose farms were not only their homes but also their capital stock. These farms generally averaged from 75 to 150 acres with a value of £300 to £1,200."[21]

In all the colonies, money made in trade or manufacturing found its way into land—urban for immediate income, back-country acreage for future appreciation. Writing in 1768 from Philadelphia, the most prosperous business center of the colonies, an investor said, "It is almost a proverb in this neighborhood that 'every great fortune made here within these fifty years has been in land.' "[22] In fact, immediate or prospective values of land served as the security for much of the credit that, over the course of American history, financed industry and transportation.

BUSINESS AND AGRICULTURE IN THE SOUTH

The plantation economy that grew up on the Southern seaboard was only in part a business-oriented society. Business considerations were obviously necessary to the planters who produced staple crops by large capital investment in slave labor. In the early years Southern land was easy to acquire through "head rights," and many sea captains and small traders realized the goal of becoming landed businessmen, buying and selling properties, and perhaps, ultimately settling down as commercial planters. In fact, all but a few of the men who ultimately became great planters had yeoman or middle-class origins. But, whereas in the North, rising farm operators aspired to be regarded as good businessmen, in the South they desired to be seen as landed aristocrats with attitudes similar to their English counterparts. Paradoxically, while successful planters were in reality among the colonies' biggest operators, they preserved the facade of leisure befitting a landed gentry.

The facade, however, had chinks through which business obtruded to a degree that made Southern plantation society of the late colonial period appear far more influenced by business considerations than was that of English or European manors. "The men who founded the aristocracy of colonial Virginia," says Louis B. Wright, "were working gentlemen busy with the supervision of their estates and occupied with the commerce which resulted from the sale of plantation products and importation of manufactured goods from overseas.... If any evidence were needed of the preoccupation of the Virginia cavaliers with trade, that evidence would be supplied by the Carter Correspondence."[23] Bridenbaugh emphasizes the mingling of business, even of separate mercantile establishments, with the ownership of plantations.[24] Aubrey C. Land notes that as early as the end of the seventeenth century the wealth of successful Chesapeake Bay planters "stemmed from entrepreneurial activities as much as, or even more than, from their direct operations as producers of tobacco."[25] Visitors from both the Northern colonies and Europe commented on the preoccupation of the South Carolina planters with trade.[26] George Washington and other large planters were active investors in Western land. In spite of the British Proclamation of 1763 prohibiting settlement beyond the mountains, Washington warned his friends that if they did not seize the opportunity to mark out holdings in the forbidden area "they will never regain it." Four years later he wrote "the greatest estates we have in this colony were made ... by taking up and purchasing at very low rates the rich backlands...."[27] The plantation South, therefore, made a unique contribution to the business of farming and land investment in America, but the effects of the aristocratic institutions of the region tended to keep business values beneath the surface.

EMPLOYERS AND EMPLOYEES

The paradox that the agricultural aristocrats were by our definition also among the biggest businessmen was demonstrated in the number of their employees. By 1770 the system of producing staples, chiefly tobacco, by the labor of Negro slaves had proved its effectiveness. In that year, more than a quarter of the population of Virginia, by far the largest Southern colony, and two-fifths of that of much smaller South Carolina were Negro. By 1770, Negro population was 40 percent of the total from Maryland on south.[28]

It is needless here to take up the controversial question of just how indentured Negro servants gradually became slaves in the later seventeenth century. By 1700 the process of social segregation, discriminatory provincial laws, and ultimately statutes defining slavery had taken place all over the colonies.[29] While a handful of families owned land and some were free urban artisans, well over four-fifths of the Negroes appear to have been slaves.*

The rice planters of South Carolina became the largest employers of labor in colonial America with work forces, by 1730, as large as 500 blacks.[30] While the total of slave labor in agriculture was largest in Virginia, individual tobacco plantations used less labor than those growing rice. In both regions the largest

---

* There are no reliable statistics on free Negroes in the Colonial period.

operators divided production into a number of separate plantations, each under a white overseer. The usual practice was to pay this local manager with a percentage of the return on the crop, a system that gave immediate rewards for harmful exploitation of both the work force and the soil.[31]

It is best to postpone further analysis of this peculiar business institution until the nineteenth century (Chapter 4) when much more information is available on routine practices that do not seem to have changed substantially from those of the earlier period. But one surveying early business should not overlook the fact that the managers of slave plantations were dealing with the most numerous single type of employees of the late colonial period.

The total population of all cities at the end of the colonial period was considerably smaller than the number of Negro slaves in the South, but the cities, largely Northern, were more the progenitors of later business institutions. As in later America, small enterprise was the norm; perhaps as much as half of the working population of the cities were independent shopkeepers or artisans. Many of them employed no labor beyond their own families and one or two apprentices. The line between "worker" and "self-employed" was not difficult to cross, or in more technical language, the functions of labor and management were not clearly separated. There were few journeymen because it was so easy, both economically and legally for a young man completing his apprenticeship to set himself up as an independent operator.[32]

There is no accurate way of estimating the number of white common laborers for city or village tasks such as portering, digging, or menial service, but is was probably not large.* In some Northern cities in the early eighteenth century, Negroes, either slave or free, did most of the lowlier tasks.[33] Southern planters believed slave labor to be more economical than free, and Charleston, where skilled Negroes kept out white artisans, seems to have illustrated the validity of the belief.[34] A visitor to Boston in the late seventeenth century thought mistakenly that every home had one or two Negro servants.[35]

The main body of white labor in the Northern cities was unquestionably in the seagoing occupations such as boatmen, fishermen, and sailors. While a ship was a business enterprise employing as many as a score or more workers, under either a proprietor or a manager, the conditions of work were so different from those on land that they fall outside the developing tradition of employer-labor relationships.

Since the colonial cities were small, the large numbers of skilled immigrants from Northern Ireland, Scotland, and Germany produced a temporary surplus of craftsmen in the seaports in some years of the eighteenth century. In time, the partly idle found their way to employment in the towns of the interior, but the

---

*
Among 275 persons in the Middle Ward of Philadelphia in 1774, Sam Bass Warner, Jr., finds only seventeen "laborers" and four "porters," but the total is less than 80 percent complete, and those for whom there is no information are likely to be in the lowliest occupations: *The Private City*, Warner, 18.

intermittent wartime booms and post-war recessions also led to periods of unemployment in colonial cities, particularly in New England which depended so much on commerce.

Aside from the maritime trades, the largest employers of free labor, as well as slave, were farmers and planters. Most of the indentured servants sold in Philadelphia, the chief eighteenth-century market, were bought by farmers. The large Southern plantations were self-sufficient communities in themselves, often employing indentured white carpenters, builders, butchers, weavers, and other skilled craftsmen. Next to the large plantations in scale of total employment were iron furnaces, forges, and shipyards. But in these diverse types of employment, it is hard to discern a "business policy" toward labor. Such uniformities as there were came largely from government regulations regarding maximum wages and conditions of apprenticeship and indenture.

On the worker's side, organization or concerted policy was also lacking. There were a few small-scale Negro rebellions, and toward the end of the period some local strikes by skilled journeymen, such as tailors. But one cannot speak of a labor movement, or a self-conscious proletariat.

THE SPREAD OF BUSINESS INSTITUTIONS

The relatively small numbers of full-time nonagricultural businessmen should not obscure their widespread influence. The fur trade had been looked to as a principal source of wealth by the early colonists of all nationalities.[36] Soon there were traders, peddlers, millers, and agents of land companies even on the remote frontiers of the Mohawk and Susquehanna. Settlements with stores, taverns, smithies, and other services followed close behind, or occasionally moved in front of the pioneer cultivator. The county seats, particularly in the newer regions in the eighteenth century, swarmed with lawyers manipulating land titles and seeking fortunes by whatever business came to hand. Anticipated increases in wealth and population gave these various businessmen energy and optimism.

In the handful of substantial cities not only the merchants in foreign trade, whom we will shortly discuss in detail, but also men in many other types of business acquired moderate wealth, prestige, and influence. Benjamin Franklin, printer and publisher, is a striking example of the rise of urban businessmen in nonmercantile lines. Shipbuilders, producers of ships supplies, distillers of rum, ironmasters, and craftsmen operating large shops all became important citizens.

Business relations were face-to-face between people who knew about each other. With few exceptions, proprietors had a paternalistic attitude toward their small number of workers. Administrative problems were a thing of the future. Industry remained at the artisan level, similar in technology or structure to that of past generations. The typical producing unit in both town and city was the small workshop on the ground floor of the family home, in which apprentices and journeymen, if any, were boarded and lodged. Members of the proprietor's family, however, usually constituted most of the work force. By the mid-eighteenth century, some candle or furniture makers or silversmiths shipped goods to other cities and developed a volume of business requiring a score or more employees, but such instances were rare. Shipyards and ropewalks occasionally employed over 25 men, but only in iron production were enterprises necessarily large, sometimes employing over 100 workers, on what were called plantations.[37]

The pattern of small enterprises with many proprietors meant a relatively large group of businessmen in relation to other citizens in the towns and cities. In 1687, for example, Boston with a total population of about 7,000 had over 500 skilled artisans and a roughly equal number of shopkeepers, masters, and merchants.[38] A century later in nearby Newburyport only 16.6 percent of the adult male population lacked a business or a skilled craft.[39] The cumulative total of this business influence was no doubt of much more importance than that of a few leaders. "The backbone of maritime Massachusetts," writes Samuel E. Morison, "was its middle class: the captains and mates of vessels, the master builders and shipwrights, the ropemakers, sailmakers and skilled mechanics of many different trades, without whom the merchants were nothing."[40] "Philadelphia," writes Sam Bass Warner, "was a town of entrepreneurs."[41]

The simple utilitarian character of the initial settlements, their continual expansion, and the resulting rise in the price of urban and suburban land generated an emphasis on business values by all property-owning groups. Ezra Stiles' resolution while at Yale—"Endeavor to make the business of your life your pleasure"—is a reflection of a serious and devout work ethic.[42] This subtle modification of English or European traditional culture with its aristocratic and agrarian values toward an American culture appropriate for a business society appears to have been in progress from the beginning.

Some of the democratic practices that arose in the simple and relatively egalitarian early colonial society aided the spread of business interests. Primogeniture, for example, often regarded as essential to an enduring aristocracy, was seldom practised. Opportunities for further expansion of wealth seemed sufficient, even if large estates were evenly divided among the heirs. While equal division may also have been induced by the lack of careers in army, church, or government to take care of the younger sons, it, in turn, tended to discourage the creation of such sinecures. Even at the end of the colonial period, British staffing of the army, navy, and imperial civil service left only a few prestigious positions at the disposal of the royal governors, and these posts were generally given to men of wealth and power rather than as a support for indigent aristocrats. As a result, even the sons of leading planters might be apprenticed to seaboard merchants in order to learn how to acquire wealth from trade.

THE MERCHANT

The most important type of nonagricultural businessman in an economy that depended largely on foreign trade was the exporting and importing merchant.

Although the greatest long-run source of wealth on the seaboard was rising land values, the successful merchant was able most rapidly to amass mobile capital that could give him influence in economic, political, and social affairs. Since success as a merchant in the late colonial period was judged to require about £2,000 in initial capital, few of them were self-made men. Usually they were aided by family connections or came to the colonies with capital from abroad. Occasionally a smart supercargo, the merchants's representative on a trading voyage, could acquire capital by honestly or dishonestly selling small amounts of goods on his own account. But wages alone, in all occupations, were too low to permit saving on any such scale.

Throughout the colonial period, the absence of many specialized forms of business drew the merchant into numerous essentially different activities. His ships supplied public transportation; his warehouses held the country's reserve supplies; his stores distributed the essential imports; his foreign agents supplied news of the rest of the world; his credit abroad made him the chief source of capital; his credits and debits at home took the place of scarce currency; he underwrote insurance, financed retail stores or peddlers in both cities and back country; and he often organized subsidiary manufacturing or service enterprises. Government contracting, usually for military supplies in the numerous wars, was one of the most lucrative trades of the merchant with political influence.

Many forces affected the way in which the merchant carried on his manifold functions, but two major ones—a static technology and dependence on English credit—tended to inhibit innovation and change. In a country that depended on importing and exporting most of the luxuries, and a few of the necessities of life, the most important technological device affecting the merchant was the sailing ship. Colonial business life was built around the ship. Roads were almost nonexistent, and those that were maintained were, during some seasons, mere streaks of mud, unfit for hauling heavily loaded wagons for any distance. The flatboat on small streams, the sloop on rivers, bays, and sounds, and the schooner or ship on the ocean were the usual means of moving goods.

The business world of the sailing ship was a slow-moving world. If all went well, a round voyage to England or Europe would consume about three months. Credit terms of six months or more suited the speed of ships. Selling also proceeded at a leisurely pace. Between 1752 and 1767 one of the leading merchants of New York averaged only five transactions a day in his busiest year.[43] Even though it is clear that in his major activity of importing and exporting, the merchant was under little daily pressure for important decisions, he went to the office early in the morning and generally interested himself in an increasing number of subsidiary enterprises.

Many of these enterprises stemmed from the desire of the conservative merchant to balance inevitably high maritime risks by the security that comes from diversification. Investment in land, houses, and shops was an almost universal recourse, as soon as capital could be spared from trade. To lessen the need for the latter and also to spread risks, individual voyages were often set up as partnerships between from two to six or eight cooperating merchants. No doubt the heritage of building new communities with scanty capital had emphasized such cooperation, but it was also part of the Puritan tradition of New England to do things in cooperating groups.[44]

Arrangements between the members of these groups were informal and highly personal. The merchants of the small cities could talk with each other every day, and complex partnership arrangements were entered into without any written documents.[45] Bookkeeping was often an equally informal business record, involving mixtures of family and commercial accounts and lacking some items that were simply kept in the merchant's head.

America's unfavorable balance of payments and England's lack of a central banking system capable of supplying sufficient currency of stable value for empire trade "doomed her overseas merchants to a frantic scramble for what the eighteenth century called bills of exchange and what we consider to be bank checks drawn on business accounts."[46] Such notes that could be used in international trade took many forms with differing market values. The most speculative were bills drawn by an American merchant against the English trading house that supplied him with goods, because the American was usually overdrawn, and the notes might only be accepted in England at a substantial discount. One would think that bills on the British government issued by the proper authorities of the armed forces would by completely secure, but this was not the case because frequently the army spent money not yet appropriated by Parliament. Consequently a promissory note issued directly by an important Bristol or London trading firm was generally the best form of exchange.

In their activities as individual foreign traders, merchants were involved in many additional uncertainties. They had no lasting control over any market, no patents, and no large permanent organizations. On the other hand, they had few trading assets that could not readily be liquidated. Each voyage was a separate speculation with both very substantial hazards and the possibilities of large profit. So many pounds were received for the outward cargo, so much invested in return cargo; when the latter was sold for a certain figure in the market, the venture was completed. At the end of the voyage the ship as well as its cargo could be sold, and the cash received could be used for any purpose.

Continued success depended largely on the merchant's personality and judgment. As he received credit from mercantile houses abroad on the basis of his personal integrity, it was best that he should know his correspondents as friends and cultivate a reputation for conservativism and caution. The success of overseas ventures depended largely on his estimate of the capability and reliability of captains and supercargoes who had to work at a distance. Ability to bargain was a desirable quality in supercargoes, but honesty was absolutely essential. Hence in Massachusetts, as Morison says, "This position . . . was often reserved for Harvard graduates, merchants' sons, and other young men of good family."[47] Selling the imported goods at home involved extending credit, often for long periods of time, and receiving many payments in kind; both of these practices demanded knowledge and judgment.

While the merchant needed a large warehouse to store the goods that came by ship and the produce taken in trade from local shopkeepers, he did not need a big office or a large staff. A porter and watchman could take care of the warehouse, one or two clerks could copy letters and serve the infrequent customers, and a single bookkeeper had ample time to keep the accounts in order. When Thomas Hancock was one of the greatest merchants of Boston, his "store must have looked very like the general dealer's shops in a small village today."[48] For the smaller retail customers he had a shop around the corner run by a young protégé. He not only received produce in payment for imports from retailers all along the New England coast, but he also sold goods on consignment for some of these customers.

With good fortune the profits of foreign trade might be high. Hancock, for example, made £100,000 between his start in overseas trade in 1728 and his death in 1764, much of it from providing military supplies. However, the risk of total failure with a private cargo was also great.[49] Many of the products of the Northern colonies were not wanted in England, so that sterling exchange with which to buy in the British market had to come from selling elsewhere. Maritime gossip and reports from foreign agents about gluts and scarcities guided a continual search for products and markets. Since the information could not be acted on in less than two or three months, conditions had often changed disastrously before the cargo could reach its destination. To the hazards of bad calculation and lack of exchange were added those of shipwreck and double dealing. Supercargoes might sell for their own account at first, and for their employer only when prices had fallen. Stephen Girard started his great fortune, at the end of the colonial era, by private trading while acting as a supercargo. Such activity was not necessarily dishonest, but to the merchant at home it must have seemed likely that the supercargo got some of the best bargains for himself.

Complicating the trade situation still further were the British navigation acts. While protecting Americans from foreign competition and stimulating some trades, the laws also forbade trades that were profitable and led respectable merchants to assume the risks of smuggling. That this unethical activity was to some degree condoned is shown by the election of Thomas Hancock to various public offices at a time when his smuggling was widely known.[50]

In addition to his quest for security through diversification, the merchant's own business operations led him into subsidiary activities. His vessels often carried goods for other shippers. His shop took care of retail as well as wholesale customers. Money owed them by other businessmen drew successful merchants into outside ventures. They took partnerships in iron plantations, shipyards, ropewalks, and candle factories, and they financed retailers, fur traders, fishermen, and whalers. More than in England and Europe, the American merchant was a general entrepreneur, alert to the chance of making a few pounds in any type of venture.

In the afternoon, when not driving about inspecting their property, merchants often went "on change." That is, they congregated at certain markets or coffee houses where they exchanged information, and in negotiating financial deals no doubt tended to many of the other activities of their metropolitan center. Because before the mid-eighteenth century, at least, the colonies lacked banks, investment brokers, and insurance companies, the merchants assumed these functions. They paid interest for money placed on deposit with them, investing it in mortgages or well-secured loans. They met at certain places to buy and sell insurance on their voyages. If a colonial capitalist wished to invest in British government bonds, the only common type of security, he asked a merchant to buy them for him. By the end of the colonial period, merchants in the major cities had built substantial "exchanges."

To make long-run provision for the welfare of himself and his family, the successful merchant usually invested extensively in land. Success at trade required special abilities and loyal foreign connections, neither of which the merchant's son might inherit, but good city lots or nearby farming land went up in value each generation. So the real estate interests of many merchants became large and absorbed much of their time in land management and speculation.[51]

With these manifold activities in a new environment one might expect that the rising American merchants would have innovated in the direction of new business forms. In many ways, however, the situation was not conducive to novel mercantile experiments. To begin with, the pressures from surrounding physical change, the fear of falling behind technical progress, scarcely existed. Compared to later periods, technology in America from 1607 to 1783 was static. No important alterations were made in the sailing ship; no major canals were completed; no new power machinery upset the tempo of production. Except for a few large operators in crude iron or shipbuilding, manufacturers were at the social level of skilled artisans. No other businessmen as a group challenged the prestige of the leading merchants.

The colonial merchant's success depended largely on good credit with English houses. The big British mercantile firms that handled American colonial trade were conservative, and unlikely to favor a correspondent who was regarded as over adventurous or slightly "unsound." The banking and brokerage aspects of the American merchant's activities required that he have, as well, a domestic reputation for caution and dependability. Successful merchants also adopted the social habits of the upper class which inescapably involved support for traditional attitudes.

Probably no set of business practices is ever stable over as long a period as a century and a half. There were small changes taking place in the role of the colonial merchant, but they appear to have been more connected with the gradual development of the surrounding society than with the conduct of his essential business operations. The first generation living in a crude, small frontier society was unable to amass the wealth or develop the varied interests of its descendents. By the end of the seventeenth century, however, successful merchants had become rich, and well-connected English traders came to the colonies to make fortunes, some with the idea of returning with them to the homeland. In 1720 London merchant Thomas Amory, for example, deciding that Boston was the busiest port in the world, moved his office there. He died in Massachusetts leaving a fortune of $100,000.

As a result of his widely varied functions, the merchant stood at the center of the colonial business world, and his well-defined social role reflected the responsibilities of such a position. Like the bankers in later years, he was expected to be grave and dignified, to have a personality that inspired confidence. Since he often handled other people's goods and money over long periods of time, his honesty had to be beyond question. More than any other citizen he represented the ties with the mother country. He was expected to have influential friends in London and other English cities and to be able to help colonials abroad. Being, even more than a newspaper editor, a source of information on world events, he was looked to for guidance in public and business policies.

But the role also reflected aristocratic pretensions and manners which belonged to an older order; these tended to inhibit innovation and were out of tune with the long-run trends of American culture. While the merchant's wealth was built on meeting economic needs that would continue, his political and social influence rested partly on exotic transplantings from European culture that were to be uprooted in the half-century after Lexington and Concord.

BUSINESS CREATES MORE COMMUNICATION

Late in this period, businessmen began to enter into intercolonial arrangements for market information, voluntary regulation of quality and measures, and promotion of trade that knit the coastal cities together. All of these developments depended on more and easier communication. By 1740 there were post roads from Portland, Maine, to Charleston, South Carolina; for part of the year mercantile travel from Boston to New York and Philadelphia was quicker by land than by sea. More social and business contacts led to intermarriage among the leading merchant families of the principal cities, which, in turn, bound the business world of the colonies still closer together. By the mid-eighteenth century, family ties were creating some of the community of interest achieved by corporate devices in later centuries.

The first enduring trade association, that of the Philadelphia House Carpenters in 1724 was soon followed by similar organizations in other major cities.[52] Information on price scales and presumably also on wages was passed from city to city. Meanwhile, master artisans and small manufacturers entered into regulatory organizations.

The most elaborate intercolonial industrial organization was the United Association of Spermacetti Chandlers. Formed by manufacturers of candles in Boston, Nantucket, Newport, and Providence in 1761, it fixed prices for head-matter, the scarce raw material, apportioned quotas for amounts to be bought, and set the price of candles. The association which lasted until 1775 was gradually extended to include new works in Philadelphia and New York. While the organization suffered all the problems of later trade agreements or pools, such as secret price cutting or buying and selling, its achievement from the standpoint of strengthening business institutions was that of putting the manufacturers in close touch with each other. Agents in each city spied on their competitors and reported various rumors and probabilities.

Associations to promote their areas by better business practices appeared near the end of the colonial period. The Boston Society for Encouraging Trade and Commerce, 1761, was followed in New York by a Society for the Promotion of the Arts, 1764, and a chamber of commerce in 1768. Philadelphia, which was doing better than its rivals in these years, did nothing, but Charles Town formed a chamber of commerce in 1773.

Merchants and general entrepreneurs like the Browns of Providence saw the entire coast as one business area. The Browns, for example, carried on extensive correspondence with their agents or representatives in Boston, New York, Philadelphia, and Charles Town, as well as in lesser ports. As James B. Hedges writes, "So regular, so vital, and so long sustained were such transactions that they could not fail to bring businessmen an awareness of interdependence. Such a community of interest in economic affairs was but a preliminary to inter-colonial action in the political realm."[53]

THE COLONIAL HERITAGE

The colonial dealer in land was the new American businessman. Yet, this pursuit was so ubiquitous that it was scarcely institutionalized as a separate business; farmers, merchants, and artisans were all dealers in real estate. Joint stock associations formed expressly to buy and sell land only appeared at the close of the period.

In general, ease of entry into small business was the most important difference between the Old World and the New. Skilled journeymen could readily go into business for themselves, unhampered by difficulties in securing a municipal license or gaining admission to a guild. With rapidly expanding local markets, the chance for success was good. Therefore, in contrast to the tendency for hereditary succession to occupations in England, America offered far more choice of activity. The other side of the coin was that master workers seeking to expand their operations had a hard time finding and holding competent journeymen. The colonial situation thus presaged the continuing American pattern of scarce labor, high wages, and many entrances into and exits from small business.

Merchants were forced to be relatively conservative in their business practices, not only because of their ties to English connections, but also because of imperial regulations which prevented them from forming land banks and probably from developing banking as a specialized business. Possibly the regulations also discouraged mercantile diversification through investment in industry, but it appears that the effect was slight, since putting surplus capital into land seemed safer, easier to manage, more prestigious, and hence more generally attractive.

Obviously, diverse occupations and levels of wealth and prestige have continually prevented businessmen from constituting a coherent social class. In the colonial period they ranged in status from the itinerant peddler, distrusted by most sedentary people, to the great landlord or merchant at the apex of the social pyramid. This was to be true, of course, throughout American history; the small retailer of the late twentieth century is far removed in status from the chief executive of a great corporation. In consequence, an interpretation of American history emphasizing the conditioning force of business has to be based more on the complex Weberian conceptions of business and social spirits or attitudes and the requirements of administration in bureaucracies rather than on Marxian class conflict.

From the seventeenth century on, in contrast to Europe, business in America was strongly represented on the top levels of prestige. While many of the large landlords both in England and on the Continent were involved in various kinds of business, they were able to carry on such activities without loss of prestige only because of their secure status derived from hereditary land ownership. In America there was a single pyramid of status based on property in any form that was held for a generation or more; regardless of its origin, conspicuous wealth qualified a family for membership in the upper class. The successful, to be sure, liked to imitate the European aristocracy through ownership of mansions and country estates, but this was also a matter of wise investment, and outside the South not strictly necessary to maintaining their place in society.

CHAPTER 2

Shaping the Culture

The dramatic contrast between fertile, unpopulated America and completely settled England and Western Europe no doubt underlay most of the cultural differences between the two regions. Subsequently, the effects of numerous physical differences became cultural forces in themselves, working for still greater deviation. Customs brought across the oceans were buffed against the hard demands of practical utility in a new environment. In America expectations regarding the future took on different meaning, novel practices had to combat less resistance from established custom, while men were forced to find solutions to new problems.

The institutions for preserving and transmitting traditions and customs, chiefly the family, the school, and the church, were themselves altered in adjustment to the new enviornment, reshaped more than their participants realized at the time. Children, adjusting more rapidly and easily than adults, in a sense, educated their parents in how to meet the challenges of a land in which "Every aspect of their existence combined to produce disorder" in the mores and folkways that had been carried across the ocean.[1] Yet it is easy to exaggerate the "cultural shock" of coming to this new environment. The seventeenth-century settlers were still trying to reconstruct civilization as they had known it in Europe, and many elements such as class distinctions, manners, and religion fell back nearly, if not quite, into their traditional places.

CHILD REARING AND THE FAMILY

Although continuing high rates of immigration meant that a considerable, although diminishing, portion of the population had been brought up in Great Britain or Europe, by the eighteenth century it seems certain that a majority of the people were native born, and had reared families adjusted to the American environment. The family, the chief agency in the transmission of culture, had to meet the challenge of reconstitution on a somewhat different basis in altered surroundings.[2]

One general drift of familial change was in the direction of making it a more efficient business or economic unit. As noted earlier, the neighborhood kinship system with its characteristics of traditional careers, well-established roles, and mutual economic support was broken by the ocean voyage and seldom reestablished in as adequate a form. In contrast to the mature unmarried children in England who still lived with their parents, and even after marriage perhaps remained in the same village, abundant land and continual movement toward the interior scattered the offspring of colonial families too widely for much continuing contact.[3] In contrast to Western Europe, and England in particular, where the supply of labor exceeded the demand, each male child in the colonies must have expected that a livelihood was not only available to him in his local area, but that his labor could be sold in other places, and that he might hope to acquire property.

Modifying this picture of careers chosen rationally in response to economic demand, was the widespread practice of apprenticeship or binding-out. At the ages of ten to fourteen children were bound-out in service to neighboring families, either to learn a trade or farming, for periods up to seven years. Even families aspiring to upper-class status would apprentice sons to merchants and daughters to other women of high status to learn housekeeping.[4] Edmund S. Morgan, who has studied the family in the contrasting environments of New England and Virginia, believes that parents thought they would be too lenient with their own children and fail to give them the best training.[5] The very small percentage of sons who headed for college avoided these rigors, and were able to choose careers at an age when they were better informed.

Binding-out, not a uniquely colonial practice, vested rational choice of a career more in the hands of the parent than the child, but it also indicated a strong commitment to rigorous discipline for economic success. The biggest difference between the old and new societies came at the end of the apprentice period: America offered greater opportunities because the demand for trained journeymen far exceeded the supply.

There is not much accurate knowledge about the details of early home training, especially among the middle to lower classes. The sources of information are largely the admonitions of preachers and writers on child rearing, and occasional private letters discussing traits to be inculcated in the young. Too often the authors of this literature lived in New England and belonged to the elite of either learning or wealth. Consequently, these maxims indicate what certain leaders of society thought desirable, rather than actual practice, and those from the Northern colonies also tend to illustrate the attitudes of the dissenting Protestant churches.

Understanding of the colonial family is aided, however, by the presumed similarity of major relationships to those of both England and America in later periods. Factors such as better feeding, and consequently stronger bodies and earlier maturity in America probably lay at the basis of the changes that did occur in family relationships. Healthy, strong children who could look after themselves from an early age, parents busy with a surplus of activities, and less crowded or traditionally controlled communities probably led to more permissiveness in parental ralations with children. Although discipline appeared to have been stricter in New England than Virginia, to upper-class foreign observers all American families seemed lacking in parental discipline. Aside from these related factors, many practices carried from the Old World persisted in the new environment. From the seventeenth to the nineteenth century the American middle-class family probably had continuing patterns of paternal and maternal authority, religious admonitions, obligations and duties toward relatives, and emphasis on obedience and diligence.

The colonial environment encouraged the cultivation of characteristics useful for business. A major theme heavily emphasized in colonial child-rearing literature was that all possible time should be devoted to work. "Time and the day were given for Work and Business," said a writer addressing "little children."[6] According to Benjamin Franklin, "Idleness is a sort of non-existence."[7] "Be always ashamed to catch thyself idle."[8] The Reverend Samuel Willard told the parents of children "to set them their business and see that they attend it, whether in attending schools for their instruction or applying themselves to labor, when fit for it . . . . "[9] "If the Protestants, especially the Puritan elements in Protestantism," says Louis B. Wright, "did not invent the gospel of work, they adopted it with such enthusiasm that it became a cardinal point in their social doctrine."[10]

Country children were given farm chores as early as possible, and city children shared household tasks along with schooling. Orphans and the children of pauper families were bound-out to work by the authorities.[11] Children were told to be honest, temperate, frugal, industrious, and silent. Each of these qualities was justified on moral grounds, but their economic value was also stressed.[12] While children's books were chiefly devoted to Christian virtues and spelling, they also emphasized industry and thrift.

Closely allied to the doctrine of the duty to work was a growing emphasis on utility and practicality. The paddle, a home-teaching device, illustrated the alphabet by accompanying phrases. In the seventeenth century the phrases were normally religious, such as "A is for Adam in whose fall we sinned all," but by the early eighteenth century a Philadelphia paddle had the alphabet illustrated by phrases such as "A—Almanac, will you buy an Almanac. B—Buy a Broom. C—Man selling and repairing Chairs."[13] While William James did not popularize the formal philosophy of pragmatism until the end of the nineteenth century, it was in fact the rule most Americans had more or less consciously abided by since the beginning. James' statement that "You can say of [an idea] either that 'it is useful' " could have been agreed to by most Americans of the colonial period.[14] Thus the demand of the economic situation for labor and useful activity, the admonitions of the clergy, and parental emphasis on the opportunities for success by diligent attention to one's business joined in a colonial attack on youthful "idleness." This appears to be one of the most important respects in which the American environment from its origins shaped a business-oriented culture.

EDUCATION FOR SIMPLE TASKS

Families with at least one literate parent generally taught the children to read at home with the Bible as a text. Beyond the family, there were three institutions for education: the church, the school, and apprenticeship. Aside from denominational schools, the church influence, like that of most families, was stronger in shaping attitudes than in transmitting formal learning. "In its primary purpose of serving the spiritual welfare and guarding the morals of the community," writes Bailyn, "it ... furthered the introduction of the child to society by instructing him in the systems of thought and imagery which underlay the culture's values and aims."[15] That the systems of thought put forward by denominational schools coincided well with mercantile aims will be described presently.

There is little indication, however, that businessmen saw any economic value in spending public money for general education beyond the little needed for reading and writing. Leaders such as William Penn saw education as valuable in creating respect for established institutions, or what later generations would call good citizenship, rather than as an aid to business development.[16] Little office help was required, and this could be supplied from the sons of families who could afford private education. Not until the mid-nineteenth century, at least, were many businessmen interested in spreading good primary and secondary public education (Chapter 5).

At least for minimal education, businessmen chiefly relied on apprenticeship, a form of teaching within the home or shop. Except for a few scholarship students, attendance at a private academy or college which provided a classical education was limited to the upper-middle or upper class. Even in the upper classes, lawyers, merchants, and doctors learned by means of apprenticeship; for example, Samuel Sewell, the famous merchant, politician, judge, and literary man, apprenticed his son Samuel. The son, a true Puritan, asked to be placed "with a good Master, and where [he would have] fullness of employment...."[17]

As early as 1660 the Boston town meeting ruled that shops could be opened only by one who had served seven years apprenticeship.[18] In all the Northern colonies, apprentices were formally indentured, usually for a term of seven years or to the age of twenty-one. The master was bound to teach the boy his trade, as well as to read, write, and keep books.[19]

These latter tasks apparently proved irksome to many masters, for evening schools to teach apprentices appeared in New York by 1690 and probably about the same time in other large ports.[20] More urban children may have received formal education in this way than in any other.[21] In the beginning such single-master schools offered only elementary instruction in the three Rs, but by

1725 they were offering "mercantile arithmetic," bookkeeping, and other useful subjects.[22] After 1748 the unusual boy who was smart enough to learn by himself could buy a copy of George Fisher's *American Instructor or Young Man's Best Companion* which contained rules for double entry (Italian) bookkeeping and other information "which if observed, may with God's blessing make a [young man's] fortune."[23]

Apprenticeship, particularly on the merchant level, involved much informal education in the ways of the market. John Reynell, for example, wrote to his apprentice Elias Bond:

> In doing business be a little on the Reserve, and observe well the Person thou hast to do with. . . . Keep thy business to thy self, and don't let it be known, who thou dost Business for, or what Sorts of Goods thou ships off . . . Endeavor to know what Prices other People give for Goods . . . If thou finds out a Place where they Sell cheap, keep it to thy Self.[24]

The conditions of foreign trade undoubtedly put a premium on outwitting competitors, but in those days before patents all types of apprentices were sworn to strict secrecy. Thus the business tradition of intensely private and deeply secret dealings grew and was passed from master to apprentice, although perhaps no more zealously than in other Western societies.[25]

EDUCATION FOR RELIGION

Religion reenforced the desires of business in the emphasis on useful work and other economic doctrines. In ideas regarding the general content of formal education, however, the two split apart. Ability to read the scriptures was the religious aim of primary education, and knowledge of Latin and Greek a major aim of secondary. Scholars were seen as potential ministers and were educated as such. Businessmen, on the other hand, needed for themselves and their office employees literacy and some education in mathematics, geography, navigation, and bookkeeping.

In the two early Congregational colonies, Massachusetts and Connecticut, the close ties between church and state led to laws, from 1642 on, designed to insure that children would be taught to read the Bible, which inevitably increased the number competent for office work.[26] Under the new charter of 1691, Massachusetts adopted an act making it obligatory for each town to provide a school and a school master.[27] Connecticut passed three laws between 1690 and 1702 defining the duty of masters to teach servants and apprentices to read and providing for the maintenance of schools in each town.[28] The penalty for failure to observe the education laws of either colony was a fine levied against the town, and some towns paid the fine rather than support the school.[29]

That general literacy was not an insistent demand of the business community is indicated by the fact that elsewhere in the colonies efforts at public education were weaker and less successful. Although many towns in Rhode Island maintained schools, there was no established church; business interests, even in this active trading community, did not take the place of theological pressure for a compulsory public system. The same situation prevailed in the middle Atlantic trade centers. In New York and New Jersey the established Anglican church viewed education as a private concern of parents, and these colonies showed only a sporadic interest in schools. In Pennsylvania, in spite of some early support for public education, problems of a population both ethnically and religiously mixed discouraged the growth of a public system.[30] In these four colonies and in Delaware, individual churches maintained some private elementary schools. The scattered rural population of the South worked against school attendance, although by the later colonial period, Maryland and Virginia had systems of public education for those who could reach the schools.[31]

Thus, regardless of its extent or semicompulsory character, this early public education was promoted by the church rather than by business; as religious zeal diminished, and population in areas such as Pennsylvania became more mixed in creeds and national origins, the emphasis on public education weakened.[32] The first quarter of the eighteenth century was a period when the religious drive in the Northern colonies was nearly spent, and the mercantile pressure for more adequate schooling had scarcely begun.[33]

Yet the low level of rural education for the great majority of the people should not obscure the progress made in a few major cities. While business leaders were not actively working for public education or endowing schools, in the eighteenth century the opportunities open in the growing American cities to a young man who could read, write, and keep accounts produced middle-class pressure for a more adequate education. This interest joined with that of the churches in spreading public education in Boston, Newport, and Philadelphia in the later colonial period. Bridenbaugh thinks that no town in England or Europe had as good a public education by 1720 as Boston, and that Newport and Philadelphia were ahead of cities of similar size in the British Isles.[34]

THE CONTENT OF EDUCATION

Public education, however, taught little beyond the three Rs. The major growth of primary and secondary education suited to business needs depended on private enterprises. Probably in all the urban areas, and in the Southern planting regions, the demand for rudimentary education exceeded the supply of qualified teachers.[35] Consequently, by the early eighteenth century, schoolmasters in the major cities were advertising the teaching of subjects necessary to the business technology of the day. In the *Boston News Letter* of March 12, 1709, for example, a schoolmaster advertised the teaching of "Writing, Arithmetic in all its parts; and also Geometry, Trigonometry, Plain and Spherical, Surveying, Dealling, Gauging, Navigation, Astronomy: The Projection of the Sphere and use of Instruments."[36] In New York, Philadelphia, and Charleston, the newspapers carried many similar advertisements.[37]

Even the private academies supplying genteel education for the sons of planters included commercially useful subjects. Somerset Academy on the Eastern Shore of Maryland, for example, advertised in the *Virginia Gazette* that students might "be taught the various branches of the *arts and sciences* such as geometry, logick, navigation, surveying, etc."[38]

After 1725 most Massachusetts elementary schools gave some instruction in mathematics that could prove useful in business.[39] "Even the middle classes for whom classical education had acquired a special meaning as a symbol of social ascent, justified their interest in grammar school training by reference to its moral and social utility."[40]

School books also tended to become more practical. An arithmetic text by Isaac Greenwood, published in Boston in 1759, held to be the first by an American author, has the revealing title: *Arithmetick, Vulgar and Decimal; with the applications thereof to a Variety of Cases in Trade and Commerce*. A later text by Thomas Carroll of New York included in its title: *How to purchase or sell Annuities; Leases for Lives, or in Reversion, Freehold Estates, Inc., at Simple and Compound Interest*.[41]

The single-master, private, vocational system generally limited education to one group of special subjects even more than the schools that followed the classical curriculum. What was needed was a blending of the curricula in a sizable school with a number of teachers. As in so many other circumstances, Benjamin Franklin was a leader in meeting this institutional need.

In 1749 Franklin submitted a proposal "Relating to the Education of Youth in Pennsylvania" to a number of prominent Philadelphians, most of whom were merchants. He argued for a curriculum that would teach "*every Thing* that is useful and *every Thing* that is ornamental: But Art is long, and their time is short. It is therefore propos'd that they learn those Things that are likely to be *most useful* and *most ornamental*. Regard being had to several Professions for which they are intended."[42] Thus Greek and Latin would be taught for ministers and scholars, other languages for those who needed them, English and history because they were useful to all, as well as "*Arithmetick, Accounts,* and some of the first Principles of *Geometry and Astronomy*."[43] Morality was to be taught from the angle of practical advantage: "to fix in the Minds of Youth deep impressions of the Beauty and Usefulness of Virtue of all Kinds, Publick Spirit, Fortitude, etc."[44] An enduring American business view was represented in Franklin's statement that history showed the "Necessity of a *Publick Religion*, from its Usefulness to the Publick; the Advantage of a Religious Character among private Persons; the Mischiefs of Superstition. etc. and the Excellency of the CHRISTIAN RELIGION above all others antient or modern."[45]

The academy began instruction under a colonial charter in January of 1751. Initially, the trustees had not decided on the grades to be covered beyond requiring that all students be able to read and write, but in four years the academy was chartered as the College of Philadelphia, and a generation later as the University of Pennsylvania. This first chartered, nonsectarian academy, college, and university is symbolic of the mid-eighteenth century triumph of the merchant values of utility and practicality over both the theological and aristocratic emphases on learning for God's and its own sake. Franklin urged men to keep "The Great [end] of Education in view viz. to enable men and to incline them to be more usefull to mankind in General and to their own Country in particular and at the same time to render their own life more happy. . ."[46].

Private academies offering vocational subjects expanded and multiplied in the other colonies, but the new colleges of the late colonial period, Princeton, King's (Columbia), Queen's (Rutgers), Dartmouth, and Brown all had denominational ties and classically oriented curricula. For another century the church was to control the mainstream of higher education.

In the founding of Brown, however, and one suspects in the movements for some of the other prerevolutionary colleges an external value to business was used as an appeal for support. To the businessmen of Providence and also to those of the surrounding towns, the Brown brothers promised that:

> Building the college here will be the means of bringing great quantities of money into the place, and thereby greatly increasing the markets for all kinds of the Country's produce, and consequently increasing the value of all estates to which this town is a market.[47]

Whether or not the college was a major factor, the Browns' prophecy proved correct. After the revolution, Providence supplanted Newport as the chief city of Rhode Island.

RELIGION IN THE ANGLICAN COLONIES

Although differing in their approach to educational curricula, on most issues business and religion had views that were compatible. The dissenting religions particularly sought to inspire the diligence and devotion to work necessary for economic success, and these in turn strengthened orderly habits of church attendance. The clergy of the Anglican or Episcopal church, nominally established in New York, New Jersey, and the Southern colonies, and strong in Philadelphia, were respectors of success who had no doctrinal reasons or personal inclinations to interfere with the practices of business. In England some prelates of the Anglican church had for a time denounced covetousness, usury, and market price. By the Restoration in 1660, however, the pressure of economically successful parishoners had become so strong that the church accepted business practices as in tune with the laws of nature, which were, in turn, acceptable to God. Such discussions seem scarcely to have troubled the colonists.

Virginia, as the largest and richest colony, was a mainstay of the Anglican church in America. Here, in the absence of local bishops, ministers were appointed for annual terms by the vestrymen of each parish. The vestry, a self-perpetuating body of the principal landholders, was not beholden to any higher authority. Such "freedom of action, which became an inherent principle in the development of the Virginia parish, brought about the predominance of the laity in church policy."[48] In this aristocratic but acquisitive society, ministers found it best either to conform to the surrounding pattern or be circumspect in their opinions.[49] The same practice of control and financial support by the local vestry was the rule in the other colonies.

In both England and America the Anglican church was associated with aristocracy and conservatism. Many merchant families that started as adherents of one of the dissenting sects, upon achieving wealth desired the more prestigious status of members of the Church of England. As a result Anglicanism, for no theological reason, became the faith of a large part of the wealthy business community.

TROUBLES IN NEW ENGLAND

Only in early Massachusetts, where both ideological differences and personal problems were expressed in terms of religion, was there a conflict between the mercantile group and the church. Not only was the ruling Puritan theocracy authoritarian in its social and economic beliefs, but it recognized that survival and progress in its unpromising geographic area required discipline by the state and cooperation by citizens. Since the state did not always act on the basis that what was best for businessmen was best for the society, merchants frequently became critical.[50]

The Puritan leaders of the early seventeenth century insisted that "the life of business be placed within a structure whose proportions had been drawn by the hand of God."[51] The religious and political leader John Cotton, for example, proposed that the governor and one or more members of the council fix prices on all imports, that selectmen of towns fix prices on their commodities and also limit the wages of labor.[52] While only certain prices were in fact regulated, the prosecution of the important merchant Robert Keayne by both church and state for overcharging illustrated not only the specific conflict between the concept of price set by the free market and that of a "just price" controlled by moral responsibility, but also the more general conflict within many citizens between economic freedom and religious conformity.

Keayne had taken advantage of a shortage of goods in the late 1630s to charge prices that seemed to both consumers and the magistrates to violate the principle of a "just price." Yet he was a deeply devout Puritan whose avocation was writing on religion. After being fined by the magistrates and admonished by the clergy, he wrote thousands of words explaining that diligence was not avarice, that the just price was the market price, and that the church elders should defer in these matters to the judgments of the merchants.[53]

In 1662 the "Half Way Covenant" allowed some people, not able to testify to the experience of personal conversion, to maintain partial affiliation with the church and to baptize their children; mercantile habits and values were undermining the old sanctions.[54] The clerical response to worldliness and conspicuous consumption was to deliver "jeremiads" condemning the new ways of life and calling for a return to the old virtues. But to Perry Miller "one remarkable fact emerges: while the ministers were excoriating the behavior of merchants, laborers and frontiersmen, they never for a moment condemned merchandizing, laboring or the expansion of the frontier . . . . That every man should have a calling and work hard at it was the first premise of Puritanism."[55] Yet the clerical view was not necessarily hypocritical: "The jeremiads were the voice of a community bespeaking its apprehensions about itself."[56]

Essentially the Puritan clergy were trapped by the doctrine of the calling. As expressed by the Reverend Cotton Mather at the beginning of the eighteenth century, a man had two callings: his general calling "to serve the Lord Jesus Christ," and his personal calling or "Particular Employment by which his Usefulness to his neighborhood is distinguished."[57] A man could not get into heaven, Mather held, unless he had "some *Settled Business*." At his business "a Christian should . . . spend most of his time, and this, so that he may glorify God by doing of Good for others, and getting of Good for himself."[58] "Would a man *Rise* by his Business? I say then let him Rise to his Business."[59] By making business God's work, the clergy gave it an aura of importance and authority. As a result as merchants grew strong enough to assert their independence of the early clerical restraints, the church had to respect the proper and essential character of the businessman's pursuits.

Under the new Charter of 1691 merchants came to control the governor's council in Massachusetts and wield the kind of influence earlier exercised by the theocracy.[60] Meanwhile, growing secularism and the grim farce of the Salem witch trials in 1692 weakened the prestige of the clergy. But as early as 1686 the Reverend Samuel Willard had couched his preaching in the language of trade in order to give it public appeal. "If you neglect to buy the truth now," he warned,

> shortly it will not be bought; not only will the price rise . . . but the market will in a little time be quite over with you . . . . One saving truth really purchased, makes the man more wealthy than if he had engrost the *treasure* of both the Indies . . . . If our negligence should provoke God to shut up the market, New England's Glory is gone.[61]

By the end of the first quarter of the eighteenth century, the clergy had faced the fact that there were certain contradictions between Puritan ethics and what succeeded best in the market place, contradictions that most men found operative within themselves. "Enormities among us show our departure from native simplicity and justice of the first generation in New England," held the Reverend Peter Thacher in 1729.[62] Yet the clergy lived in a society supported and held together by merchants. The results were a number of clerical explanations of how private gain led to public good. "How apt would Mankind be to indulge themselves in Laziness," wrote the Reverend Andrew Eliot in 1744, "were it not that they have a love of the World, and some Desire to have a large portion of things in it. Nor can I see any evil in such desires, so long as our Love of these subliminary Enjoyments is subordinate to our Love of God."[63] The Reverend Charles Chauncy, of Boston's First Church, also emphasized the need for combatting sloth: "If Persons possess ever so great an Abundance . . . still they ought not to be idle . . . . We are made for Business."[64]

Cotton Mather in 1710 specifically stated the doctrine of the "Stewardship of wealth," which was to become popular with business leaders more than 150 years later. "The rich man," he said, "is the Lord's Steward and is charged with the sacred trust of 'Charity.' " He further suggested that the good stewards were frequently rewarded in this world.[65]

While the rich were constantly exhorted to dispense charity, a far stronger justification for wealth in growing America was that "Each man coveting to make himself rich, carries on the Public Good." This argument was elaborated in detail by the Reverend Joseph Morgan two generations before the publication of Adam Smith's *Wealth of Nations*.

> A rich man is a slave to others while he thinks others are Slaves to him. He is a great Friend to the Publick, while he aims at nothing but serving himself. God will have us live by helping one another and since Love will not do it, Covetousness will.[66]

Other arguments for the merchant being a benefactor, in spite of himself, were advanced by the Reverend Benjamin Coleman:

> Christianity has been greatly served by Trade and Merchandise, by means whereof a great part of the World has been gospelized . . . . And to add yet one more Benefit of Commerce; it enlarges Peoples Hearts to generous things for the support of Divine Worship and Relief of the Poor.[67]

In addition to justifying wealth from trade, the clergy offered some direct help to business. The greatest continuing problem of the well-established merchant was domestic credit. Goods were sold to retailers and consumers on terms of six to nine months, while the merchant himself owed money to others, including his English correspondents. To collect enough in payments, often in produce, to meet his domestic and foreign obligations was a continual struggle. Yet, no merchant could do business on a strictly cash or even a commodity basis. The financially strong Thomas Hancock had to sell on nine-months credit with the additional clause that "if not paid then, after that to pay interest until all is paid." To secure these overdue debts, he asked for a personal note or "bond." By 1755 he held perhaps £10,000 worth of such bonds, granted by debtors as far away as North Carolina."[68]

Responding to this perennial business problem, the clergy in the eighteenth century waged a concerted campaign against overindebtedness. Of a group of forty-two sermons published in Boston or New London between 1700 and 1775, virtually every one attacked the problem of debt.[69] Cotton Mather defined the problem in 1716:

> Some debt is to be allowed of. Yea, without some debt there could be no trade carried on .... No body is hurt, if the Debt wherewith Trade is carried on, ... be kept under a Suitable Regulation .... (But) when men have brought, perhaps necessary, debts upon themselves, their *Delay* to get from under them, is what ... amounts into a crime, for which they are to be indicted, as *not having* the fear of God before their Eyes.[70]

In the course of sermons on debt, the Reverend Samuel Moody provided a guide to sound business. "Depend not on Probable Gains or Increases, as if they were Certain," he warned, "consider what you have in Hand ... not what you have only in Hope."[71] All moral justification lay with the creditor. "Debts must be Paid tho All go for it."[72] "It is no sin to be Poor," he concluded, "but to lie in Debt, is a Sin."[73]

The forms or rituals as well as the sermons of the New England churches were inevitably influenced by the attitudes of their increasingly wealthy business parishioners. These conservatives favored "refined, decorous, formal, rather than emotional evangelical services."[74] They also favored unity and efficiency in church organization as against the multiplication of small sects. Supporting the "Standing Order" that controlled the Congregational church in Connecticut and the Puritan establishment in Massachusetts were the group of businessmen and local officials who represented the chief property interests. When division over doctrine was threatened in Connecticut, "the entire conserving force of the colonial government and all its institutions were rallied gainst the helpless Separates."[75] The issue of church unity was fought with extreme bitterness only in Connecticut and to a lesser degree in Massachusetts, but there seems little doubt that the substantial merchants in all the colonies were on the side of the established religious institutions.

The church in eighteenth-century New England aided the chief businessmen in many ways, and they in turn, continued to manifest devotion. Thomas Hancock instructed a captain: "See that Divine (Service) is often performed ... without which you cannot hope for success." [76] Yet in association with this piety, there seems little question about the force of business values. The Reverend Andrew Eliot, for example, suspected the authenticity of the pious protestations of merchants. "What are your thoughts employed about?" he demanded; "Is it not how shall I buy and sell and get gain?"[77]

THE MEETING HOUSE AS A BUSINESS ORGANIZATION

Quaker thought in Delaware and Pennsylvania had much in common with that of the Congregational clergy of Connecticut and Massachusetts, but it also showed some striking differences. The lack of a Quaker ministry meant that the church was led, de facto, by merchants and a few large landowners. Therefore a contest between the church and business, such as that in Massachusetts before 1685, could scarcely occur. William Penn, a landowner on a scale that made him a big businessman, was always concerned with the promotion of trade. In his famous "No Cross No Crown," drafted in the Tower of London where he was imprisoned for his liberal views in 1669, Penn wrote, "True Godliness don't turn men out of the World, but enables them to live better in it."[78] He advised his children that "Diligence is . . . a discreet and understanding Application of one's Self to Business and it avoids Extremes of Idleness and Drudgery . . . . Shun Diversions: think only of the present Business, till that be done." From Proverbs 22:29 he quoted: "Seest thou a Man diligent in his Business he shall stand before Kings."[79]

Penn's feeling for business was illustrated in the early administration of Pennsylvania. He sold shares in a Society of Traders, and each of the first 100 purchasers received a 5,000 acre bonus in land. In attracting merchant capitalists to his colony, "Penn worked carefully to present Pennsylvania not only as a religious refuge . . . but as a field ripe for economic exploitation as well."[80] "Hardly a position of influence or profit in the early years was allowed a man without a 5,000 acre investment in the province."[81] The interested merchants urged on Penn the conservative frame of government that denied the lower house power to initiate legislation. Subsurface conflict between "simple," idealistic Quakers and those more interested in the security of investment is suggested by the query of Penn of liberal Quaker Benjamin Freely: "Who has turned you aside from . . . good beginnings to establish things unsavory and unjust?"[82]

In spite of this strong merchant influence, the Friends emphasized coopera-tion more and individual success less than the Congregationalists, and poverty was not regarded as a punishment by God. The Philadelphia monthly meetings collected donations for the poor, and the Yearly Meeting appointed substantial Friends to visit families "where they think there is occasion to suspect they are going backward in their Worldly Estates."[83]

The Meetings regulated the economic life of the first generation of settlers in Philadelphia much as the Massachusetts General Court had regulated that settlement a half-century earlier. The leading members of the Meeting controlled the Pennsylvania legislature which passed wage and price-fixing laws. The Meeting lent money for working capital, organized an employment service, and provided for the mediation of legal disputes.[84] But there was a significant difference between the Massachusetts theocracy regulating the activities of merchants whom it regarded with suspicion, and the Quaker merchants regu-lating affairs to suit themselves.

The Quakers were even more rigorous than the Congregationalists in con-demning overindebtedness. The Yearly Meeting of 1688 in England issued an Epistle, duly observed in Philadelphia, warning people not to "launch forth in

Trading and Worldly business beyond what they can manage honorably and with Reputation . . .that their Yea may prove Yea and their Nay may be Nay indeed."[85] In 1692 an Epistle of the Philadelphia Meeting advised that the "Payment of Just Debts be not delayed by any Professing Truth, beyond the Time promised and agreed upon . . . . And that all Friends concerned, be very careful not to contract extravagant debts."[86] That domestic debts remained in Philadelphia as elsewhere a major mercantile problem is shown by the continuance of admonitions to pay. In 1735 another Epistle held it:

> Our Duty to renew our former Advises, that Friends everywhere take diligent care to prevent Persons professing with us defrauding their Creditors of their just dues to the great Scandal and reproach of our holy profession.[87]

Since Quaker emigration from England diminished after the Toleration Act of 1689, by the end of the colonial period they were a small minority of the Pennsylvania population. Complete toleration had made the province attractive to many persecuted sects, as well as to Catholics and all the major Protestant denominations. Although some rich Friends became Episcopalians, Quakers continued to play a leading part in business affairs. By 1769 Quakers were only one-seventh of the population of Philadelphia, but they accounted for more than half of those who paid taxes of over 100 pounds.[88]

No one can say whether admonitions for good business practice by religious bodies and the clergy had the same effect as later fears of a bad rating in Dun and Bradstreet. Perhaps losses from bad debts were proportionally less in the colonial period than they were to be in the booms and collapses of the early nineteenth century when business was first reaching into the Ohio and Mississippi Valleys. But, in any case, colonial merchants could scarcely have asked for more cooperation from the institutions of religion than they received from eighteenth-century Congregationalists and Quakers.

BUSINESS IN A TRANSITIONAL CULTURE

Of the principal forces acting on the British culture brought to America, new economic opportunities probably had less effect during the colonial period than in the years thereafter. Aside from real estate, business went on much as it did in the older nations. Yet, one should remember that all over the Western world, commercial capitalism was becoming an increasingly powerful force for cultural change. Thus, some of the effects of new business opportunities on American family life, education, and religious practice were, no doubt, also present in England and on the Continent.

Where the physical environment and migration reenforced business influences as in early maturity of the young, freer choice of careers, and greater prestige for commercial pursuits, the differences from England or Europe were marked. America was in truth developing a society with more equal opportunity to make money, and on that basis, to rise socially. In these initial decades of life in the new surroundings, the base was being laid for the altar to success at which so many would eventually worship.

Losing in transit some of the armor of custom that had arisen from a more settled agricultural and aristocratic society, all social institutions became more susceptible to the new influences. Families came to think of the most profitable rather than traditional careers for children, education became an economic asset for getting ahead, and dissenting religions sought to inspire the diligence and devotion to work necessary for economic success in the new environment. Social mores based on the values of business were overcoming the older aristocratic, educational, and religious traditions, as they were also to do in Europe in the course of two ensuing centuries. In many areas of American life, however, the businesslike customs took over by the default of a confused and uncertain opposition.

CHAPTER 3

Power and Prestige

Although the institutions of the home, the school, and the church are basic in shaping ideas and attitudes, they have not normally been the agencies for direct and specific exercise of power in American society. The early Puritan and Quaker churches were exceptions to this statement, but their periods of effective control were brief. Usually the agencies of power in America have been based on political organizations, private wealth, or a combination of both. Since private wealth operates in numerous and subtle ways, the power of businessmen in American society is a complex question. Insofar as the business spirit permeated the hopes and dreams of commercial farmers as well as urban artisans and merchants, it underlay all phases of colonial public affairs. Since, however, planters, prosperous farmers, and rural landlords had economic interests different from those of city dwellers, there were political conflicts between these two groups of businessmen based more on differing economic interests than on any contrary ideology. The general political success of the rural groups through weight of numbers has to be balanced against the less obvious influences of business on all institutions.

BUSINESS AND AN EMERGING LAW

With law, as with other institutions such as education and the family, it is difficult to distinguish between the effects of a primitive environment demanding simple labor-saving procedures and the pressures of business for practical rather than traditional action. The English law was the general basis of the legal understanding most of the early colonists brought with them, but this was not a simple, well-codified body of rules. There was customary local law that varied from one part of England to another; the law of the King's justices or "common law"; ecclesiastical law governing probate and inheritance; the "law merchant" for trade; and equity law which might make exceptions to the doctrines established by any of the other types.[1] Furthermore, each branch of law had its own courts. The well-educated colonists were likely to bring with them Sir Edward Coke's *Institutes* and Michael Dalton's *The Country Justice* (London, 1618).[2] In contrast to the maze of English case law that only trained lawyers could hope to use intelligently, Coke and Dalton provided the principles and rules of action of the common law. In other words, the colonists brought over and respected the essential substance of English law without attempting the mastery of its details.

Untrained laymen applying the law to new situations, in a single set of courts, inevitably shook off an immense amount of technicality and procedure, much of which had been inherited from the middle ages. As a New Hampshire justice observed in the mid-nineteenth century, "We regard the ignorance of the first colonist . . . as one of the most fortunate things in the history of the law . . . we happily lost a great mass of antiquated and useless rubbish, and gained in its stead a course of practice of admirable simplicity."[3]

During the seventeenth century, justices, even in the highest colonial courts, were generally laymen, a good knowledge of English law was rare, and decisions were more likely to follow the "laws of nature" or of God than common-law precedents.[4] A Maryland wit said of its high court that "Twice a year does gravely meet/Some to drink and some to eat/A swinging share of County Treat." Until 1680, Virginia barred attorneys from practice before its courts.[5]

In early Massachusetts there was a better understanding of English law—John Winthrop and Nathaniel Ward had studied at the Inns of Court in London—and also an added readiness to modify the common law to suit local situations and to follow Puritan religious precepts. The Code of 1648, established by the General Court of Massachusetts, was a "lawyerly piece of work," but it broke with the common law in "many striking features."[6] For example, from the earliest days the property of intestates was divided evenly rather than given to the eldest heir, and such matters were decided in lay, not church, courts.[7]

As the capitalistic attitudes of American farmers were the most important colonial manifestation of the spirit of business, so the evolution of a simpler and more practical law regarding property in land was the most important legal development. The law was rather quickly changed from one that had evolved in England to protect traditional tenures, to one aimed at achieving easy transfer of ownership, ready salability, and the promotion of equality of distribution through equal inheritance among heirs. These considerations led to the easy "docking" or breaking of entails, the device by which estates were held together generation after generation.[8] There was also a direct business pressure involved in this last change, because entailed property could not be used as security for mercantile credit. Frequent buying and selling of capital assets in land was no doubt one of the factors behind the American habit of talking in terms of capital values rather than income.

In the eighteenth century, the increasing needs of mercantile business for legal protection—particularly of creditors against recalcitrant or absconding debtors—led to greater use of English precedents and to more trained lawyers. But even in the city or Mayor's Courts of the early part of the century, trained lawyers were few. In the 1730s only eight lawyers were permitted to plead before the Mayor's Court of New York. Although the number of qualified attorneys had grown by the 1760s, the cost of legal education, and the great need of landed Americans for legal services in the buying and selling of property, together with the involvement of so many of these landlords in trade, made the law an aristocratic profession in colonial America.[9] In the relatively small American cities, judges, lawyers, merchants, and landowners formed an elite that had many interests in common.[10] In the case of New York, at least, Julius Goebel, Jr., finds this bar of the merchants and landlords learned but lacking a "close relation to the life of the community."[11]

Although still in its infancy in all of the colonies, by the mid-eighteenth century law was emerging as a profession. To a considerable degree professionalism and knowledge of English law grew with law libraries.[12] In Philadelphia, which led the American bar, Tench Francis, for example, was notable because he possessed a law library of as many as 300 volumes.[13] These more technically expert pleaders continued nevertheless to alter the common law to fit colonial needs. To quote another nineteenth-century state jurist: "By degrees, as circumstances demanded, we adopted English usages or substituted others better suited to our wants, till at length before the time of the Revolution we formed a system of our own."[14]

In England the late seventeenth and eighteenth century was a period when the "law merchant," developed in the middle ages to protect foreign traders, was being slowly assimilated into the common law.[15] While businessmen in individual colonies such as New York, that had acquired the practices of the more advanced Dutch laws, may have had some influence in this development, on the whole the change was one brought about by the merchants of England. Until after the first quarter of the eighteenth century, colonial courts, lagging behind those of the mother country, tended to distinguish all of the "Law Merchant" from the doctrines of the common law.[16]

The major development in statutory business law in England during the colonial period was the Promissory Note Act of 1704, which made notes in writing, not witnessed or sealed before a notary, assignable for the benefit of the trade and commerce of the realm.[17] As we have seen in Chapter 1, such promissory notes, together with bills of exchange ordering payment of money or credit on deposit somewhere else, were essentials of colonial trade. By assignment these notes could perform some of the functions of currency.

Colonial statutes diverged even more than the case law from traditional English doctrine.[18] And in this new area of statute law, colonial business influence was strong. Since the city representatives in the assemblies were normally merchants or their lawyers, and the rural representatives were likely to be uninterested in matters not affecting land or agriculture, the business interests were usually able to enact the few regulatory or procedural laws or ordinances they thought needed. The growing volume of correspondence on such matters between the merchants of the different seaboard cities helped to make the colonial laws governing commercial practices fairly uniform.[19]

That colonial laws benefitted employers as against employees was partly a result of the widely recognized economic need, in most years, to hold down the price of scarce labor. Merchants also sought to insure uniformity in exported commodities and fair trading in domestic markets by fixing prices and measures for basic products. For certain types of semipublic employment, the local selectmen or magistrates in all the colonies set maximum wages. These occupations included porters, carmen, dragmen, millers, smiths, chimney sweeps, grave diggers, and pilots. Fees for services such as slaughtering, sawing wood, and grinding corn were customarily fixed by the authorities.[20] Such regulations were generally based on provincial laws empowering the localities to act. No doubt magistrates often thought that they regulated both wages and prices with an even hand, but there were many more local restrictions on workers than on businessmen. A few early efforts were made in New England and New Netherlands to control profits, but this form of legislation does not seem to have proved effective.

BUSINESS CONTROL OF CITY POLITICS

From the early days of the colonies until the nineteenth century, merchants, by personal participation in local politics, controlled the municipal corporations, or in New England the boards of selectmen, which ran the cities. Of the five major cities, Philadelphia and New York were incorporated, practically from their beginnings; Boston and Newport retained the town-meeting form with an elected board of selectmen; and Charleston was run by the colonial assembly. It cannot be said with certainty that the Northern cities were run by and for the business community as a whole, because as always there were diverse interests, but their governments, at least, represented the dominant urban businessmen in contrast to the landed interests of county commissioners or colonial assemblies.

Up to 1731 the mayor, aldermen, and councillors of New York and Philadelphia were either appointed officials or self-perpetuating bodies. In New York a new charter in 1731 provided that councillors be elected from wards by voters qualifying under a property franchise. In Philadelphia the ruling body remained out of the reach of the electorate until 1775. To provide for limited self-government and greater efficiency than could be expected from the aristocratic merchant councillors, the colonial assembly established elected boards for special purposes such as tax assessment and care of the streets.

In Boston and Newport annual town meetings, attended by those who could meet certain property requirements, elected about 200 local officials. It is a mark of the traditional deference to wealth and position in eighteenth-century society that in spite of a majority of small merchants, shopkeepers, and artisans in the meeting, leading aristocratic merchants always were a majority of the elected board of selectmen.

These urban administrations, led by merchants, sought to promote both business and the economic growth of the community. On occasion, they offered free construction labor, from the workhouses for the able-bodied poor, as an inducement to entrepreneurs to locate mills or other works in a town.[21] Following English precedents, the assemblies were willing to grant monopolies to groups which would carry on essential operations. These grants took two forms: chartered craft guilds of master-workers who sought to control their trades locally by apprenticeship regulations and administered prices; and groups of merchants given a monopoly to encourage supply of a special product. Of the first type, craft guilds for shoemakers and coopers were chartered for a brief period in mid-seventeenth century Boston, but they found it impossible to perpetuate control of their trades; Philadelphia shoemaker's and tailor's guilds, chartered in 1718, soon disappeared. While the major cities continued the European practice of charging masters for a license or "liberty" to work, the fees were small.[22] Grants of the second type, for monoplies of supply, were also rare. To encourage exports needed by England, the government of Connecticut in 1705 gave seventeen partners a monopoly to sell naval supplies for five years.[23]* To start paper production, Thomas Hancock and four partners were able to get an act passed in Massachusetts in 1728 giving them a ten-year monopoly provided they met certain levels of production.[24]

In addition to such legally created associations and monopolies, craftsmen and merchants formed a few voluntary associations. The Carpenters Company of the City and County of Philadelphia in 1724, and similar associations in New York and Boston, often organized to meet particular issues, are examples of membership associations that sought to control competition.[25] The United Association of Spermacetti Chandlers of New York and Rhode Island (Chapter 1), a group really run by the merchants who supplied the whale products, effected a private control of their market in the decade before the revolution.[26]

POWER IN THE GOVERNORS' COUNCILS

While within the cities the businessmen could legally or voluntarily control economic life, they and their representatives in the assemblies were a minority in the colonies as a whole. The wealthy merchants, however, benefitted from the fact that the upper house of colonial legislatures was a small council, which, except for Rhode Island, was either appointed by the governor or elected by the assembly. The councils, where merchants shared power with lawyers or land-lords, represented the interests of wealth and could block unfavorable legislation initiated in the lower house. It should also be remembered that in these groups of small communities, the wealthy were widely connected by marriage.

Election of the councils by the assemblies in the three southern New England colonies lessened the influence of the urban businessmen. Wealthy Connecticut

---

* This was part of a British policy to encourage naval stores in the Northern colonies.

merchants, however, divided power in the council with the Congregational clergy, lawyers, and large landowners. While the power of the merchants was growing, it was not dominant before the revolution.[27] In mid-eighteenth century Massachusetts, the council lists were literally a who's who of the trading community.[28] While the mercantile interests lacked a majority of the assembly, they provided a large part of the leadership, and the house was often attentive to the desires of the merchant-led boards of selectmen of the seaboard cities or towns.[29] In agrarian-democratic Rhode Island, the influence of urban business was less than in the neighboring colonies.

In New York, while the landed and other up-state interests were represented on the council, the closely knit group of New York City merchants and lawyers, often relatives of the up-state landowners, were in the majority.[30] The Pennsylvania pattern, discussed in relation to Quakerism, led to a "small nucleus of wealthy merchants who . . . played an important role in its religious and political life."[31] These merchants usually made up a majority of the council.* In 1700, in New York and Pennsylvania, "it is not misleading to regard the Governor's Councils as. . .acting on behalf of this powerful class."[32]

In the South, merchants were important politically only as they were allied to the planters. But in the colonial period, at least, there seems to have been little divergence in interest between local, as distinct from English, merchants and the tidewater plantation group that generally dominated politics.

Merchants were rewarded in several ways for the time and money spent in government. Being the close friends of the governor, the councillors had the first choice in land grants. Cadwallader Colden wrote of Governor Fletcher of New York that he was "a generous man [who] gave away the king's lands by parcels of one hundred thousand acres to a man, and to some particular favorites four or five times that quantity."[33] There were also many minor offices at the disposal of the governor, from which underlings or relatives of the councillors could collect fees. In return for these favors the governor, on occasion, appealed to the councillors personally for emergency funds.[34]

Those close to the governor also had an advantage in securing provincial or English government contracts. England or France, whose respective colonies faced each other across the uncertain Canadian border, were at war most of the time from 1689 to 1763. Thus, war contracting was a lucrative business, dependent on political influence either at home or in England.[35]

This direct participation by some of the big merchants in the councils of the colonies, administrative or judicial posts, or advising the governors, contrasts with the practice in latter centuries when the business pressures in politics were exerted chiefly through lobbyists or contributions to party organizations. Personal participation by leading businessmen does not seem, however, to have greatly altered the institutions of colonial government. Merchant influence was highly individualistic, conservative, favorable to limitations on the powers of the

---

* The council, however, had less power than in the nonproprietary colonies.

assemblies and to the maintenance of aristocratic English traditions and customs. The merchants who remained active appear, in Massachusetts at least, to have been motivated more by personal political ambitions than class interests.[36]

RURAL-URBAN TENSIONS

In spite of their strong position in New York and Pennsylvania and their considerable influence in Connecticut and Massachusetts, merchants and other urban businessmen fell far short of controlling most of the provincial governments. On the basis of population, the cities were generally underrepresented in the assemblies, and on the basis of wealth the discrepancy was still greater. Fortunately for the urban business group, there were not many important issues between country and city.

A continuing complex of issues between urban merchants and the rural majority revolved around debtor-creditor relations and control of the supply of money. While merchants and tradesmen were both debtors and creditors, owing each other as well as foreign houses, they were in general creditors of their inland customers. In addition, inflation was upsetting to contracts, book credit, and other long-term business relationships, whereas it could easily benefit and scarcely hurt the farmer. Yet merchants also suffered from lack of currency, and had differing attitudes toward its issue through the formation of land banks. This device was in reality a loan office run either by a private group or a colonial government, where currency would be created and loaned, secured by mortgages on property. Repayment of the mortgage within a fixed time was to retire the notes. The line-up of interests on the issue of creating such banks differed between New England and the middle colonies.

Before the land bank system was inaugurated, paper currency had already been issued by the legislature in Massachusetts. In 1690 the colony printed notes in order to fit out a military expedition in advance of anticipated revenue. This initial issue of currency relieved a severe monetary shortage in the colony and appeared to aid business; hence from 1702 to 1714 a group of merchants pushed the idea of continuing paper money through a private land bank. The governor and council were amenable, but the legislature disapproved of putting power over the currency into private hands.[37] In 1714, after defeating the private interests, the Massachusetts legislature, spurred by petitions from towns in all parts of the colony, passed an act for a government land bank. During the following generation, large note issues were not redeemed on schedule and consequently depreciated. Many merchants then turned against such paper money, as an element upsetting to long-run business transactions.

A bitter struggle between most of the seaport creditor interests on one side and back country debtors supported by a few businessmen on the other, occurred in Massachusetts between 1739 and 1741. A plan to lend £60,000 in new provincial notes to responsible investors, the system used in Pennsylvania, was defeated in 1739. The next year the legislature chartered a privately run land bank to issue £100,000 in currency, although existing notes had depreciated to 5 to 1 in terms of sterling.[38] Claiming they had power to create corporations or associations, the general court did not submit its action to the governor and council, but put the bank into immediate operation. In an ensuing election featured by farmer-debtor demonstrations, a pro-bank assembly was elected; this assembly nominated probank councilors for the governor's approval. Governor Belcher and the existing merchant-led council appealed to England for help.

The value of the empire to conservative businessmen in both England and America was now illustrated; the British government might interfere with some trades, but its great economic interest was in protecting and furthering "sound" mercantile enterprise. Parliament extended the "Bubble Act" to the colonies, making corporations not authorized by Parliament illegal; and Governor Belcher refused to seat the new councillors. Deprived of legality before the courts, the bank collapsed with the loss of much of the money of its backers.[39] In this emergency, Massachusetts merchants opposed to inflation had successfully invoked imperial power to protect the value of their credits, but they were not able to check continuing issues of currency by the provincial government.[40]

In Rhode Island the governor, the deputies or council, and the assembly were all elected by the people on the basis of a moderate property qualification and a system of town representation. Furthermore, there was no mention in the charter of need for royal approval of legislation. In this situation, the Newport merchants were powerless against the farmers. The latter wanted inflation and secured it by one land bank after another. In 1750, with £525,335 already outstanding, the assembly authorized another bank. Seventy-two leading merchants of Newport signed a petition to the crown asking for prohibition on further emission of bills of credit.[41] The next year Parliament forbade all "banks" of paper money in the New England colonies. Bills of credit could only be issued for current expenses or to meet the costs of war. Again the larger merchants had been aided by the power of the imperial government.

The fact that the Act of Parliament of 1751 was confined to New England attests to the more orderly history of land banks in the other colonies. Between 1723 and 1740, Pennsylvania and New Jersey had put, respectively, £80,000 and about £90,000 in notes into circulation. In 1737 New York issued £40,000. On the basis of population in 1740, the amount issued by New Jersey was roughly comparable to the £250,000 issued in Massachusetts during the same period, but these middle-colony mortgages, supported by more productive land and higher internal prosperity, were generally well-managed and repaid by successive borrowers.[42]

In contrast to those of New England, merchants in the middle colonies saw such moderate internal lending as an aid to economic development rather than a menace to long-term business agreements or to their claims as creditors. Undoubtedly there were a number of money-lending merchants in these colonies who resented the competition of loans from the provinces at 5 percent interest or less. But they could weigh against this the stimulation given to consumer purchasing and the saving that the land bank revenues brought to large taxpayers. Hence, in spite of bitter opposition in the British Board of Trade, concerted pressure by the colonial agents of New Jersey and Pennsylvania, helped by the governors and several merchants with important English connections, succeeded in winning approval in London for middle-colony paper issues.[43] James Pemberton, a leading merchant of Philadelphia, is said to have expressed a popular view when he wrote "paper currency hath proved of singular service in advancing the interest of all parties."[44] Large debts in paper, built up in the Southern and to a lesser extent in the middle colonies for local support of the French and Indian War, led the British government in 1764 to forbid further emission of paper that had the status of legal tender in all the colonies. But the paper was still so useful to the business community in New York and Pennsylvania that government-run land banks were continued, and their paper was accepted without the status of legal tender.

Conservative in effect, the business influence was not static or wholly bound by traditions and fixed principles. Businessmen—mercantile, manufacturing, or agricultural—took a pragmatic view of their own interests. As illustrated by the land bank question, merchant support or opposition depended on the practical operation of the system, and usually their private interests could be protected, if necessary, by using one branch of government against another.

RISE OF BUSINESS OPPOSITION TO BRITISH POLICY

In view of benefits to many businessmen and restrictions on others, the impact of British imperial policy, as a whole, on colonial business, and the influence of Americans in shaping that policy are extremely intricate subjects. Unquestionably the British imperial system put American merchants in a dependent status, forcing them to adjust their activities to rules over which they had little control. But often the arbitrary rules did the merchants more good than harm. In general, the British system sought to meet situations that were deemed unfavorable to English enterprise only as they arose. Curtis P. Nettels calls the British program of bounties for naval stores the "major experiment in state planning of the early eighteenth century." When this experiment failed to produce satisfactory results, the mercantilists in London turned to "a purely negative policy."[45]

It was the rather abrupt abandonment of the negative policy in 1763, largely as a result of the imperial financial burden arising from the Seven Years War, that aroused opposition among some business groups in the colonies. One of these groups, the Sons of Liberty, represented a mixture of small businessmen and urban workers. These young artisans, shopkeepers, journeymen, and apprentices physically resisted the Stamp Act in New York and Boston and later engineered the tea parties. The leaders were generally lawyers who were not sharing the governor's favors and some merchants whose trade, legal or illegal, was threatened by the new regulations. The cities were also centers of an ineffective loyalist opposition led by some of the wealthiest merchants who felt that both their social positions and business interests were best protected by England.

British policy regarding the West and the fur trade, designed in London to bring peace and order to governing the interior of America, affected a number of urban businessmen interested in Western land as well as wealthy rural speculators. The Proclamation of 1763 cutting off land investment in the Ohio Valley was a matter of serious interest not only to Virginia planters but also to Philadelphia merchants who had plans for the development of that area. These groups turned to London to seek a way of reopening Western land for purchase by companies, possibly by the creation of a new interior colony. Neither group was successful, and the Policy of 1774 restricting land grants and raising quit-rents struck a further blow at these entrepreneurs. Finally the Quebec Act placing the administration of the lands north of the Ohio and west of Pennsylvania in the hands of the province of Quebec not only conflicted with claims to this area by several colonies, but transferred the legal administration of the principal fur trade from New York to Canada.

In view of the years of good imperial relations and unprecedented colonial prosperity from 1770 to 1773, it cannot be said that the revolution resulted from a continuous and rising small-business agitation. But a considerable number of middle-class businessmen opposed the policies that England pursued between 1773 and 1775. These somewhat educated artisans and tradesmen read the newspapers, heard speeches and in the Northern cities, particularly, many responded to the appeals of American nationalism, home rule, democracy, and no taxation save by their own representatives. Enough substantial lawyers and merchants whose trades had suffered from the new regulations were caught up in the atmosphere of resistance to join with the dissatisfied Virginia planters in supplying respected leadership for the revolution.

SOCIAL STATUS AND SOCIAL LIFE

In spite of the participation of some of their leaders in the revolutionary agitation, the social attitudes of the wealthy businessmen were strongly conservative. Their Old-World heritage in private life was one of the caution and conformity that had come from generations living in the shadow of the powerful institutional structures of the church, the military, and the aristocratic landlords. Even in America, before the mid-nineteenth century, business was scarcely strong and secure enough in social prestige to oppose openly the manners and customs established by these older institutions. Admiration of the self-made man in America was not part of the colonial tradition. In the earlier period, the middle-class businessmen who became rich adopted the manners of the old aristocracy, insofar as they could discern them, and made little conscious effort to restructure aristocratic roles. Buying estates and investing in land, the successful businessmen illustrated the sociological hypothesis that "the several major bases for stratification tend to go along together."[46]

While aristocratic and by the mid-eighteenth century clearly stratified, the colonial class system was open and fluid in comparison with contemporary Europe.[47] Even in the late colonial period, a very successful skilled craftsman, particularly in lines such as coach building, portrait painting, or silver smithing that supplied the upper class with luxuries, could win social acceptance by large merchants and landowners. A number of Philadelphians, for example, continued to be active at their crafts after becoming rich through land investments.[48]

Since up to the end of the first quarter of the eighteenth century, the colonies were relatively poor, and struggling to establish viable economies, upward social mobility in this period may have been slow. In the more propspeous later years of the colonial period, increasingly rigid class distinctions may have presented an added barrier.[49] But the great obstacle to one seeking entrance to the prestigious status of merchant throughout the period was the need for an amount of capital that few self-made men could acquire. Probably a large number of the merchants who succeeded in the early years got their start through family connections.[50] At all events, evidence on social mobility even in the later colonial period is still inadequate for generalization.[51]

An analysis of late colonial Newburyport shows that craftsmen and shop and tavern keepers were over half the male population.[52] This majority group of businessmen would, on any scale of stratification, be regarded as middle class. Below them the less affluent or skilled, those whose trades demanded strenuous physical activity, were referred to as "inferior mechanicks."[53] These made up part of a lower class composed, in addition, of some but not all indentured servants, journeymen and apprentices, unskilled laborers, and Negro slaves. Above both groups was the relatively small number of merchants, landlords, and professional men (lawyers, doctors, and ministers) whose families had enjoyed wealth for a generation or more. In all the cities the families of this gradually increasing group intermarried and tended to erase social distinctions between landed and business wealth.

Looking at the colonies as a whole, the planter-businessmen of the South, together with their relatives in the coastal cities who were primarily merchants, made up the largest part of the colonial upper class. If a new preoccupation with dealing in land was the major contribution of the colonial period to the traditional forms of business, the planters were innovating businessmen. From the modification of ancient laws to leadership in the conflict with England over Western land grants, the big planters, of Virginia particularly, were men reshaping their environment in the interests of business. They were also among the largest operators in the colonies, yet ironically plantation living developed a traditional aristocratic way of life different from the businesslike customs of later American elites, and therefore makes the planters of less interest for later history than the elites of the Northern cities.

As the urban upper class, both North and South, became wealthier, they sought more and more to imitate the customs of the Old-World aristocracy. By the end of the colonial period, the leading merchants carried swords and drew them if not granted proper respect by inferiors. Their wives and daughters wore the latest London fashions and were painted by the highest priced artists. The prestige of the title of merchant is indicated by the fact that at the close of the seventeenth century, 11.5 percent of the adult male population of Boston strove for social recognition by giving this as their occupation. But probably only a third of this group, those who "owned an increasing portion of the province's shipping," could meet the level of wealth necessary to maintain the highest status.[54]

As time went on, much of the wealth of mercantile families came to be in land. As noted in Chapter 1, land near seaports was regarded as a more secure family heritage than capital employed in trade, and for many families this choice was abundantly justified. Consequently, the "old rich" of the colonies, North as well as South, came to be landlords, and thereby to fit more closely to the worldwide pattern of landed gentility.

Since the behavior of the colonials who regarded themselves as upper class was consciously modeled on that of the English aristocracy, there were both broad similarities as well as minor variations in the merchant role in all cities.[55] According to William Penn's initial plan, Philadelphia city lots were only granted to those purchasing 5,000 acres of provincial land, hence the early merchants were also landlords.[56] The commanding position of Quakers in civic affairs created the atmosphere of the city and the character of its business roles—quiet, industrious, luxurious, but unostentatious. The great Philadelphia merchant Isaac Norris said to his son on his first trip abroad: "Come back plain. This will be a reputation to thee and recommend thee to the best and most sensible people."[57] While Boston, by the late colonial period, had outgrown its simple Puritanism and welcomed luxurious living, New York was the most cosmopolitan city, with its merchants consciously trying to act like Londoners.

A few other types of businessmen, such as distillers of rum, producers of iron, or shipbuilders, made fortunes large enough to establish their families in the upper class. Each generation produced a number of businessmen on the rise, who lacked well-to-do parents. These men could become leading civic and political figures, although they probably could not gain acceptance in the most exclusive social circles. Thomas Hancock and Benjamin Franklin were of this type, until the latter became a great world figure.

Franklin, a successful publisher, grasped the fact that urban problems, both business and civic, required organized collective action. Perhaps inspired by the example of the Quaker meetings, he led the way in forming a tradesmen's club, the Junto, that neatly combined stimulating discussions of public affairs with mutual business favors. When the original club established half a dozen associated clubs in the late thirties, Franklin wrote that among its other advantages were "the promotion of our particular interests in business by more extensive recommendation, and the increase of our influence in public affairs, and our power of doing good by spreading through the several clubs the sentiments of the Junto."[58] His well-known leadership in organizing a circulating library, the American Philosophical Society for Promoting Useful Knowledge, the Pennsylvania Hospital, and the Academy and College of Philadelphia illustrates Franklin's business efficiency applied to the social problems of a growing metropolis.

While the mercantile elite failed to acquire Franklin's vision of the growth of urban institutions, they did assume the traditional upper-class responsibilities for civic improvement and patronage of architecture and painting. An observer wrote that among the initial contributors to the Society of the New York Hospital in 1771, for example, all but twelve were merchants, and there were no nonmerchants on its board of governors.[59]

Apart from support of public institutions needed by all classes, there was little mercantile interest in philanthropy. The doctrine that was to characterize the mainstream of American thought up to the Great Depression of the 1930s—that poverty was a punishment for personal vice and inadequacy—was widely held in the colonial period. Since areas such as eastern Massachusetts suffered several periods of rather severe depression, ways of dealing with the urban poor became well established. The able-bodied indigent, and also orphan children, were either put in workhouses or bound-out to those who could use cheap labor. In spite of such efforts to make the poor pay their way, there was widespread complaint in the depressed 1760s over the increasing cost of public care of the indigent, and local regulations were passed to prevent impoverished strangers from entering cities. The moral stigma attached to poverty continually checked philanthropic efforts to establish more adequate forms of relief.[60]

The attitudes toward patronage of the arts developed by merchants in the North and planters in the South were to remain for at least two centuries as cherished norms of American culture. Those arts that were wanted by the merchants or planters aspiring to upper-class status flourished, and those not so patronized languished. Oliver W. Larkin writes of the merchants, "They believed in art but believed in it with reservations."[61] To satisfy his desire to be a gentlemen, the developing aristocrat wanted a fine house and carved furniture. Portraits were also a mark of family distinction, and occasional landscapes both pleased the eye and bespoke affluence. A large part of the best painting in the colonial period, the work of Smibert, Feke, and Copley, depicts merchant families of the New England coast. Architecture, interior decoration, and painting, therefore, flourished after a fashion in both Northern and Southern urban mansions and manor houses. In contrast to heavy reliance on English imports by the Southerners, the artist-craftsmen of the Northern cities produced house furnishings that tempted the local buyer.

The gradual evolution of a Massachusetts family from the level of austere artisans to that of great merchants committed to aristocratic luxury can be traced in the evolution of the Royal house in Medford. The first Royal of the early seventeenth century was a cooper, and the house was a simple one of two stories and six rooms. The Royal of the next generation was only a carpenter, but his son became a successful merchant. Meanwhile the house grew in size but scarcely in elegance. Isaac Royal, of the fourth generation, remodeled the house to give it genteel elegance. The facade became one of the most impressive of the Georgian period; there were rooms with carved woodwork, and walls hung with Fekes and Copleys. To add the final touch to the family's aristocratic status, Isaac was an Anglican and a Tory who fled to Nova Scotia in 1775.

THE NATURE OF BUSINESS INFLUENCE

In all the colonies, wealth could lead easily to political influence, particularly at the higher levels of government. Taking the merchants as representative of business wealth, however, they appeared to have had only limited occupational interests in politics. Zemsky finds the political pressure of merchants like John Hancock to have been confined to government contracts, currency, and taxes. Those like Thomas Hutchinson who were continuously active politically worked for personal prestige rather than economic legislation, for ego rather than interests.[62]

Merchants had the usual attitude of successful American businessmen toward change: technological or managerial innovations which promised profits were welcomed, but they preferred a social and political system that stayed the same. Business planning is inevitably easier if other things remain equal. Since there were few important technical or procedural innovations in business during this period, there was little to inspire the merchant to alter any aspects of his role.

Granting that the merchant's role was the most prestigious in urban business, what were its influences on the development of American society? It obviously emphasized money and wealth; it fostered a limited amount of utilitiarian education; it broke down provincialism and furthered national organization; it stimulated painting and architecture; and it also perpetuated attitudes of feudal aristocracy. It moved America along the road to a more business-oriented culture, although not exactly the type of business culture that was to be the rule in later periods. Specifically, the merchant role did not accord with at least two of the major sets of American values agreed upon by scholars studying ensuing centuries. In contrast to the values later accorded to equalitarian democracy and social progress, the merchant's role was aristocratic, patriarchal, and unconducive to a sense of social mission.

But merchants were a small minority among men of business. Probably the majority of artisans, manufacturers, miners, and small traders promoted practicality, readiness to try new methods, and conservation of time and labor, characteristics also encouraged by migration and the needs of new communities. As Boorstin writes

> American men . . . had become versatile through force of circumstances. They were not "universal men" but "jacks of all trades."

Their tasks and opportunities made their interests broad and fluid. The "businessman," not the virtuoso, was the prototype of American versitility, for the businessman took his clues from his opportunities.[63]

From the standpoint of influences on the development of American culture stemming from the colonial period, the heritage of changing values from artisans, manufacturers, merchants, and shopkeepers is probably less important than the legacy of a commercialized agriculture passed on by planters and farmers. The view of land as transferable capital rather than a family heritage, and the selection of careers on the basis of anticipated pecuniary return rather than familial tradition, affected the nine-tenths of the population that was rural, as well as the small minority in the cities. Business in land and the local mixtures of land investment and artisanship or shopkeeping permeated the whole society.*

* Sachs and Hoogenboom in *The Enterprising Colonials*, 57, say that latter-day Massachusetts town proprietors were "out and out speculators," often absentee.

Part II

TRANSITION, 1775-1850

CHAPTER 4

National Business: Continuities

Before 1850 the United States was to develop very substantial industrial equipment rivalling that of France and fast catching up with that of Great Britain. But most of the change toward an industrial society came late in the period. For the first fifty years after the revolution, business life went on much as before, revolving around the concerns of trade and investments in land and slaves. In this and later periods the new should be seen against the background of many continuing occupations and procedures, especially those connected with handicrafts and marketing that for the rural or small-town majority constituted business.

On the other hand, one must not neglect the stimulating effect of the promise of new industrial enterprise and power transportation that inspired dreams of American economic greatness, even when the reality was still around the corner. While the average income of individual Americans did not advance rapidly until the middle part of the century, every local booster was sure that better roads, canals, and railways would bring factories in their wake and transform his farming center into a metropolis of great wealth and power. As Albert Gallatin observed, early in the century, "The energy of this nation is not to be controlled; it is at present exclusively applied to the acquisition of wealth and to improvements of tremendous magnitude."[1] Meanwhile, the immediate social changes of the period up to the 1840s was more due to the general rise of complex business in marketing, insurance, trading, and transportation companies than to the coming of "tremendous" improvements or of factories to the countryside.

MERCANTILE EXPANSION, 1775-1830

The revolution severed some of the mercantile ties with Britain and permitted the rise of banking and chartered corporations in America, but it did not greatly alter the social position or business functions of the large merchants. During the war, enterprising merchants such as Robert Morris in Pennsylvania, William Duer in New York, or Silas Deane and Jeremiah Wadsworth in Connecticut exploited new opportunities in French and Dutch trade, army supply, and privateering.

Other more conservative mercantile houses were hurt by the war, and many of their partners left the country and sought reparation from the British government. When the war was over, therefore, while the large merchants were still the chief businessmen, many were newly rich. In spite of such mobility and an egalitarian revolution, their social influence was still conservative and aristocratic.

The period from 1790 to 1807, coinciding with almost continual war in Europe, brought overseas mercantile activity to a peak of prosperity, with rates of profit running up to 20 percent or more a voyage. The China trade, in particular, brought riches to New England merchants, and to some in New York and Philadelphia, far beyond the wealth of earlier periods. It seemed as though some great houses like those of Girard, Astor, Derby, Gray, or Perkins might perpetuate a dominant position in ship ownership and foreign trade. But government policies, if nothing else, prevented this. From 1808 on, embargoes, restrictions, and war by the United States interfered; following the long period of European wars, the return of normal competition cut the rate of profit to a point where internal investment was more attractive. The China trade came to depend chiefly on smuggling Turkish and Indian opium into the Empire, and although the traffic continued until the 1840s, mainly in the hands of Boston firms, the Chinese government made the operations hazardous.

Even at the peak of their business, the trading houses never developed substantial managerial staffs. Writing of the great China houses of Perkins and Company, and Russell and Russell, Jacques M. Downs says that they "carried on business with one or occasionally two partners and the same number of clerks. In neither counting house was there any clear separation between the work performed by apprentices and that of the members."[2] Except for the opium traffic, the bigger houses abandoned world trading between 1812 and 1830 and shifted their capital to internal ventures such as banking, transportation, acquiring Western land, and manufacturing. Thus, the most successful merchants became manufacturers or financiers without ever having built up any great commercial organizations like the India companies of Europe. As railroad executives or manufacturers, they had to learn to handle the problems of large-scale management from the ground up.

Meanwhile special kinds of business had been separated from the broad functions of the earlier mechants. Since these activities had been parts of the merchant role, the new enterprises were largely developed by men from the mercantile ranks who did not immediately alter their policies or ideas. Insurance gradually became a separate business. The Philadelphia Contributorship, a mutual company, started fire insurance before the revolution, but a second mutual company did not appear until 1784; the first two stock companies, for fire and marine insurance, were formed ten years later. Promoters in New England had organized nearly half of the national total doing business in 1800.

While some of these early companies would write life insurance policies, this part of the business was unimportant.

Specialized stock brokerage houses appeared in the 1790s with the organization of "stock" exchanges in both Philadelphia and New York in 1792. Previously, investors had traded securities in a number of taverns or merchants' exchanges, and establishing an "exchange" simply meant concentrating the business at one location. Most of the securities traded were government bonds, and no distinctions were made between markets for bonds and stock. Except for government-financing during the War of 1812, stock exchanges were not an important business institution before the 1820s.

New transportation enterprises also knit metropolitan businessmen from Baltimore to Boston into self-conscious and competing groups, each of which sought ways to divert trade from its rivals by better connections with the back country. Wealthy men, therefore, subscribed to shares in turnpike, canal, and bridge companies as a community obligation, without too careful a weighing of probable returns. Such men influenced their states and municipalities to subscribe heavily to these stocks or bonds.

George Washington and his friends led the way by establishing the Potomac River Company in Virginia in 1784 to canalize the river. Work was slow, and the first of the new enterprises to finish an improvement in transportation was the Charles River Bridge Company chartered in Massachusetts in 1785. The Philadelphia and Lancaster Turnpike Company, formed in 1792, was followed by a great boom in the private building of hard-surfaced toll roads. Canals, partly state-owned, were ultimately to produce bigger companies and more complicated business problems than either bridges or turnpikes. But this phase of business development came after 1820, and meanwhile industrial growth had altered the business world and given the economy greater resources for new investment.

EMERGENCE OF THE BANKER

Among the immediate offshoots of the old merchant role, none were more important than investment and commercial banking. In the beginning of specialized banking, the mercantile connections were clear and dominant. By 1780, state and congressional currency, issued in immense quantities to pay for the war, had so depreciated in value that it no longer served business as a source of credit or medium of exchange. Some new system for mobilizing the capital of the community was needed, and the success of the Banks of England and Sweden made chartered banks the obvious answer. In 1780, Robert Morris and other merchants opened a nonprofit Bank of Pennsylvania, which was absorbed the following year by the Bank of North America, a private, profit-making Pennsylvania corporation. Success in Philadelphia led the merchants in New York and Boston in 1784 to open, respectively, the Bank of New York and the

Massachusetts Bank. By 1800 there were 28 banks in operation, and by 1811 the total was 88. Suspension of specie payments during the War of 1812 encouraged the opening of unsound banks and raised the total to 208 in 1815, many more than in any European nation.

While the role of banker initially stemmed directly from functions that had been performed by the large merchant, banking was but a first step into a new world of industrial finance. With the cashier as the only full-time executive, eighteenth-century banks were run directly by the merchants on their boards of directors. As the banks prospered, it became necessary to have a full-time president, to departmentalize the banks operations, and gradually to create a distinct business of banking. Used almost exclusively by other businessmen, rather than small depositors, even a big bank needed only eight or ten employees.[3]

Unlike the colonial merchants, who had been tied to the seaports, the presidents and cashiers of banks could play leading roles in cities throughout the nation. Since credit for loans or mortgages was the life-blood of an expanding community, the banker's opinions were carefully respected. The Greek temple design in the architecture of nineteenth-century banks symbolized the antique nobility of the banker's position. He considered the mundane requests for aid during the week and administered spiritual concerns as head of the deacons of his church on Sunday. Lesser bank employees were expected to model their conduct on the decorous ways of their superiors—good manners, quiet speech, restrained dress, and an air of responsibility. By midcentury the role of the banker was similar to and as closely defined as that of his predecessor, the great colonial merchant.

Outward decorum, however, did not always insure honesty and social responsibility. Timothy Dexter, Jr., of Gloucester, Rhode Island, had by 1809 established a group of "banks" that issued $800,000 in notes with practically no backing in cash. Many honest but speculative bankers kept a dangerous amount of notes in circulation by designating inconvenient spots for redemption. Regardless of practice, these men adhered to the amenities of the banker role, since their success depended upon maintaining the confidence of their fellow citizens.

Private or investment banking grew up first in large mercantile firms, like those of the Browns of Baltimore or the Peabodys of Boston, which finally established foreign exchange and investment operations as a separate business.[4] Since these "private" bankers handled large sums of money without legal regulation of their operations, the confidence of their customers was even more important than in the case of men managing chartered commercial banks. In states that prohibited chartered banking, after the disastrous panic of 1837, the notes of trusted private bankers helped to provide the currency necessary for business.

By 1850 there were over 800 chartered banks and a much smaller, but unknown number of private banks. If one takes 1,000 as the total and estimates 5 employees per bank, this would make 5,000 "bankers" out of a little less than

8 million "gainful workers"—surely not a large percentage of the whole, but a much larger and more significant fraction of the business elite. Most bank employees were young men from good families and were probably better informed regarding business and political trends, both at home and abroad, than similarly situated men in industry, transportation, or wholesale trade.

THE CONTINUING INFLUENCE OF TRADE

Although in 1850 there were fewer than half as many gainful workers in all forms of trade as in manufacturing, the number of businessmen in trade was undoubtedly larger. In manufacturing, probably only about one man in ten or twenty represented business dealings, as opposed to tasks directly connected with fabrication, whereas in trade probably more than half the total were proprietors or managers chiefly occupied with prices and profits. While detailed statistics are lacking, it seems safe to assume that small retailers were the most numerous group in American business.

In the Middle West, as in the older regions, the earliest business interests were generally in land, but in the booms following the War of 1812 the land operators found that they needed merchants in order to establish towns and attract farmers. Consequently inducements were offered to merchants to set up stores or trading posts in advance of demand.[5] In any case the back-country storekeepers, local lawyers, and other businessmen played a major part in the life of the frontier community. These small operators showed the same virtuosity as in the colonial period, moving freely from storekeeping to other trades or farming perhaps several times during their lives. These ubiquitous, over-optimistic operators often went bankrupt or migrated in depressions, only to start again in another new area. "Storekeepers," writes Lewis E. Atherton, "constituted the central group in the development of interior villages and towns in the ante-bellum period."[6]

The large importing and exporting merchants of the seaboard cities continued to be the conservative leaders of the business community. But investing in the new forms of manufacturing, finance, and transportation, and sitting on the boards of such companies, some merchants became hard to distinguish from the new, professional corporate executives. Meanwhile, as wholesaling spread to interior cities such as Cincinnati, St. Louis, and Chicago, the term "merchant" came to be used for anyone in trade. By 1850, the beginning of a national system of specialized wholesalers, brokers, factors, jobbers, and agents receiving and distributing goods by rail and water, made the old seaboard merchants with their aristocratic traditions but one part of a large community of wholesalers with varying backgrounds. These wholesalers, the most powerful business group in the nineteenth century, were to perpetuate the old merchant influence.

The legal structure of the mercantile community changed little in the first half of the nineteenth century. Between 1820 and 1850 most of the important commercial states, except Illinois and Virginia, allowed limited liability to a partner who invested money but took no part in management. Obviously such a device made it easier for mercantile firms to raise additional capital and establish branches in the newer regions. Banking and insurance firms were generally excluded from using this form.[7]

More important to the structure and functioning of trade was the growing intensity of the business cycle. Swings in business activity caused by crop yields and wars go back beyond recorded statistics, but in the long period of international peace from 1815 on, there appeared a rhythm of ups and downs that seemed more the result of speculative investment and weak credit facilities than of the fluctuations in agriculture. There were major depression periods from 1818 to 1822 and from 1839 to 1843, as well as lesser recessions in between. With the optimistic American practice of starting ventures on a "shoestring," success might hinge on timing in relation to the business cycle.

Since the cyclical movements were more severe than in Europe, commentators regarded American business as relatively unstable. An anonymous contemporary critic estimated that between 1800 and 1840 only 5 or 6 percent of the merchants or others with bank deposits in Boston avoided failure or acquired net assets. A director of the Union Bank of Boston in 1846 said, "Bankruptcy is like death and almost as certain; they fall single and alone, and are thus forgotten, but there is no escape from it; and he is a fortunate man who fails young."[8] Yet next to Philadelphia, Boston was the most sedate and stable major American business center of the nineteenth century.

A British observor regarded American business communities as lacking in the services that increased efficiency, particularly crossed checks, overdrafts on banks, and public warehouses. "There is hustle and discomfort in offices," he continued, "fidgetiness and anxiety on the countenances, and a hurried grasping action in the movements of the New York mercantile community."[9]

Charles Dickens and Frances Trollope, both inclined to see the bad features of the United States of the 1830s and 1840s, thought that a low level of honesty that bred "Universal Distrust" and a "love of 'smart' dealing which gilds over many a swindle" were great evils in the business system.[10] A low level of reliability, however, may also have been an inevitable result of undefined roles in new situations. In the light of comparisons made three decades later, it appears that the standards of ethics were higher in the old, capital-exporting, creditor centers such as the East Coast ports, than in the new capital-importing, rapidly developing areas of the West.[11]

By 1850 these Eastern urban centers were actively exporting the capital accumulated from trade for railroads, mines, and other Western ventures. Boston, in particular, with its limited opportunities nearby and its old wealth was a leader in the development of the Central West, whereas New York was more occupied with financing trade, and Philadelphia with developing the great coal, iron, and later, oil resources of Pennsylvania.[12]

LAND: THE GREAT AMERICAN COMMODITY

In considering the transit of merchant capital to the back country, one should not forget that the great business of America, as in the colonial period, was distributing and exploiting the continent's vast resources in land. The greatest fortunes came from increases in the value of land, much of it Eastern urban and suburban property, but capital also flowed strongly into Western real estate. Not only did land trading remain a more important business than in the older, more settled societies, but ingenious entrepreneurs also found ways of substituting land for other forms of capital. Farms and urban properties were frequently mortgaged to provide funds for business ventures. Some entrepreneurs invested first in cheap land that could be developed for workers' homes, and then mortgaged the land to help provide capital for the plant that would hire the workers whose housing would give value to the land. In this way the company would gain doubly, from both manufacturing and the improvement of real estate.

In the West, reasonably quick profit from land depended on speed of settlement. To hasten and direct the process, the Western boosters transformed all possible businesses into agencies for promotion, chiefly for townsite planning and development. After studying maps of projected railroads, water routes, or post roads, a single promoter or group would buy land from the government at $1.25 an acre in a spot where a town could be developed. If the boosters could direct a turnpike or canal to the spot, or later on, persuade a railroad to come and build a station, or secure a county seat or a college, their fortunes were made. As Josiah Strong wrote many years later, "first the railroad, then the town, and then the farms."[13] These towns appear to have been the most purely business-oriented or capitalist communities the world has ever known.

Early in the process, a growing community usually attracted an editor ready to publish what was partly a news medium and partly an advertising sheet for the town. To attract the right sort of settlers, town promoters quickly arranged for the building of schools and churches. If these devices worked, and a town grew, it soon acquired a hotel for transient residents, salesmen, and conventions. Partly because of their importance in intercity competition, American hotels in the early nineteenth century led the way to new levels of luxurious living. Spacious lobbies, expensive furniture, indoor plumbing, and long, magnificent bars distinguished them from the modest inns or hotels of most of Europe. In the small city, the hotel and its bar became the community center for business and political discussion.

Securing a county seat was an assurance of substantial success for a town. This favor was generally secured by bids made to the state legislature or privately to the proper legislators. The promoters had perhaps bought the desirable sections of a six-mile square township for $15 an acre or less and, if successful, they could count on selling quarter-acre lots for $500 or more; thus, a bid of $50,000 for a county seat was conservative. The result was, obviously, many county seats, many county courts, and small counties.

The early promotion of Chicago in the 1830s produced one of the most frenzied real estate booms in American history. Men such as Gordon S. Hubbard bought land in the area made valuable by the Chicago canal and then sold the deeds in the East. In this way he kept turning over at high rates of profit both his own capital and sums advanced him by Eastern friends. Deeds, much cheaper to ship East than barrels of flour, became "the staple of the country, and were the only articles of export."[14] As the boom progressed, Eastern corporations, such as the American Land Company, sent representatives to buy and sell Chicago lots. One of these men, William B. Ogden, of lasting fame as a Chicago businessman, is said to have represented about a hundred Eastern clients. In the panic of 1837 the land boom broke disastrously for overextended, late purchasers, but many of the insiders had taken their profit and were prepared to further the mercantile growth of the newly created city. Even during the years of depression, exports of real goods mounted and imports of new capital remained surprisingly high, showing both the ephemeral aspect and lasting benefit of such a speculative orgy.[15]

In these heroic efforts at local development, all were expected to work together for the community and glory in its successes even if personally they failed to share in them. This background of intense community rivalry all over the Northern part of the nation goes far to explain the uncritical local loyalty and "chamber of commerce" mentality that were, in later years, to obscure national or international outlooks.

On a lesser scale, those with Eastern or local capital could buy, sell, or grant mortgages on the surrounding farm land. Money could be lent in Iowa in the 1840s on good security at 20 to 25 percent interest. To be safe, the lender bought the land in his own name and gave the settler a bond specifying that he could receive the deed to so many acres by paying a fixed sum and interest at a future time.[16] To secure equipment, the settler might also assume a chattel mortgage. Often the lenders were themselves people of moderate means putting their savings to use.

This small-scale finance emphasizes that not only capitalist promoters, but also "dirt" farmers were drawn into business in land. For example, while the original division of land by the first settlers at Marietta, Ohio, in 1788 set eight acres as enough to support a family, Western ambitions always ran to 160 or 320 acres.[17] As in earlier times, absentee speculators or investors in Western or "wild" land often found such ventures unprofitable, but those on the spot, the original settlers who occupied before government sale, were generally successful. Banding together in "claim clubs" when the federal auctions were held, these "squatters" were able to acquire their "improved" 160 acre tracts at the minimum price. Such a tract could then be subdivided into four ample farms and sold to later comers. If the land turned out to be near a growing town, the profits might be considerable; if the land had been poorly chosen in the beginning, they might be nil. In either case, the tendency was to sell and move on.

On the farms themselves, changes were also taking place that would ultimately make agriculture in America a business little different from other types of production. Up to about 1820, farm technology remained much as it had been in the colonial period; by 1850 the prosperous commercial farms were both specialized and mechanized. Since many farmers resisted becoming enmeshed in the market economy, change proceeded slowly and unevenly. Farmers, aware that they could probably make more money by specialization and sale of their surpluses, still preferred the simpler life of relative self-sufficiency. Buying machinery on time meant contracting debt and thereby losing a degree of independence.

Writing in the transactions of the New York State Agricultural Society at the end of the period, Horatio Seymour said of the farmer:

> He can now take advantage of the principle which lies at the foundation of success in commercial and manufacturing pursuits, of "doing one thing; doing it extensively and well . . . it enables him to methodize his business and to acquire a thorough knowledge of everything relating to the article he produces."[18]

Clarence E. Danhof cautions, however, "that the concept of agriculture as a market-focused, profit-making business was by no means universally accepted even in 1850."[19] To see the farmer becoming a businessman does not, of course, lessen the validity of the history of farm movements against merchants, dealers, or railroads. Every business group has battled others whose policies interfered with what the first group considered its proper returns, and until well into the twentieth century, such economic conflicts were accentuated by attitudes arising from different types of social life.

SLAVERY AS BUSINESS

In no other instance was the divergence from general American business attitudes by groups with differing interests and style of life as marked as in the case of the Southern slave operators. Inexorably the general nineteenth-century world of business rose around them and interfered with traditional practices. As ocean-going ships grew bigger and tidewater soil less fertile, direct visits to plantation wharfs were abandoned, and the export staples were collected at port cities. This led to more local intermediaries in the export of tobacco and cotton. These "factors" had operated in the colonial period, but not as universally as during the great days of the Cotton Kingdom when many planters lived away from deep-water transportation. By taking over all the business part of marketing the Southern staples and merely paying the proceeds to the planter, the factor converted the planter into a production manager who was paid in relation to sales, but who had little direct connection with the selling part of the operation. Freed from these duties, and living in a staid community little troubled by newcomers or innovators, the planter could devote himself more fully to politics and a life of gentlemanly leisure, thus emphasizing the characteristics that set him apart from most other wealthy Americans.

"No other profession gave a Southerner such dignity and importance as the cultivation of the soil with slave labor."[20] Apparently aloof from business details, the planters nevertheless controlled the economic and political life of the South. They sat on the boards of the local banks, controlled the machinery of state government, and administered the "peculiar institution" of slavery. This business had several aspects: Negroes could be used as field hands with relatively little training; taught to perform skilled work such as carpentering or household service; rented out to nearby mills or plantations; or sold at generally increasing prices.

Scholars are now in general agreement that the cultivation of staple crops with slave labor was economically rewarding. Kenneth M. Stampp says, "On both large and small estates, none but the most hopelessly inefficient masters failed to profit from the ownership of slaves."[21] In general, it was best to keep plantations at a size that could be run by one white proprietor or overseer, and to expand by establishing new plantations, not necessarily contiguous or even in the same area. While, in Virginia for example, the avarage number of slaves per owner remained at a little under ten from 1790 to 1860, a few planters owned many plantations with hundreds of slaves and also invested profits in Northern or foreign securities.[22]

The wise owner or manager watched for slaves who could develop special skills and reduce the need for hiring carpenters, coopers, and other building and repairmen. When not busy on their own plantation, these skilled Negro artisans could be rented out to neighboring estates. By 1850 a large part of the labor force in Southern mills, mines, and iron works were slaves, about four-fifths owned by the proprietor and the remainder rented from nearby plantations. But as industry was not highly developed in the South, only about 5 percent of the total slave population were so employed.[23]

Industry lagged in the South, not only because of the profitability and lower risks of slave agriculture, but also because the leading planters were loath to create an urban middle class and thousands of factory workers. While cities and some moderately large scale industry existed in 1850, the planters regarded both as necessary evils that should not be encouraged.[24]

Congressional prohibition of the international slave trade in 1807 helped to raise the value of slaves and in spite of smugglers made slave-breeding a profitable business. The general flow of the internal trade was from the old and declining plantations of the Atlantic coast to the expanding ones of the Mississippi Valley. While this was one of the most important businesses of the

South, the men who actually conducted the trade were looked down upon by the planters.[25]

In general, the trade was in the hands of small entrepreneurs, operating with $10,000 to $20,000 in capital. Like horse-trading, the business was rife with misrepresentation of the age, health, and ability of the slaves. The itinerant trader collected his score or two of Negroes by advertising his presence in the local newspapers of Maryland, Virginia, or the Carolinas; when he had fully invested his capital, he drove them overland to the auction markets of the southern Mississippi Valley from which the expanding plantations of the Southwest were stocked. Some operators kept permanent offices at the gathering points; the Richmond, Virginia, City Directory of 1852 for example, listed twenty-eight traders, and of these a few ran large establishments. Franklin and Armfield of Alexandria, the largest traders from 1828 to 1837, had traveling agents, branch offices, and their own ships for carrying the Negroes south.[26] Beside the legitimate trade, there was extensive smuggling from abroad, stealing slaves from plantations, and kidnapping free Negroes.

THE COMMERCIAL WORLD OF 1850

The Southern cities such as New Orleans and Charleston had much in common with Northern centers, and by 1850 both were participating in commercial activity far more specialized and complex than that of the eighteenth century. In the 1840s most of the services and forms of present-day commerce were present in at least embryonic form. Although perhaps a third of the interior retailers still made annual or semiannual trips to the Eastern centers to buy their goods, the traveling salesmen had already appeared in the 1820s.[27] In machinery and other valuable hardware, dry goods, and apparel, he sold from catalogues, sending orders back to the East or to regional agents. Deliveries could be made along the railroads in 1850 by four express companies. To protect wholesalers against dishonest or unreliable local shorekeepers, Lewis Tappan in 1841 opened a Mercantile Agency in New York to collect information regarding the credit of the "country" merchants. By 1850 the agency had branches at Boston, Philadelphia, Baltimore, Cincinnati, and St. Louis.[28]

An increasing volume of information useful to business, and advertising needed to acquaint both businessmen and ultimate consumers with what was available, was being spread by a rapid growth of newspapers and magazines. Penny newspapers in the 1830s reached a lower strata of mass consumers. The rotary press in the 1840s and growing cities pushed the circulation of some dailies above 100,000 and made newspaper publishing an important industry. Business matters, North and South, were ably discussed in *Hunt's Merchants Magazine* and *The Banker's Magazine,* both started in 1839, and also in *deBow's Review* which began in 1847. In the 1830s trade journals such as *The Railroad Journal,* and *The Dry Goods Reporter and Commercial Glance* also made their appearance.[29]

Stock and commodity exchanges, essential to the world of big business—even the first severe stock market panic (1837)—all indicated increasing economic maturity. Shares in railroad companies were actively traded in New York and on appropriate regional stock exchanges. In 1841, Thomas Jones published an American book on accounting theory which saw transactions as purely statistical; Jones distinguished between capital accounts and income or the "financial" and "business" departments of companies, presaging the approach of the more sophisticated accounting controls of the later nineteenth century.[30]

Urban offices of increasing size housed a population of clerks, bookkeepers, and minor administrators. Some of these men were young and on their way to partnerships or other positions that would lift them above the "white-collar" ranks, but all had a strong tendency to identify themselves with the successful men of business who defined these lesser roles. Reflecting the views of the business elite more than they did the earlier independent artisans or tradesmen, they helped to form an urban middle or upper middle class with businesslike social attitudes.

CHAPTER 5

The Business System:
New Developments

Alongside the old familiar ways of business that changed little from one generation to the next, basic technological change in the later eighteenth century initiated the new forms and practices required by industrial power machinery. By the end of the first decade of the nineteenth century, the demanding routines of factories and mechanized transportation intruded upon the easygoing society of farmers, shopkeepers, and artisans. Managers of the new technology altered the established routines of life and patterns of business. Factories, steamboat companies, trunkline canals, and railroads each required new types of organization and management. By 1850 the age-old business world of the merchant was overlaid or added to by that of the men of industrial power: big manufacturers, investment bankers, transportation magnates, and their specialized legal and political advisors.

The American society, that had become apparent by 1850, was not, however, simply the result of the "industrial revolution." Rather, it was the product of a complex interaction between particularly American forms of democracy and habits of migration in contact with unusual economic opportunities in land and other resources. The business entrepreneur, the agent of change, continued to be differently conditioned than his European counterpart. He expected to use government rather than to fear it, to find social leaders friendly rather than hostile to his plans, and to regard his personal success as of primary value to his community. These and other environmental influences gradually molded types of entrepreneurial personality in the industrial society of America that differed from those of England, France, or Germany.

The United States at midcentury had a "value added" by manufacture equal to more than one-half of that arising from agriculture.[1] While still only in the early stages of its colossal growth, the industrial production of the United States was almost as large as that of any nation in the world. "At the beginning of the United States industrialization in the 1840s the United States was already a wealthy nation."[2] In the last half of that decade, industrial production was in a particularly brisk upswing that had started in 1843. New devices such as the sewing machine, the rotary press, the reaper, and the telegraph promised continuing rapid growth and social change.

From 1840 on, the railroad was a chief factor in determining land values, boosting them astronomically around stations, and puncturing the balloons of speculative hope in the areas it skipped. Already the roads were greatly stimulating the growth of their main terminal cities and junction points, adding to the rapid rate of urbanization. The old census category maintained that 8,000 or more inhabitants made a center likely to possess urban characteristics; the population of such cities increased from 3.3 percent in 1790 to 12.5 percent in 1850.[3] By then, there were six cities with over 100,000 inhabitants, and fifty-six more between 10,000 and 100,000.[4] For many purposes, it is realistic to see the United States of 1850 as a web of these sixty-two urban knots with connecting strands of rail and water.

AMERICA AS A "LESS DEVELOPED" AREA

Since the modern term "less developed" chiefly implies a lack of mechanized transportation and productive equipment, the American states at the end of the revolution were, by the modern definition, obviously less developed, but it is equally obvious that they were not in the same situation relative to other nations as economically backward areas of the twentieth century. Compared to America, England and the leading nations of Western Europe were only slightly more advanced, enough to supply ideas and guidance, but not to create crushing competition.

Unquestionably, abundant natural resources in land, minerals, timber, and water power were major factors in the growth of American industrialism, and abundant agriculture, particularly in the Southern staples, also played an important part in providing money to pay for imported machinery.[5] Internally, increasing millions of small farmers, able to produce a surplus, provided a market for manufacturers. Yet, without taking into account the particular characteristics of American businessmen, these advantages seem to fall short of explaining the rate and direction of American economic development. Some American traits came, as discussed in Chapter 1, from the nature of European immigration and of continuing migration in America, resulting in a population that was more likely to innovate, less attached to tradition or custom, and more oriented toward individual success than in the Old World. The great expectation of success from wise ventures and hard work in this rewarding environment reenforced personal enterprise. Because a high return on capital was anticipated, saving was encouraged. While the hopes of quick reward were often frustrated, they nevertheless kept businessmen devoted to work. This total situation developed traits of optimism, frugality, physical activity, and quick pragmatic decision-making.

Concentration on individual success, however, did not prevent a high degree of cooperation. Individualism in the nineteenth-century American sense was less an egocentric, inward-looking, emotional assessment of situations—like the enduring type of individualism of the Spaniard or Latin American—than it was an outgoing, more "other-directed" characteristic—staunch in defense of personal rights but pliable in support of the group. Ralph Barton Perry wrote, "American individuality is the very opposite of singularity. The individual who holds himself apart, who will not 'join,' who does not 'belong,' who will not 'get together' and 'play the game,' who does not 'row his weight in the boat,' is viewed with suspicion."[6] *

This type of individualism, in part conditioned by the cooperative needs of settling and developing a continent, has been of fundamental importance in industrial development. The attitude might be called voluntary cooperationism with strong emphasis on the voluntary. Not only did it lead in the early days to a broad use of state and community resources for economic growth, and in later years to the rapid formation of pools and mergers, but it meant that United States businessmen were peculiarly fitted by their attitudes to operate the developing system of "managerial enterprise."

Confidence in the beneficent role of government in providing security for long-term investment played an incalculable part in entrepreneurial optimism. In contrast to Europe where government was largely in the hands of aristocrats often indifferent to business needs, American state governments, in particular, were servants of business, passing the laws that entrepreneurs deemed necessary for the rapid development of their areas. One business group might be politically favored over another, but no one feared obstruction based on tradition, confiscation of property, or ruinously adverse legislation. This aura of internal stability, the unique American security from foreign conquest, the assumption of a continually expanding market, gave added encouragement both to high rates of saving and investment in enterprises that might take five or ten years to complete.

The fact that England was the most industrially advanced nation was an added advantage to the United States. In spite of British restrictions on the emigration of skilled workers, the common language and the higher rewards to be won in America made English technicians willing to risk illegal migration. Although, up to 1825 England also prohibited the export of machines or their specifications, these laws were subject to many exceptions and lax enforcement. Steam engines, lathes, and other machines reached the United States when needed.[7] By 1820, American textile machinery for coarse cloth was almost as good as English.

The central government incidentally aided the process of industrialization by forceful interference with imports of finished goods from Britain. The initial

* The fact that culture is the aggregate of beliefs and habitual patterns of the persons who compose a society intimately relates personality and culture. So little work has been done on modal American personality at different periods, however, that it is necessary to derive assumptions from the better explored norms of the culture. For more on this problem see Wallace, *Culture and Personality*.

interference, the Revolutionary War, came too early in the development of technology to aid much in establishing factory processes with power machinery. Most of the increased artisan activity of the war period disappeared in the years of peace. The embargo of 1807 to 1809, restrictions on British trade from 1809 to 1812, and war from then until 1815, however, helped greatly in establishing complete textile manufacturing processes and aiding metal working and other industries. After 1800, state governments also joined in passing laws to stimulate manufacturing; New York, Massachusetts, and Pennsylvania made loans and granted tax remissions.

In view of all of these favorable conditions, one might have expected even more rapid development than in fact occurred. There were, however, a number of retarding factors—population was small and widely scattered; roads or canals for cheap overland transportation were lacking in the first half of the period; foreign competition could only be met by well-capitalized efficient plants; American entrepreneurs initially lacked both technological and managerial know-how; and even by midcentury the whole system of doing business in the United States was crude and unreliable compared to that of the leading centers of the Old World. At the time of the panic of 1837, there was little reliable credit information on "country" accounts; as late as 1850, clearing houses for bank checks existed only in a few cities; and throughout the period, inland distribution was cumbersome and hazardous.

THE CORPORATION

With independence from England, American entrepreneurs were able to use the old device of the state-chartered corporation in ways that made it a revolutionary agent of change. More than a century later, President Nicholas Murray Butler of Columbia University called the business corporation "the greatest single discovery of modern times without which even steam and electricity . . . would be reduced to comparative impotence."[8] The ability to create by charter an abstract, indestructible, immortal, and to some degree irresponsible entity that could gather the savings of a community or nation and pour them into immense works did, in truth, alter the character of the business system more than any other change of this period.

In the United States, the business corporation developed gradually between 1783 and 1850. The corporate form had been used in Europe for large foreign trading companies, such as the East India or Hudson's Bay, and for governing towns and cities, but the need for action by the central government discouraged applications for charters. In England there were scarcely more than half a dozen chartered business companies by 1800, and in France only a score. As we have seen, in 1741 the British government sought to prevent the growth of business corporations in the colonies by extension of the "Bubble Act" which forbade companies to issue stock without the consent of Parliament. While the limits of the types of charters or other corporate forms prohibited remained hazy, colonial governors used the power of incorporation sparingly except for agencies of government.

As a result, the late colonial and postrevolutionary land companies, the biggest business ventures, were joint-stock companies rather than corporations. This type of company prohibited by British law, but not interfered with by officials in colonial America, was really a broad copartnership in which the partners held salable shares of stock. One joined the partnership simply by buying stock, which generally carried votes for electing the managers or directors. Since joint-stock companies did not have to leave any legal record, it is difficult to generalize about their methods of operation.[9]

The major economic need of the new American states was social overhead capital in the form of roads, bridges, canals, and water systems. Companies for such purposes needed public franchises, and it was easy to secure a corporate charter along with the franchise. The charter was actually restrictive from the standpoint of scope of operations; a joint-stock company would have been more flexible, but restrictions on corporate activity, state recognition through a special charter, and defined methods of control and record-keeping gave the chartered corporation an aura of safety and stability attractive to the investor.

Limitations on a stockholder's liability for the debts of a bankrupt corporation developed slowly. As in partnerships, investors in joint-stock companies each had to assume unlimited liability for all the obligations of the enterprise. Since many early charters made no stipulation or had conflicting clauses, it was not clear, at first, whether this held true for investors in a corporation. Gradually the courts adopted the doctrine of a liability limited to the assets of the company (except in the case of directors guilty of malfeasance) and later charters contained such clauses.

By the 1820s the corporation had features that particularly suited it to the American environment: it was relatively easy to secure a charter from state legislatures; investors could support community enthusiasm for local development in a turnpike or canal without risking more than the money subscribed; and participation could be ended at any time by sale of the stock. This last feature particularly suited the migratory character of American investors. The Bostonian moving to a city on the Great Lakes could sell his shares in Massachusetts enterprises and associate himself with the ventures of his new community. If he remained an absentee owner in a Massachusetts company, he risked no liability for loss beyond the value of his stock.

While it was much easier to get a charter from an American state legislature than from Parliament or the government of France, it still took time and money for attendance at the state capitol and lobbying with the politicians. It cost the promoters of the Delaware and Raritan Canal Company, for example, $3,100 and two years of work to get a charter from the New Jersey legislature. To encourage the use of the corporation for religious, educational, and manufacturing purposes, some states enacted general incorporation. Under such a law a group could apply for a standard form of charter and receive it automatically upon the payment of a specified fee. In 1786 New York and New Jersey passed general incorporation acts for religious bodies.[10] In the 1790s New Jersey and Pennsylvania provided for educational and library companies.[11] The first general acts for some types of manufacturing companies were passed in Massachusetts in 1809 and New York in 1811.[12]

Two distinct concepts spurred the movement for general incorporation acts. Laws like that of New York for the incorporation of manufacturing concerns, or of Connecticut in 1817 and Massachusetts in 1830 granting limited liability, were passed to encourage incorporation. After the panic of 1837 and the long depression that followed, a wave of general incorporation acts was largely inspired by the fear that corporations were gaining too many dangerous privileges through special acts. Led by Connecticut in 1837, Maryland, New Jersey, New York, Pennsylvania, Indiana, Massachusetts, and Virginia all passed some type of general incorporation statute before the Civil War. In all cases, the laws sought to bring about uniformity and to protect the public from special privileges in the establishment of corporations. The ease of incorporation under these laws, however, was in the long run a great stimulus to the increasing use of the corporate form of organization.

In theory, the stockholders, assembled at annual or more frequent meetings, exercised ultimate control over their corporation. In a few early cases, the small investors were favored by reducing the voting power of large stockholders. In the charter of 1791 for the Bank of New York, for example, each share carried one vote up to a total of five, but then the ratio decreased until beyond ten it took five shares to warrant one vote.[13] Despite such occasional aids, the small stockholders never appear to have exercised democratic control of a corporation with widely held shares. The ability of the corporate form to mobilize savings from a broad area and the ideal of having the stockholders assemble in person and debate the policies of their company were in conflict. If the small stockholder lived any distance away, attending a meeting would cost more than he received in annual dividends. Furthermore, he would come without proper information or any organized following, whereas the management could use the office of the company to solicit votes by proxy and could present a specific program. Thus the directors initially selected became, in fact, self-perpetuating, unless some large capitalist or institution bought enough of the stock and organized enough additional stockholders to defeat the insiders. Needless to say, this was a time-consuming and costly process, and could only be carried out by a new group of financiers interested in gaining power, not by small stockholders merely interested in altering a specific managerial policy.

The emergence of about 300 chartered corporations by 1800, and probably well over 1,000 by 1815 changed the social character of some areas of business.* These companies, largely in the new mechanized types of business, tended to be larger than the old proprietorships and partnerships; they had enough money and specialization in management to provide men to lobby for their needs at the state capitals or in Washington; their directors knit the business community together by serving on the boards of other companies; their officers undoubtedly thought in terms of prestige and power as well as profit; and as corporations grew larger, their social and legal responsibilities became more difficult to define.

The large fixed capital needed, particularly for steam transportation, together with the unrestricted and secret transferability of corporate stock encouraged grave abuses on the part of unscrupulous financiers. It was possible for managing groups to gain personal profit by ruining great companies and selling out before the situation became known. Daniel Drew was perhaps the outstanding example of this kind of entrepreneur in the period before the Civil War. He bought and sold, built up or ruined properties solely for the purpose of extracting the maximum personal gain. But in the long run, the more conscientious men, who mixed pride in productive efficiency with the quest for wealth, were better rewarded. Cornelius Vanderbilt, Nathan Appleton, and Erastus Corning all branched out from the successful conduct of one enterprise to the control of many through strategic stock ownership.

Appleton illustrated most clearly the possibilities of widespread influence opened to the financier by the modern corporation. Turning from mercantile pursuits in 1813, Appleton, together with some of the Lowells and Jacksons, put his capital into large-scale textile manufacture. As the efficiently run business prospered, the profits were invested in new textile companies and many other forms of enterprise. Appleton came to be looked upon as the business leader of Massachusetts, sometimes sitting in Congress, at other times coaching Daniel Webster to look after his interests, and always writing and lecturing on the value of the protective tariff and sound banking. By 1840 he and his Boston associates had created in eastern Massachusetts a miniature of the corporate industrial society of the twentieth century. They controlled banking, railroad, insurance, and power companies, as well as great textile mills scattered all over the state.[14] It was the large "modern" corporation, controllable by strategically organized blocs of shares and virtually self-perpetuating boards of directors, that made this concentration of power possible, but it was also this device for

---

* It is impossible to give exact figures. Evans, *Business Incorporation*, 12, gives figures for new incorporations in eight states after 1800, but there is no record of incorporations or liquidations for most of the other states. Evans also used earlier estimates by Davis in *Essays in the Earlier History of American Corporations* (Cambridge: Harvard University Press, 1917)

gathering together the savings of thousands of small investors that produced rapid development.

NEW ROLES IN MANUFACTURING

Human adjustment to industrialization has involved a gradual change in social roles over a period, still unfinished, that started in America around 1790. Machines quickly brought specialized plants, but except for textiles, no large aggregations of managers and workers. In the late eighteenth century mechanized flour mills, such as Oliver Evans' on the Brandywine River in Delaware, operated with half a dozen employees. Even by 1850 only textiles and allied industries such as carpets, textile machinery, and calico printing; mining and refining of iron; and production of agricultural implements were generally at the factory—in contrast to the shop or small mill—stage of production.

The early application of machinery to textiles, and apparel such as shoes or hats, involved a combination of mechanized processes in mills with hand processes carried on at home. In cotton textiles before 1814, only the spinning was mechanized. Cleaning, weaving, dyeing, and printing were put out either to home workers or small shops. Since in England and Europe the industry was also broken up into stages of production, each with its own factories, the Waltham plant in 1814 was the first textile plant in the world to house all processes under one roof.[15]

A shortage or complete lack of many kinds of skilled labor led American entrepreneurs to think initially in terms of machine processes, even though these may have been very imperfect and wasteful. In the economist's language, it was not only a case of comparing the marginal costs of different factors of production, it was often one of substituting for an unavailable labor factor. Eli Whitney, the entrepreneur generally credited with introducing interchangeable parts early in the nineteenth century, probably never achieved true interchangeability or ever made a reasonable profit. But Whitney and many other fire-arms manufacturers seem to have given little thought as to whether skilled hand labor or investment in machinery was cheaper; they appeared to be emotionally committed to the improvement of machine processes.[16]

Industrial machinery required capital which master craftsmen lacked, and much of the needed money came from merchants. Between 1810 and 1830 many of the great merchant families of New England and the middle states moved from trade alone into various mixtures of trade, manufacturing, finance, insurance, and transportation. The low or nonexistent profits in foreign trade from 1807 to 1815 and the promise during these years of high returns in domestic enterprise, brought, as we have noted, Appletons, Cabots, Lawrences, Lowells, and other leaders of the merchant aristocracy into textile manufacture. A failure of trade profits to reach their old levels after 1815 also brought merchants into banking, insurance, and railroads.

The early mills were often built and run by managers who had formerly been skilled artisans, such as Samuel Slater, the English emigré who set up spinning mills for Almy and Brown of Providence, or Paul Moody who made the initial power loom for Francis Cabot Lowell. In all these business forms, just emerging from the mercantile-agrarian past, there was a strong tendency to rely on relatives for management. Wealthy merchants tended to place sons and nephews with inadequate training in charge of the new manufacturing operations, often with disastrous results. But even the most experienced master artisans had to make a transition to being businessmen as well as craftsmen, to becoming managers able to organize the work of others, to keeping records, and in some cases, to mobilizing more capital and marketing products. There was an "industrial discipline" necessary to management as well as to labor.

While the big iron makers and shipbuilders had had some of the same problems and opportunities in the colonial period, there had been only a few such enterprises, and they had not carried on coordinated processes, paced by machines. In the new mechanized factories, problems arose that required much more specialized attention. A man good at working in the shop might be poor at supervising production; he might be too interested in the processes and not enough in turning out salable goods. When machinery needed adjustment, for example, he might be too inclined to stop and do the job himself, at the expense of his managerial duties. The exmechanic was likely to be neglectful of proper division of authority, keeping of accounts, and preparation for meeting payrolls. These jobs, in turn, were too demanding to allow proper time for promoting sales.[17]

Thus in the years between 1775 and 1850 not just one but several distinct business roles emerged from the mill and factory system. One was that of the expert operating man whose role called for organizing production and maintaining good rapport with his workers, a role, however, which made few demands for social relations with his peers, community responsibility, persuasive salesmanship, or financial forecasting and manipulation. The cult of American efficiency owes its expansion in large part to the impact of increasing numbers of these men on society. Another new role required familiarity with banking, real estate deals, mortgages, and bookkeeping in order to secure and handle money efficiently and plan for expansion. Both types of men and their descendants would increasingly need specialized education or training. A third new type of role was adjusted to the needs of the marketing structure. It required cultivation of external contacts with suppliers, agents, and customers; it spread, if it did not originate, the salesman type of personality that sought to manipulate people. This role was generally divided into that of the manager who handled sales and marketing at the factory and traveling men who visited brokers, jobbers, wholesalers, and large customers. As time went on other subtypes, each with special attitudes and orientations appeared, but production, finance, and sales remained the basic divisions of both the structure of management, and the types of personality or social roles arising from industrial processes.

Each of these three types of social role was different from those of the old artisans or merchants. There were no traditional prescriptions for how the roles should be played, and as a consequence there were bound to be wide differences in performance. As usual in new situations, the habits of past conditioning persisted; former artisans, for example, who became part owners of factories readily grasped the importance of the production machinery, but not the organization of a factory. The merchants who were used to distributing goods and acting as factory agents lacked understanding of the needs and problems of machine production. In general, the early manufacturer was engrossed in too many tasks to do any of them expertly or to take much part in social and political activities. Right up to the twentieth century, the small manufacturer has remained one of the busiest of businessmen, less likely than other types to be involved in any activities outside the immediate demands of his business role.

The partners in early manufacturing enterprises who took over the roles of accounting or selling carried on activities allied to those of office or sales workers in trade, finance, or transportation. But in manufacturing these roles were held to a minimum. Large companies were rare, even by 1850, and those that existed were run by small managerial and clerical staffs. The McCormick Harvester Company plant in Chicago, for example, had 300 workers, but was run by Leander McCormick and four foremen. A big textile factory employing several hundred workers might have only two or three people in the office, and a dozen foremen in the plant. Frequently an exmerchant, assisted by one or two clerks, handled the finances of several mills from a city office. Distribution was customarily through independent agents who added the mill's products to their other lines of merchandise.

EMPLOYEES IN THE PRODUCTION PROCESS

Thus, the small but growing number of manufacturers had rather undefined or ambiguous business roles. Probably their personal attitudes and the impact of these on society did not differ greatly from those of the more substantial master craftsmen of the colonial period. But in disciplining increasing numbers of supervisors and workers to the demands of machinery, the manufacturers were highly important in shaping new social attitudes and customs. Punctual reporting for work every day, concentration on a repetitious task, care in handling expensive machinery, and attention to work schedules and quality all had to be taught by managers and learned by workers.

Efficient factory production by employees working out of sight of the boss, or even their immediate supervisor, depended upon what Reinhard Bendix calls an "internalized ethic of work performance." "In the West," he says, "two hundred years of moral and religious education preceded the rise of modern large scale industry."[18] Certainly, if this was the major factor, New England was uniquely prepared for factory work. While Americans have perhaps adjusted to industrial needs about as rapidly as the people of most other nations, the process has been a slow and painful one for all people accustomed to the very different requirements of agriculture. Women and children readjusted their habits more easily than men, and in the declining agricultural areas of the

Northeast, they were in plentiful supply. But, regardless of the inherent abilities of those recruited, work of uncertain quality or consistency was so likely to result from hands newly recruited from surrounding farms that in the early nineteenth century, mills sought patronage by advertising that they had skilled British employees.

As firms grew bigger, the relations of businessmen to their own employees became an increasingly important aspect of the social structure. Except for a very few operations, such as shipbuilding or the production of crude iron, eighteenth-century labor relations, on land, had been those of a master to one or two journeymen, or to apprentices, who were likely the young sons of his neighbors. The employers' part of the relationship was to meet customary standards in wage rates, sometimes fixed by law, and articles of apprenticeship. As journeymen and former apprentices tended to set up shops to work for themselves, the contacts in the shop were personal and usually of limited duration.

Yet it was in these small employer trades, not in the new factories or transportation companies, that employees first organized to improve their status. The pressure for organized action came partly from the loss of personal intimacy as urban shops grew larger, and partly from keener competition that squeezed wages or piece rates. As in England, collective labor action was regarded by the courts as illegal combination. In 1816 an association formed by master cordwainers (shoemakers) successfully prosecuted the striking Journeymen Cordwainers of Philadelphia as a common-law conspiracy in restraint of trade. But resort to the courts was tedious and costly; normally it was better to deal with a strike either by shutting up shop, if trade was slack, or by hiring strikebreakers if orders were pressing.

In the great boom of the mid-1830s, unions spread to cover most of the skilled handicrafts, particularly the building trades, in the major cities. There were central city councils representing all of the organized crafts, annual meetings of representatives from these city councils, and some national associations of particular crafts. The chief issues were not only those of wages, hours, and conditions of apprenticeship, in a time of inflation, but also social reforms such as free public education, an end to compulsory militia service, and exemption of a worker's tools from attachment for debt. Labor parties were attempted, unsuccessfully, in New York and Philadelphia.

Unemployment in the long depression following the panic of 1837 put intolerable pressure on these early unions. Losing their militancy, some survived as insurance and benevolent associations. The return of prosperity in the mid-forties was accompanied by vast waves of Irish, German, and French Canadian immigrants that flooded the urban labor markets and discouraged the revival of direct union action against employers.

Meanwhile, the managers of factories and contractors building canals or railroads had prevented the rise of unions among these less-skilled workers.

Strikes by ad hoc organizations of the unskilled were regarded by both employers and local governments as riots and were broken up by use of the police power. In 1842, when strikes and union activity had temporarily almost disappeared as social issues, a case involving the legal status of a trade union made its way to the Supreme Court of Massachusetts, where Chief Justice Lemuel Shaw ruled that combination and resort to a strike for a purpose that was not in itself unlawful, was legal.[19] This, to be sure, was only a decision in one state, but that state was the leader in matters of law, and, in general, the decision discouraged conspiracy prosecutions until after Congress passed the Sherman Anti-Trust Act in 1890. The American decision was also notable for preceding similar actions in England.

Such a brief sketch of these social relations overemphasizes the element of conflict. Even in large factories there were seldom as many as two hundred employees, and the conscientious manager could know each by sight and personally take care of unusual difficulties such as illness or injury. This system of paternalism by the owner, which grew up in America and elsewhere in the Western world, was one of the elements most obnoxious to union organizers, because it, in effect, granted many of the union benefits without the cost of union dues. How satisfactory proprietary paternalism was for the worker is impossible to judge; the scanty histories of uneventful labor relations necessarily rely on the records of the companies.

THE BEGINNING OF MANAGERIAL ENTERPRISE

Canal corporations such as the Delaware and Hudson or the Lehigh Canal and Navigation Company, that owned natural resources and ships as well, were the first to employ thousands of men working over large areas and to face the other problems of modern big companies. By the 1840s management problems of the same type were also present on the larger railroads. In these transportation companies the roles necessary to a hierarchical system of management were evolving. Soon there came to be vice-presidents and executive vice-presidents, general managers, and general superintendents, superintendents of motive power and maintenance, freight and passenger agents, division superintendents, auditors and general counsels, as well as many lower administrators. Even the conductor of a train was an administrative type of employee, in charge of valuable company property as well as of the lives and welfare of passengers. Applying the phrase "managerial enterprise" to corporations in which the salaried employees rather than the large stockholders on the board of directors make the important decisions, these transportation companies were the first important American examples. Just as it became impossible for the small stockholders of a big company to exert their democratic rights of control, so in a big complex organization it became increasingly difficult for directors who met no more often than once a month to know what should be done. President George Bliss of the Western Railroad remarked in 1846 that "one principle . . . which, from daily and habitual experience and observation, has been impressed on my mind more indelibly than any other ... is that ... the President ... devote all his time and faculties to the service of the company."[20] Only in this way could an officer know enough to inform the board correctly of the decisions that should be made; in general, the members had to trust their informant.

The power of professional management, of salaried careerists, however, was held in check for many decades by the presence of powerful capitalists on boards of directors, men whose help was needed in raising capital and in relations with other companies. These men could not participate intelligently in the large number of routine decisions that frequently shaped long-run policy, but when an important policy decision was to be made by the board of directors, the opinion of a man like Nathan Appleton, representing Boston finance or Erastus Corning of the New York railroad interests, might be decisive.

The combination of managerial enterprise and the corporation was to have profound economic and social effects which will be discussed in later chapters, but the change that was almost immediately evident was that the managers, including the directors, were in the position of trustees operating with other peoples' money. The power of the directors and officers in a railroad company, or even a big bank, in which they owned only a small percentage of the common stock, depended on their ability to mobilize a majority of the votes at the annual stockholders' meeting. Managing more of the stockholders' property than their own involved new problems in ethics and risk-taking. The participation of officers and directors as stockholders in many different corporations could frequently put them on both sides of a bargain.

Little progress had been made before 1850 in erecting codes of ethics or proper practice to fit the new conditions. As Nathan Appleton, called by his associates "Nathan the Wise," remarked in 1841, "There is, in the nature of things, greater danger of mismanagement in such an institution, where the interest of the managers is comparatively small, than in institutions of less capital immediately under the direction of parties more deeply interested."[21] Investors, in general, were fearful that officers would not work as hard for the stockholders' interests as they would for themselves.

The immediate social effect of the big company in finance, canals, local public utilities, and railroads was to produce a small but new social strata of well-paid, and generally well-educated careerists. They were not usually rich, but were influential in the business community because of the power of their corporations. While as citizens their social roles were, for the present, indistinct, their attitudes toward society had much in common with those of the rapidly growing ranks of lawyers, journalists, accountants, and engineers who served corporations in auxiliary ways.

Beside creating new social types, use of the corporation for large ventures also coincided with movements toward controlling competition between such highly capitalized forms of enterprise. Early in the century, steamboat operators formed associations to fix rates and limit competition. Large-scale New England enterprise in finance, insurance, textiles, and railroads was dominated by a few coalitions of Boston investors. Smaller manufacturers were beginning to form regional trade associations. Far more than in the colonial period one could now speak of the political and social pressures or organized business.

But even in 1850, the census still placed 60 percent of the "gainful workers" in agriculture. The business influences on their lives seldom came from big corporations or big cities. The country store, the store boat, the miller, the artisan, the peddler, and an occasional specialized salesman were the carriers of business mores in most of the area of the United States.

SOCIAL INFLUENCES ON THE BUSINESSMAN

"In this culture," writes James Willard Hurst, "every presumption favored the moral worth and social contribution of the shrewd manager of men and resources."[22] Such social sanctions added to the effects of abundant natural resources, scarce capital and labor, and continual migration in shaping the personality of American businessmen. By midcentury a modal type of entrepreneurial personality was emerging. Great value was placed on action. The man who did not just stand there but did something was applauded, even if what he did turned out to be wrong or wasteful. Even the philosophical supreme court justice Oliver Wendell Holmes observed, "Life is action, the use of one's powers. As to use them is our joy and duty, so it is the one end that justifies itself."[28]

Men with this optimistic activist type of personality were inclined to impatience in demanding immediate results: the long run tended to be overlooked in favor of short-range immediate market gains; experience was more valued than theory; and there was strong managerial aversion to "book-learning" and intellectual speculation. Richard Hofstadter's *Anti-Intellectualism in American Life* is a penetrating comment on this aspect of personality. The pragmatic attitudes were possibly efficient up to the end of the nineteenth century, but less so since that time.

In addition to the coming of industrialism, migration and rapid growth, both involving continuous change, made for opportunistic, loosely structured social roles. This meant that American entrepreneurs prided themselves on a high degree of independent action, doing what they wanted to do regardless of law, order, or tradition. Novelty and innovation were often positively sanctioned, and profitable change was seldom opposed. These Americans, often highly conservative in religion and social philosophy, were not really as independent as they thought, but in general there was enough leeway in business roles to allow an entrepreneur to perform economic functions in novel ways. This is perhaps equivalent to saying that America was economically a "young" country, in contrast to "old" ones where roles were more defined and hence produced stronger socioeconomic rigidities.

Increasing political and social democracy in the society as a whole were reflected in business roles. The colonial merchants had been sword-carrying aristocrats; the managers of the new transportation and manufacturing concerns of the early nineteenth century were generally hard-driving, simple men who mingled freely with their workers and expected egalitarian forms of address and manners. No doubt the relative scarcity of labor up to 1837 and the ease with which good men could get other jobs served to increase the respect accorded them. In contrast to cultures in which executives avoided contact with workers, many early proprietors of manufacturing firms spent too much time with men in the plant and not enough time in the office dealing with business problems.

We have already noted how the continual need of migrants for cheap durables or semidurables led to an American business interest in the mass production of simple utilitarian commodities. This type of market reenforced scarcity of labor in encouraging the use of machinery wherever possible, not only because it promised goods at cheaper costs, but in many cases, because skilled labor was too hard to get and to keep in sufficient quantities.

The smallness and competitiveness of early state governments made them easier for business to deal with than a remote and less interested national establishment. This encouraged the use of incorporation and led to much state aid to private ventures. The competitive economic interests of neighboring states also encouraged assistance to business and the provision of necessary services at public expense when the cost was too high for private capital.

The mixture of state and local enterprise may at times have been wasteful, but it supplied the "infrastructure" necessary for rapid development. As the mixed system of transportation and finance began to pay off by bringing crops grown on rich Western soil to market by canal and railroad, Americans realized that they were headed for great wealth. The "higher standard of living," signifying economic and social progress came to be a leading value and an ultimate sanction. Generation by generation, this value became stronger and more pervasive. Later philosophers and theologians have said the "American Way of Life" *is* the American religion, and the higher standard of living is its central component.

CHAPTER 6

Cultural Continuities

In such basic institutions as child rearing, schooling, or religion, national independence had little immediate effect on the slow processes of cultural change. As English connections became more remote, American attitudes generated by migration and the new environment became more influential; most of these, such as the condemnation of leisure and the virtue accorded to work, were part of the complex of values associated with business attitudes. Thus as time went on, the culture became manifestly more businesslike. Perry Miller believes that about 1815 business civilization became "the dominant theme of American History at the expense of other value systems."[1] In the same vein James Willard Hurst writes "the getting of income. . .could easily become an end in itself."[2]

FAMILY LIFE AND CHILD REARING

Elimination of the extended local kinship group as the result of migration to America was one of the major alterations that had taken place in family life and outlook before the rapid spread of urbanism in the nineteenth century. The long-run effects of the relative isolation of the nuclear family, reenforced by continued migration within America, became more obvious with the passage of generations. Writers of books on the family in each period, sensing the magnitude of these forces, held that drastic changes were taking place and that child rearing and the transmission of cultural traits were no longer the same as in earlier generations. But with the advantage of a retrospective view, the alternations in the period from 1775 to 1850 seem gradual, partly because writers now see "American characteristics" as originating much earlier.[3] In the brief discussion which follows, much of the change can be seen as an extension of colonial practices and attitudes. America had probably always been "a society which deemphasized personal ties and emphasized social and geographical mobility. . .in the interest of economic progress and correspondingly one inimical to strong family ties or dependence on kin."[4] The same forces also appear to have weakened the strength of nonfamilial personal ties. Amos

Lawrence, a Boston Brahmin of the older generation, said in 1840, "I practiced the maxim 'business before friends.' "[5]

The principal new directions of change in the family and child rearing, resulting from the progress of industrialism and urbanism in this period, are generally assumed to be a rise in the position of women and children in relation to the father, and an increased emphasis on the proper use of time. The movement of industry out of the home to specialized shops, and the rapid migration of country people to towns and cities lessened the economic importance of the family household and compelled internal readjustments. While most Americans before 1850 were still brought up on family farms, a majority of boys succeeding in business may have spent their youths in towns or cities.

Arthur W. Calhoun sees estrangement from the father as arising also from the business demands of the competitive American environment: "Men were too busy to know their little ones, to enjoy much of their wives' society, or to lavish affection."[6] The Reverend John S. C. Abbott, for example, wrote, "The father. . .eager in the pursuit of business toils early and late, and finds no time to fulfill. . .duties to his children."[7] Murray G. Murphey finds estrangement from, and resentment of, the father arising also from the fact that he ordinarily administered the severe punishments.[8] "I'll tell your father when he comes home," was the mother's ultimate resource. According to Murphey's analysis of both child-rearing theory and the accounts of familial discipline by foreign visitors, this practice led to enduring aggressiveness toward threatening males.[9] While the practice was undoubtedly present in other cultures, it may serve everywhere to explain the joy in winning a battle in the market place and doing-in a business adversary. It has no doubt provided some of the emotional content that has made business so exciting a pursuit.

Although Murphey's data on parental authority is from visitors to the Middle Atlantic states, and New England practices were probably stricter, severe punishment seems to have been rare, at least among the urban upper-middle class. Foreign observers who found American business roles loosely structured, were also struck by what seemed to them a high degree of permissiveness in American child rearing. They commented on lack of strict discipline, little use of corporal punishment, and an absence of enforced deference for elders. Undoubtedly there were areas such as toilet training and sex, on which the visitors failed to report, where stern measures may have been the rule.[10] Yet, the visitors had to agree that, on the whole, this training produced independent, precocious children who soon reached maturity. These qualities may have been more valuable to the business world of the mid-nineteenth century than was training by strict discipline. But submission to hierarchical authority became more important as firms grew larger, and child-rearing books usually put strong emphasis on obedience. "Prompt, faithful and willing *obedience*," writes the

Reverend John Hersey, "is the foundation upon which the hope of your children's future happiness must be laid. . . . Your word *must* be respected—your commands *must* be obeyed or your children must be ruined."[11]

Factories and railroads introduced a new emphasis on time. Daily routines now went by minutes rather than hours, and children must be trained not to waste time and to be punctual. To a considerable extent, the new emphasis merely continued colonial admonitions against wasting time. "A rational principle of economy will admit no waste of *time* or *money* or *property*," said Hersey, "children should be taught to avoid the sluggards bed; teach them to consider idleness as the fruitful source and parent of every evil."[12]

Thus saving time was joined with homilies on the virtue of work. "Industry was seen as "the surest guard against vice."[13] The well-known minister Lyman Beecher cautioned, "It would be endless to describe the wiles of idleness—how it creeps upon men. . .where it has its way it sinks and drowns employment."[14] The virtue of work should not be obscured, he again cautioned: "A hearty industry promotes happiness. The applause of conscience,. . .the manly joy of usefulness, the consent of every faculty of the mind. . .constitute a happiness superior to the fewer flashes of vice in its brightest moments."[15] Hersey warned parents, "You cannot drive your children into habits of industry by frowns and by force, but by reason, by persuasion and example; but when these means fail, you must then resort to coercion."[16]

As business success became the goal of the middle to upper class Americans likely to peruse such literature, the child-rearing manuals imply an emphasis on the children as a means of achieving parental ambitions and raising their family's social status. "The young child was the future businessman or citizen, equally capable of earning a million dollars or aspiring to the presidency."[17] Hope for business success was coupled with beliefs in man's power to control the environment, and in child rearing as a rational process for achieving desired traits of character.[18] The emphasis on getting ahead of others appears at least as early as 1790 when the Reverend Enos Hitchcock wrote that children "should be fired with a spirit of emulation to equal or excell others."[19] By the mid-nineteenth century, emphasis on success had become the general theme of admonitory literature of many types.[20] Ministers urged parents to "encourage a child to amass, that he might use, and use well, what he gains."[21]

As early as the 1830's, Mrs. Edith Sigourney in *Ladies Magazine* was protesting against this set of values based on the accumulation of wealth.[22] As time went on, both the values and the protests grew stronger. According to a twentieth-century writer, editor Sarah Hale's campaign in *Godey's Ladies Book* was so persuasive that "the resulting tension between the values of the success ethic and those of Mrs. Hale's crusade did little to further domestic solidarity. . . . The home and the market place became the foci of opposite sets of values, one stultifyingly static, the other recklessly dynamic,"[23] No doubt, many of the devoutly religious men who also acquired wealth were conditioned always to be conscious of the obligation to further good works.[24]

In this economy which greatly needed capital, it is not surprising that child training in frugality and saving were as strongly advocated as training in industry and profitable use of time. "While the habits of industry. . .prepare the way for the practice of every virtue," said Hersey,

> In every stage of domestic education, children should be disciplined to restrain their appetites and desires. Let nothing be wasted; this motto should not only be written on the title page of your child's memory, but it should be engraven on the tablet of their understanding. . . . Do not permit your children to run in debt for anything; there is more waste and extravagance connected with the system of credit than people are generally aware of. . . . Real economy admits of no negligence or carelessness as these lead to waste.[25]

He also stressed the Calvinist doctrine of the sacred duty of everyone to choose a proper calling, holding guidance in their choice to be one of the family's obligations to its children. "It must. . .form an important item in your parental account to select a suitable trade or profession for your children."[26]

In summing up the virtues expected in young Americans, Beecher said, "The reputable portions of society have maxims of prudence by which the young are judged and admitted to their good opinion. *Does he regard his work? Is he industrious? Is he economical? Is he free from immoral habits?*[27] Samuel Goodrich's list of necessary virtues that parents must inculcate was "Truth, Justice, Cheerfulness, Fidelity, Industry, Courage."[28] The primacy given to truth or reliability in both lists indicates the importance of this business problem in the nineteenth century. The desire for quick success, loosely defined business roles, and the untraditional character of business situations in new areas all tended to erode accepted canons of honesty. As we have seen (Chapter 4), the credit exporting areas of the Eastern seaboard deplored the irresponsibility of debtors in the interior. Merchants would fail in one community and disappear with the cash on hand to try their luck elsewhere, while peddlers from the East cheated the back-country people with bad merchandise. The severe critic, Mrs. Trollope, wrote, "after four years of attentive and earnest observation and inquiry, my honest conviction is that the standard of moral character is very greatly lower than in Europe,"[29] While not as serious a fault as hostile critics made it appear, business dishonesty was a continuing problem, perhaps stemming from high geographical mobility and not curable by large doses of childhood admonition.[30]

PRIVATE ENTERPRISE IN EDUCATION

The view, inherited from England and Europe, that education was not a responsibility of the state continued outside New England and most businessmen remained uninterested in public education. Everywhere in the new states, the revolution had a "disastrous" effect on schools.[31] Many public, charity, and private schools, abandoned during the war, failed to reopen. Businessmen, thinking of office employees in terms of rising middle-class youths, saw no need for financing their education. The desirability of a well-educated working class, which had in fact much less economic value than in later periods of more complex technology, was seldom recognized. Those few who did advocate more general education based their case on indoctrination for the protection of property and orderly government.

Outside New England there were few provisions for schools in the early state laws. New York and seven other states made no mention of education in their original constitutions. In spite of the speeches of a few leading statesmen regarding the value of education, "in actual practice there was little evidence that schools were generally considered as necessary means of solving political, economic, and social problems of the day."[32] What had started as neglect because of an emergency gradually crystalized into a laissez-faire policy regarding public education. No one contradicted men like the famous Dr. Benjamin Rush of Philadelphia who favored a free school in every township, but no one in authority took up the cause.[33] In 1824 James G. Carter wrote of the public schools, "The decline in popular education among us, or rather the comparatively retrograde motion of the principle means to it, has been more perceptible during the last twenty or thirty years, than it ever was at any former period."[34] Meanwhile, as opportunities for the unskilled in factory, mill, and construction work led to a decline of the skilled handicrafts, apprenticeship—the usual form of education for ambitious urban youth—was becoming less important.[35]

While public education suffered from general neglect, private education in academies spread rapidly. In 1790 private academies, often starting with the elementary grades and continuing through high school, were "to be found throughout the nation."[36] By 1850 they formed a national system of secondary education, supported in part by state grants and remission of taxes, but largely free from public control. The inadequacy of the system, apart from the matter of tuition fees, can be inferred from the fact that in New England, where the academy had its highest development, there was an average of only 1.6 teachers per school—little improvement over the one-room country schoolhouse.[37] Yet it was not generally recognized that these understaffed academies could not keep pace with the growing educational needs of the world of business. For example, in 1807 at the new Warren Academy at Morristown, New Jersey, decimal currency, the official money system of the country since 1775, was not taught; neither were geography, history, nor geometry.[38]

Increasing opportunity open to those with only a rudimentary dame school or home training, and the relatively low prestige of intellectual pursuits worked against all types of education. Children went to work early to increase the family income, middle-class boys left academies as soon as they could secure promising jobs, and few who were not intending to be lawyers or ministers finished college.

As Mrs. Trollope remarked in her invidious way, "At sixteen, often much earlier, education ends and money-making begins; the idea that more learning is necessary than can be acquired at that time, is generally ridiculed as absolute monkish bigotry."[39] In view of the fact that "higher" education consisted largely of Latin and Greek, there was much to be said for the youthful dropout.

By 1825 social reformers in the ministry, the law, and politics, and a few businessmen, were becoming certain that it was dangerous to neglect the education of the masses.[40] Some of these leaders of opinion seem also to have seen the problem that the more the economic system progressed, the less fit the ordinary man was for contributing to the advance. Abbott Lawrence, the founder of the textile mills at Lowell, was one of those who in contrast to general business opinion, held that successful operation of factories in competition with the British required educated employees.[41] In 1842 educator Alonzo Potter urged that for advancing the nation "education is unspeakably more important than a luxuriant soil, fine climate or noble rivers."[42] Eastern businessmen dealing with the interior were anxious that Westerners should be indoctrinated with sound views of political economy. Edward Everett, soliciting aid for a school in the West, warned New England businessmen:

> Let no Boston Capitalist. . .who is called upon to aid this Institution in the center of Ohio, think that he is called upon to exercise his liberality at a distance, toward those in whom he has no concern. . . . They ask you to contribute to give security to your own property.[43]

A few individuals like Timothy Claxton of Boston who made school equipment obviously had an interest in furthering education, but during most of the period before 1850 it was difficult to contend that free education was essential to the conduct of business.[44]

As a consequence, in spite of the exhortations of leaders like Everett or Lawrence, or of the supporters of factory schools like that of T. W. Dyott at Dyottville, Pennsylvania, businessmen did little to further public education.[45] A committee of the senate of Massachusetts, the most advanced state in educational matters, reported in 1825 that in most industrial towns of the state, children employed in factories were receiving no schooling. Some of the manufacturers held that schooling for factory children was undesirable and refused to release children for attendance at school.[46] In Philadelphia the Pennsylvania Society for the Promotion of Public Schools had among its fifteen-odd council members several businessmen interested in philanthropy, but its officers and a majority of its members appear to have been men interested in political office. In spite of the interest in education of the well-known economist of industry, Matthew Carey, the society could not be called a "business" pressure group.[47]

By 1830 several journals devoted to education were calling attention to the deficiencies of the American system compared with those of the leading nations abroad. Reports on the Prussian public school system which Francis Bowen of Harvard called "the most complete system of common schools which had yet been devised in the civilized world" were making some Americans uneasy.[48] France and Scotland were also held up as models that the United States should seek to emulate.

It was against the background of rapid industrial and urban growth, general business complacency regarding the educational *status quo,* a rising demand by organized labor for free education, and the superior progress of some foreign nations that the campaign for public schools finally gained momentum. From 1825 to 1850 free education was one of the continuing major issues of the day. "Old friends and business associates parted company over the question," writes Ellwood P. Cubberley, "lodges were forced to taboo the subject to avoid disruption, ministers and their congregations often quarreled over the question of free schools, and politicians avoided the issue."[49] While among eighteen groups listed, Cubberley has no category for businessmen, city residents—which would include most of the business community—are recorded as favorable.

From the literature on the struggle for free schools, it would seem that businessmen probably divided for and against along liberal-conservative lines and cannot be said to have had any group attitude. Horace Mann, a believer in state action, who gave up a profitable law practice and a seat in the legislature to become the first secretary of the new State Board of Education of Massachusetts in 1837, thought that the best persuader was to show that "education has a market value; that it is so far an article of merchandise, that it may be turned to a pecuniary account; it may be minted, and will yield a larger amount of statutable coin than common bullion."[50] In his famous Fifth Report in 1842, widely read in other states, Mann made a particular appeal to businessmen, which may have been one of the factors awakening many of them to the need for better education. An educational authority said in 1863 that Mann's report had "probably done more than all other publications written within the past twenty-five years to convince capitalists of the value of elementary instruction as a means of increasing the value of labor."[51]

By this time more leaders of business were strongly in favor of public education. Thaddeus Stevens of Pennsylvania, iron-maker and politician, urged the legislators to vote for free public schools since they would cost less than half as much as private schools. Abbott Lawrence in Massachusetts counseled his fellow businessmen to "Let your common school system go hand in hand with the employment of your people."[52]

Yet the strong admonitions of a few businessmen had little effect politically. At the end of the period there were inadequate "public" schools in Connecticut and Massachusetts, partly supported by rates or small fees per child; still more inadequate pauper schools existed in the middle states, with local option for free public schools after 1830. It is notable that in the 1830s most rural communities in these states were offered a partial subsidy. In some areas opposition was based on religious objections to secular education.

That before 1820 there was practically nothing beyond pious pronouncements regarding public education in the West suggests lack of local business demand for a tax-supported system. In 1825 Ohio laid the foundations for a public system modeled after Massachusetts; two years later Michigan territory, which included the future state of Wisconsin, passed similar legislation. In Illinois and Indiana, where New England influence was less, action on public education lagged until after 1840. The Southern pattern varied between no provisions for a state system, and free schools for paupers only. In all, Edwards and Richey estimate that in 1840 about half the children of New England, one-seventh of those of the middle states, and one-sixth of those of the West had free education.[53]

Businessmen whose sons were educated in the many private academies were not anxious to pay taxes to support public high schools. While there were a few such schools in New York, Pennsylvania, and Connecticut, only Massachusetts had a law, passed in 1827, requiring high schools in towns of 500 or more families. But the schools opened under this law were of doubtful merit. Up to 1852, in the high school at Lowell, for example, "the bulk of the pupils were studying arithmetic and grammar, while not one had studied moral science for three years and only two had done anything with higher Mathematics in the same time."[54] There were few indications of helpful influence from the more advanced foreign schools on the development of American high schools before 1840.[55]

BUSINESS INFLUENCES ON CURRICULUM AND TEXTS

In many schools, however, the curriculum gradually became more secular and utilitarian, which meant more responsive to the needs of business. The pressure for such courses was not new. In 1786 Dr. Rush had written,

> If we consider the commerce of our metropolis (Philadelphia) only as an avenue of wealth for the state, the study of it merits a place in a young man's education, but I consider commerce in a much higher light when I recommend the study of it in republican seminaries. I view it as the best security against the influence of hereditary monopolies of land, and, therefore, the surest protection against aristocracy.[56]

Some of the older academies appear to have moved toward more utilitarian education before 1800. In 1788 Phillips Academy at Exeter, New Hampshire, was offering algebra, geometry, and ancient and modern geography.[57] Two years later, the Church-of-England School in Newburgh, New York, offered geography and history to those willing to pay 12 shillings a quarter instead of the 8 shillings charged for the three R's.[58] In a speech at Darby Academy in Hingham, Massachusetts, in 1796, the Reverend David Barnes called business arithmetic the international common language. "It proves a facility of commerce, and seems to have been intended by Providence in some measure to limit the dissocial effects of the confusion of tongues."[59]

As academies spread rapidly in the first half of the nineteenth century, the same trends continued. By 1815, for example, Woburn Academy in Massachusetts had added bookkeeping to its curriculum.[60] Six years later the English Classical School of Boston offered bookkeeping, navigation, surveying, mensuration, and trigonometry.[61] In 1837 the Board of Regents of the State of New York listed, in addition, courses in statistics, technology, architecture, drawing, civil engineering, mapping, and stenography.[62] Presumably, each course was taught in at least one approved school in the state.

Textbooks followed the same trends as the curriculum. R. R. Robinson found that religious subjects made up 85 percent of the content of readers published before 1775, and only 22 percent in those published between 1775 and 1825.[63] The famous *New England Primer*, for example, when first published about 1690 was highly pietistic, but by 1800 it was becoming secular in its examples: admonitions such as B stands for "Heaven to find, the Bible to mind" were replaced by B "was a Blockhead who ne'er learned his book."[64] Noah Webster wrote in 1840 that when he was young (the 1760s), "the books used were chiefly or wholly Dilworth's Spelling Books, the Psalter, Testament, and Bible."[65]

The publication of Webster's texts—the speller in 1783, the grammar in 1784, and the reader in 1785—were major educational events. Other new texts such as Jedidiah Morse's geography in 1784 aided the inadequately equipped teacher. Curti notes that "Webster's social philosophy included the astute doctrine that real power always consists in property and held that 'the laborious and saving, who are generally the best citizens will possess each his share of property and power.' "[66] While Webster's texts had broad influence, the circulation of other early books is uncertain. *The American Classbook or a Collection of Instructive Reading Lessons adapted to use in the Schools,* for example, taken from the works of Hugh Blair, a Scottish clergeman and professor at Edinburgh, had a strong emphasis on business—Topics near the end of the book were the coal mines of England, the iron works of England, and manufactures, including detail on those of paper and porcelain—but its readers may have been few.[67] Arithmetics frequently had sections on business operations such as discount at compound interest, annuities, rules for adjusting partnership shares, and other useful applications.[68]

The famous McGuffey readers began to appear in 1836. The fifth reader in 1844 completed the group available before 1850. Differing in no outstanding fashion from their competitors, they did not immediately sweep the country.[69] Webster's reader of 1785, for example, held a good market for nearly a century.[70] These first McGuffey readers present a general philosophy of self-help, natural rights, the sanctity of private property, and Christian morality, salted with admonitions such as "When a man resolves to do his work himself, you may depend upon it that it will be done well," and "Do your task at once; then think about it," or "One doer is worth a hundred dreamers," all of which values were highly regarded by men of business.[71] These and the other widely-sold readers, such as those of Caleb Bingham, Lindley Murray, John Pierpont, or Noah Webster, however, show also that the traditional religious and literary themes of American and English culture dictated much of the content of what was "good" for a child to read.

SPECIAL EDUCATION FOR BUSINESS

Education whose aim was to transmit the knowledge and skills needed by business may be divided into two branches: the continuing spread of part-time schools for business techniques, that came to be called "business colleges"; and the beginning of education in science and engineering. Small proprietary night schools that had started in the early eighteenth century (Chapter 2) began around 1820 to call themselves "business schools or colleges" and to appear in almost every city. James A. Bennett opened a bookkeeping school in New York City in 1818, and two years later published the *American System of Practical Bookkeeping adapted to the Commerce of the United States and Exemplified in one set of Books.* By 1833 this text was in its fifteenth edition.[72] Run as profit-making enterprises for their masters, by the 1840s the more successful schools developed chains of affiliates. H. B. Bryant and H. D. Stratton, and R. Montgomery Bartlett were leaders in this type of enterprise. In 1850 there were about twenty private business schools in cities of the East and Middle West, offering courses that usually ran for three months.

The students were generally young white-collar employees of mercantile firms, not manual workers.[73] For the latter, it appeared that free courses at "mechanics institutes" might be the way to a better educated and more skilled labor force. But after the first few years in the 1820s most such organizations, supported largely by donations, died away from both lack of attendance and lack of funds.[74] Some of these were absorbed in the lyceum movement for public lectures. A few such as Franklin Institute in Philadelphia (1824), Maryland Institute in Baltimore (1826), and Mechanics Institute in Cincinnati (1828) attracted enough private support to become, ultimately, centers for museums, exhibits, lectures, and research.[75]

Scientific schools had had a long history in Europe. The School of Mines in Freiberg, Saxony, for example, was opened in 1665. By the mid-nineteenth century, educator Daniel C. Gilman thought that "The material prosperity of many European countries is manifestly dependent upon the extent and character of their systems of scientific education."[76] Possibly the United States lagged behind Europe because its rich ores near the surface had raised few mining difficulties, and engineering problems regarding canals, hard-surfaced roads, and bridges came only after 1790. It may also have been that Americans, too fond of relying on experience, undervalued even strictly technical learning.[77]

No specialized school to impart engineering or scientific knowledge was established by any American state or private groups until 1824. Meanwhile, the United States Military Academy at West Point, started in 1802, had provided a few men with engineering training. Rensselear Polytechnic Institute, the first specialized American scientific school, was founded by a landed aristocrat, Stephen van Rensselear, who probably had his attention called to the need for such education through his interest in canals and his service on the New York Canal Commission. The original plan was to "instruct the sons and daughters of farmers and mechanics...[in] the application of science to the common purposes of life." Listening to lectures was to be mixed with experience in performing scientific operations.[78] Although its sponsor considered it primarily a school of applied chemistry, the institute was led by the coming of the railroad into the field of civil engineering.[79]

Even though science and mathematics became more important in curricula, the industrial revolution was over half a century old in the United States before there was a second, enduring private scientific school. Abbott Lawrence explaining his gift of $100,000 to Harvard in 1847, which founded the school named after him, stressed not so much the need for technologists as the desirability of more fully developing the talents of young, educated Americans. "I believe the time has arrived," he said, "when we should make an effort to diversify the occupations of our people."[80] Thus both of these scientific schools were established by philanthropists thinking of the general welfare of the nation and its people rather than in direct response to the immediate needs of business, although no doubt the latter played a part.

THE HIGHER LEARNING

While religious missionaries provided the educational push behind the proliferation of small American colleges or "universities," the money needed for land, buildings, and faculty came largely from local businessmen, who continued to regard colleges as valuable economic assets. Every growing city aspired to a college, not only for the additional consumers it would bring to the area, but because in the keen intercity rivalry an institution of higher learning was symbolic of the success and importance of the community in competition with its neighbors. Consequently, the more energetic cities were willing to raise substantial sums of money to attract colleges of any of the popular religious denominations.[81] As a result, the college became a competitive institution of the frontier like the local bank, newspaper, and railroad project, not one serving any large population in need of higher education. Before 1870, for example, twenty-one colleges were founded in Illinois and thirteen in Iowa.

Most colleges, like other small businesses, failed—700 before the Civil War, and only one college in five started in that period existed in 1930.[82] Since in some cases the state charters where acquired by rival institutions, many colleges can trace an ancestral line under several different names.

The older private establishments, except for the University of Pennsylvania, were denominational and saw the training of ministers and spread of the denomination as their major roles.[83] While some fifty new colleges were established between 1780 and 1829, including some state universities, sectarianism remained the rule. Even the larger colleges, such as Harvard, Yale, or Union, were small. Probably none had more than about 400 students, and some "universities" had well below 100. An estimate of the mid-1820s placed the annual number of college graduates at about 750.[84] Only a handful of colleges or universities had more than two or three professors, including the president.

Until well into the nineteenth century, college performance suffered from the same loss of interest in intellectual matters that was weakening both public education and support of the old orthodox churches. In the period 1789 to 1829, Joseph Dorfman finds that "meagre salaries, ill-trained teachers, multitudinous subjects under one instructor, shortened programs and nepotism were admitted evils."[85] During this period the interaction between business and the content of higher learning seems to have been slight. The beginning of a more active business interest appeared in the 1830s when college-educated merchants began to appreciate the value of proper academic courses and of pursuasive texts on economics for preserving social stability.

At Columbia University in 1831, John McVicker taught one of the earliest courses in economics.[86] The missionary character of most early economic teaching is suggested by the designation of the courses as "moral philosophy." Of all the textbook writers who supported the existing economic order, Francis Wayland, economist, minister, and president of Brown University, was probably the most influential. Calling his study "moral science," he found its two basic principles to be personal liberty and private property. His *Elements of Political Economy*, published in 1837, became the leading text, and imparted doctrine that has been called "clerical laissez-faire." The major emphasis was on the beneficent and automatic operation of the laws of the market. Market price was in general a fair price because departures from labor cost would be quickly corrected. Regulation for any purpose was generally uneconomic.[87]

While the economics text was developing as an intellectual and moral justification of business practice, the institutions of business came under vigorous attack from leading nonacademic New England intellectuals. Channing, Emerson, Parker, and Thoreau, as well as a host of lesser figures, saw the emerging industrial society as a menace to older and better customs and values. Except in the case of Thoreau's idealistic individualism, the attack was not basically radical; it was rather a criticism of businessmen as lacking in humanitarianism, imagination, and other finer qualities. Channing saw the main energies of the generation centered "On property, on wealth. High and low, rich and poor, are running the race of accumulation. . . . Our danger is from the habits of drudgery."[88] Emerson found that state papers and debates, lectures and sermons, and especially newspapers

> recommended conventional virtues, whatever will earn and preserve property; always the capitalist; the college, the church, the hospital, the theatre, the hotel, the road, the ship of the capitalist—whatever goes to secure, adorn, enlarge these, is good, whatever jeopardizes any of these is damnable.[89]

Whereas Emerson condemned business for "meanness and sterility," Parker saw dishonest businessmen as the corrupters of public morals. "The devil of the nineteenth century," he held,

> has gone into trade and advertises in the papers. He makes money; the world is poorer by his wealth. . .his patron saint is Judas. . . . In politics he wants a Government that will ensure his dividends; so asks what is good for him, but ill for the rest. He knows no right only power; no man but self, no God but his calf of gold;[90]

While ministers like Emerson and Parker might entertain large audiences with their rhetoric, they were exceptional from the standpoint of both the church and higher learning. In colleges and universities, where mercantile trustees and a clerical faculty maintained harmonious relations, business and religion re-enforced each other. In preaching "We estimate the value of a thing by its usefulness," the Reverend George W. Bethune spoke for both groups.[91]

But all-in-all, the connection between classical college education and the immediate needs of business was so obscure that once a college had been brought to the community, businessmen made relatively small donations to the struggling private institution. Many self-made businessmen thought college produced indolent aristocratic habits and preferred not to hire graduates. The relatively large number of college men who became the heads of big companies was more an indication of the connection of higher education with upper-class family background than of the value placed by businessmen on the higher learning.[92]

Thomas Hamilton, an English visitor, wrote in 1843,

> In all the knowledge that must be taught, and which requires laborious study for its attainment, I should say that the Americans are considerably inferior to my countrymen. In that knowledge, on the other hand, which the individual acquires by himself by actual observation, which bears an immediate market value, and is directly available in the ordinary avocations of life, I do not imagine the Americans are excelled by any people in the world.[93]

This seems a wise observation on the state of education in the northern United States, at least, in the mid-nineteenth century. The businesslike culture emphasized sharp observation and the use of experience, and deemphasized reading and theoretical approaches.

BUSINESS AS EDUCATOR

Hamilton's statement also calls attention to the educational role of business institutions themselves, reaching far beyond the training provided for apprentices. Chief among these institutions was the country general store.

Small groups of squatters, generally the first residents in areas west of the old seaboard colonies, were initially served, if at all, by itinerate artisans, peddlers, and teachers, but close on their heels came the general storekeeper. "Such establishments appeared at the earliest possible chance for survival and compensated for the limited extent of the market by performing as many economic functions as possible."[94] If the storekeeper was successful enough or the land salesmen were pursuasive enough, a town developed around his shop. As an example, Lewis E. Atherton cites Magnus S. League of Bluff Springs, Virginia. "In 1823 he opened a general store in connection with a ferry across Big Black River. League also operated a sawmill, a gristmill, and a distillery. As the community developed he provided a post office, schoolhouse, Masonic-lodge building, church, and a site for a cemetery from his neighboring landholdings."[95]

The general store necessarily became the social and civic center of the frontier or country community. Here the little news that came in from the outside world would be brought by travelers, newspapers, or by the merchant himself. He sold what new books and periodicals his customers saw, and he let youngsters read them in the store. He had not only cloth, but fashion books with patterns for the home dressmaker. He had whisky and a warm stove for sociable afternoons or evenings. The general store was the academy and college of the frontier youth brought up in a lonely wilderness.[96]

The history of the Lincoln family, so meticulously investigated, illustrates the educational process on the frontier.[97] Unsuccessful at both business and farming, Abraham Lincoln's father Thomas sank lower and lower in the economic scale until in 1818 he reached the frontier in southern Indiana "Rite in the Brush," where he erected an open-face camp. It was two years before the Lincolns had finished an eighteen-by-twenty-foot log cabin. Meanwhile Thomas Lincoln, the two children, his wife, and her brother relied mainly on game for food and made only feeble efforts at farming. Abraham Lincoln lived in such circumstances from the age of eight.

Yet in this environment Lincoln acquired an education and knowledge of the culture that fitted him for an active role in local affairs and politics in small-town Illinois as soon as his family moved to that state in 1830. He learned to read and write during 1818-1819 when a wandering teacher held school some two or three miles away for a single winter. In two later years Lincoln again went to a school, but the family legend has it that altogether Lincoln attended school less than one full year. Another source of education was the small supply of books that his stepmother brought to the cabin when she came in 1819. Lincoln was a continual reader and also sought books from the libraries of lawyers at the frontier villages of Rockport and Boonville.

But a large part of his contact with the culture of the more settled parts of nineteenth-century America came from the store in nearby Gentryville. This town began to develop about 1820 when James Gentry started to sell store goods at his farm house, and later opened a general store. "To this backwoods hamlet young Lincoln would speed like a homing pigeon when work was done for the day," wrote Albert J. Beveridge.[90] "For there gathered other youths and men who craved companionship and the story-telling, talk, and discussion which took place in country stores." His contact with Gentry led to Lincoln's being hired to help take a flatboat of goods to New Orleans. When the family moved to Illinois in 1830, Lincoln soon became a store clerk in nearby New Salem, a job that apparently grew out of his earlier association with Gentry. Until Lincoln became village postmaster of New Salem in 1833, therefore, his principal connections had been with storekeepers. In view of his limited formal schooling, it seems reasonable to say that, apart from reading, the general store was the principal educational influence in Lincoln's early life: that as a frontier youth his school was the emporium of retail trade.

Thus business institutions and American business culture moved into the West scarcely behind the man with the rifle. If one tries to assess the origins of the culture of the fairly mature frontier, of regions settled ten years of more, it is hard to say whether the farmers or the townspeople, such as the lawyers, storekeepers, millers, and artisans, had contributed more. While the farmers were in somewhat greater numbers, they were less articulate, less likely to innovate, and less able to influence others. The men who went to the towns were presumably better educated, in contact with large numbers of clients or customers, and conscious readapters of Eastern practices to Western necessities. That the towns ran the countryside was obvious by the later nineteenth century, but it seems probable that the period when this was not true was so brief in most areas that it was culturally unimportant.[99] And the entrepreneurs of Main Street represented American business as truly as the financiers of Wall or State Street.

THE ENLIGHTENMENT IN THE EAST

Independent of any influences from business, the immediate effect on religion of the political excitements of the eighteenth century, at home and abroad, appeared to be a weakening of the older Protestant churches. From 1775 to 1800 the young were not brought up in the strict religious or social decorum of the late colonial period. The upper classes, as illustrated by college student opinion, showed a loss of interest in religion. The period has been characterized perhaps too strongly, as one of "spiritual deadness among all the American churches. . .the lowest ebb-tide of vitality in the history of American Christianity."[100] Of the five major denominations in 1800, "only the Presbyterians had a truly national constituency in addition to. . .an educated clergy."[101] Yet while the kind of religion favored by the established elite appeared to be weakening, two new faiths—Baptism and Methodism, with more evangelical appeal and more flexible organizations than the older churches—grew rapidly.

It is difficult to say whether, on balance, the value of the institutions of religion to business declined. Superficially the churches that were attended by the well-to-do appear to have suffered most from the postrevolutionary loss of enthusiasm. It seemed that businessmen, for a time, failed to realize the importance of vigorous Calvinist churches to a young capitalism. The colonial churches had failed fully to mirror the rationality, individualism, and optimism of American business. The discrepancy became greater as postrevolutionary businessmen saw in the new nation an economic promised land, too great a gift to come from a God who regarded most men as irrevocably damned. "Calvinism," writes Russel Nye, "seemed to have very little relevance to an expanding mercantile society which believed in natural rights, social contracts and foreign trade."[102] The weakened appeal of the older theology opened the way for the influence of European Deism on the ministry of the leading urban Congregational and Presbyterian churches, and among their prosperous and influential business parishioners. The new doctrines, such as recognition of the ability of the individual to interpret his relationship to God and scripture, and the essential goodness of man, helped to inspire Unitarianism and later Universalism in the Congregational church, as well as the New School Presbyterians.

A small group who might be called business intellectuals of the late eighteen century wrote in favor of Deism. Thomas Paine, who had been an able public-relations man for the Pennsylvania Bank in the 1780s, returned to France and wrote *The Age of Reason* in 1794. He exhorted men to study God through his works. Denounced by conservatives, the American edition was nevertheless a best-seller, and the Episcopal Parson Mason Weems saw no harm in carrying it on his book-selling travels.[103] John Fitch, pioneer entrepreneur of the steamboat, formed a Philadelphia Group of Deists. Stephen Girard, soon to be the richest man in the United States, collected the writings of Voltaire in many editions. Joel Barlow, poet and promoter of Western land, wrote as a Deist of the perfection of individualism:

> Look through earth and meditate the skies
> And find some general law in every breast
> Where ethics, faith, and politics may rest.[104]

Franklin, while sympathetic to the Deist view, took little part in spreading the doctrine, and died before the publication of the *Age of Reason*. The limited excitement over Deism, as such, died away in the early years of the new century, but the harmony of more liberal religious ideas with optimistic business attitudes may help to explain the swing of Boston mercantile wealth to Unitarianism. According to Harriet Beecher Stowe, "all the trustees of Harvard College were

Unitarians. All the elite of wealth and fashion crowded Unitarian churches."[105] Vernon F. Parrington says, "The commercial dominated the intellectual and emotional in their prim and somewhat cold congregations."[106] Seldom has a religious heresy received such solid financial support. Nathan Appleton, the sage of Boston finance, wrote,

> The Unitarian party embraces the most intelligent and high-minded portion of the community. It is my opinion that the views of the Unitarians are the best and only security against the spirit of infidelity, which is prevailing so extensively amonst the most highly educated and intelligent men of Europe.[107]

Octavius B. Frothingham, looking back on the days of his youth, said of Unitarianism,

> "This influence was strongly conservative of the existing order, and threw the weight of public opinion against agitation or reform."[108]

Somewhat more gradually the same doctrines of individualism and optimism penetrated the Presbyterian church. In 1801 the Connecticut Congregational and Presbyterian churches entered into the Plan of Union for supplying new churches with ministers. While the Plan was joined by the two denominations in the other New England states, it was never accepted by theological conservatives. By the late 1820s irreconcilable differences divided the Old School Plan of Union or New School Presbyterians and weakened them as a missionary force for businesslike Calvinism in the West.

THE CHALLENGE OF THE WEST

Decline of the old Calvinist theology, however, had other effects less acceptable to business. Deism or its liberalizing influences in the Congregational or Presbyterian churches had little appeal to the uneducated parishioner who preferred a more emotional religion. A revival of fundamentalist religion started in the 1790s in some Congregational and Presbyterian churches of New England, but the churches best able to provide this type of experience were the Baptist and Methodist. Rebels from the Church of England, more on social than theological grounds, these churches allowed lay preaching and ordained ministers without requiring special education. No intricate system of apologetics was required; belief in Christ and the literal authority of the Bible were sufficient. Baptist and Methodist "circuit riders" in the South and West were the chief missionaries of a "Second Great Awakening." Men like Francis Asbury, a Methodist, preached in hundreds of small communities every year. Camp, or revivalist, meetings brough people from many miles around, who stayed together for days, listening to hell-fire and damnation sermons, usually by lay preachers, while also enjoying social activities and doing some business.

Businessmen, however, found many of these newly awakened Western Baptists and Methodists hostile to the orthodoxies of commerce and to the accumulation of wealth. Exhorting nearly self-sufficient farmers, the evangelical lay preachers extolled honest poverty and did not see material possessions as a sign of God's grace.[109] In place of a religion favoring entrepreneurship, the West was in danger of developing a religion of resignation to a humble role.

Both liberals and conservatives in the New England churches and many Eastern businessmen felt challenged by the spread of evangelical faiths to Middle Western settlers. Furthermore, the Congregational and Presbyterian churches by 1800 lacked enough ministers for Eastern pulpits and had no surplus to send West.[110] To make the best use of scarce resources, liberals in the two churches, cooperating through the Plan of Union, tried to supply the ministers needed to win the West to a more orthodox Calvinism. But, in spite of new seminaries established by both sects, the supply of ordained clergy remained inadequate.

By 1810 the conservative leaders of the Eastern, and particularly the New England, Congregational and Presbyterian churches were deeply disturbed by developments both East and West. Unitarians and uneducated Baptists and Methodists were seen as misinterpreting and ignoring the educated clergy, the only qualified interpreters of God's meaning. Men like Lyman Beecher, perhaps the leading intellectual among the conservatives, Herman Humphrey, president of Amherst, and Timothy Dwight, president of Yale, were sure that God had a divine mission for the United States, but that it could only be realized under strict religious guidance.[111]

While the Unitarians mirrored the optimistic, individualistic, expansive side of business thought, the strict Calvinists shared the businessman's fear of radical social change and his reluctance to put too much faith in human nature. Undoubtedly most businessmen agreed with President Humphrey in ascribing all poverty to moral causes such as "want of capacity," "prodigality," "pride," and "intemperance."[112] Furthermore, the Unitarians were not prepared to do much about the lapse of the people of the interior from what the New England theologians regarded as proper tenets of faith, and from what New England businessmen regarded as commercially reliable, acquisitive views favorable to the development of the interior markets. To rectify the situation the old guard of the Congregational and Presbyterian churches swung into action.

In addition to preaching and writing, the orthodox group established local societies to win back the people of their own states, and national societies to carry the Word to other parts of the country. The American Education Society (1815), the American Bible Society (1816), the American Sunday School Union (1824), the American Tract Society (1824), the American Society for the Promotion of Temperance (1826), and the American Home Missionary Society (1826) were not led by businessmen, but they received substantial mercantile support as did the parallel spread of New England education to the West. Between 1815 and 1850 the societies supplied the West with Bibles, tracts, and libraries for their Sunday Schools. Lyman Beecher thought the societies the most powerful instrument in the service of the church. One indication of their effectiveness is the violent opposition they aroused among Baptists and Methodists in the West.[113]

To many Eastern Calvinists the laxity of Western morals was due to lack of a serious, devoted interest in moneymaking. A Quaker merchant from Massachusetts hoped to encourage "industry, temperance, morality and love of gain" in the population of Ohio. "With a population governed by such habits," he wrote, "the state must necessarily advance in improvement at a rapid rate."[114]

By the 1820s, the societies and other New England influences had to compete with migrants from Europe as well as the South in efforts to translate God's design to the West. By dominating education and tirelessly asserting their ideas of morality, more perhaps than through the societies or the churches themselves, the New Englanders were remarkably successful. But the economic forces in the situation also swung toward the conservative Calvinist side. As long as new settlements lacked reasonably cheap transportation, farmers had to be largely self-sufficient, and moneymaking was virtually impossible.[115] In such surroundings there was little support for a business-oriented morality. But as steamboats, canals, and ultimately railroads opened transportation routes, wise farmers, millers, and storekeepers became prosperous. In the new environment, wealth came readily to the shrewd and ambitious. As men achieved fortunes, they were undoubtedly more inclined to favor the order and diligence associated with the Puritan or Yankee. The leading citizens might not leave their earlier churches, but gradually they influenced the original "frontier" Baptist and Methodist preaching to conform to the doctrines of frugality, hard work, and acquisition. Thus the American environment joined with Calvinism in winning the West for business.[116]

RELIGION, THE "PARAMOUNT BUSINESS"

The environmental forces that helped to win the West continued to influence the Eastern seaboard, giving the nation a religious atmosphere that was Calvinistic and missionary. As a Congregational minister saw it: "In the discovery and settlement of this country, God had some great end in view."[117] The nation was thought to be God's new Isreal with a divine destiny. "Religion," wrote de Tocqueville, "directs the manners of the community, and, by regulating domestic life, it regulates the state. . . . Thus while the law permits the Americans to do what they please, religion prevents them from conceiving, and forbids them to committ what is rash or unjust."[118]

Reading the sermons of the first half of the nineteenth century inevitably gives too strong a reflection of the views of Calvinist sects of the Northeast. These well-educated urban ministers of both orthodox and liberal ideas published sermons, letters, and autobiographies, exceeding in quantity and quality the output of the less literate clergy of other churches and regions. Yet, one suspects that this bias in the sources may reflect their nationwide influence. The Northern writings emanating from the old centers of learning must have supplied much of the reading matter and many of the ideas for the literate preachers in other areas. It may be no exaggeration to say that if the northeastern seaboard did not dominate the behavior of other regions, it supplied most of the themes for formal or serious thought.

These Eastern sermons illustrate again the pervasiveness of the business context of American culture. "All the people of New England without an exception, beside what is created by disease, or misfortune, are men of business," said President Dwight of Yale. "The business of a clergyman it is here believed, is to effectuate the salvation of his flock, rather than replenish his own mind with superior information."[119] The usual language of sermons was businesslike and practical rather than philosophical or theological. The Reverend Gregory T. Bedell of Philadelphia, for example, admonished his congregation: "Religion is a business with you, either unthought of or followed as a something undefined and indeterminate. You have never taken hold of it as the one paramount business."[120] The effective Reverend Charles G. Finney emphasized to "professors of religion" the persuasive value of business language. "Illustrations should be drawn *from common life*, the common business of society. . .the manner in which merchants transact business in their stores."[121

The same emphasis on the value of employment and the moral danger of idleness that characterized the sermons of colonial Calvinists continued without regard to the orthodoxy of the preacher. "A man's business ought to be a part of his religion," said Mr. Finney,

> He cannot be religious in idleness. He must have some business to be religious at all, and if it is performed from the right motive, his lawful and necessary business is as much a necessary part of his religion as prayer, or going to church or reading his Bible. . . . A life of business is best for Christians as it exercises their graces and makes them strong."[122]

Bedell writes in the same vein: "What is the nature of happiness, of heaven? Judge it from its business. I cannot imagine anything like happiness apart from some kind of business or employment."[123]

The virtue of conscientious activity for the businessman blended with emphasis on the necessity of labor for all. The Reverend Nathaniel L. Frothingham, an advanced Unitarian, spoke of God as the "great taskmaster,"[124] The Reverend George W. Bethune, sometime Presbyterian and Dutch Reformed minister, said, "Labour is the irresistible law; inactivity a violation of it that cannot occur."[125] Quaker John Jackson cautioned: "There is no time for us to stand idle in the marketplace saying 'no man hath hired me.' "[126] The Reverend Henry Ward Beecher told young men "A hearty industry promotes happiness. . . . The poor man with industry is happier than the rich man in idleness."[127]

Admonitions for devotion to business and labor were, of course, accompanied by reminders of the primacy of God and religion. "We cannot devote ourselves to two masters, to both God and the World," cautioned Episcopalian minister Henry A. Onderdonk; "We may labour for wealth; but if so doing engrosses our thoughts and cares, our labours become sin."[128] The famous Theodore Parker, transcendental Unitarian minister, held that "The real test of religion is its natural sacrament,—is life. To know whom you worship let me see you in your shop, let me overhear you in your trade."[129] Finney saw "having too much worldly business" as one of the frequent causes of "backsliding." "Business is a duty. . .which God requires. . . . But to get into business that will encroach upon secret prayer and eat into religion, is all worng."[130] "Covetousness," said Bedell, "is pronounced by the eternal God to be Idolatry. . . . 'For love of money is the root of all evil.' "[131]

A logical result of the paradox of working hard—for God but not for money—was the stewardship of wealth. In this period, however, the stewardship appeared to mean honesty and benevolence in transacting business and recognition of the presence of God, rather than the careful use of accumulated capital for social welfare. Mr. Finney, for example, formulates the doctrine in this way:

> Sinners transact business to promote their own private interests and not as God's stewards. . . . Should All men's business be done as for God, they would not. find it such a temptation to fraud and dishonesty as to ensnare and ruin their souls.[132]

Among sixteen types of business sinners listed by the Reverend Mr. Finney were "all those who lay up their surplus income," instead of putting it to economic use.[133] In another sermon he says, "Men are God's stewards and He never employs them so that they cannot have time to commune with Him."[134] As the Reverend Mr. Frothingham saw the rich Unitarians: "There was no interpretation of charity but giving, and that was mainly private. The idea of humanity as a whole, and of the individual's relation to it, was unfamiliar."[135]

The Reverend William Ellery Channing, Unitarian pundit and lecturer, saw business as a missionary force for Christian civilization. "Commerce is a noble calling," he said; "It mediates between distant nations, and makes men's wants, not as formerly, stimulated to war, but bonds of peace. . .it carries abroad the missionary, the Bible, the Cross, and is giving universality to true religion."[136]

There was, of course, a good deal of discussion about bringing Christian morality to business. "The opening of vast prospects of wealth to the multitude of men," said the Reverend Mr. Channing, "has stirred . . . a feverish insatiable cupidity, under which fraud, bankruptcy, distrust, distress are fearfully multiplied, so that the name of America has become a by-word beyond the ocean."[137] The Reverend Theodore Parker saw religion as a cure for this widespread dishonesty: "If religion is good for anything, it is as a rule of conduct for daily life, in the business of the individual and the business of the nation."[128] The Reverend Mr. Wayland emphasized that our obligation to obey God "extends to every action of our times."[139] Similar statements may be found by random opening of any collection of sermons.

CONTOURS OF A BUSINESS SOCIETY

Seymour Lipset argues that "it is the basic value system, as solidified in the early days of the new nation, that can account for the kind of changes that have taken place in the American character and in American institutions, as these faced the need to adjust to the requirements of an urban industrial bureaucratic society."[140] An element in the continuity was that people faced with frequent environmental change treasured old beliefs to which they could hold fast, although at the same time they wanted the developments that promised personal betterment.[141] Thus, from the eighteenth into the twentieth century, American society carried a dual heritage of conservatism and progress, of fundamentalism and innovation.

That migration was a major element in this ambiguous configuration was clear to the people of the time. Congressman S. P. Marsh of Vermont told the House in 1846, "We are legislating for an age, a country, a people, whose great characteristic is movement."[142] Migration to cities strikingly reenforced the old and emphasized the new. Nuclear families living in strange urban environments, without the support of a circle of relatives, undoubtedly clung defensively to their household mores; however, the absence of complex and enduring family ties and the early departure of children to jobs also set the stage for the rise of the doctrines of self-help and the superior virtues of the self-made man.

In spite of modest actual accomplishments in the form of public schools, urban America gave such verbal support to the idea of free public education that foreign visitors were overly impressed. At midcentury, Anthony Trollope was led to believe that Americans knew they had to provide good education. "They did so, the unrivalled population, wealth and intelligence have been the result."[143] Regardless of such exaggeration, the pattern of recognition of free education as a public responsibility had been established.

In spreading a national culture that included emphasis on religion, hard work, and material success, New England rather than the Middle Atlantic states became the generating force. The more fertile middle states lacked the same degree of economic pressure that was driving the rural population of rocky New England westward. With great natural resource to exploit within its own boundaries,

Pennsylvania lacked the New England interest in capturing Western markets, while New York prospered as the middleman between Europe and the American hinterland.

The drive to make the West part of Greater New England was total: economic, religious, intellectual, and social. The relatively dense population and limited resources of Connecticut, Rhode Island, and Massachusetts produced a surplus of people, goods, and intellectual energy that flowed westward across the nation. These missionaries of all types, business, educational, and religious, spread the "sound" business doctrines of Calvinist belief. In spite of liberal religious movements such as Unitarianism and Transcendentalism among stay-at-home Massachusetts intellectuals, the type of belief exported to the West stressed not only industry, frugality, and piety, but also initiative, aggressiveness, competitiveness, and forcefulness.[144] These qualities carried by businessmen and ministers, and backed up by the outpouring of New England teachers, resulted in a paradox: as Puritanism became more permissive in the East, it transferred its rigors to the West, where they took root as part of the enduring cultural pattern.

CHAPTER 7

The States Promote Business

Businessmen of the early national period were accustomed to a large number of government regulations. Price fixing for basic commodities, regulation of markets, inspection requirement to establish grades of purity, and wage ceilings were the rule. While colonial businessmen had objected to British imperial regulations, they had cooperated in passing and upholding provincial measures, and they sponsored similar activities by the new state governments. The regulations could be regarded as largely promotional, designed to hold down costs and to insure honesty and predictable market conditions.

Such regulations contrast with the internal tariffs and monopolies of European nations which were, in general, levies to benefit a favored class or government bureaucrats. Such burdensome regulations spawned the extreme interpreters of Adam Smith, who insisted that the economy should be self-regulating; early Eurepean laissez-faire, however, does not appear to have had strong political followings in the northern American states.[1]

THE EARLY CONSTITUTIONS

In observing the merchant's and other conservatives' fear of the popular will reflected in most of the initial state constitutions, it should be remembered that control by the people with no check in the form of ultimate veto had never been tried in America or any other extensive nation. Consequently, the needs of business, which were to assume considerable importance fifty years later, seemed a minor matter compared to the dangers to all property inherent in a completely unchecked democracy. When it came to drawing up state constitutions, landlords and merchants thought alike in terms of protecting private rights, personal liberty, and the control of property from the pressures of the lower classes, and did not consider detailed causes defining the relations of government and business as necessary. In other words, the battles were over limitations on democracy and the power of democratically controlled organs of government rather than specifically over more or less economic freedom or aid to enterprise.[2]

The Northern back country, with its more uniform distribution of wealth between working farmers, and its commitment to agriculture, generally championed greater democracy. In Connecticut and Rhode Island, the influence of the back-country towns was strong enough to preserve as constitutions the colonial charters, which greatly overrepresented the rural areas. In New York, the rural interests dictated the legislative clauses, but the combined mercantile and landed aristocracy won a conservative check on popular pressures in the form of a Council of Revision which could disallow legislation.[3] In New Jersey and New Hampshire, the conservatives making the most of good advance organization, secured constitutions that appeared safe to the merchants. But in Pennsylvania, the Delaware Valley interests were overwhelmed by the rest of the state. The Pennsylvania Constitution of 1776, referred to as the "leveling constitution," put ultimate power in the hands of a single-house legislature elected annually on the basis of a liberal franchise. Although a Council of Censors with power to review legislation gave some protection to the Eastern merchants, the latter worked to bring about a new constitutional convention in 1790 that adopted a more conventional and conservative document.[14]

The most prolonged and interesting conflict between the seaboard towns, wealthy from fishing and trade, and a relatively poor agricultural back country occurred in Massachusetts. In the coastal towns, which were dependent on the interior for food, there was "a deep resentment toward the farmer harbored by rich and poor alike."[5] The first constitution was drawn up by the legislature, continuing under the forms of the colonial charter, and submitted to the towns for approval in 1778. Pleasing to neither the mercantile nor the agricultural interests, the document was overwhelmingly rejected. Essex county, led by the lawyers of Newburyport, now held a local convention which published *The Essex Result*, illustrating the kind of basic law desired by the seaboard lawyers and merchants. The Lockean doctrine of inalienable rights, an enduring safeguard for free enterprise, was strongly asserted, and a bill or rights was proposed. The legislature was to be bicameral, the upper house representing "gentlemen of education, fortune, and leisure," and other property interests, and the lower house "the bulk of the people." The legislative, judicial, and executive branches should be independent of each other.[6] The people were only to vote for electors who would then choose the representatives and the governor, and there was a moderately high property qualification for voting for senatorial electors. The distrust of the direct democratic process, so clearly shown in this lineal ancestor of the first Massachusetts constitution, has been shared, as we shall see, by at least a strong minority of successful businessmen in each generation. But in later years it was not politically expedient to argue for such restrictions.

The proceedings that led to the Massachusetts Constitution of 1780 show how a well-organized minority who devoted their time to a cause could prevail. The legislature called upon the town meetings to elect delegates to a convention, but some interior towns took no action. The expense of coming to Cambridge for the sessions further reduced the attendance from the back country. Long debate meant mounting living costs, and within two months about two-thirds of the members had drifted away. Adjourning in November and attempting to reassemble January 5, 1780, the convention waited twenty-one days for a quorum. No ballots were recorded by delegates, and the record does not show how many actually took part in adopting important clauses, but it is logical to presume that the seaboard towns were well-represented and the interior much less so.

The document which emerged from the convention was largely the work of Boston lawyer John Adams. It followed the general principles of *The Essex Result*, but eliminated indirect voting. There were property qualifications for suffrage and a senate apportioned according to taxable wealth. The towns voted for the new constitution, but offered a number of amendments. The convention reassembled, however, and after counting the votes, declared the constitution in effect as originally drafted. The business interests supported by other conservatives had achieved a triumph for republicanism against direct democracy, in what is widely regarded as the best and most stable constitution of the revolutionary era.

In the South, the political struggle was generally between a combination of merchants from the few seaports with large planters of the tidewater section, on one side, and inland planters and farmers on the other. Fearing the executive power because of their experience with gubernatorial and royal vetoes, the back-country or "democratic" group advocated a governor with a few powers. As might be expected, North Carolina went the farthest by stripping the governor of the veto and all important powers of appointment and electing him annually. In Maryland and Virginia, and still more in South Carolina, the merchant-planter coalition, aided by the overrepresentation of the eastern areas, was able to maintain its influence. In Georgia, British occupation so confused the situation that brief generalization is impossible. Allan Nevins' summary of the new constitutions is that "everywhere the main outlines of state governments followed those of the colonial governments."[7]

The group chosen by the state legislatures to assemble in Philadelphia in 1787 to draw up a federal constitution included more landed aristocrats than in the case of the Cambridge convention, but their general ideas regarding a proper government were not much different. Nearly all were men of substance, and the majority favored sound money and a strong, moderately conservative government. Differences between merchants and planters, between investors in securities or business properties and investors in land appear minor in relation to broad major areas of agreement.[8] It is certain that merchants desired the clauses forbidding the states to violate the sanctity of contracts, issue currency, or interfere with interstate commerce, and it is similarly true that the power to levy all forms of indirect taxes was a boon to security holders. But these provisions were also supported by conservative nationalists as necessary to effective central government. By creating a secure national market for both investment and trade, the constitution was to be even more valuable to business than could readily have been foreseen in 1787; but these conditions obviously benefitted other Americans as consumers, property owners, and interstate migrants.

DEFINING THE COMMON LAW

By taking over the common law, the states in theory continued the same everyday principles of legal control, but the judges were changed, the ultimate sanctions differed, and new state statutes altered old precedents. Thus the immediate effect of the revolution was to create confusion in regard to what was the law. The uncertainties harrassed merchants and other businessmen and put a premium on the services of persuasive lawyers. In Massachusetts, the feeling against procedures that "afforded Encouragement to mercenary lawyers to riot upon the spoils of the people" was particularly strong.[9] Similar situations, however, developed throughout the new states, South as well as North.[10]

Because of a general failure to keep or preserve court records, colonial laws and decisions were often inaccessible, and new editions of colonial or state statutes were slow to appear.[11] Court reporters were lacking, and justices relied on judgment rather than precedent. James Kent said that during his nine years as chancellor of New York, from 1814 on, he never heard an opinion of one of his predecessors cited.[12] * Uncertainty was increased by low popular esteem for the law with its consequences of meagre judicial salaries and mediocre, untrained men on the bench. The rising value of legal ability at the bar ultimately corrected the situation by producing a large group of able lawyers by midcentury, but the older businessmen of the revolutionary generation had suffered greatly from rapid changes in constitutions, statutes, and the American versions of common law.[13]

Not until the beginning of the second quarter of the ninteenth century was there any reliable guide to the common law, other than Blackstone's *Commentaries* (Philadelphia, 1771-1772), which could lead to uniformity in state decisions. Massachusetts and New York, states with many business problems and a strong tradition of legal literacy, took the lead in making precedents and principles available. In 1823, Nathan Dane, an elderly, retired lawyer and politician living in Beverly, Massachusetts, published the results of thirty years of study in the *General Abridgment and Digest of American Law, with Occasional Notes and Comments* in eight volumes. The monumental work was soon added to by the publication in New York of James Kent's four-volume *Commentaries on American Law.*

The rise of effective legal education is interestingly involved with both Nathan Dane and Joseph Story from nearby Salem. Story illustrates the many

---

* In Rhode Island the courts could be overruled by the legislature, and judges preferred to give oral decisions through the period to 1850 (Coleman, *The Transformation of Rhode Island,* 252).

activities possible for one man in this simpler, less specialized society, as well as the relatively light docket of the Supreme Court. While an associate justice of the United States Supreme Court from 1811 on, he was also president of the Merchant's Bank of Salem (1815-1835), vice-president of the Salem Savings Bank (1818-1830), and after 1825, a fellow of the Harvard Corporation. Some of this incredible vigor may be credited to the fact that he was only thirty-two years old when he became an associate justice. Meanwhile, he saw nothing amiss in drawing up a published brief for the merchants of Salem in favor of altering certain congressional regulations on trade, and also serving as a delegate to the Massachusetts Constitutional Convention of 1820. In 1828, Nathan Dane persuaded this banker-statesman-jurist to become the first Dane Professor of Law at Harvard. There, while still the leading nationalist intellectual on the Supreme Court, he is credited with having been the chief early builder of the Harvard Law School, which was the first to institute continuous university legal education. He also gave a striking example of the effectiveness of an able practitioner teaching law.[14]

The impact of the legal scholars such as Kent and Story, of the decisions of the United States Supreme Court led by John Marshall, and of the rulings of leading state justices was an emphasis on individual rights in property and contracts. This was a reaction against the arguments for legislative sovereignty in Blackstone's *Commentaries* and in the American revolutionary movement. The process of building the law, as business interests desired, into a structure of precedents resistant to legislative or popular attack is illustrated in the decisions of men like Theophilus Parsons, chief justice of Massachusetts from 1806 to 1830. Clearly and concisely combining the local usages of real estate, contracts, and the law merchant with the enduring structure of the English common law, he exerted a strong influence on judges all over the nation.[15] As debt-ridden state legislatures lost prestige after the panic of 1837, the emphasis on individual property rights and business freedom continued to grow to perhaps the greatest extent in any Western nation.[16]

Actions concerning land and commerce were the main business of law officers, and as in earlier periods, the most important specific changes in American law arose from litigation over land.[17] "It was the land law," says Howard J. Graham, "that profoundly affected and shaped the law of the land."[18] Judges in Western states did not seek to be legal innovators; in fact, they tended to be conservative, and both bench and bar quoted Chancellor Kent's views to each other. The impetus for change came from the compounded confusion of state land titles. The holdings of absentee owners were unfairly taxed by the states, and the taxes frequently were not paid, or because of poor mail service and changing county jurisdictions, could not be paid. Then the state would auction off the land to pay the tax liens. It is said that the new states drew 90 percent of their revenue from taxing or despoiling absentees. In defense of the investors, Western attorneys gradually won broader interpretations of the meaning of "due process of law" and "the equal protection of the laws," and helped make these doctrines the pillars of a new common-law protection of property, one that was to become important for all business by the late nineteenth century (Chapter 12).

THE USE OF GOVERNMENT BY BUSINESS

Although later generations of businessmen would try to curb state action, to those men born in a mercantilist atmosphere and brought up during a revolution, government was a utility to be used when needed for the development of the new commonwealths. Merchants and small manufacturers did not favor unlimited government activity, but each interest group wanted the activities that would aid them and disapproved of less favorable activities, not on principles of liberalism or laissez-faire, but on the basis of expense. To these men, the new phrase "laissez-faire" probably represented a meaningless doctrine. Rather, they stood for dispersed private activity when the capital required was within the grasp of the individual, state initiative where the capital required was too great for a small group of individuals, and at all times, public policy favorable to maximum exploitation of economic opportunities with minimum capital expenditures.[19]

In the three largest Northern states, policies were quite similar. "Massachusetts drew freely upon the normal legislative power, a power to which it recognized no limits but those set by feasibility and utility."[20] In Pennsylvania, "the objectives of government were pervasive and they played a daily part in the activities of businessmen."[21] In early New York, "the legislature frequently intervened between buyer and seller, debtor and creditor, or simply asserted itself as a force in the economy."[22] Few businessmen tried to curb such activity, because "no one was secure enough to demand a limit to state action who on the morrow might also need assistance."[23] New York and Pennsylania, less burdened by early debt than Massachusetts and blessed with better sources of revenue, did more to promote internal commerce and manufacturing than any of the New England states.[24]

The provincial regulatory activity of the colonial period continued, much of it in response to the needs of good business. For example, money of account was defined; laws of agency and contract enacted; codes of conduct for masters and men; rules of trusteeship, bankruptcy, and probate were established; weights and measures were set; and inspection of quality provided for in commodities usually exported. In addition, the public interest was protected by licensing acts for such activities as innkeeping, liquor selling, piloting, auctioneering, legal practice, and brokerage.[25]

The colonies and early states had granted about a dozen monopoly patents for inventions by legislative act. While this was a function that obviously should have been performed by the central government, businessmen and farmers alike were harrassed by the inadequacy of the federal act of 1793 which provided for the issue of patents by the attorney general for any new device without requiring proof of novelty. In 1826 a congressional committee reported that "None of the patents have been recorded, as the law requires, from 1802. . .owing to the want of the requisite assistance of clerks in the office."[26] Partly because of the lax laws, Americans were taking out more than 500 patents a year—three times the number in Britain. The law not only provided no real protection for the bona fide inventor, but opened the way for repatenting devices already in use and endless threats of suits for infringement against necessarily uninformed manufacturers or users. The prevalence of the patent racket in the 1820s led to congressional investigation, and by 1836 to an adequate law which set up a proper office and required proof of exclusive priority.* The earlier chaos was another example of the failure of government, as well as business, to appreciate the need for adequate systems of control.

PROTECTING RISK TAKERS

Relations between debtor and creditor were another area of law needing redefinition in a society vitally concerned with ventures of high risk. As business risks increased in England in the late eighteenth century, a fundamental distinction was made between bankruptcy, which applied to debts contracted for business purposes, and insolvency which applied to personal delinquency.[27] But of the laws existing in the American states, only the Pennsylvania bankruptcy statute of 1785 specifically limited application to "merchants, scriveners, bankers, brokers or factors."[28] The latter type of law reassured risk-taking entrepreneurs, whereas relief for those imprisoned for personal insolvency was a matter of humanitarian social reform, not so directly concerned with economic growth.

Difficulties over bankruptcy law illustrate one of the handicaps to business of the federal system. Article I of the Constitution of the United States giving Congress the power "to establish uniform laws on the subject of bankruptcies," immediately following the commerce clause, was apparently inserted for business purposes.[29] The constitutional provision led to a broad federal bankruptcy act in 1800; this act failed to safeguard creditors against fraudulent manipulation by rich debtors and was repealed in 1830.[30] Subsequent state action was hindered by federal judicial decisions, such as *Sturgis* v. *Crowninshield* (1819), which made it appear that states had no right to pass insolvency laws applying to either past or future contracts. This interpretation was not clarified until the Supreme Court in *Ogden* v. *Saunders* (1827) affirmed the right of the states to legislate regarding future contracts.[31] Thus, in spite of business pressures, passage of needed commercial bankruptcy legislation by the states was checked by apparent unconstitutionality, plus fear of fraud.[32]

The deep depression following the panic of 1837, and the chaotic condition of state laws led President Van Buren to recommend a bankruptcy law confined to banks. In the four years of congressional debate that followed, the business-

---

* When the patent office burned in 1836, Congress commissioned a publication of earlier patents, based on local records, and allowed patentees to reconfirm those that had value.

minded conservatives, such as Webster in the Senate or Storey on the Supreme
Court, expressed themselves in favor of a bill providing for both voluntary and
involuntary bankruptcy for all classes of debtors including corporations, but it
was difficult to secure a majority in either house.[33] Some Eastern mercantile
creditor areas as well as some Southeastern planters opposed release of debtors
through bankruptcy; strict constructionists and states-rights advocates believed
federal action, particularly if applied to corporations, unconstitutional; and
finally the presidential request was, of course, labeled as Democratic and
therefore to be opposed by many Whigs. Thus, in spite of a need for uniform
bankruptcy legislation recognized by farsighted businessmen, during nearly four
years nothing was accomplished.[34]

In August of 1841, about the worst period of the long depression that lasted
from 1837 to 1843, Congress finally passed a Whig-sponsored act that provided
for both voluntary and involuntary bankruptcy, but excluded corporations. The
act remained in force only a little over a year, but 34,000 persons with $441
million in debts took advantage of its provisions.[35] It is a testimony to the
severity of the depression that the debtors surrendered property worth less than
10 percent of their indebtedness. With the return of prosperity in 1843, pressure
for new federal or state action died down, not to be revived until after the panic
of 1857.

Meanwhile, stay laws, exemption of parts of a debtor's property from
execution, and the gradual limitation of imprisonment for debt had been
meeting the most pressing problems of personal insolvency in the states. These
laws came mainly in the major depression periods, such as 1784-1787,
1807-1809, 1818-1822, and 1837-1843. The usual function of stay laws was to
prevent the sale of property by foreclosure for a certain period of time unless it
brought a half to three-quarters of its appraised value. The early laws exempting
certain types of property from liens were the result of demands by labor leaders
for protection of workers' tools; later laws also exempted dwellings of low value
and certain amounts of farm acreage from seizure to satisfy general, as opposed
to specific or chattel mortgage, indebtedness.[36]

The effect of laws making it possible to gain release from debts and make a
new beginning was undoubtedly important in stimulating entrepreneurship in
most nations of the Western world, but such rebirth was particularly important
in the United States where the settlement of new areas and attendant risks
promoted many starts in business and many failures. Viewing the new world of
competition, Emily Dickinson wrote in 1852,

> Mortality is Fatal
> Gentility is fine
> Rascality heroic
> Insolvency sublime.

Several of the most prominent nineteenth-century American entrepreneurs, such
as R. H. Macy, used the "sublime" recourse one or more times before ultimately
achieving a great success.

ADJUSTING TO THE CORPORATION

While government regulatory and judicial policy toward corporations and their charters affected only a small segment of the business population, the precedents were vitally important for the era when corporations would account for most of the national product. The chief points at issue were the conditions under which charters should be granted, the enforcing of charter provisions, and the modification or revocation of charters by subsequent legislative action.

As noted in Chapter 5, the trend was toward greater ease in securing charters, but powers were more narrowly defined. Much of the discussion in Massachusetts before 1830 was over the question of whether or not the charter asked for would benefit the commonwealth, but with annual or biennial changes in legislative personnel, a persistent charter-seeking group could usually get what it wanted. The early charters often provided for broad powers such as unlimited assessment of stockholders, the right to issue notes that could pass as currency, or certain monopoly privileges.[37]

The enforcement of charter provisions became particularly important in relation to both early banks and transportation companies. In incorporating banks, "the state tried all degrees and types of control involving proprietary interest or not, but always involving restrictions and regulations. ... The impression was general that the exercise of the banking function without express authorization from the sovereign power was improper."[38] This inevitably involved bankers with both state legislation and the decisions of the courts. "In some respects," says Bray Hammond, "the law, parent-like, could not keep up with the banks but followed them with ineffective commandments and prohibitions."[39] Legislators, judges, and bankers were almost equally uncertain as to what was sound or what was reckless, what was for public good and what for long-run private profit. The Handlins conclude that the Massachusetts practices regarding banks gave "an appearance of supervision which really did not exist."[40] In the recession following the War of 1812, the Pennsylvania legislature revoked the charters of ten banks that had suspended specie payments, but this was not a general policy.[41] Although enforcement was weak and uncertain, by the 1820s all the states regulated banking corporations to some degree. Alarmed by failures after the panic of 1837, agrarian-minded legislators prohibited the incorporation of banks in Arkansas, California, District of Columbia, Florida, Illinois, Iowa, Texas, Wisconsin, Minnesota, and Oregon.[42]

Most of the major canal systems and a number of the early railroads were publicly financed state corporations. Saying in 1811 that "by the tests of efficiency, economy and financial capacity private enterprise was incapable of building the Erie and Champlain canals," a commission headed by New York financier Gouverneur Morris appears to have expressed the feelings of many entrepreneurs regarding participation in large transportation ventures.[43] Between 1815 and 1840, the Middle Atlantic and Middle Western states invested heavily in canal and railroad corporations, and the New England states, chiefly

Massachusetts, limited such activity only through fear of the cost to governments already in debt.[44]

Public corporations and the multitude of privately owned bridges, turnpikes, and particularly railroads presented courts and legislatures with new issues. Litigation concerning the inviolability of charters, and contractual rights of states and their corporate creations, demonstrated the importance of the federal constitution. While before 1820 states had frequently altered initial charter provisions by subsequent acts, in the Dartmouth College case the Supreme Court of the United States gave corporations federal protection from state modifications of their charters.[45] But the upholding of this colonial charter hinged on the personnel of the Court. By 1835 the Court, altered by Jacksonian appointments, was ready to consider some state actions in protection of public health, or other aspects of the police power, as superior to the sanctity of contracts. Furthermore, following the Dartmouth College decision, new state charters usually had specific provisions permitting modification by legislative action.[46]

In 1837 the Supreme Court decided that a charter granting a corporation a transportation route, in this case the Charles River Bridge from Boston to Charlestown, did not mean that the privilege was exclusive unless the charter said so specifically.[47] In the light of the long antimonopoly tradition of America, the decision seems routine. However, it took the Supreme Court many years to decide, and the case for the monopoly right of the original bridge company was strongly argued by Daniel Webster.[48]

Equally important in its effects on business institutions was the decision in *Bank of Augusta* v. *Earle*. The United States Circuit Court in Alabama had ruled that a corporation could not enter into contracts or, perhaps, even do business outside its home state. That decision, according to Justice Story, "frightened half the lawyers and all the corporations of the country out of their proprieties."[49] Webster arguing against the circuit court decision said that "no part of the commercial system of the country would be free from its influences."[50] The newspapers favorable to national business strongly condemned the decision, while the Jacksonian Democrats mirroring localism and states rights praised it. In the Supreme Court, Chief Justice Roger B. Taney handed down a decision that in the absence of any statute to the contrary a corporation might make contracts and do business in any state.[51] While the decision left the door open for exclusion laws, in fact they were not enacted, and corporations were given the security necessary to exploit the national market.

The many state courts and jurisdictions robbed state decisions of the drama and historic importance of those of the Supreme Court. In general conservative and guided by precedent, the state courts often evaded major issues for many years. "Wisconsin law," writes Robert S. Hunt, "failed to recognize the need for anything more than the time-tested techniques of an agricultural society."[52] Yet little by little, corporations and railroads in particular, by forcing the courts to give "specific interpretations in case after case gradually undermined and transformed the law."[53] In general, change was in the direction of more sovereignty for the corporation and less state control under the assumptions of the common law. Thus, in making use of the corporation, business appears to have benefitted from the federal system.

While the effect of the railroad on the common law and judicial process has had little study, its effects on statute law were obvious and important. Railroads were in fact local monopolies whether or not they were granted such a privilege in their charters, and to lay out their routes they required the right of eminent domain.* It was inevitable that private corporations possessed of such powers would be regulated by the states that created them. New England, with the largest amount of track in relation to its area, was the first to meet most of the problems of railroads as public utilities.

Eminent domain had been used by transportation companies and public utilities such as waterworks before the coming of the railroad. But the rapid growth of railroad companies and public excitement about the powers of monopolistic corporations in the Jackson period brought the right into question in the Middle Atlantic and New England states. In 1833 a Massachusetts law prescribed the method by which railroads might exercise eminent domain, and in 1844 New Hampshire provided for appeal to a board of three commissioners who could fix valuations and assess damages.[54] But the more general attitude, which prevailed in the three middle states, was that charters were self-enforcing, subject only to appeal to the courts.[55]

While for any given area the exercise of eminent domain was a passing problem, that of rates and conditions of service remained. The first state railroad commission in 1839 came as a result of the question of whether a railroad, the Boston and Providence, was open to use by a separately owned connecting line. While the immediate issue was settled by the Boston and Providence buying the line in question, the problem led to the creation of a five-member Rhode Island Railroad Commission.[56] In New Hampshire, questions involving eminent domain, which was not granted in the state's early railroad charters, led to a railroad commission in 1844.[57]

Gradually all the New England states and New York found it impossible to handle railroad problems through charters and legislation alone. "By the fifties," writes Edward C. Kirkland, "it was apparent that governors, attorney-generals, legislatures and their committees, judges, and county commissioners were not able to deal continuously, expertly and successfully with a powerful, expanding, novel railroad interest."[58] For the next thirty years, the usual state solution

---

* The first three Massachusetts roads were specifically granted thirty-year monopolies.

was to establish a railroad commission, empowered, in some cases, to regulate rates.[59]

BUSINESS IN STATE POLITICS

The pervasiveness of attitudes inspired by interest in moneymaking enterprise makes it difficult to draw firm lines between business and nonbusiness interests in politics. The planter influence in national affairs, for example, may be validly regarded as representing the agricultural export business; yet planters were also part of a subculture that deliberately deemphasized the business aspects of life and looked down upon the "capitalist ethic." Although the planter might in fact spend some of the day on business calculations, he saw himself as a country squire, a supporter of the traditional graces of honor and gentility as opposed to the utilitarian attitudes of the Northern merchant or manufacturer.[60] Hence it is possible to speak of political contests between planter and business interests, even though both parties were, in a real sense, businessmen.

In the North, the same type of division could be found between farmers, who were only part-time businessmen, and the full-time entrepreneurs of the towns. But the Northern farmer, at odds with storekeepers and millers, did not see himself as part of a superior subculture; his differences were simply matters of dollars and cents. With some exceptions, therefore, such as the early Southern migrants to the Middle West, the rural population of the North came to have many interests and attitudes in tune with those of its businessmen. Furthermore, many Northern and Western farmers had interests in town activities, or sons or daughters who worked in shops or mills.

The great majority of full-time businessmen, however, carried on their operations from towns or cities. Thus much of the political power of business-men in "agricultural" states rested on their control of town politics and on the political importance of the country town. The county seats and other large towns were political centers; the local party committees met there, the large campaign contributions generally came from there, and lawyers and other local businessmen to whom politics was an alternate career lived there. While many farm boys like Lincoln rose to political eminence, they had usually become town boys early in their careers. Comprising a small minority of the people in farm-state constituencies, the representatives of local business nevertheless wielded a powerful influence.[61]

Under such circumstances there was a tendency for small-town or city entrepreneurs to dress their policies in rhetoric that would appeal to the farmer. Furthermore, business was usually more involved in government policy than was agriculture. The problems brought before the farm-state legislatures in the early nineteenth century were not what to do about the conduct of farming so much as they were how to implement the theme of material progress, how to build canals and railroad, and when to charter banks and other business corporations: that is, the upbuilding of the state for the benefit of all residents was necessarily entrusted to businessmen who had the essential knowledge or skill. James Primm writes of the frontier agricultural state of Missouri,

> As in Massachusetts, Pennsylvania and New Jersey, the state took an active, positive role in the economic affairs of its citizens during the period before the Civil War, and was not hampered appreciably in this course by laissez-faire or non-intervention theories. In so far as negative ideas found expression they tended to be directed at federal rather than state economic activity.[62]

The truly back-country areas occasionally demanded equality for all, interpreted as each constituency receiving its share of the state aid. When Illinois voted extensive subsidies for internal improvements in 1837, for example, $200,000 was appropriated to compensate counties in which no railroad or river improvements took place.[63]

There were, of course, party divisions on matters of state promotional policy, but the split was usually not between those for and those against, but between Whigs in favor of aid alone and Democrats favoring aid and state regulation.[64] A third alternative, state construction and ownership, was largely confined to costly canals or railroads, such as the Erie Canal in New York, the Ohio Canal, the Pennsylvania mixed transportation system, the Western and Atlantic Railroad of Georgia, or the Michigan Central Railroad. In the South, the planter influence made politicians less ready than in the West to subsidize manufacturing by either local or state aid, but both farmers and merchants were actively interested in canals and railroads that would open up the back country.[65]

In all parts of the nation, there were small businessmen, farmers, and politicians opposed to state expenditures for improvements that would not directly serve their areas. Similar antagonism existed between proponents of state aid to one type of transportation, such as highway improvement, and those who wanted the money used for a canal or railroad.[66] The battles in state legislatures seem to have revolved more around the issue of who would benefit from what than over any principle of state planning or ownership as against free enterprise.

In the legislative battles, promotion of agriculture, as such, seems to have played a relatively minor role. Probably all assumed that in farming the forces of nature were dominant. In Primm's volume on economic policy in Missouri from 1820 to 1860, agricultural policy takes up less than seven pages, devoted chiefly to laws to insure reliable products by tobacco and hemp inspection, and to small-scale subsidization of agricultural societies and fairs.[67]

State efforts in New York, Pennsylvania, and New England to encourage manufacturing and trade had the support of agricultural as well as urban constituencies. From 1790 on, New York granted small loans and a limited amount of tax exemption to potential manufacturers. After the embargo of 1808, the size of the loans "from a sympathetic legislature" increased. Later, the state profits from the Erie Canal were also used as a development fund.[68]

Pennsylvania lent money to farmers, industrialists, and corporations, granted bounties, and invested heavily in the shares of over 150 companies.[69]

The support of these varied state development programs in the North by farm county representatives, as well as those from urban business constituencies, reveals the power of the town; it also shows how, in this region, the promise of new industry and mechanized transportation temporarily soothed the tensions between seacoast and interior, country and city, merchant and farmer, and big business and small. This enthusiastic Northern confidence in both business and government promotion appears to have reached its height in the period from 1790 to 1837. The nation's first great depression, from 1837 to 1843, ended the honeymoon period of agriculture and industry. After that came failure of banks, decay of uncompleted transportation routes, and temporary insolvency of states heavily burdened by loans for internal improvements, such as Illinois and Pennsylvania; these adversities weakened faith in miraculous progress, demonstrated administrative failures, and reawakened conflicts of interest.

Distrust of state politicians contrasted with earlier attitudes, when the successful creation of new governments, to which the ablest members of society lent their energies, had given state politics and public office high prestige. During the same period, the fumbling efforts of early business management in the new areas of industry and large-scale transportation could not provide material for a doctrine of business efficiency. The balance probably began to change in the 1820s, as democratic ideas of the competence of the common man and rotation of office, "the spoils system" lessened the chance of the states developing able and prestigious administrative bureaucracies. Meanwhile, the better-run private corporations began to create a legend of administrative competence.

By the crisis of 1837, the time had come when the business administrators might hope to succeed in an attack on state regulation and administration. "If the administrative record of private enterprise was also bad," writes Hartz, "nevertheless the prestige of the business entrepreneur was rising while that of the politician was in decline."[70] The main public effect of the financial difficulties of state-owned or mixed companies was not a demand for better state administration, but rather the rise of a movement to get the state out of business.

Underlying the ultimate success of this campaign, which led to the sale of state-owned railroads, such as the Pennsylvania and Michigan Central in the middle 1840s, was the growing strength of private capital. With recovery in 1843, it became possible to sell private stocks and bonds on a larger scale than ever before, and soon to attract foreign capital, not to state bonds as earlier—they now had a bad reputation—but to the bonds of well-placed railroads and utilities. In a broad sense, business no longer urgently needed the state and now mounted a campaign to get rid of annoying participations and regulations. "What was it our fathers wanted to secure by the Revolution?" asked John Blanshard of Pennsylvania of his fellow congressmen in 1846. His simple answer was, "Independence in their business."[71]

EARLY BUSINESS SUCCESSES IN NATIONAL POLITICS

National politics, more limited by the Constitution in economic scope, and more divided along geographical lines of interest, mirrored these shifts in business desires less clearly than states. In general, when demands for federal action had behind them a combined mercantile and industrial support from most areas, they were successful, but these instances, such as the first tariff and the first bank, were rare. Usually, federal policy was a tortuous compromise between the conflicting demands of different sections and different interests in which it is impossible to speak of the pressure of "business" as a single force. More often, special business lobbies gained limited objectives that were either regarded as in the national interest or were, at least, not strongly opposed by other groups.

Land policy is an early illustration of the success of business pressure when relatively unopposed. Urged on by able lobbyists, the last sessions of the Continental Congress aided some land companies by free grants, others by grants at what appeared to be nominal cost, and all by a system of government for the West that would check local democracy until the period of initial sale and settlement was past. This latter policy enacted by the famous Northwest Ordinance of 1787 was an excellent example of the triumph of the relatively unopposed forces of business in government. Congress had before it a Committee Report of 1784, largely the work of Thomas Jefferson, which was vague and unsatisfactory as to just how government was to be carried on at the start, and which provided for democracy at an early stage. Businessmen like Manassa Cutler of Massachusetts, representing the Ohio Company, and William Duer, the New York entrepreneur on the Board of Treasury, wanted a well-defined administrative form of government capable of protecting property, before they and other promoters put large sums into Western development, As a result, a new ordinance was framed with the real problems of initial sale and settlement in mind. Until an area attained the relatively large population of 5,000 adult males, government was to rest in the hands of a governor and three judges appointed by Congress; even after that period, direct representation of the resident property holders was to be limited to the lower house of the legislature. Thus the business decisions to buy land only if political and social stability were assured directly shaped the territorial policy that would be applied to each new section of the United States. Or to put it another way, only business pressure produced an act of permanent importance from the dying Continental Congress.

Acceptance of business aims and methods is illustrated in the long history of congressional land laws. Whether from the desire of certain Eastern Federalists to slow down Western settlement, or the pressure of states with a great deal of land to sell, or the continuing interests of land companies, the first laws for the sale of land were designed to keep the central government out of the retail market.[72] Federal competition was almost eliminated by requiring the buyer to take too large a tract, at too high a price, and to carry out the transaction at the national capital. From 1784 to 1800, federal sales to actual settlers were unimportant. In the latter year, the nonvoting congressional representative of

Ohio territory, the only region in which federal sales were an issue, was William Henry Harrison, the son-in-law of the major Ohio land seller John Cleve Symmes. Torn, no doubt, between popular demand and family business interests, Harrison appears to have made a skillful compromise. His father-in-law was protected by keeping the price of land at $2 an acre, a policy also held to discourage speculation and benefit the treasury, but otherwise the desires of his constituents were largely met. Three hundred and forty acres, still too much for a family farm, was made the minimum quantity, payments could be made in installments, and land offices were established in Ohio.

Apparently, the settler now had a chance to buy direct from the government, but original sale at public auction still strongly favored companies when it came to securing the best land, and this remained the procedure until 1862. As a result, most men found it easier to go beyond the limits of land open for sale and trust to the political and physical force of themselves and their neighbors to secure title to their farms at a later date. Families with money found that it paid to buy good land from companies rather than take a chance on securing the acreage they wanted at auctions that were distant, badly run, and often corrupt.

To this extent, business organized the westward movement in the interest of large-scale investment in land. In assessing the effect on the settler of this intrusion of a middleman in the land-selling process, two basic economic facts must be kept in mind: first, the government minimum price of $2 an acre up to 1820 and $1.25 an acre thereafter was far less than the market value of the best land; and second, there was plenty of inferior land. In no large area was all the land disposed of at the initial auctions. There always remained good acreage for sale at the land office at the minimum price. But since the cost of land was small comparied to the other costs such as moving, clearing, plowing, building, and fencing, it was worth paying even $10 an acre for rich, well-located land at the office of a "friendly company" ready to advance credit, rather than $1.25 cash for unsold land at the government office. The land company was, in effect, receiving a fee for selection and convenient marketing. At times the fee was high, but many land companies lost money on wrong guesses as to the future course of migration, and were eaten up by the cost of holding the property and administering sales. While land remained an attractive investment, some of the shrewdest financiers thought that "wild" land was a poor gamble. John Murray Forbes, one of Boston's great financiers and large landowners, wrote of tracts in partly settled Michigan in 1848: "Even when they are sure to rise as on the line of the Mich. R. Road. . .it would cost more trouble in managing them than the profit would pay."[37]

The Hamiltonian programs of the 1790s are striking examples of the ties between business and the Federalist party, but year after year in less spectacular ways, there were indications of the strength of the mercantile and financial interests in both Congress and the administration. Assumption of state debts, tax and subsidy policies, a treaty for trade, and other policies favorable to Great

Britain rather than France all pleased the mercantile interests. Hamilton would also have aided the embryonic manufacturers with higher tariffs and many subsidies, but here the merchants joined with the planters in dissent, and Congress could not move far in these directions.

In the early years of the republic, merchant and planter interests in federal action were much the same. Both groups were socially conservative and in favor of stimulating foreign trade. Behind the facade of a national government headed by aristocratic planters from Virginia, merchants and a few manufacturers wielded a good deal of influence. Desiring a second bank of the United States in 1814, for example, New York merchant John Jacob Astor sent Theron Rudd, one of the earliest full-time congressional lobbyists, to Washington and wrote interested parties to get in touch with him.[74] In 1816 their efforts were crowned with success, and Astor became president of the New York branch of the Second Bank. The same year Congress struck at Astor's British competitors by limiting the fur trade to United States citizens. This law, like that chartering the Second Bank, may be seen as part of a postwar outburst of American nationalism, but men like Astor, Girard, and Lowell played a part in channeling the force. In 1822, after a long campaign by Senator Benton of Missouri, Congress ended federal government competition with the Astor companies in the fur trade.

Meanwhile, the rise of industry had mobilized strong business forces behind a protective tariff. Here again, industrialists needed only to support ideas that grew from the war. When Francis Cabot Lowell of the Boston Associates went to Washington in 1816 to lobby for a tariff, "he had no difficulty in making himself agreeable to two of the most prominent leaders of the war party, Calhoun and Loundes."[75] Lowell skillfully manipulated the congressional committee to provide a high minimum duty on cottons that would protect the coarse products of his own company mills, but not the calicos of Rhode Island.

In the economic fluctuations that followed the return of peace, the tariff of 1816 failed to protect American producers from British competition, and associations to encourage aid for domestic manufacturing gained strength. Nationally there was a Society for the Encouragement of American Manufactures; on the state level Connecticut, New York, New Jersey, Pennsylvania, and Kentucky formed societies; and in the cities, societies were started in Cincinnati and Philadelphia.[76] The state societies that won such aids as tax exemption, loans, and subsidies for manufacturing enterprises from their legislatures had much of their backing from large farmers who saw in industry the development of a home market for agriculture.[77]

After the failure of these loosely organized societies to gain added tariff protection in 1820, the Philadelphia group, renamed the National Institution for the Promotion of Industry and intellectually guided by economist Matthew Carey, became the central organization for national propaganda and action. With the support of thoughtful students of economic growth such as E. I. du Pont de

Nemours, it published the *Patron of Industry*, devoted to arguments for protection.[78] In 1827 the Pennsylvania societies organized a national convention at Harrisburg; thirteen states sent over 100 delegates, many selected by state conventions.[79] The year was also marked by the appearance of the German emigré Friedrich List, a learned theoretical champion of protection, whose subsequent articles in the Philadelphia *National Gazette* were widely used by other protectionist newspapers. His small book *Outlines of Political Economy* became the protectionists popular manual for education.[80] In the tariff acts of 1828 and 1832, the protectionists temporarily triumphed in Congress.

The tariff battles of the 1820s were fought largely over the textile, particularly the woolen, schedules. While the manufacturing interests were able, through good organization, to get increased duties on finished products, they won only through the support of the large agricultural businessmen, such as the merino sheep raisers and the Kentucky hemp planters. The latter expected equal favors in duties on their products, and often through direct participation as political leaders, they secured what they wanted. Thus the tariff rose higher and higher, to the disgust of Southern exporters, but because of the nature of the political coalition, increases for the manufacturer were often negated by advances in duties on his raw materials.[81] Only this combination of agricultural and industrial business interests and their Washington lobbies, however, could have brought increasingly high protection to a nation that was overwhelmingly agricultural and commercial. The sheep, hemp, and home-market agriculturalists of the Middle Atlantic and Middle Western states, including Kentucky, joined the manufacturers in an "American System" to win victories by narrow margins over a solid South and a divided New England.[82]

The tariff of 1832 produced a better balance for manufacturers between the duties on raw materials and finished products, but in doing so, it drove the most aggressive leaders of Southern free trade to forceful opposition. Nullification by South Carolina, and the resulting compromise tariff of 1833 that progressively reduced duties over the next ten years, are well-known episodes of national political history. While the Whig majority in Congress was able to pass a higher tariff in 1842, its work was undone by the Democrats in 1846. The country remained on a basis of tariff chiefly for revenue until the Civil War. These vicissitudes of the protectionists illustrate the point made by Lee Benson in his study of New York, that there were not many voters who would make tariff the primary issue. His conclusion applies to business as well as nonbusiness voters. The battles over the tariff were not between business and nonbusiness interests, but between well-organized protectionists and a less-organized segment of the business community that probably comprised the majority.

GOVERNMENT AS A UTILITY

That most Americans in the period before 1850 were farmers scarcely hindered the emerging forces of business in industry, trade, and transportation from making effective use of law and government. Analysis of voting records indicates, even in the older areas, much agreement between town and country.[83] While there were keen regional rivalries, there was little dispute over most economic issues; everyone stood for local progress.[84] As the common law took more tangible shape and the states expanded statute law, both were chiefly responsive to the developing needs of business. In the East as well as in the West, keen interregional rivalries made the bench as well as the bar favorable to local enterprise.

In comparison to the rigid aristocratic control of European national states such as Prussia, the American state and federal governments served as agencies for business promotion. The difficulties experienced by entrepreneurs seeking aid came chiefly from the rivalry of opposing economic interests, as in the case of the tariff, or from fear of excessive cost to the taxpayer, as in the decision of Massachusetts not to build a western railroad at state expense. In general, however, if the local business community was reasonably united, it could get what it wanted from the state legislature.

While the total of federal aid, aside from the unmeasurable effects of the tariff, was relatively small, it was often of considerable importance in activities deemed essential to the national security. The first Congress granted subsidies to the codfishing fleet; from the 1840s to the Civil War, high-speed passenger steamers crossing the Atlantic were dependent on federal subsidies; some early turnpikes, canals, and railroads received grants of public land; and the railroads were continually assisted by mail contracts. In addition, the development of the frontier was stimulated by the money spent in maintaining army posts.[85]

Government actions, state or federal, merely reflected the intensely businesslike character of Northern and, particularly, Western American society. "It is hard," says Hartz, "for a later age, accustomed to comparatively mild chamber-of-commerce mentality, to appreciate the intensity of the passions which the regional rivalries of this period evoked."[86] It is perhaps equally hard for later generations, more disillusioned by history, to realize the enthusiasm, hope, and confidence of the naive promoters of towns and railroads to whom the future seemed as boundless as outer space. The developing fringe of the Middle West had a society such as the world had never seen.

> Kentucky of the 1800's was a microcosm of the age of enterprise, a lawyer's paradise where everyone speculated in land or risked in commercial and manufacturing ventures money that was only for the moment his, relying on his lawyer and his representative in the legislature—often one and the same man—to keep him out of trouble.[87]

CHAPTER 8

Business Reshapes the Social Structure

The glorious age of the independent farmer, the lord of the soil, hailed by Jefferson and Jackson, was in fact the Indian summer of a dying order. Up to the early 1800s the colonial type of society persisted, with landowning farmers in the great majority, slave-owning planters a regional minority, and trade and handicraft confined to a few centers. But from then on, new social groups living by machine production or transportation grew up around the old order, and in the North particularly, they altered habitual customs year after year until by midcentury there was a new society different from the American past or the European present.

The new society of the North and West was seen by European visitors as a business-oriented democracy striving relentlessly for material progress.[1] The lack of a similar degree of change in the South—where the old plantation system rather than a new business society spread to the Southwest—and the continued political and social dominance of the slave-owning planters meant a widening of the cultural divide between the sections. The Civil War may be seen as a result of the uneven progress of the values of business, capitalism, and democracy in the major sections of the nation.

In the North, several processes were involved in the gradual change in values and attitudes. Not only did factories, steamboats, and trains give wealth and influence to industrial enterprisers, but promotional development of the West created a new, more businesslike agricultural region whose needs and opportunities also colored Eastern thinking. The wealthy merchants of the Eastern seaboard, social perpetuators of the colonial business elite, dominated both developments. This meant that while the business scene was changing in tempo and action, in fundamental ways the merchant "aristocracy," either old or new, continued to hold the financial reins and to enjoy the highest social prestige. Thus the intellectual and artistic life of the North was influenced by a mixture of the traditional mercantile, social, and religious views, modified by impulses coming from the new democratic and intensely capitalistic West.

A SHIFT IN THE BASIS OF PRESTIGE

The change toward democratic capitalism inevitably involved a readjustment in the traditional prestige accorded to the ownership of land. As early as 1812, in one of the first geography textbooks, the Reverend Elizah Parish appears to have forgotten the owners of great estates when he writes, "Though there is no distinction by law in the United States, fortune and the nature of professions form different classes. Merchants, lawyers, physicians and clergymen form the first class; farmers, and artisans, the second; workmen who let themselves by the day the third. In public amusements these classes do not commonly intermix."[2]

During the period between the revolution and the major depression from 1837 to 1843, landowning in the Northern states underwent a status revolution. While large-scale foreign trade had been prestigious before the revolution, landowning was still the traditional, unquestionable basis for high social status. Merchants who made fortunes invested in land as a mark of social position, as well as for security. By 1850, landowning on a scale that assured wealth was still highly prestigious, but it was more because of the money represented than the land. In the Northern states, at least, the trading or commodity aspect of land had overcome the feudal glamor of the great estate. The successful merchants in scores of Northern cities were large landowners, but the land was held for future sale, and the landlord lived in a house on main street.

More than in earlier times, the rural regions in the North were dominated by their market towns or cities. The farmers were still more numerous than the townspeople, but the lines of economic, political, and social power intersected in the towns. The merchants who handled the farmers' products and sold them their goods, very likely on credit, lived in the town; the politicians who represented the area in state and nation were town lawyers; and the men with the most substantial fortunes, and hence the highest social prestige, had made them from commerce and the manipulation of urban property.[3] The coming of steam transportation by water and rail increased the strategic importance of the commercial centers, and further removed the truly rural man from political and social influence.

In 1844 Moses Yale Beach, publisher of the New York *Sun*, compiled a list of residents of New York City worth over $100,000. Dixon Wecter characterizes the list as "lawyers, merchants, auctioneers, newspaper publishers, tailors, patent medicine manufacturers."[4] Again, the land is not mentioned, but also a usually important category, "bankers," is omitted. In contrast, at midcentury, "economist" Lyman Atwater of the College of New Jersey said that the bankers had become "the potentates of the land, and the stock exchange, as in England, is 'the real seat of empire.' "[5] Since most of the largest merchants participated in the control of banking, the operating bankers could in fact be regarded as representative of the old mercantile community.

Thus, by mid-nineteenth century the cities of the northern and western United States had, with some exceptions, made the transition that in Europe required another century, the shift toward a strictly pecuniary or business society where "wealth became the measure of man's importance and social standing."[6] Some members of older status groups in the professions or modest landholding, now lowered by the rise of the new men of business wealth, deplored the situation. The *New Englander* in 1843 carried a long article lamenting that "where wealth and accidental circumstances were the only principal objects of respect, society could not be otherwise then vulgar."[7] But outside of a few Eastern areas, usually those that energetic young people were leaving, Americans gloried in the first thoroughly capitalist society. "The characteristics which Christianity in its present state seems to require," proclaimed the Reverend Henry Noble Day, "are chiefly vigor of invention, skill in execution and subscribing to the true end of industrial arts—utility."[8]

THE MERCANTILE CITY

While the towns dominated the countryside, the urban regional or "metropolitan" centers were the generators of the new business influence. At the time of the revolution, only the East Coast ports and a handful of interior towns such as Hartford, Albany, and Lancaster were such regional urban centers. In 1790, there were still only six cities with more than 8,000 inhabitants. Therefore, of the eighty-five cities in this category by 1850, more than 90 percent were new, and the rate of growth of the Northern seaports had been so great that Baltimore, Boston, New York, and Philadelphia were far more new than old. Remains of the New York of 1800, for example, with its 60,000 inhabitants, had to be searched for in the midcentury city of over half a million.

While every expanding city grows from in-migration, a new city must obviously grow almost entirely from this source. Thus each of the inland cities reproduced the in-migration aspects of the original colonies or the "frontier." This meant that for some years there was a preponderance of young men and young families imbued with the urge for success, wealth, and progress. Tolerant, by necessity, toward differences in nationality, religion, and education, these young arrivals joined in promoting their community. By the 1840s steamboats and railroads were bringing migrants longer distances, and heavy immigration was adding to the racial mixture, as well as to the skills and abilities that could be put to work.[9]

A large fraction of the migrants stayed but a few years in any one place before seeking new opportunities.[10] Such movement operated as a selective device; successful merchants were inclined to become permanent residents, whereas the less successful moved on. Those who prospered and remained nearly always invested in city or near-city property and in local industrial ventures that needed some personal supervision. Hence, while mercantile wealth was generally more important than industrial, there was no sharp distinction in ownership. The leading merchants, in more or less close association with each other and the local manufacturers, controlled the early nineteenth-century cities.[11] "Throughout the West," writes Richard Wade, "the pattern was everywhere the same, with city-council lists reading like the local business directory."[12]

While the contrast between a dominant group of sedentary merchants, with expanding family connections, and the mass of migrant population may have been most striking in the West, it was present to some degree in the older cities. In Boston, for example, the established merchants "utilized an elaborate web of kinship ties which made the family a potent institution."[13]

In the West, where the businessmen were originally migrants rather than heirs of established mercantile families, they saw the whole city as a business operation, and themselves as a group of merchant adventurers. Their profits depended on increasing trade, manufacturing, and land values; their costs were those of improvement and municipal administration. The businessmen, who dominated the early city councils, saw the cost of government as similar to overhead cost in a firm, a charge that should be kept to a minimum. With this prevailing bias, city councils were slow to invest in needed improvements or adequate protection for health and safety.

The friendly legislatures of the Western states cooperated with the city entrepreneurs in minimizing overhead costs by giving the municipalities very limited powers.[14] The major local expenditures were for creating market-places, paving essential streets leading to the markets, building wharves, and occasional creation of new land by drainage of marshy areas. In the rapidly growing cities, these needs greatly exceeded municipal revenues and occasioned many bond issues. This made it still less likely that nonessential social services would be undertaken. But even among old Eastern cities Constance M. Green finds that only Boston demonstrated an interest in urban social problems.[15] The rest were essentially laissez-faire ventures, in which the merchant community assumed the risk that other things would remain equal or take care of themselves while business expanded.

The most notable exception to early urban laissez-faire was regulation of markets. Just as colonial merchants had found it wise to build the reputation of their city for reliable products, fair weights, and reasonable prices through regulations and chambers of commerce, the merchants of the interior found such measures valuable in interurban competition. These "market ordinances in Western cities were strikingly similar": they sought to prevent impure or unwholesome food, false weights or measures, or raising prices by monopoly.[16] Those who attempted to corner or rig markets were denounced as "hucksters."

Looking at cities from the economist's point of view, primarily as markets, the inland cities of the early nineteenth century, with government held to the minimum, military expenses nil, and social services scarcely existing, were as purely economic centers as any that have ever appeared.* Yet, in spite of, or perhaps because of, this strict market orientation, mistakes stemming from lack of thoughtful planning and careless overoptimism were frequently made. Markets with attendant streets and squares were overbuilt or wrongly located.[17] The same types of mistakes were made by both municipal government and private enterprise. Blocks of office buildings were constructed to house businessmen who bypassed the city, housing developments were started for population that only arrived a generation later, and investments were made in local canal and railroad projects that never reached fruition.[18]

In the rapidly growing older cities, planning was also inadequate. The surveyor for the New York gridiron plan that was adopted at the beginning of the nineteenth century justified its unimaginative rigidity as best for "buying, selling and improving real estate." Years later Edith Wharton called it the work of "a society of prosperous businessmen who have no desire to row against the current."[19] Of adjustment to growth in the nation's second city, Sam Bass Warner, Jr., writes, "Philadelphians clung to their traditions of privatism, failing where privatism doomed them to failure, succeeding where privatism and community could be brought into harmony."[20]

Bigger cities and more complex urban problems led to the rise of a group of professional politicians, quite distinct from the prosperous amateurs who had given up time to serve themselves and the community. The new professionals participated in and were strengthened by the trend toward universal suffrage which began in the 1820s. Engrossed in its expanding business affairs, the merchant community gradually ceased direct participation in the increasingly large and complex problems of municipal government. The professional politician who took the merchant's place had primary interests in developing a stable party organization and in building a personal political career, matters that had been of minor importance to the merchant. This meant the rise of men thinking not solely in terms of the welfare of business, but also of policies that would gain mass approval from the citizenry. As most voters thought in material terms of the growth and prosperity of the community, the difference was not striking, but it did mean that such services as police protection, street lighting, fire protection, public health, and education were likely to receive more consideration.[21] The mercantile elite had not been indifferent to these matters, but it had regarded them as subordinate to more direct economic employment of scarce resources.

Professional politics in the cities necessarily brought about the same breakdown of community of interest noted earlier on the state level. The business group continued to be influential, but now they used their power *through* the political bosses rather than directly. For this purpose it was wise to have a place

* Some of the frontier cities gained greatly by supplying army outposts.

to hold preliminary caucuses, such as a chamber of commerce or the board of governors of an exchange. Representatives of such agencies, sometimes full-time administrative secretaries, could now speak with the voice of the "business community," of which the large merchants were still the most important members.

THE MERCANTILE SOCIETY

Outside the plantation South, urban merchants set the highest levels of consumption, taste, and manners. In some centers educated lawyers, clergymen, professors who had married or inherited money, and an occasional literary man leavened the sameness of material preoccupations. In Boston, in particular, the mercantile elite, viewing themselves as a republican aristocracy, assumed a certain responsibility for good manners, morals, and education.[22] It is easy, however, to exaggerate the commitment of the mercantile elite, the "Brahmins," to human welfare or the arts. Thomas Jefferson Coolidge, a Brahmin sage, looking back on the days before the Civil War, wrote: "Everybody was at work trying to make money . . . the only real avenue to success."[23] The poets and writers, such as Emerson or Parker, now so precious a part of the American heritage, were not highly regarded by the contemporary men of wealth and power.[24] Yet, in all the old cities some leading merchants, at least, saw themselves not only as architects of material progress but as men whose activities spread civilization and appreciation of the arts.[25]

In most cities the merchants' influence on improving the intellectual or artistic tome of social life was largely submerged in the more utilitarian interests of American society. New Yorkers, according to novelist James Fenimore Cooper, talked of wine, money, and lots. While several cities beyond the Appalachians called themselves the "Athens of the West," they did not divert many dollars to achieve such a reality. As noted earlier, institutions of learning were generally regarded as economic assets. Transylvania University, for example, was founded in 1820 partly as a cure for the deep depression in Lexington, Kentucky. Making the city a cultural center, argued one of the newspapers, will "fill her empty streets, it will people her tenantless houses, it will afford a market to her manufactures and the produce of that charming and fertile country with which she is surrounded."[26]

Merchant patronage of the fine arts followed the patterns of the colonial period: those arts such as portrait painting, decorative landscapes, and architecture that were part of a prestigious scale of living were patronized by rich merchants. Nowhere was this more the case than in Boston. Architects Charles Bulfinch and Samuel McIntire produced modified copies of English houses that had the elegance and simplicity of some of the best architecture of London or Bath. Even the stores and wharves of the port of Boston were rebuilt to lend "a magnificence to commerce."[27] While Western centers such as Cincinnati and St. Louis failed to keep pace with "the hub of the universe," the same trends toward a decorative architecture for commerce and banking were present throughout the nation.

In promoting the less prestigious arts, leadership probably came more from wealthy lawyers and occasional well-to-do doctors or clergymen than from merchants.[28] Small-business or public support of any of the arts was slight, and as in later times, imported art objects conferred more prestige upon their owner than those executed by native Americans. Only in the literary arts, where patronage by the rich was not essential, was American production well regarded in Europe.

In 1858 Freeman Hunt, the editor of the principal business review, *Hunt's Merchants' Magazine*, published two volumes of *Lives of American Merchants*. Merle E. Curti has analyzed these biographies to see their social-psychological implications, both as they reveal the ideas of the writers, frequently lawyers or merchants, and as they interpret the attitudes of the subjects. Regardless of inherited wealth, the merchants were seen to be as acquisitive as the rest of the society. The great merchant-financier Nathan Appleton wrote, "Some modification of the selfish principle may be said to lie at the root of all human action, but nowhere is it so naked and undisguised as in the profession of the merchant, whose direct and avowed object is the getting of gain."[29] But the successful were also seen as men of principle and character who recognized their social responsibilities and took a leading part in civic affairs and personal philanthropy. "Generally speaking," writes Curti, "the social role in philanthropy played most fully was giving to religious organizations, to education and to institutions for caring for the unfortunate. In these philanthropies, wealth was clearly and directly redounding to the benefit of the general good; the Christian concept of the stewardship of riches was being spelled out."[30]

Since other social institutions did little to help the poor, business support was sorely needed. Except for county poor houses, filled with the crippled, senile, or mentally disturbed, and some outdoor relief distributed partly for political purposes in the large cities, government was inactive. In the scheme of Calvinist justification, poverty, unless deliberate, was a sign of lack of grace and an indication of laxity or sin. This, combined with the widespread opportunities of nineteenth century America, produced an attitude of moral condemnation toward the poor that was scarcely modified before the rise of social work around 1900. and probably continues to be held by many American businessmen in the latter half of the twentieth century.

The rise of small-scale private charity appears to have come largely from individual religious or status motives or a blending of the two. Giving to spread morality to Westerners, Indians, Negroes or benighted foreigners not only kept one's peace with God, but conferred standing in church and community. "By 1815 the wives of leading merchants and professional men had established female benevolent associations in every city to aid the poor through relief and religion, using a vocabulary that smacked of noblesse oblige."[31] Church and charity as family stepping stones to keep social status abreast of business success were to become increasingly important for the rising middle class. By mid-century Philadelphia, for example, had over one hundred associations devoted to various forms of welfare work.[32]

A few wealthy merchants or their descendants granted substantial funds for schools, charitable institutions, and libraries. Among self-made merchants, Stephen Girard endowed a school for orphans in Philadelphia and John Jacob Astor left a small fraction of his great fortune for a library in New York. Although such giving was restricted to a relatively small number of individuals, it was held to be larger than in contemporary European nations.[33]

Merchants also gave financial support to many of the social reform movements that swept the North between 1810 and 1850, but they generally left active leadership to the clergy and other professional men. The likelihood that this would be the rule increased as business demanded more and more of the entrepreneur's full attention. Yet, at the same time, the larger operations returned bigger revenues and made the businessman more of a "steward of wealth." While many of the wealthy sponsors had religious or idealistic motives, they also thought the reforms would help to create a safer and more prosperous society.

One such reform, organized temperance, had an obvious appeal to those interested in worker's productivity. A Connecticut Society for the Reformation of Morals and a Massachusetts Society for the Suppression of Intemperance were both founded in 1813. The American Temperance Society was organized in 1826 by the same conservative or nonrevivalist religious groups,[34] including not only the rich Unitarian merchants of eastern Massachusetts but also many members of the orthodox Congregational and Presbyterian churches. Thus, temperance had the support of many of the New Englander business families who had been Federalists in an earlier day. These families were alarmed by the menace to property inherent in the advance of manhood suffrage, particularly if the lower class was drunken and irresponsible. In 1826 Lyman Beecher warned his fellow conservatives: "As intemperance increases, the power of taxation will come more and more into the hands of men of intemperate habits and desperate fortunes; of course the laws will gradually become subservient to the debtor and less efficacious in protecting the rights of property."[35]

This essentially upper-middle and upper-class movement to keep workers and voters sober was a moderate one, generally not opposed to wine or beer, and received most of its political support from the National Republicans or Whigs.[36] But in the 1830s, the evangelical churches began to join in a nationwide prohibition movement that advocated total abstinence. As growing industrial cities faced the effects of the heavy drinking of much of the unskilled laboring population, more businessmen joined the movement.* Since the Irish and German immigrants brought with them their convivial habits of drinking, by

---

* It should be remembered that in order to cut down surplus federal revenue the Jackson administration repealed the excise taxes and liquor became extremely cheap.

the 1840s prohibition became in part a movement of respectable middle-class native Americans against those people they considered to constitute an irresponsible lower class and immoral foreigners.

In cities like St. Louis, Cincinnati, and Milwaukee, where the German population was large, the split between prohibition and nonprohibition tended to be ethnic; the prohibitionists were labeled as "Yankees," which many of them were.[37] While such rifts divided business, temperance on the whole had the support of both older merchants and new industrialists. Foster Rhea Dulles writes, "The church easily fell in with the attitude of the merchant-manufacturer class, whose sole objective was to get as much work as possible out of its employees."[38] Certainly the levels of drinking reported by commentators on the 1830s would seem intolerable in an industrial society.

In accounting for social responsibility in the role of the merchant, in particular, it must be remembered that not only was a reputation as a man of principle an important trade asset, but also that the aristocratic traditions of the mercantile-financial complex carried with it ideas of social leadership and paternalism. In addition, the succcessful merchant increasingly had more capital at his disposal than he could employ in his trading ventures. In terms of social theory, the merchant role had been well-defined over the course of centuries; it had standardized patterns of résponse to recurring situations; it had anticipated attitudes and beliefs, manners, and ethics; and it insured some uniformity in the type of man who succeeded. Habits and practices of social responsibility, which had hardly entered the roles of newer types of businessmen created by economic development, tended to persist in this generally sedentary and conservative group.

CRYSTALLIZING CULTURAL TRADITIONS

By the mid-nineteenth century, American businesslike culture in the North had developed characteristics that were to shape it in later generations. It had acquired the patterns implied in such clichés as "the American way of life" or "American individualism." Based on a high degree of both internal migration and economic opportunity, the culture differed significantly from that found in any of the nations of Western Europe or their overseas colonies.

Scholarly analysts of this emerging system of cultural values see major emphasis on such themes as achievement and success; activity and work; moral justification based on Protestant Christianity; efficiency and practicality; material progress; equality and democracy; and freedom; combined with external conformity, nationalism and patriotism, and respect for the rights of the individual. Of this group, which most social scientists would accept with minor modifications, the normative values placed on achievement, success, activity, work, moral justification, efficiency, practicality, and progress were all fostered by the conditioning force of business.[39]

Such slogan-like words are, of course, open to many interpretations. The values associated with words such as "individualistic," "independent," "responsible," and "self-respecting" differ between nations. American "individualism," for example, has differed markedly from the same trait in Latin cultures, and probably somewhat from one period to another in the United States. Consequently, when a group of social analysts writes, "A note of individualism sounds through the business creed like the pitch in a Byzantine choir. . . . It is the keynote of the classical creed, around which the themes of freedom and equality are woven," further definition is needed to establish any historical reality.[40] For example, research in Spanish types of culture indicates that individualism means an internal, unique spiritual independence from one's immediate environment. In the United States in means, among other things, an insistence on respect for one's equality and rights in relation to a social group.[41] Similarly, "responsible" in Latin cultures means primarily responsibility to one's true self and one's family, but not reliability in keeping social or business engagements or carrying out cooperative programs, as it does in the United States.[42] "Self-respecting" to Latins and many other European peoples means, again, an inner respect for the dignity of the human being, whereas in nineteenth-century America, it came increasingly to mean socially well-behaved or conforming.

There is an important underlying distinction in these contrasts: the American cult of the individual was shaped to fit the needs of the community and of economic development, to fit the vigorous, assertive, but generally reliable businessman. These cultural norms, however, did not necessarily control individual behavior. Nearly all intelligent businessmen subscribed to, but did not always honor in their conduct, the moral slogan that "honesty was the best policy"; and in the new areas, where cooperation in the interests of the community was most stressed, reliability, undermined by overoptimism, might be lamentably low.[43]

The type of equalitarian democracy proclaimed as an ideal in the Declaration of Independence, and given more substance by the political evolution of the 1820s and 1830s, was not an essential part of the system of business roles or values. Rather, it grew up alongside expanding business, and each system adjusted to the other. In business, democracy meant equality of initial opportunity, absence of rigid class lines, easy communication between worker and manager, and more effort to provide good working conditions than, for example, in England.[44] But this utilitarian democracy in the plant did not alter the principle that ownership carried dictatorial rights over the use of property. "Liberty" to the American businessman, whose personal liberty had never been menaced, meant chiefly the right to control and dispose of his property.

Business writers insisted that American free enterprise was in fact bringing about greater democracy. Henry C. Carey of Philadelphia held that "the ideals of the Declaration of Independence were being fulfilled in the economic sphere by the essential justice with which wealth was distributed in a system of free economic enterprise."[45] Curti concludes that "instead of repudiating democracy as the southern proslavery apologists were to do, the champions of rising industrialism interpreted it in such a way as to make it sanction the influence of wealth."[46] Two scholarly writers stress the inverse relationship: "There are formidable reasons for concluding that the development of American small-town enterprise (and by extension, of urban capitalism) is most centrally—organically—connected with that of American political democracy."[47]

Since according to American belief, the road to wealth through diligence and hard work was open to anyone, increasing belief in equalitarian democracy made the self-made man appear more virtuous, more truly American, than the one born rich. The power of the regard for success through self-help was strikingly revealed in William Henry Harrison's campaign for the presidency in 1840. This scion of five generations of Virginia aristocrats was successfully pictured as a man who rose from a humble log cabin to national prominence. The rags to riches myth became a standby of politicians, clergymen, and business leaders in proclaiming the democratic character of American institutions.* Even the hard-headed Dr. Oliver Wendell Holmes "believed that after ten years of patient and diligent labor any enterprising young man might rise into this elite."[48]

Gradually the opportunity for success was translated into a duty to succeed which became part of the training of American children, and has been assumed to be an important characteristic of a modal American personality.[49] Of value for economic growth, this urge to succeed may have produced alienation and neurosis in many who, in spite of vigorous efforts, failed in the contest for wealth. Unconsciously thinking only in terms of the North, Sir Charles Lyell called the United States "a country where all, whether rich or poor, were laboring from morning until night, without ever indulging in a holiday . . . . In no country are the faces of the people furrowed with harder lines of care."[50] "It was natural," says F. R. Dulles, "that Americans should not entirely escape the shadow of work in their play, should carry into it something of the competitive spirit which characterized their other activities."[51] According to a writer in *Hunt's Merchants' Magazine*, even in daily work diligence was carried to a point where it produced inefficiency. "The detail of the business is not left to subordinates, but occupies, most unprofitably, the attention of the principal."[52]

While the values put on striving, success, and hard work made Americans strongly competitive, there were also factors in the American heritage that encouraged a high degree of cooperation. Certainly from the earliest days of the colonies, the common needs of migrants in new areas and the problems of building new communities worked in this direction. De Tocqueville was impressed with the cooperativeness of Americans; and a century later, Albert Hirschman, after intimate observation of less cooperative Latin types of personality, rated cooperativeness as one of the major factors in American economic growth.[53]

---

* Referred to as a myth because career line studies indicate that most men at the top had come from favorable backgrounds. See Miller, *Men in Business* and Cochran, *Railroad Leaders.*

Willingness to join, conform, and cooperate strongly supported business needs in later decades and produced a peculiarly American type of large-scale enterprise and managerial capitalism. The high development of these qualities again illustrates the complex interaction of the social and economic needs of the American environment with the values of equalitarian democracy, Calvinist religion, and competitive business.

The American environment also produced a need for cheapness and utility which, in turn, stimulated mass production. To meet the high demands of a rapidly expanding society for new consumer durables, such as pots and pans, or capital goods in the form of tools or farm equipment, American factories were designed to turn out cheap articles in large quantities. The users of these goods, frequently on the move, wanted short-run utility and easy replacement. Fine quality was a luxury for the rich and could be secured by importation.

Reenforcing this emphasis on the value of quantity over quality was the large scale of the nation itself. The need for many more miles of road, canal, or railroad than in European nations led to building for quick and cheap completion, that is, for quantity rather than quality. The light iron rails and inadequate grading were not necessarily the result of frauds or mistakes in construction; they represented the cheapest and quickest way to secure railroad service over long distances with small numbers of customers. Improvements could come later when traffic warranted them.[54]

New communities, and a nation that saw itself as young, necessarily thought of the future more than the past. In the Old World, antiquity was highly esteemed, but in America, newness was a virtue. A ten-year residency was considered long standing in thousands of American communities. A people on the move discarded ancestors and ancestral homes, and thought in terms of the new house they would someday build. Nevertheless, readiness to accept innovation and change was only a matter of degree as compared with Europe or even less developed areas. In every older American community, there could be strong opposition to innovation, often led by entrepreneurs whose interests were menaced and by many conservative fundmentalists of one type or another.[55] The school board of Lancaster, Ohio, for example, saw dangers to the immortal soul in technological change: "Such things as railroads and telegraphs are impossibilities and rank infidelity . . . if God had intended that his creatures travel at the frightful speed of fifteen miles an hour by steam he would clearly have foretold it through his holy prophets."[56] Yet, the type of effective resistance offered by privileged groups abroad was generally prevented by the basic belief of most influential Americans in the inevitable working of the laws of the market. The initiators or controllers of technological or physical innovation were to a large extent businessmen. Migration made farmers, laborers, and white-collar workers tolerant toward change; skilled workers might be the chief inventors, but it was the entrepreneur who was generally the architect of progress. Stimulated by a new environment and many opportunities, he saw things differently and played his essential roles in new ways.[57]

Such innovation was not likely to be in the field of general ideas or scientific theories, but rather in practical methods of fulfilling economic needs. Hence, as the economic system surged forward, American political and social ideas and practices might fail to keep up with new situations or problems resulting from business or technological change. The successful innovators in business generally had wealth and prestige on their side; the proposers of the new in intellectual, political, or social matters were less likely to enjoy this advantage. Hence, while industrialism and exploitation of the West were creating grave regional tensions that would lead to the nation's bloodiest war, and mushrooming cities were already afflicted with slums, ghettos and corrupt governments, no group felt responsible for the advance of the troubles or capable of arresting them.

Part III

INDUSTRIALISM, 1850-1915

CHAPTER 9

*The Pattern of Industrial Business**

"The consumption of iron is a social barometer by which to estimate the relative height of civilization among nations," said Abram Hewitt in 1856.[1] Obviously by his standard the United States was already a leader, but the patterns that were to characterize American industrial supremacy were only beginning to emerge. Few companies sold in a national market, few aside from transportation and public utilities were large, and the codes and practices of corporate management were still to be formulated. While urban population had grown rapidly in the previous half century, the reciprocal process of industry creating cities and cities building industry was to be still more important from 1850 on.

From an economic standpoint, the years from 1850 to 1915 cover the initial exploitation of the great natural resources of the interior of the continent, a process that was to make America first among the industrial states and her corporations the world's largest private enterprises. It is not surprising that this powerful national drama obscured most other elements in American social development, that material success became the highest goal, that the ablest young men plunged without question into the business of developing the country, and that politics and social morality adjusted to the needs of the grand process.

No one stood successfully against the development of the country and a higher standard of living as primary goals, and few people tried. Rapidly expanding markets and resources led to the breakdown of local or regional efforts at cooperation and hence to a period of intense, harsh competition, in which businessmen suffered from high risks and uncertainties even though they commanded the social, intellectual, and economic resources of the nation.

These forces, combined with a continuance of the Calvinistic approach to work as a duty and a service to God, produced a hard-driving type of entrepreneur who felt that he was fulfilling his obligations to society by devoting himself fully to his business. In contrast to the carry-over of mercantile gentility

* Parts of this chapter and the next have appeared in Qualey, *Thorstein Veblen.*

that had graced much business life in the previous era, most of these industrial and mining entrepreneurs lived chiefly for the excitements of business achievement. In general they left politics to lesser men and other social relations to wives. Observing the men around him, the famous banker of the Civil War, Jay Cooke, remarked, "Through all the grades I see the same all-pervading, all engrossing anxiety to grow rich. This is the only thing for which men live here."[2]

For the fortunate, America of the late nineteenth century handsomely rewarded the desire to be rich. Within twenty or thirty years fortunes rivalling those of the great landlords of older civilizations were accumulated, and they became a new force in American society. Such wealth gave a few hundred businessmen the power, had they used it, deliberately to bring about political or social change. With few exceptions, however, the great changes they wrought were unplanned results of using their money-power in ways strictly associated with their business.

As we have seen (Chapter 5), the generations that were mature leaders after 1850 were not brought up to value either classical or theoretical learning. With few exceptions, they saw experience as the great teacher and hard work the proper school. Middle-class boys entered offices after grammar school and succeeded by alertness, judgment, and luck in seizing opportunities. Only in the small world of big business were preparatory school and college ties important in success. Or one might say, only in the area of railroads and large-scale finance was the chief emphasis on getting ahead within the organization or system rather than directly participating in profit-making, that is to say, upon careerist rather than market-oriented behavior.[3]

THE BUSINESS SITUATION

The growth of big companies to supply a national market tended to obscure the continuities in the American business scene. The storekeeper, plumber, carpenter, salesman, and real estate or insurance broker were still the types of businessmen in contact with the nonbusiness public and with each other. The number of these proprietors and partners, plus the managers and administrators of larger firms, had increased rapidly from the beginning of improved transport and machine industry. Each decade, from at least 1820 on, the total social influence of such businessmen seems to have grown. Increasing opportunity in nonagricultural business accords with the general structure of developing industrialism. While a few hundred firms in a score or more highly capitalized industries became big and semimonopolistic, thousands of new firms started each year either in the many lines of manufacturing continually opened up by new technology or in the much larger areas of trade and service that arose from expanding markets and growing levels of consumption. Between 1880 and 1910, the number of firms listed by Dun and Bradstreet doubled to over 1,500,000, and the total including those too small or transitory to have a credit rating was doubtless over 2,000,000. Retailers continued to be the most numerous full-time businessmen; the total of any other type was small compared to the number of stores. But undoubtedly the average members of this group exercised less influence on business, political, or social thought or practice than did the leaders of large corporations or suppliers of semiprofessional services such as accounting or brokerage.

Like other Americans, the small enterprisers, equalling perhaps 6 percent of all gainful workers in 1890, were a mobile population. Their ventures often became insolvent within a year or two and the entrepreneurs moved to another state, escaping small creditors who found it too expensive to pursue debtors with legal processes. Few debtors went through formal bankruptcy proceedings.[4] Failure usually did not mean an end to the proprietor's entrepreneurial activity, but merely that he reopened in a new area or became an employee until he found a new opportunity. Since men also moved to make profits, the firm that had the same name, proprietor, and location for over five years would be the exception, as was the Middle Western farmer on the same farm at the end of five years.

This mobility was partly caused by the continual settlement of new communities that promised less competitive markets than the older towns. Merle E. Curti notes that in his frontier county of Trempealeau, Wisconsin, "Only a very small number of the non-agriculturally employed stayed from 1860 to 1870."[5] Most of the businessmen for whom information was available in Trempealeau county formed partnerships; "many partnerships, however, were shortlived."[6] Thus continual movement of small enterprisers helped to spread the relatively uniform business culture across the continent, influencing the manners and attitudes of the farmers, who were still two or three times as numerous as the commercial and industrial entrepreneurs.

THE GREAT BUSINESS OF REAL ESTATE

The railroad not only added enormously to the area of commercial agriculture, making market-oriented businessmen from millions of farmers who grew staples in the Mississippi Valley and Great Plains, but it gave a new maturity and complexity to the major business of dealing with land. No part of the broad and fertile plains was too remote to be reached by a railroad which could turn homestead claims into valuable acreage. "Towns," writes Leslie E. Decker, "sought penitentiaries, normal schools, colleges and county seats partly to prevent the railroad from by-passing them."[7] He estimates that between 1872 and 1880 Kansas and Nebraska towns spent $22 million to attract railroads.[8] To raise these sums and to provide improvements such as schools and public buildings that would attract settlers, the land operators used the borrowing power of the town and county governments. "On the mid-continent frontier, then, almost all the early comers to any area were speculators first and home seekers second or not at all."[9]

The continuing federal practice of opening only limited tracts of land for sale by public auction at any given time meant that there were always many real or presumptive settlers establishing squatter or preemptive claims in areas not yet open for legal acquisition of title. Some of the most active trading was in such claims, the whole group protecting themselves, as earlier, by forming a "club" that would intimidate, if necessary, any outside bidders at the eventual government auction. The Homestead Act of 1862, giving a settler 160 acres at the end of five years, did not greatly change practices as there remained too many other means of initial acquisition.

The chief operators in the buying and selling of claims were probably professional realtors, nearby businessmen with $10,000 to $20,000 in capital. In the old port cities, these men would have been risking their money in trade or urban real estate, but in the West they subordinated banking, trade, or the practice of law to rapidly rotated investments in farm land. "Subordinated" is perhaps the wrong word, for these entrepreneurs were busy at all types of moneymaking activity—they "lived business."

Robert T. Swierenga has explored the occupation of 292 residents of Iowa who entered claims for over 1,000 acres each in central Iowa at midcentury. Just over 40 percent are classified as "realtor-banker-lawyer"; nearly 30 percent as "merchant-manufacturer"; and the rest scatter among categories such as "county, township, city official," physician, and other professional or skilled people. The same major categories also included over 80 percent of the 83 non-Iowa residents who entered claims at this time.[10]

Since land continued to be the chief form of nineteenth-century investment, nearly all the members of the community who had substantial liquid resources were real estate operators. The business was one which the whole community understood; the absentee buyer worked through local real estate men, the latter refrained from bidding at auctions against actual farmer-settlers, while the newspaper advertising and other promotion carried on by the big investors was welcomed as raising the value of everybody's land and helping local business in general.[11]

"By the 1860's the attitude that borrowing capital should be avoided was no longer widely held."[12] Men without capital could sell their labor to earn a down-payment on a farm. Of 145 farmers in an Iowa township who appear in the census from 1860 to 1880, only 39 were not mortgagors. Allan Bogue thinks that landowners generally encumbered one-third to one-half of their land with mortgages during the first generation.[13] Thus between mortgage interest and payments on an increasing amount of farm machinery bought on credit, the commercial farmer was in much the same economic situation as other small businessmen.

In the 1880s, the business machinery for agricultural lending was so well developed that packages of Western mortgages could be marketed to insurance companies and other large investors in the East. As is usual with debtors, many farmers operating on mortgages complained of grasping money-men, but in the absence of government farm loan banks, such middlemen seemed essential to rapid agricultural expansion. In the words of Howard J. Graham: "Successful speculators often were the planners of a planless society . . . middlemen performing a social function that had been abdicated by government."[14]

THE BUSINESS OF THE SOUTH

While railroads, mortgage money, and new methods had much the same effect on land operations and farming in the South and Southwest as in the North, the sudden ending of slave production caused special problems. An obvious recourse for the plantation owner would have been to hire the exslaves as paid labor, but this required an amount of working capital that was unavailable. Local banks were either closed or in very weak condition, and there were more attractive investments for Northern capital in rebuilding the devastated areas. The usual solution to the dilemma was to rent the old plantations in small parcels to Negro families who would pay with a share of their cotton or tobacco crop.

As in colonial days, mercantile credit was widely substituted for bank loans. The share croppers, and other impoverished farmers received the necessities of life from a local merchant and repaid him when the crop was marketed. As in all such risky extensions of credit, the concealed costs were very high; the storekeepers prospered and the borrowers remained poor. As capital accumulated in the hands of the merchants, many of them went into banking, and small "country store banks" spread throughout the South.

By the 1880s, these and other readjustments in the Southern economy had been made, and a degree of prosperity was returning to the area. Industries previously discouraged by the slave-plantation system were springing up, and business in the South was becoming more like that of the older states of the West. Yet excessively small enterprise, a weak credit system, poor transportation, and much absentee ownership, particularly in larger operations, continued to be the rule and to hold back development.[15]

Entry into business remained difficult for Negroes. Denied the experience of responsible jobs in existing manufacturing companies, and also lacking the capital necessary for promoting factories of their own, they were confined to handicraft or service operations catering largely to other Negroes. In the latter, particularly in banking, and sickness and burial insurance, they achieved some mild successes but also many failures.[16] The first bank operated by Negores, since the demise of the Freedman's Bureau in 1873, was the Capital Savings Bank of Washington, D.C., opened in 1888, followed the next year by others in Richmond and Chattanooga. In 1900, forty thousand Negroes were listed in a wide variety of financial and service enterprises. At that time a National Negro Business League was organized, which according to newspaper accounts five years later, included "prosperous bankers, real estate and insurance agents, editors, publishers, managers of steam laundries, manufacturing establishments, and an opera house; and owners and operators of a street railway and electric light and power plants."[17] But judged by census figures, the capital resources of most of these enterprises must have been pitifully small.[18]

THE IMPORTANCE OF MARKETING

All over the nation the businessmen most often seen by the average citizen were inevitably the small tradesmen. They were the lowest or basic level of an increasingly complex structure of national marketing. Commission merchants, brokers, agents, jobbers, and salesmen channelled goods in various ways from producers or importers to wholesalers and retailers. The meaning of each title varied from one activity to another, but most such middlemen avoided the accumulation of a stock of goods. They bought, even in carload lots, only for prompt resale. Manufacturers' agents also arranged for delivery of the products from suppliers they represented directly to whosesalers and retailers without taking possession of the goods. Either hiring salesmen or performing this function themselves, these expediters of marketing could work out of small offices. Wholesalers, on the other hand, bought the goods of many producers and stored them in warehouses for resale over a considerable period, and many direct agents for manufacturers supplying the national market did the same with the products of their particular firms.

The traveling salesman was ubiquitous in the whole system. Journeying by rail he represented manufacturers to middlemen, middlemen to retailers, and suppliers to the general public. To many small cities and towns he was the personification of the outside world of business, and he was built into the culture by the usual method of jokes and tall stories. He represented "slick" urban culture, the sophistication that came from travel and knowing many people and, necessarily, the mores and folkways of national business. Most famous of this new breed of Americans was Diamond Jim Brady, who sold railroad equipment. He pleased his customers, whose purchases ran into the millions, by lavish dinners and entertainment that emphasized the carryover of personal relations into the world of marketing.

By 1890 signs of a trend toward more direct marketing of consumer goods were present. An increasing number of branches, staffed by employees of the firm making the goods, sold directly to individual consumers in local markets. In the 1880s sales from the mail-order catalogues began to grow rapidly. Big companies like Montgomery Ward and Sears Roebuck could deliver goods from their producers by mail, for cash, more cheaply than the consumer could buy through the usual marketing channels. Before 1900, chain stores such as Woolworth and A&P appeared in notions and food. In each case, smaller retailers, tied to the system of independent wholesalers and jobbers, survived by making more efficient arrangements for supply and by offering service and credit.

New ways of marketing led to an increasing volume of communication between business and the general public. Talks with salesmen, reading newspapers, which were business enterprises, and perusing catalogues and advertisements all became a larger part of everyday existence. Advertising, for example, was as old as American business, but until the 1840s it had been held back by the high cost of paper and printing and the local character of most markets. By 1870, rotary presses and pulp paper made magazine and newspaper space cheap enough for lavish display, and firms trying to capture a national market for their brands began extensive advertising. In most firms, however, advertising was regarded as a minor department until at least the 1890s, and advertising men were treated with condescension or suspicion, as individuals whose occupation was suggestive of show business, huckstering, and slightly dishonest ways of attracting patronage.

But from 1890 to 1900, advertising expenditures grew rapidly, and its agencies and specialists became respected members of the business community. Agencies hired artists and consulted psychologists, while popular magazines became, from the business angle, primarily advertising media. Trolleys, elevateds, subways, and suburban trains made car cards important, and the bicycle and automobile gave new life to outdoor advertising. By 1910 the total of advertising expenditure reached 4 percent of the national income, a figure never substantially exceeded.[19]

Advertising knit business activities more tightly together. By appealing directly to consumers through advertising, a manufacturer could force wholesalers and retailers to carry his product. Supplying most of the revenue for newspapers and magazines, large advertisers exerted power for considerate treatment in the field of publishing, and in general made the media conservative, cautious, and nonpartisan. Through trade associations, the advertising agencies and the media added their influence to many others that were bringing local businessmen together in weekly or monthly get-togethers, partly social and partly business.

The majority of advertising specialists in this period believed in rational human beings who could be won over by describing the virtues of the product. The advocates of hidden persuasion were still a minority.[20] Regardless of underlying psychology, the types of appeal developed by advertising experts tended to reenforce the folklore and values of high-level consumption, and to inflate marketing slogans or attitudes into stronger forces for public education and conditioning. For example, the ultimare desirability of a Packard, and of the largest one rather than the smallest, was a lesson in values more readily learned by the young man of the early 1900s than the desirability of intelligent participation in local politics.

From recognition of the force of advertising copy in creating values or social attitudes, public relations was emerging as a professional technique. The conception of building favorable opinion for an industry or a firm, without emphasis on selling any paricular product, had beginnings in the United States with publishers' agents in the 1840s; iron, steel, and wool association lobbyists from the 1850s on; railroad executives after the Civil War; and electric traction and utility representatives at the end of the century. By the first decade of the new century "publicity agencies," as distinct from advertising agencies, began to appear; among these pioneers the work of Ivy Lee for the Telephone Company, the Pennsylvania Railroad, and the Rockefeller interests was the most notable.[21] Viewing the business scene as a whole, public relations before 1915 was more a portent than a major factor, but it was to develop steadily from then on. The sharp increase in goodwill toward American business in the 1920s may have owed much to this focused effort to create attitudes and values favorable to particular industries that inevitably were also favorable to the aims and customs of business as a whole.

COMPANIES GROW WITH THE MARKET

The demands and opportunities of selling in a market that grew from less than 25 million relatively isolated people in 1850 to 100 million people bound together by rails and highways in 1915 led to the rise of industrial giants. Nationwide competition and large-scale operation were as new to the generation growing up after 1850 as atomic power and outer space were to their descendents 100 years later and of greater immediate importance to businessmen. The pressures that a national market imposed on production and selling, and the opportunities such a market opened to the shrewd and fortunate were all new and uncertain. In addition, some entrepreneurs were becoming familiar with the uses and abuses of the corporation, many of which were still mysteries to the ordinary businessman or politician.

As technology improved and lower railroad rates intensified competition, the rapid adjustments required to maintain a share of any given market were made more difficult by generally falling prices. In addition, between 1873 and the end of 1878, and again from 1893 to 1897, the nation suffered from continuous depression, and manufacturers from great overcapacity. When markets had been local or regional, it had often been possible to control prices by tacit agreements or by accepting the leadership of one firm—the processes later known as monopolistic competition, and what Thorstein Veblen, no doubt, had in mind when he wrote, "It is very doubtful if there are any successful business ventures within the range of modern industries from which the monopoly element is wholly absent."[22]

Goaded by the dire situation of the 1870s, new and more systematic efforts were made to maintain prices by agreement. While such voluntary associations went back to the merchant guilds and the Hanse, in earlier America they had generally been confined to single cities or at the most to limited areas, such as the Hudson River Steamboat Association. Now worsening conditions of competition hastened collective action in all industries with large fixed capital. High capital intensity did not necessarily mean large-scale operation, but merely a large investment in plant and equipment in relation to wages and the value of the products. A small distillery, for example, might have fixed capital, and wage and income relations similar to a large railroad; whereas, a big textile mill might have relatively low fixed capital and have wages as its principal factor of cost.

Cooperation to control the market was a solution to the cutthroat competition that menaced returns on fixed capital, and Americans, superficially at least, were highly cooperative. If they sometimes prevented mergers, it was through placing too high a value on their enterprises, not because of family pride or fear of loss of identity.[23]

Survival by a combination of independent companies in close association was quite a different solution from merger into a single corporation or trust. A group of small manufacturers pouring their goods in fixed quotas into a pool were attempting a method of restriction that would keep the least efficient producer alive, as the pool would dispose of the goods at prices sufficient to cover the highest individual cost of production. In the whiskey pool, for example, production was apportioned among some eighty distilleries.

By using similar devices, small business was kept alive in England and Western Europe. But belief in the free market and legal hostility to "restraint of trade" made the United States pools and other price-fixing associations imperfect and unreliable. Operating outside the law, pacts to control competition had only the force of "gentlemen's agreements," and every large group included many who could not be counted on to behave as gentlemen. Consequently, none of these manufacturing agreements gave more than temporary relief from bitter competition.

Consolidation into one single company had obvious advantages in legality and efficiency over any of the extralegal methods of association. For example, in 1885 when the whiskey distillers agreed to merge into one firm, known euphemistically as the Cattle Feeders and Distillers Corporation, they were able to close down more than seventy distilleries and supply the market from the dozen most efficient plants. But it was often hard to bring a large number of competitors together voluntarily, and some big companies such as Standard Oil grew by what might be called conquest. In many types of production, the firm that first achieved a large scale of operation could produce each unit more cheaply and make better bargains with the railroads for handling its larger volume of shipments. Thus, the leading firm could set prices below the costs of smaller competitors and force them to sell out. On occasion, as Henry Demarest Lloyd noted, these market pressures were reenforced by threats and violence.[24]

Before 1889, however, the general incorporation acts of the states did not allow one corporation to hold the stock of another. Therefore, a merger involved either forming a new financial structure, or finding some legal way of attaching the purchased firm to its new parent. In railroads the solution was for a larger interest to buy the controlling securities of a company and then lease it for a long term, as when the Vanderbilts bought control of the Canada Southern in 1877 and subsequently leased it to their Michigan Central company for ninety-nine years. In manufacturing, when no such long-run stability was visualized, the device of trusteeship was used. The term "trust" technically meant that the shareholders of the merged companies put their stock in the hands of a board of trustees and received trust certificates in return. S. C. T. Dodd, the lawyer of the Standard Oil trust, is credited with having first applied this system to a corporation in 1879.

In 1889 a New Jersey general incorporation act permitted a company to own the stock of other companies. Ten years later Delaware passed a law even more liberal than that of New Jersey; in fact, the whole operation could be performed without any stockholder of the new corporation taking the trouble to travel to Delaware. The old "trusts," by this time under attack from state and federal courts, soon became "holding companies" with New Jersey or Delaware charters, but the term "trust" continued in popular usage.

THE ATTACK ON BIGNESS

By 1890 railroads and some public utilities were already large companies, and in many places they were also local monopolies. In manufacturing or processing, the size of companies was increasing rapidly, and several trusts had been formed. Production of refined petroleum and sugar, cotton and linseed oil, matches, tobacco, whisky, cordage, and lead were each dominated by a single large firm.[25] These companies varied considerably in the control they could exercise over their markets, and may *in toto* seem peripheral to the main types of production and distribution, but the alarming thing to contemporary observers was that they had all appeared within about a decade. If the movement were to continue and to grow, it would not be long before each type of production was monopolized, and the worker and consumer reduced to the status of serfs in an industrial feudalism.

Doubtless the movement against trusts gained strength from the general anxieties of the day. National enterprises, that were neither trusts nor monopolies, were nevertheless putting competitive pressure on small regional producers. Salesmen from big city distributors were reaching the customer previously served from wholesalers nearby. Robert H. Wiebe believes that by about 1885 "local America stood at bay . . . . Among the components of crisis, none found fuller expression than the belief that the great corporations were stifling opportunity, and no one cried his resentment more persistently than the local entrepreneur."[26] This was the climate of opinion that led associations of small businessmen, farm organizations, and journalists like Henry Demarest Lloyd to devote their energies to combatting the trusts.

Such pressure was almost irresistible politically, and states and the federal government passed antitrust laws. In the bold and sweeping language of the Sherman Anti-Trust Act, passed by Congress in 1890,

> Every contract, combination in the form of trust or otherwise, or conspiracy, in restraint of trade or commerce among the several states, or with foreign nations, is hereby declared to be illegal . . . .
> Every person who shall monopolize, or attempt to monopolize, or combine or conspire with any other person or persons to

monopolize any part of the trade or commerce among the several States, or with foreign nations, shall be deemed guilty of a misdemeanor.

The law was a criminal as well as a civil statute; it provided fines and imprisonment, as well as triple damages to injured parties.

Obviously, such a drastic law was partly a gesture by legislators to reassure their farm and local business constituents. Prior to 1960 no big business executive ever went to jail for violation of the Sherman Act, but its interpretation by the Supreme Court had by 1911 established certain ground-rules for business agreements or mergers. Any agreement among a number of firms to fix prices, or allot production or territories was illegal, as was any effort by labor or others to boycott particular firms. Nearly complete monopoly, unless based on the limited duration of particular patents, was also outside the law, but the percentage of control of the market that constituted illegal monopoly would be decided by the Court in each case, on the bases of the justices' conception of the effect on the public interest.

This latter view, called the "rule of reason," put forward in the Standard Oil case of 1911, was strongly objected to by the representatives of small or medium-sized business. They could point to a number of occasions on which committees of Congress had declared in favor of exact and literal interpretations of the law. As a result, the Congress elected in 1912 passed the Clayton Act (1914), more carefully defining the types of action that constituted restraint of trade or monopoly. Among the actions forbidden were "directly or indirectly, to discriminate in price ... where the effect of such discrimination may be substantially to lessen competition," to tell a wholesale purchaser that he "shall not use or deal in the goods ... of a competitor," to acquire the stock of "another corporation ... where the effect of such acquisition may be to substantially lessen competition."[27]

THE ASCENDANCY OF FINANCE

Big companies, such as railroads, public utilities, or industrial "trusts," generally raised their capital by public sale of securities. Hence, as these companies grew and multiplied, so did the business of marketing securities carried on by investment bankers. In general only well-to-do businessmen and speculators bought common stocks. Bonds were the conservative investment for ladies or those of limited means. Thus, sales in foreign markets and to financial trust and insurance companies were important in selling large issues of securities.

By the 1870s, investment banking houses such as Drexel, Morgan; August Belmont; Winslow, Lanier; Lee, Higgenson; or Kuhn, Loeb formed a substantial and powerful part of the financial community. To handle railroad issues running into tens of millions of dollars, they formed syndicates with each other and with their foreign correspondents. At this time the English and Western European security markets for high-grade bonds were bigger, and better for the seller, than in the United States where new security offerings tended to outrun the savings available for this type of investment. Consequently the strongest American houses were based on reliable foreign outlets. Drexel, Morgan, for example, had its own partners in both London and Paris, as well as close relations with the great English firm of Baring Brothers. Kuhn, Loeb could draw on the resources of the Deutsch of Berlin, while August Belmont and Company represented the ubiquitous Rothschilds.

In a nation hard pressed for funds to meet the obvious needs of a geographically expanding economy, these controllers of the supply of security capital, who were also figures of international importance, became leaders of a new business elite. Like the importing merchants of the earlier periods, they had influential overseas connections, they were the best informed about what was going on in the world, and they could greatly influence what was undertaken by big business.

While there was no regularized hierarchy of power, and all the partners in the major investment houses shared in an aura of mysterious international influence, from about 1890 to 1913 J. Pierpont Morgan acted as a de facto leader. His influence rested on local financial resources second to none, strong foreign connections, a dominating personality, and willingness to take responsibility. In 1889, for example, he persuaded the leading investment houses to withhold financing from Eastern railraods that cut rates, and called the railraod presidents to his library to announce the rule. He talked, said President Roberts of the Pennsylvania, as though "we, the railroad people, are a set of anarchists, and this is an attempt to substitute law and arbitration for anarchy and might."[28] So influential was Morgan's role in big business and finance that these years around the turn of the century have often been called the "Morgan Era." In no period before or since has the influence of one man been so widely recognized in American business.

Much of the Morgan eminence came from the increasing power of the entire financial community. The big New York City banks such as National City or First National, and the big trust companies such as Bankers and Guarantee, shaped commercial banking policy more than ever before. National City Bank had a gold reserve rivaling that of the Treasury and held deposits for more than 200 large out-of-town banks. During these years, the presidents of the chief New York City banks conferred and cooperated closely with Morgan and other leading investment bankers.

In the nineties, life insurance companies became important customers of the investment bankers. As the assets of the "big five" of these companies rose from under $400 million in 1890 to about $15 billion in 1900, their annual premium and investment income, plus that of dozens of smaller companies, offered a major market for new securities.[29] Investment bankers also wanted to restrain the big insurance companies from eliminating financial middlemen and dealing directly with the corporations needing capital. Consequently Morgan and the other leading bankers bought controlling blocks of stock in the "big five" and took seats on their boards of directors.

This concentration of financial power in the hands of a few New Yorkers, evident in the panic of 1907, led to a congressional investigation by the Pujo Committee. Its report, issued just before J. Pierpont Morgan's death in 1913, called him the leader of a "money trust." The aim of the "trust," if it could be said to have any agreed-upon aim, was to keep investment finance sound, conservative, and essentially noncompetitive, thus making the overly speculative American security markets safer for the buyer of high-grade bonds. That this could not be accomplished altogether, or that the effort may have had bad side effects in slowing the expansion of useful enterprises, could be seen as part of the price that had to be paid for lack of any official central banking system before 1914.

The Morgan Era capped the gradual development of more reliable financial mechanisms that were leading the upper-income group to risk their savings in stocks and bonds as well as in real estate and mortgages. Furthermore the size of this group grew so greatly that by 1900 some stock and bondholding was characteristic of the upper-income families in both business and the professions. While no figures on the number of security holders can be assembled, the increase in the maximum number of shares of stock traded in a single day on the New York exchange—from 700,000 in 1879 to 3,281,226 in 1913—suggests a high rate of growth.[30]

Accompanying this rise of security capitalism was the spread of trust companies to manage estates and of financial lawyers to protect the interests of trustees, banks, and corporations. John B. Dill began a lecture at the Harvard Law School with "I am the lawyer for a billion dollars of invested capital."[31] Unfortunately, the census does not show the increase of such occupations, but numbers would be no guide to the great social influence wielded by both Morgan and Dill who were close, in one way or another, to the allocation and control of thy capital represented by securities, or by others who were developing new types of advice or auxiliary services, thereby greatly increasing the number of business roles.[32]

AMERICAN BUSINESS CHARACTERISTICS OF THE
EARLY INDUSTRIAL AGE

The earlier influence of abundant natural resources, migration, and rapid growth in population were accentuated in the late nineteenth century, and a new factor was added, the effect of a national market. By opening the entire country as a single market, the railroad, as we have seen, made manufacturing highly competitive. Mail order houses and factory salesmen brought some of this competition to bear on wholesalers and retailers as well.

Added competitive pressure probably increased the tendency of most entrepreneurs to think in terms of short rather than long-run profit. To them, research and conservation of resources seemed needless expenses. As late as the 1870s, Andrew Carnegie claimed to be the first steelmaker to hire a chemist.[33] The attitude of strict economy for immediate ends, and disinterest in planning for development affected entrepreneurs even in companies not menaced by cutthroat competition. A writer of 1871 noted that "it has never been the custom of those managing the Eastern Railroad to place any reliance upon telegraphy in directing train movements."[34] In part this "seat of the pants" type of entrepreneurship, which Arthur H. Cole has more elegantly labeled "empirical," has been true of the early stages of industrial development in all nations. But the American environment of keen competition and cheap resources probably perpetuated it beyond its normal period.

The earlier opportunistic or unethical approaches to obligations also persisted and foreign visitors continued to comment on American dishonesty. Cole is uncertain about the explanation of business failure to "devise procedures whereby crooks were driven out and their power minimized . . . . Why didn't the political structure of the business world evolve in a manner favorable to social needs and its own good repute?"[35] Again, one may resort to an answer based on factors such as excessive opportunities for sharp practice offered by unfamiliar types of enterprise, rapid movement of population, more impersonality in business dealings, the unexplored possibilities of the corporation, and the uncertainties as to what was the law.

The American situation of a "people in motion" emphasized impersonal, strictly market-oriented decisions, thereby creating another temptation to dishonesty and a striking feature of American practice. This type of decision-making was in direct contrast to the ways of businessmen in old, settled, agrarian communities, where successful business agreements were many times based on a degree of friendship. Late in the period, a Chicago executive told his salesmen: "Don't make any intimate acquaintances . . . . A stranger can always do more business than one who is well known."[36] One doubts the truth of so extreme a statement, but such an example would scarcely be found elsewhere in the world.

To Europeans, American businessmen had always seemed in a hurry, but the railroad brought time into business as never before. The months formerly allowed for delivery and payment both shrank to weeks, and appointments and travel became geared to train schedules. The telegraph, telephone, and standard time zones, all established in the late 1870s, conditioned men to think in hours and minutes, and often to dispense with the time-consuming process of writing letters.

By the end of the century the vast American domestic market, the largest in the industrialized part of the world, was contributing, along with the forces of law and competition, to produce the biggest corporations. The ease of formation of such giants by the merger of smaller family firms again emphasizes both the impersonality, or economic rationality, of American decisions, and how experience in building new communities had fostered attitudes of ready cooperation in joint efforts. There were exceptions, of course, some of whom were foreign-born entrepreneurs who had not gone through the American process of continuous movement. In addition to any tendencies produced by social conditioning, the legal doctrines that made associations of independent companies impossible were a powerful impetus toward merger into an economically profitable number of larger firms.

In the "Progressive Era" before World War I these hurrying, competitive, sharp entrepreneurs were being forced by a conjunction of circumstances to give more attention to political and social problems. The great cities produced by industrialism and railroad transportation needed more efficient government; overly competitive markets would benefit from regulation; and better public education and welfare would in the long run help business. Advanced business leaders were coming to recognize that for security and order a certain amount of social accounting was needed alongside the traditional market calculations.

CHAPTER 10

New Business Problems

To many contemporary observers of America at the turn of the century, big corporations were the most important feature of American business, or at least the one that most differentiated it from that of Western Europe. There were, in fact, only about a thousand companies large enough to pose managerial and social problems distinctly different from those of smaller firms, but their chief executives and counsellors were the recognized leaders of American enterprise, regarded with mixed awe, fear, and admiration by lesser businessmen, journalists, and politicians.

FORERUNNERS OF A NEW CAPITALISM

The internal administration of the big corporation was in truth a new world of business. Professional salaried managers who controlled companies without a substantial share in ownership had, of course, been present from early in the nineteenth century. However, few of the first big companies—which were chiefly those in transportation—had developed to a size where the special characteristics of the very large corporation could be discerned: i.e., an organization permanently employing thousands of men, with a life of its own that could not readily be understood or meddled with by an outsider, even though he might be a member of the board of directors. The growth in power of railroad managers, for example, in relation to their boards of directors in the last half of the nineteenth century was not based on lack of power to enforce their views, as was to become frequently the case in the twentieth century, but rather on the outside capitalist's lack of the knowledge necessary to make decisions.

The fact that salaried professionals got ahead by being good administrators in a complex social organization like the big corporation inevitably led to tests of fitness different from those imposed by an impersonal competitive market. They had to be men who could exercise leadership by winning the loyalty and respect of their associates. In this careerist competition, the well-spoken man with a good family and educational background had an advantage over the slightly educated self-made man.[1] In a period when the percentage of all businessmen with some college education was negligible, some 40 percent of the top-level corporate elite of the last third of the nineteenth century appear to have attended college. The "old school tie" joined with family friendships in providing visibility for the young man in the big company.

Operating as trustees for other people's money, the managers developed a code of business ethics that differed from that of the man working for himself. This new code evolved gradually during the last half of the nineteenth century. Its cardinal principle, from which many others stemmed, was to avoid being on both sides of a bargain. In the 1850s, highly respected executives saw no harm in having companies they owned sell to corporations they managed, but by the late 1880s, President Henry B. Ledyard wrote that he had "long since made it a rule not to have any pecuniary interest in any company or corporation which has any arrangements whatever with the [Michigan Central Railroad] company."[2] The situation became more complex where managers were interested primarily in only one of several types of company securities, such as the bonds of a supplier, and progress was much slower.

In the matter of giving stockholders money for community purposes, the attitude of executives varied with the type of corporations. Railroads, for example, were necessarily regional development companies and could be relied on for at least moderate assistance in projects for advertising or building up communities along the tracks. But when it came to support of religious, educational, or social service, both company presidents and the law courts thought that there should be some clear connection with the welfare of the corporation. John W. Brooks wrote,

> Our mission is not that of aiding institutions of learning or religion because they may commend themselves to our personal judgment . . . . We can properly help . . . when it is clearly for the pecuniary advantage of our stockholders that we should do so, as for instance, if it would raise the price of adjacent land belonging to the company we could make a donation of land for the location of an educational institution.[3]

Limited use of the stockholders' money, however, was thought justifiable for supporting organizations such as the YMCA that preserved social stability or improved the performance of workers. The narrow view of the interests of the stockholders was also generally expanded in railroads to include—if the cost was low—the maintenance of a good public image of the company. For this purpose management gave free or reduced fare transportation to ministers, editors, and influential educators.

While between 1890 and 1915 a number of industrial and public utility corporations and a few banks and insurance companies joined the railroads in the ranks of managerially-run big business, the total of all their policy-forming officers was probably under 250,000 men. This small group of professional executives represented the most important emerging force in American business, a group that seemed destined to grow steadily in numbers and power. Hence, the evolution of the managerial social role as a force in society, and as a device for reflecting outside social pressures inside the corporation was of great potential importance. Even by the first decade of the twentieth century, the businessmen most active in national affairs were likely to have a big company background. George W. Perkins of United States Steel, Robert de Forrest of the New Jersey Central Railroad, Edward H. Harriman of the Western railroads, Frank Vanderlip of National City Bank, and scores of other men whose influence was strongly felt in political and civic affairs had risen by the professional career ladder, even though some of them came from leading families and had amassed considerable private wealth in the process.

The uniformities of the executive role tended to give these men certain qualities less common in the older types of American businessmen. The ablest were becoming accustomed to computing general effects in the fairly remote future with a calculus that integrated long-run factors with immediate pecuniary gain. They realized that their actions could affect both politics and society, and that they had to have an interest in each. In contrast to the antagonism of most businessmen toward theorists, they welcomed special education and expert knowledge. They tried to cultivate an "objective" view of business situations in which company welfare was expected to supersede personal desires. In short, they represented an emerging institutional, status-oriented type of capitalism in contrast to the individual, market-oriented type of earlier centuries.

In addition to policy-making professional executives, the big corporation introduced another new business character, the functional or specialized "middle manager." Trained to think in terms of efficient execution of policy, these men seemed to economist Thorstein Veblen to represent the great new factor which industrialism contributed to production. The cumulative growth of technological rather than market habits of thought that accompanied the machine process, he called the "industrial arts," and he believed that in the end the men with such mentalities—the professionally oriented specialists—would take over business. Relatively unimportant in the nineteenth century, such men did, in part, fulfill Veblen's expectation, but they still remained subject to chief executives, more oriented to the company position in the market.

The future importance of the big business executives, however, should not obscure the more immediate social effect of the new legions of medium and small businessmen and of the professional and administrative middle class in the growing towns or cities. With few exceptions, this latter group could be regarded as unconsciously probusiness in values and outlook. In one sense, these townspeople were no different from other Americans who evaluated alternatives on the basis of what would pay most, but the urban middle class could increasingly be counted on to support business values in labor disputes and attitudes toward legislation. By the end of the period, far-sighted company executives were also recognizing the protection from government interference that might be gained by enlisting the middle class as stockholders.

BUSINESS AND NATIONAL UNIONS

The rise of big impersonal companies, the increasing location of plants in large cities, and dangerous high-speed machinery brought modern problems in labor relations. Prior to 1850, businessmen had given little thought to labor as an impersonal mass, class, or economic problem. Aside from textiles, most factory operations were small enough for the proprietor to know his workers personally. The early "labor movement" was participated in and often led by middle-class believers in various types of cooperative communities, and the terms radical and agrarian were often applied interchangeably to the extremists. Industrial, mining, and transportation businesses had few relations with such movements.

The renaissance of skilled-craft unionism in the boom of the 1850s brought new types of employers in contact with the "labor problem" and labor leaders. In addition to typographers and members of the building trades, the locomotive engineers and the skilled workers in iron making organized. Employers were convinced that unions violated the economic laws of the market in seeking higher wages by organized action, and also endangered the managerial control of production necessary for survival in interregional competition. Businessmen in construction and small-scale manufacturing had increasingly adjusted to unions, because 8 percent of the nonagricultural labor was organized by 1904. In the major business areas of trade and finance, however, unions were practically nonexistent, and employers as a whole never accepted unions as either desirable or necessary.

In the late nineteenth century, community and political attitudes toward unions varied. Middle-class and journalistic opinion was strongly against large-scale strikes. In the railroad strikes of 1877 and the Chicago disturbances of 1886 the public, as represented by the newspapers, displayed a panicky fear of union leaders. Labor organizers and strike leaders were pictured in the press as foreign or outside agitators who made their living unethically by creating social disturbance. Although in this period of massive immigration, it was true that many labor leaders came from the more mature trade union movements of the United Kingdom and Germany, and some supported the doctrines of anarchism, many others such as Eugene V. Debs and John Mitchell were native Americans, committed to building unions.

Education contributed its share to the hostile attitude toward organized labor. "With one exception," writes Ruth Elson, "there is absolute unanimity among schoolbook authors on the evil results of labor unions . . . . No attempt is made to define 'union,' 'strike,' or other related terms used in the texts . . . . Very often strike and riot are used interchangeably . . . . To question American labor conditions was un-American."[4]

Despite the educated public's generally unfavorable reaction to the activities of the minority of organized workers, a manufacturer in a small or medium-sized city might find that the public was against him if his plant was struck by labor.[5] The old middle class in towns that were developing factory industry were jealous of the wealth of the manufacturer, who was often a newcomer as well. The local politicians, recognizing that workers were a majority of the voting public, might also be loath to use the local police force—made up, perhaps, of relatives of the striking workers. Local newspapers, with advertising chiefly from the old merchants and artisans, not the new manufacturers, could also respond to the same forces. Hence the instances where state troops were called for could indicate lack of community support for the employer rather than local desires for suppression of union action by military force.

The rapid gain in membership of the American Federation of Labor between 1897 and 1904 produced a new wave of alarm, particularly among small employers. Operating under conditions of severe competition, such men objected to discussing wages and hours with anyone but their own employees, and some manufacturers either closed down for long periods or moved to other localities when their plants were struck by strong, national unions. The growing fear among these smaller enterprisers also led to an abrupt shift in policy by the National Association of Manufacturers (NAM). By 1902 the original proposals of the NAM for promoting trade had been largely achieved, and the international traders who had controlled the organization were displaced by Middle Western manufacturers anxious for a major attack on labor unions. David M. Parry, James W. van Cleave, and John Kirby, Jr., led the militant antilabor forces, and successively held the presidency of the NAM over the next dozen years.[6] Under their leadership the power of the organization was directed chiefly to opposing the closed shop, collective bargaining, and exemption of labor from the Sherman Anti-Trust Law.

In combatting unionism, the NAM was aided by a score or more employer associations that had come into existence since 1880. Organized to help the small employer deal with the big union, these associations ranged from those based on employers in a single industry such as the United Typothetae of America, for printing, through those like the National Metal Trades Association covering a variety of activities, to a top coordinating association for all employer resistance, the Citizen's Industrial Association of America, set up in 1903 by the NAM.[7] Within a few years internal difficulties developed between the CIA and the NAM which led the latter to withdraw its financial support, and to build up a new subsidiary, the National Council for Industrial Defense, with James A. Emery as its Washington counsellor.[8] His office became the center for NAM lobbying activities. He assured members that the staff "keeps track of all legislation in the States and in the National Legislature of interest to manufacturers . . . . It represents them in opposition to such legislation as they oppose, and in promotion of such legislation as they express a formal interest in."[9] Emery was so effective in political persuasion that President Kirby of the NAM boasted in 1909: "I can assure you that no objectionable bill will pass through the hands of any committee after Mr. Emery has had a chance to tell them what it means . . . the bill is dead from that moment."[10]

These organizations successfully combatted the closed shop in medium-sized cities by bringing employers together to support common policies. When the A.F. of L. hatmakers union sought to aid their Danbury, Connecticut, local by a nationwide boycott of the products of a struck plant, the employer groups finally won a decision of the Supreme Court convicting that national union of violation of the Sherman Anti-Trust Act.[11] The lawyers of these groups also helped employers to secure a number of court injunctions prohibiting picketing or other interferences with strike breakers.

Meanwhile Samuel Gompers, president of the A.F. of L., was trying to pursue a policy which he called "business unionism." He stood against government interference in matters affecting union labor, and for long-term contracts governing hours and wages freely negotiated between the representatives of employers and employees. In 1900 he entered into the formation of a National Civic Federation made up of leading businessmen, labor leaders, and representataives of the "public," that would act as a fact-finding and mediating agency in labor disputes. Unfortunately for its general influence in labor affairs, the federation gained a reputation for directing its chief energies against socialism.

By 1908 the limitations imposed on the American Federation of Labor by its craft structure, the depression of 1907, and the effective work of the Citizen's Industrial Association and other antiunion organizations had thrown the closed-shop campaign into reverse and checked the growth of organized labor. At the peak, in the decade before World War I, unions were still largely confined to the building, metal, and garment trades, plus some other skilled crafts, such as those in brewing, mining, trucking, and the operation of railroad trains. By 1915 the A.F. of L. represented some two million workers, and the Railroad Brotherhoods and a handful of independent unions about half a million more. With a total nonagricultural labor force of over 20 million, employer's policies regarding wages, hours, lay-offs, and security were obviously more important to society in the nonunion than in the union sectors. Undoubtedly, union bargains had an indirect impact on nonunionized shops, but the total effects are almost impossible to estimate. Real wages advanced moderately during both the relatively nonunion period before 1897, and the period of union growth thereafter.

THE SECURITY OF WORKERS

In the rapid industrial expansion of the nineteenth century, low wages and low consumption seemed economically necessary in order to provide adequate capital from the personal and business savings of owners and managers. Business leaders varied between those who took the classic view that workers should be hired as cheaply as possible, to those who were willing to pay as much as their competitors—often a distinction without a difference.[12] Occasionally, a hiring official recognized the value of better morale, achieved by fewer lay-offs or maintenance of wages in depression periods, but such men appear to have been a small minority.[13]

Seasonal lay-offs, which were the rule in construction and much factory production, probably worked less hardship than might be presumed from looking at statistics. The general sixty hour, six-day work week, seven days in a few industries such as brewing and steel, left workers with need for considerable time off. Some of the slack periods were seasonal and predictable, and workers had other part-time jobs for those periods. Plants, such as breweries, could use most of the steady employees released from brewing and malting for repair work. Seniority appears to have been observed by good employers, at least, in providing all-year-round work.[14] But in many industries, particularly those in big cities, lay-offs were a great hardship.

Security against the infirmities of old age was regarded as a moral responsibility of the individual worker, who was supposed to save, rear dutiful children, and perhaps join in some insurance plan. With average wages less than $9 a week for "lower skilled" workers in 1890 and only $10.65 in the substantially higher-priced year of 1910, it was hard to expect much in the way of insurance or saving. Even workers in manufacturing, the highest paid group except for building construction, received only $15 a week in 1910.[15] "Dutiful children" might be a recourse in case of accident, illness, or dismissal because of age, but continual migration tended to separate children and parents and make joint arrangements difficult. The Chesapeake and Ohio railroad in the 1890s was considering a pension plan, but a general move in that direction did not occur until World War I.[16]

Avoidance of injury from accidents was also regarded as a personal responsibility of the worker, and many executives of big firms in hazardous industries regarded safety devices as an unwarranted use of the stockholders' money. Railroads, for example, were slow in adopting the lifesaving airbrake and automatic coupler on freight trains, even when required to do so by a federal law of 1894. Meanwhile, adequate personal insurance in such industries was prohibitively expensive.[17]

Yet, in spite of the grim figures of 25,000 annual deaths and a million injuries from industrial accidents by 1910, the situation was not as universally intolerable as it appeared. In firms headed by owner-managers, which probably hired over four-fifths of nonagricultural workers, hardship was dealt with through the charity of the boss. An injured worker might be given a sedentary job as a doorman or watchman. The families of dead or sick workers were kept track of and assisted.[18] But in companies with more than a thousand employees, big-city locations, and many branches, such informal social security broke down.

Several alternatives were possible: companies might voluntarily subsidize insurance by adding to the worker's contribution, compulsory state compensation laws might be passed, which would force all companies to contribute; or unions could be made strong enough to raise and administer adequate benefit funds. Voluntary company plans were, of course, the solution favored in principle by executives, but companies were slow in acting. Railroad leaders talked about such plans from the 1870s on, but few roads did anything. When plans were adopted, they were far from adequate.[19] Starting in 1893, the Pabst Brewing Company, for example, matched employee payments of between 25 and 40 cents a month for a fund to pay funeral expenses, and half wages for up to a year in case of injury.[20] Many businessmen and associations came gradually to favor insurance, if compulsory by law, Between 1910 and 1915 the leading industrial states passed workmen's compensation acts that forced employers to carry what was deemed to be adequate liability insurance.

CHANGING CONDITIONS OF WORK

The major changes in conditions of work that affected business relations with labor took place primarily in the limited spheres of manufacturing and railroad transportation. In 1870 these sectors made up a little over a fifth of the labor force, and in 1910 a little over a quarter. Inclusion of the relatively static building trades would add from 6 to 7 percent to these figures, and mining, where some changes took place, an additional 2 to 3 percent. Yet these four areas providing employment for roughly a third of the labor force colored the public and much of the business view of what was happening to conditions of labor. In fact, the conditions of employment of the 10 to 12 percent of the labor force that worked in manufacturing shops, large or small, was the focus of most of the voluminous public discussion of the Progressive period.

One of the controversial issues between workers and employers in these years was incentives to productivity, which, in turn, involved democracy versus autocracy in shop management. In the late 1880s, a number of members of the American Society of Mechanical Engineers such as Henry R. Towne, Frederick A. Halsey, and Frederick W. Taylor began to study working conditions in manufacturing plants and methods of pay in relation to productivity. Beginning with studies of the motions of the individual worker, Taylor had by 1903 worked out a system that he called "scientific management." Soon he and a number of disciples and imitators were advocating, wherever possible, a system of incentives for faster performance through pay based on the units completed.

On the surface, such changes should have improved the worker's morale and his relations with management, but when the leading plants in an industry introduced the new system the tendency was to depress prices, which, in turn, led to reductions in piece-work rates. Soon workers equated scientific management with "speed-up"—harder work for the same pay.[21]

The new ideas also put additional strain on the tensions already created by placing men educated in the schools in democracy, in rule by the majority, under an autocratic system of "scientific" plant management. For the workman, cooperation in the system meant "to do what they are told to do promptly and without asking questions or making suggestions . . . the worker . . . had merely to obey the 'laws.' "[22] Trade unions that might speak for the worker in resisting change were not approved by Taylor and his followers. While the system was never widely adopted, workers, social reformers, and foreign observers regarded it, unduly, as symbolizing the emerging attitudes of American factory managers.

The executives of the large corporations were as opposed to the closed or preferential shop as were small employers. Through blacklisting workers known to be organizers, forcing employees to sign contracts that they would not join a union, some espionage, and the shifting of work to other areas in times of labor trouble, the big companies with many plants remained open shop and dealt with no unions aside from a few special crafts.

In order to check the threatened spread of trade unions, thoughtful employers also experimented with ways of attaching the worker more strongly to the company. Studies suggested that in many jobs as much work could be produced in eight hours as in ten, and that better lighting and other improvements in the environment of the worker more than paid for themselves in both productivity and improved morale. Employee representation plans were started by three companies in 1904, but were not widely adopted until World War I. While the leaders of such "company unions" were all on the payroll, meetings gave an opportunity for expression of grievances. Other means of creating loyalty to the company were stock purchase plans, profit sharing, pension plans, recreational facilities, and employee magazines. None of these devices were widely used before 1915. Meanwhile the craft structure of the A.F. of L. made it ineffective in organizing big, multiplant companies that embraced many different skills. Most of the union controversies and the experiments in workers relations were by medium-sized employers in competitive industries who saw "welfare" as a means to higher productivity per dollar of pay. Taking the same view, workers feared the impact of such plans on employment as well as on the speed of work.

UNSOLVED PROBLEMS

Thus, strong unions with a foothold in many industries that still employed skilled craftsmen had grown up alongside large corporations that demonstrated their ability to prevent unionization of the rank and file of semi- or unskilled workers. But the situation did not represent a stable or satisfactory solution for the relations of manual workers to the big company, and there was bound to be trouble at some future time.

In general, managerial enterprise before World War I was only a portent of its more mature form. The managers themselves were not fully aware of the many social, political, and business issues involved in directing the policy of organizations so large that single company decisions might affect the national welfare. The executives were also in the early states of learning the political science of the big company: how to wield power effectively in ways that would not disturb the harmony of the organization and bring about reprisals; how to formulate policies that would have to pass through several layers of management; how to treat stockholders and consumers. These and many other skills were needed by the successful executive.

CHAPTER 11

The Old Order Weakens

The "dominant value profile" of American culture, as seen by anthropologists, may not have changed much between the early colonial settlements and the twentieth century.[1] Such American "focal values" as material well-being and optimistic belief in the effectiveness of individual effort were historic middle-class values of Western capitalism and also among the incentives to that basic element in shaping American character—migration. But the manifestations of such values in a primarily rural agricultural setting differed from the outward forms they would take in an urban industrial society.

Max Lerner says that in the 1840s and 1850s America became a "market society, in which the great crime is to be 'taken in,' and the great virtue is to be tough and illusionless. This means resisting the pitfalls of fellow feeling and breaking whatever it is that ties person to person in the web of a common plight . . . . The result is the desensitized man whose language is the wisecrack and whose armor is cynicism."[2] Without necessarily accepting Lerner's precise dates, these were the strictly rational, or economic, patterns of behavior that were strengthened everywhere by the rapid rise of industry, mechanized transportation, and urbanism. After 1840 they appeared to many observers to be undermining the old agrarian order and its central institutions such as the family, religion, and the small personalized community, even though no great change appeared to be taking place in the underlying value system.

SUCCESS AND SELF-HELP

As employment in urban occupations increased, the deeply rooted American hope of getting ahead came to be defined more specifically as success in business. The literature exhorting the young to adopt this goal through personal effort was spreading rapidly by the 1840s, while children's readers were full of admonitions on the duty of Americans to succeed.[3] Foreign visitors, mainly aristocratic to be sure, were impressed with the universality of the American aim of success through commercial achievement. Looking at America of the mid-1880s the perceptive James Bryce said, "Trade and manufacture cover the whole horizon of American life . . . . They . . . are the main concern of the country to which all others are subordinate."[4] "Business is a passion with the

Americans," wrote the Pulskees, "not the means but the very life of existence."[5] They also observed how the utilitarian attitudes necessary for material success were stressed in the earliest training of children, and reaffirmed continually at home and at school. As Count Vay de Vaya and Luscod saw it: "The practical cast of American intelligence is its most prominent trait. From infancy mental faculties are directed to the purely utilitarian point of view. No one has either the leisure or taste for other questions."[6] As early as 1853 Harper's *New Monthly Magazine* affirmed that "to to vast majority of Americans success had long since come to mean achievement in business and making money."[7]

Even in earlier periods, as we have seen, there had been no strong competitor to business as an avenue of success. The new note sounded in the exhortations to the young in the last half of the nineteenth century was the virture of, and the hope of, winning success through one's own efforts. While it is doubtful that in fact a "self-made" man enjoyed higher prestige than an equally able and important citizen who had inherited wealth, the emphases on equal opportunity and self-help were good democratic doctrines and a consolation to parents who had nothing to give their children save good advice.[8] The doctrine that most successful industrialists were self-made men became firmly established in the last quarter of the century, and was particularly in evidence in sermons, commencement addresses, and other literature aimed at the young.[9] The assumption that the training of the young at home was for success in the commercial world pervaded middle-class family life so generally and subtly that it seemed a part of the natural order of things.

FAMILY TRAINING FOR BUSINESS

The combination of emphasis on success in business through one's own efforts and the movement of many families to urban surroundings gradually altered family relationships. In farming, the chief rural occupation, the family was a functional economic unit providing employment and much of the education for the children within the confines of the homestead.* In the town or city, jobs as well as education were normally outside the home, and the family lost some of its social functions. With the lessening of his direct economic controls, the father's authority was probably weakened, and with much activity away from home by both parents and children the mother's influence may also have become less. As early as 1869, the *Nation* noted the disappearance of the old-fashioned family.[10] *

* In many "rural" areas, the assumption that family farming was the chief form of economic activity may not have been true. Construction, exploitation of mineral and other resources, and employment in nearby towns provided jobs outside the home for both children and adults.

* There is a good deal of exaggeration about the "old-fashioned" family assumed to have a large number of children. The average household of 1850 was 5.5 people as against 3.5 in 1950.

By European standards, the American middle-class family had always seemed, and continued to seem, permissive in its treatment of children. A French visitor of 1883 observed that the family was a monarchy in the Old World, a repulbic in the New.[11] Modern psychologists have seen in these characteristics possible connections with the drive for success. Brewster Smith suggests that warm but dominating mothers increase achievement motivation, whereas dominating fathers diminish it.[12] William J. Good adds that "It is in the family with a wider dispersion of authority that the achievement-seeking son is more likely to appear," and that emotional support from the mother is important.[13] These hypotheses suggest that other things being equal, the increasing percentage of urban middle-class families with frequently absent fathers and less arbitrary authority may have increased motivation for achievement. Because of lessening authoritarian discipline, the average American of the early twentieth century may have been more highly motivated for achievement in business than his grandfather of 1850.

Present-day theorists give little support to inculcating emotional attitudes by intensive pressure for the desired responses. "A parent," says Robert White, "can try to foster independence and achievement in a child, and get instead a docile guilt-ridden intimidated individual."[14] But in the late nineteenth century, middle-class families increasingly sought to produce the qualities regarded as desirable for success in business by more intensive training.* Since the child's initial job would presumably be as an employee, ready obedience and disciplined habits, qualities not found in American children by foreign visitors, but always stressed in child-reading literature, were essential. Writing in 1871 on *Gentle Measures in the Management and Training of the Young*, Jacob Abbott exemplifies the continuing emphasis on early training in obedience "on the principle of simple submission to authority."[15] In terms such as "every child ought to be trained to conform his will to the demands of duty," such advice was repeated by many writers.[16]

Parents were also urged to extend the business system into family affairs. Abbott suggested that parents set up a system of debits and credits for advances to the young in order to lay "permanent foundations for their children's welfare and happiness throughout life by training them from their earliest years to habits of forecast and thrift and the exercise of judgment and skill in the management of money."[17] The advantage of a book account was that interest could be debitted and credited, which would add to the instruction in how to be good managers.

At the end of the period, Edwin A. Kirkpatrick devoted a substantial book to training children in the use of money. "It is important," he urged, "that the

---

* While one hesitates to generalize from relatively scanty evidence, there seems some parallelism between the rise of more hierarchical business structures and a new emphasis on training for obedience.

financial training of children should begin early and should be conducted so as firmly and clearly to establish the idea of money as a product of effort and a means of satisfaction . . . . Children should rarely if ever be given pay for doing something that has not a commercial value of some kind."[18]

The idea of training for "character" in general was also closely tied to the aim of success in business. In 1892 a writer suggested as a conditioning device, a "bank of character" where good behavior would result in credits and bad behavior in debits.[19] Character meant not only honesty and reliability but concentration on the task at hand. "It is called for in play as well as in work," Caroline Benedict Burrell cautioned parents: "You must train systematically, you must practice a certain length of time each day, whether you like it or not, you must play hard to the final innings or you won't win."[20]

Similar overly simple ideas of character formation from special training permeated the new psychology of adolescence developed by President G. Stanley Hall of Clark University, who believed that adolescents could be trained to be a new breed of human beings.[21] In response to such ideas, twenty-two organizations for influencing youth were formed between 1900 and 1920, among which the Boy Scouts of America (1910) was the most important. The scout masters were generally skilled workers or small businessmen who aimed, through medals, ranks, and other rewards, to motivate their charges for personal success and achievement.[22]

The application of science to both child rearing and business were part of the rising general belief in the possibility of a scientific society. Social Purity, temperance reform, dietary reform, and many other movements had their scientific—or perhaps, pseudo-scientific— bases. Writers complained that parents were "called to fill this vocation without any real training for it."[23] Such advisors would presumably apply a type of Taylor's "scientific management" (Chapter 10) to the home. By training in the observation of functional principles, average parents could produce efficient children, just as average foremen, properly trained, could run an efficient shop.

Christian morality or the laws of God or nature were frequently replaced by invocations of the laws of science as the ultimate sanctions for child discipline. The rise of belief in psychology as a guide to a profession of child rearing came rapidly from about 1890 to 1920, just as did the somewhat allied faith in collegiate or graduate business education as the creator of a profession of management. As late as 1887, a specialist in child rearing could still write, "Unity in nature and man is the moral, pedagogical and religious solution of our time."[24] But by the middle mineties, examples of the new "scientific" attitude are numerous. The editor of *Childhood Magazine*, for example, writes, "Parenthood is already looked upon by the more advanced minds as a profession; the time must come when its duties will be reduced to an exact science ignorance of which will be inexcusable."[25] In 1914 George W. Jacoby had the temerity to publish *Child Training, an Exact Science*.[26]

BUSINESS DOUBTS REGARDING PUBLIC EDUCATION

The famous Boston financier and philanthropist Henry Lee Higginson held that we must educate "to save ourselves and our families and our money from the mobs!"[27] Probably Higginson was not altogether clear as to what he meant by educate. Certainly American business leaders, in general, were not insistent on employees being well educated. Most of them seem to have approved of a "useful" amount of education, one that would fit the worker for his proper role in life, but not one that would waste time on unnecessary learning or create a desire for scholarly leisure.[28] Consequently, American education prior to the 1890s progressed unevenly, and judged by what could have been possible, slowly.

In 1880 the schooling of the average American was reported as less than four years, and illiteracy at 17 percent. Recent studies suggest that at this level of education the citizen will have only a neighborhood or small-community view of society, that he will be incapable of understanding the decisions that must be made in a large urban, industrial state. Yet in spite of the urgings of Horace Mann and others, the American social elite did not in general relate corrupt government, the self-defeating type of dishonesty in business, or lack of social responsibility in men of power to inadequate education. The rapidly growing urban upper classes did not see that in cities the school must take over many of the educational tasks previously performed by the family, the surrounding community, or years of apprenticeship.[29]

It is far easier to chart the course of change in American education, the subject of countless monographs, than to assess business opinion regarding education and its actual influence in the schools. Apparent changes in business attitudes toward secondary and higher education around 1890 make it convenient to look at the period in two parts. In the earlier part, at least, general secondary education was moving away from the immediate interests and needs of business. Not only the new public high schools, but also most of the older and more substantial academies emphasized the classical and traditional subjects needed for college entrance. Since the colleges, in turn, were generally affiliated with churches, this meant an atmosphere in secondary and higher education more congenial to religion than to business.

The situation arose and continued because business opinion of all types was uncertain regarding the value of secondary or higher education. E. E. White, commissioner of education for Ohio, said in 1881 that the capitalist aristocracy "asserts that popular education is a tax on capital . . . . Ignorant labor has few wants to supply and is content with low wages."[30] Four years later, H. C. Baird, an industrial publisher in Philadelphia, said, "Were the power with me no boy or girl should be educated at public expense . . . beyond grammar school, except for some useful occupation."[31] Edward C. Kirkland and other scholars who have examined such opinion think that businessmen, and other Americans, favored increasing education as long as it was aimed at moral improvement and utility. Obviously this did not include precollegiate Greek, Latin, and philosophy, and left secondary education a debatable area.

But urban businessmen had little direct influence on public education. Except for Massachusetts after 1882, and a handful of other states by 1915, schools were supported by the taxpayers of local districts, and even in 1915 children of school age were predominantly rural. Farmers saw little practical need for more than rudimentary education. Ellwood P. Cubberley, writing at the end of the period, held that "any marked educational progress was impossible under the district system."[32] The businessman who favored adequate primary and secondary education would have a hard time winning increased taxes in his particular district, if the surrounding areas continued as before. The needs of cities, the growth of the white-collar middle class, and professional educators were the forces behind the movement for more general education.[33]

In the cities, however, the child over ten or twelve could be working if not in school, and what economists call the "opportunity cost" of education discouraged attendance. The percentage of children working outside the home, therefore, rose with urbanism. The private contribution provided by parents foregoing the possible earnings of children exceeded all public expenditures for education in the late nineteenth century.[34]

In expenditure for education as a percentage of gross national product, the United States from 1880 to 1900 was behind Germany, but about 20 percent ahead of England or France. The structure of the educational system was so different, however, that comparisons are not very meaningful. It can only be concluded that all these Western industrial nations were putting an almost equal emphasis on public education.[35]

While only a few businessmen were leaders in educational improvement, teachers and educational administrators sought to inculcate in students values favorable to business. Educators emphasized the school as a molder of the industrial capability and character of children, taking unto itself educational functions formerly performed by home and shop.[36] In the elementary grades, the teachers probably stressed moral character and duty more than substantive learning. Analysis of readers at about the fourth-grade level, the average terminal year for nineteenth-century Americans, shows a continual increase in what the authors term "achievement imagery."[37]

A study of all nineteenth-century school books illustrates how elementary education, as in any nation, reenforced the dominant value system, and in America, how closely that system fit the attitudes of businessmen. The text writers saw industrial development as "the first fruits of American liberty and industry." While there is a pervasive religious emphasis, it "sanctions virtues likely to lead to materialism rather than other worldliness." Not only are riches "the baggage of virture," but at times "virtue would seem to be the by-product of riches." Since poverty is regarded as the fruit of idleness, in most cases, it is also identified with immorality.[38]

It is impossible to tell what views were expressed in classrooms by the relatively uneducated and transitory female teachers, but the professional educators who spoke at the annual meetings of the National Education Association (NEA) pictured the school as a conservative social force. The president of the NEA in 1877 hold that "the public school alone had saved the country from the terrors of the French Commune."[39] Similar sentiments were put forth by successive presidents. In 1881, for example, James H. Smart said that the free school did more "to suppress the latent flame of communism than all other agencies combined."[40] A speaker claimed that the high school, not particularly popular with businessmen, "detects and exposes the fallacies of socialism; the poor learn that they have an interest in respecting the property of the rich."[41] Superintendents justified the increasingly elaborate urban school administrations by reference to business experience with the value of abundant supervision.[42]

Organized labor found the school administrators unsympathetic to their methods as was the middle class generally. Strikes, condemned by the major newspapers, were also denounced by educators. The Knights of Labor, the most active national labor organization of the 1880s, regarded the high school as an unsympathetic middle-class institution—as no doubt it was. School textbook writers were nearly unanimous in denouncing unions and strikes. The former were pictured as un-American organizations promoted by foreign agitators, the latter as the equivalent of riots. The good worker who got ahead accepted the wages that were offered.[43]

TOWARD MORE SYSTEMATIC BUSINESS EDUCATION

In contrast with Germany which set out systematically to train men for industrial occupations, the prevailing American attitude seems to have been that the able man could learn on the job. Another deterrent to social investment in vocational training was the ease with which skilled workers could be imported from Europe. While private manual or industrial training schools or institutes had started in the 1820s (Chapter 5), their spread had been only moderate. In 1876 when the Centennial Exposition in Philadelphia stimulated new interest in the industrial arts, the NEA first established an Industrial Department. The response of the school system, however, was slow. Cubberley gives 1884 as the first high school manual training department. No doubt students who wanted particular manual skills offered some resistance to studying the rest of the classic high school curriculum.

While businessmen were strongly in favor of training schools, organized labor opposed them as a new menace to the dying apprenticeship system. A few businessmen were sufficiently interested in vocational education to set up private or company schools. Peter Cooper founded the Cooper Union in New York City in 1857 to teach the mechanical arts. Among company schools were those of the Hoe Printing Press Company in the 1870s and the National Cash Register School of Salesmanship in 1894.[45] In contrast to Germany, however, the vocational education movement was still small scale in the United States by the end of the nineteenth century.[46]

The teaching of office skills such as bookkeeping, penmanship, and later typewriting was quite a different matter. In the mid-nineteenth century, as business offices rapidly grew larger, it was found that the needed skills could be taught more efficiently by a specialized school than by supervisors on the job. This led to a period of vigorous private enterprise in business schools or "colleges" from 1850 to the 1890s, after which the public school system moved into the field. Courses in the private schools usually ran about three months and could be taken in the evening, but some more elaborate schools such as Packard Business College came to offer fifteen-month courses covering subjects such as commercial arithmetic, business English, geography, and navigation.[47]

By 1866 there were chains of business colleges of which Bryant-Stratton, with its fifty schools, was the largest. Branch schools were opened by "partners" who shared profits with the parent organization. All these enterprises were in keen competition with each other, and national meetings were held to discuss educational problems and systematize the trade. Reporting the 1866 convention, *Harpers Weekly* said, "The sphere and limits of business education have been as clearly defined as those of law, medical, and theological schools."[48] In 1878 the commercial group organized a Business College Teachers and Penman's Association which held annual meetings.

The element of "opportunity cost" gave the business college an advantage over the public or private high school. In either of the latter schools the student, in order to receive a degree, would have to attend four years of daytime classes which would preclude a full-time job. The business college could offer the grammar school graduate a degree for one winter of evening work. As competition between business colleges, and between them and the public high schools, increased, the costs of advertising and solicitation reached 25 to 30 percent of business college revenue, and made them more vulnerable to public school competition.

A few enterprising public schools, such as Philadelphia Central High, had introduced bookkeeping courses in the 1850s. Because of the influence of the business colleges, and the middle-class college preparatory character of high school education, however, there remained a strong opposition to any substitution of commercial subjects for those of the classical curriculum. In 1893, as business pressure for more utilitarian secondary education began to mount, the entrenched teachers and supervisors won appointment in the NEA of a Committee of Ten, made up of representatives from ten other committees and headed by President Charles W. Eliot of Harvard, to report on desirable curricula for high schools. The committee, of course, strongly favored a curriculum centered on mathematics, Greek, and Latin, but agreed that an acceptable but less desirable one could emphasize English and history with the inclusion of drawing, bookkeeping, and commercial arithmetic.[49]

In 1895 the business college enrollment of 96,000 was still nearly four times as large as the number of students taking a commercial curriculum in public high schools, but the NEA had, at least, established a Department of Business Education.[50] Although nothing important resulted, the proper aims and curriculum for business high schools now became a subject for discussion at the annual convention of NEA.[51] In 1898 the New York Chamber of Commerce led similar organizations in passing a resolution in favor of both secondary and higher public education for business.[52]

BUSINESSMEN AND EDUCATORS MOVE CLOSER

By the end of the century, the increasing demands of office work, the growing complexity of machine technology, and the deteriorating social and political conditions in American cities were all leading businessmen to take a more active interest in promoting education. This was one of the important factors stimulating the passage of compulsory education laws between 1885 and 1915. On the whole, the rural areas resisted laws providing for schooling up to from thirteen to sixteen years of age, and because of the strong rural power in state politics, the state superintendents of education might support the farmers. Resisting action in Pennsylvania in 1894, Superintendent Shaeffer said that many of the schools were "waste places," and "forcing children into such school rooms and surroundings by compulsory law makes one think of Herod who slaughtered the innocents of Bethlehem."[53] But the combined forces of urban business and professional leaders and progressive educators ultimately triumphed in Pennsylvania and most of the other states. By 1915 only a few Southern states lacked effective compulsory education laws.

Within the educational system itself, the ideas of the German educator Johan Herbart and the American John Dewey were guiding education in utilitarian directions acceptable to business. The ideas of Herbart regarding education for good citizenship were particularly suited to the businesslike society of the United States. He emphasized interesting the child in useful information such as political history and geography, and studying the particular child, both of which ideas were congenial to American utilitarianism, individualism, and the developing ideas of the scientific management of children. Although Herbart had died in 1841, educators studying in Germany in the 1880s were impressed by the applicability of his ideas to America. A Herbartian Society was formed in the United States in 1892, and its utilitarian influence, which included approval of commercial education, began to spread through the school system.[54]

John Dewey, as professor of educational psychology and director of the Experimental School at the University of Chicago, went further and more rigorously along the lines initiated by Herbart. In part, his philosophy, elaborated from the midnineties on, seems deceptively like that which might have been formulated by the thoughtful American businessman. He emphasized learning by experience the things the child needs to know for "making the most of the opportunities of present life." First the child would be exposed to experiences; "the next step is the progressive development of what is already experienced into a fuller and richer and also more organized form, *a form that gradually approximates that in which subject matter is presented to the skilled mature person.*"[55] The concealed difference between Dewey and the business educators was that the former assumed that the child would be exposed only to subjects with important intellectual content.[56]

Although the Dewey ideas involved relaxation of strict discipline and intensive study of the individual child to degrees that seemed impractical to the businessman and also to many educators on school boards, the emphasis on experience, useful subjects, and preparation for success in the outside world spread rapidly through the public school system and was carried to extremes not contemplated by Dewey. As early as 1907 an educator, W. C. Bagley, in a book called *Classroom Management*, that went through thirty editions in twenty years, treated the running of classes as a business problem.[57] In 1915 savings bank plans were teaching thrift and banking to students in 1,500 schools.[58]

Businessmen needing more skills in plant and office were also becoming interested in sponsoring both vocational and commercial education. The increasing business interest was paralleled by a shift toward the control of school boards by local businessmen. This, in turn, affected the outlook of school administrators. Raymond E. Callahan holds that up to about 1900 the latter had identified themselves with professional scholars, as on the Committee of Ten; now they began to identify with efficeint businessmen.[59]

The forces of Progressive reform were also pushing secondary education in the direction of utilitarian training. Compulsory school laws in the advanced industrial states generally put the minimum age for leaving school at sixteen years. This meant that whereas in 1900 perhaps 80 percent of the whole age group from fifteen to nineteen were out of school, with the percentage of fifteen-year-olds unrecorded, now a majority of this latter age group were forcefully kept in school. High school curriculum, therefore, needed to be designed to hold the attention of below average intellects and convey to them something useful.

The changed situation was dramatized in a new report to the NEA of a Committee of Nine on the Articulation of High School and College. In contrast to the Committee of Ten in 1893, no member of the new group had a reputation for scholarship. Most of the members were high school teachers, and the chairman was from Manual Training High School in Brooklyn, New York. Their report urged "the early introduction of training for individual usefulness, thereby blending the liberal and the vocational," with greater attention to the "mechanic arts, agriculture and household science" for all boys and girls

(Chapter 18). The report held that "by means of exclusively bookish curricula false ideals of culture are developed. A chasm is created between the producers of material wealth and the distributors and consumer thereof."[60]

Cubberley, a diligent worker for better education, defined the role of the schools in 1915 in the language of business:

> Our schools are, in a sense, factories in which the raw materials (children) are to be shaped and fashioned into products to meet the various demands of life. The specifications for manufacturing come from the demands of the twentieth century civilization, and it is the business of the school to build its pupils to the specifications laid down. This demands good tools, specialized machinery, continuous measurement of production to see if it is according to specifications, the elimination of waste in manufacture, and a large variety in output.[61]

The utilitarian pressures led to ten general types of high school curricula: ancient-classical, modern-classical, English-history, scientific, business, manual arts, household arts, agricultural, teacher training, and special vocational courses.[62] Some of the courses were given in special schools, particularly in the case of manual training and agriculture. Practically all public high schools offered training in business or "commercial" subjects.

In addition, the private business "colleges" continued to thrive by offering quicker and more convenient training than in the four-year high school. In 1915, some 850 business colleges reporting to the United States Bureau of Education claimed a registration of 95,000 men and 88,000 women, while 209,000 students followed commercial curricula in the public, and 18,000 in private secondary schools.[63] Edmund P. James, a leading student of business education, called the private "colleges" the best of their kind in the world, perhaps not high praise, but indicative of their secure place in the educational system.[64] As noted earlier, the saving to the student in opportunity costs was far greater than the short-term tuition of the "college," and traditional humanistic learning was, after all, a useless luxury fit only for those who could well afford it.

HIGHER EDUCATION

As businessmen gave generously from fortunes beyond the dreams of earlier generations, they came to exercise a major influence not only in private universities and colleges, but also in many theological seminaries. Between the 1870s and World War I, business leaders, including lawyers, largely replaced the clergy in controlling higher education. In the older denominational colleges and universities, private or state, the shift was a gradual one that became obvious around 1900. The effect on the theological seminaries was not to make them more businesslike, but rather more independent from denominational control. The Morrill Act of 1862 gave early impetus to the change. Thirty thousand acres for each senator and representative in Congress were granted to every state, the proceeds of which should be used to form an endowment for at least one college "where the leading object shall be . . . to teach such branches of learning as are related to agriculture and mechanic arts."[65] In the new universities created by this act, lawyers and businessmen dominated the boards from the start.

Until the end of the nineteenth century denominational missionary zeal and local boosterism continued to be the major forces behind the location of numerous small private colleges. The willingness of local boosters to put up money generally determined the location of the new state universities created by the Morrill Act, and in some instances the community bids ran very high. By an act of 1867, for example, the Illinois legislature formalized the bidding for the location of the new university. Jacksonville submitted the highest bid, $491,000, but Champagne, assisted by the Illinois Central Railroad, put more of its money into buying the favor of politicians and won the award with a bid of only $285,000.[66]

While a college or a university might be an important community asset, businessmen before the 1880s were not much interested in what was taught, and widely regarded any course other than engineering as a waste of time that would probably hinder the student in his future business career. Andrew Carnegie in donating a library to Braddock, Pennsylvania, said, "In my own experience I can say that I have known few young men intended for business who were not injured by a collegiate education."[67] Similarly, lumberman Henry W. Sage, after many years on the board of Cornell University, thought that, "If a man were to enter the realm of 'affairs' he would manage as well if not better without college training."[68] Other businessmen who believed abstractly in the value of liberal education questioned the utility of the American system of small, local institutions. "Beward of colleges," cautioned railroad executive John Brooks, "One of the blighting influences upon higher education in the West is the multitude of colleges (so called) where the untried, lean, hungry and cadaverous professors are undertaking to run down the 'freshman class of one.' "[69]

In a society in which the values accepted by business increasingly came to be those held by the middle class in general, such contempt for, or disapproval of, the traditional classical curriculum had a damaging effect on the internal morale of the liberal arts college. As the religious rationale which had justified higher education in earlier periods was succeeded only by the concept of acquiring mental discipline, the student body came to regard much of what the faculty knew and taught as irrelevant to their lives, and the undergraduates turned to more immediately rewarding activities such as campus politics and athletics, bringing to these pursuits the intensely competitive attitudes of nineteenth-century business.

Few writers on higher education at the turn of the century have been able to resist quoting the penetrating description of Yale, written years later by Henry Seidel Canby. "The cry of our undergraduate world," he says, "was always 'do something,' 'what does he *do*?':

> Freshmen hurried up and down entry stairs seeking news for the college paper, athletes, often with drawn, worried faces, struggled daily to get or hold places on the teams, boys with the rudiments of business ability were managers of magazines, orchestras, teams, or co-operative pants-pressing companies. Those who had a voice sang, not for sweet music's sake, but to 'make' the glee club. Long throats went in for social drinking, glib minds for politics; everything but scholarship was in my day an 'activity', and called 'doing something for the college'. Fraternities read off each meeting night their record of successful achievement, where credit for study meant only that the brethren had kept out of trouble with the faculty.[70]

Dean William C. DeVane of Yale writes that undergraduate scholarship declined steeply and probably reached its nadir about 1904-1905.[71] While the socially elite Eastern colleges may have given more of a foretaste of the business life to come than some of the more religious colleges of the back country, the rift between faculty and students, between traditional learning and preparation for business success, seems to have been nationwide.

Ultimately, starting about 1910, the undergraduate curricula followed the general educational trend toward more utilitarian courses, but, meanwhile, specialized technical or professional schools were the recourse for increasing numbers of students. Engineering schools, either separate entities, such as Massachusetts Institute of Technology, or affiliated with universities, such as Columbia School of Mines, both founded in the 1860s, spread rapidly before World War I. Increasingly, potential businessmen also saw a law degree as a valuable asset, and in general, little or no liberal arts undergraduate education was required for entrance to these professional schools.

Management was regarded by most of its practitioners as more an art than a science. Railroad executives, the earliest large group of big businessmen, thought that their problems had to be solved by experience rather than by reading or theory. "The most important qualification in a superintendent," wrote the early engineer and management specialist John B. Jervis, "is the ability to discriminate character."[72]

In view of such opinion, no doubt even more pronounced among small business employers than among the big business elite, Joseph Wharton, representing old mercantile wealth, was ahead of his time in giving $100,000 in 1881 to the University of Pennsylvania for the Wharton School of Finance and Economy. Partly, his aim was to give business training to wealthy young men who would not learn by hard experience. He specified that accounting, mercantile law, money and banking, industry, commerce, transportation, political science and history should be taught. The Wharton School probably gained more popularity from offering a modern social science education than from the belief that successful business management could be taught.[73] Not until 1898 was there a second business school, and this was at the advanced and experimental University of Chicago. From this time on, other major universities added business schools, Harvard on a strictly graduate level in 1908, until by 1914 twenty-five business schools were in operation, with a combined enrollment of 9,000 students. Reflecting the trend toward education for business purposes, the number of degrees granted at Pennsylvania by the engineering schools overtook those given by the college in 1906, and Wharton School became the leader in 1916.[74]

Businessmen and business ideas also became dominant in the administration of higher education, particularly in the big universities. As the first generation of American millionaires began to make substantial gifts to universities, they, as prudent investors, took positions on the boards of trustees. Often the influence of one such businessman who contributed both time and money became dominant in university affairs. Henry W. Sage, for example, who gave Cornell between $1 million and $2 million during his lifetime, largely dictated university policy, first as a member of the board from 1870 on and from 1875 to 1897 as chairman of its executive committee. President Andrew D. White referred to him as "our Millionaire Master."[75]

Often Sage's influence was not in the best interests of the university, and because of the character of the conflicts, one may assume that the troubles were fairly common to universities directly controlled by businessmen. In order to rationalize his power over the faculty, it was necessary for Sage to degrade their practical intelligence. Although he was friendly with many professors, he was condescending toward them in matters of the real world, which he obviously regarded as more important than those of the intellect. His opinion was no doubt shared by the American public that regarded teachers as "infinitely below the financial men, political figures and lawyers who now began to be a majority of the college board of trustees."[76] Commenting on an unsucccessful installation in a college building Sage said, "Like nearly all professor's work, it has to be done again by somebody who *knows how*."[77] He did not hesitate to hire and fire professors as well as presidents and other administrators. He saw the major function of the university as teaching Protestant Christian morality, and himself as a servant of God in maintaining this aim.[78] The result of such policies by Sage and hundreds of other authoritarian, self-confident business leaders was to drive the board and the faculty apart and to make administration a separate operation whose practitioners were regarded by business members of the board as hired men, usually considered inferior in ability to the executives they would rely on in their own companies.

The easy capture of university control by businessmen was a logical result of the American situation. Starting with the University of Pennsylvania in 1779, a large number of institutions of higher learning had university charters, but they were in fact small colleges, accompanied by one or two professional schools such as law or medicine. According to English and other European standards, true universities only developed in the United States after the Civil War. By this time the major educational influence was German, which favored professional administration, centralization of control, and specialized study. This was a more congenial tradition to businesslike America than the English one of universities composed of decentralized separate colleges, emphasizing preparation of well-rounded gentlemen. American institutions, even including Harvard, lacked firmly established traditions as universities and were easily manipulated by men of wealth, who, often for reasons of conscience or prestige, were willing to finance change and growth. As a result, Dean DeVane says, "By 1900 the pattern of the American university . . . was a close adaptation of a complex and sophisticated business firm." It saw as its first task the training of the professionals the country demanded.[79]

Wealthy businessmen were also beginning to influence higher education through the establishment of foundations. In 1902 John D. Rockefeller, Sr., started the General Education Board, which, within a generation, gave over $60 million to colleges and universities. The board decided which institutions were worthy of support and which might be allowed to perish.[80] The decisions in this case, and in similar foundations established by Andrew Carnegie and a few other very rich businessmen, were made not by the business leaders themselves but by professional foundation executives, similar to the managerial careerists in other types of large corporations. The influence, therefore, chiefly served to align academic policy with the general views of the growing professional business elite.

EDUCATION BY MASS MEDIA

Students of child conditioning have decided, logically, that everyday ideas and attitudes come from family and personal contacts, while ideas regarding remote matters and infrequent experiences come chiefly from texts, schooling, and mass media. In the late nineteenth and early twentieth centuries, newspapers were unquestionably the most powerful influence in continuing or adult education. Formal adult education came largely from special lectures, or summer courses such as those at Chatauqua, New York, normally attended by the upper classes. The hundreds of little magazines probably reached about the same audience. Judging from estimates of total circulation, however, by the 1840s at least daily or weekly newspapers were reaching a broad cross section of the population, many or most of whom read nothing else.

Since there is a relatively high degree of consistency in the attitudes and beliefs of every stable culture, one would expect to find them reflected in a representative social institution such as the newspaper. Consequently, the fact that eighteenth- and early nineteenth-century newspaper publishing was conducted by small printers on hand presses did not prevent such papers from being means for cultural reenforcement. While these small enterprises reflected the political partisanship of their proprietors, those whose partisan feelings mirrored the views of mercantile or business interests prospered more from advertising than their opponents. If the local party in power was the one not favored by most businessmen, lack of commercial patronage of the party press might be compensated for by government printing and advertising. Obviously, in either case the "independent," partisan journalist was reflecting the opinions of a section of the elite. Furthermore, in most developing communities beyond the Alleghenies, the newspaper was regarded as an agency for bringing new business and population to the town, a sort of chamber of commerce advertising sheet.

The Fourdrinier machine that lowered costs by making paper from poor quality rags, and the increasing urban population made a one-cent mass circulation newspaper possible in the mid-1830s. Depending on a broader circulation and patent medicine advertising, the publishers of these journals in the four big East Coast cities were farily independent of the pressures of politicians or advertising by leading businessmen. Yet, it is not clear that they in any significant way departed from the broadly accepted mores on the business society.

Other developments were moving big-city newspaper publishing more completely into the realm of big business. The Hoe rotary press perfected in 1847, costing a minimum of $20,000, eliminated the small job printer from the metropolitan daily newspaper business. While H. J. Raymond and his backers started the *New York Times* with $69,000 in 1851, the average cost of establishing a metropolitan daily was around $100,000.[81] As the cities grew, the circulation of the leading dailies and weeklies grew even faster. In 1860 the *New York Weekly Tribune* ran 200,000 and the *Weekly New York Ledger* twice that. By the early 1870s, the circulations of the biggest dailies ran from one to 200,000, and as business firms they were worth $1 million or $2 million.

While American newspapers were said to carry more advertising than any others in the world, it is not necessary to argue that editorial and news policies were dictated by advertisers in order to assume that the papers spread the attitudes of successful big business. The metropolitan dailies were themselves big business.[82]

The late nineteenth century is still looked back upon as one of "personal" journalism, of editorial giants like Charles A. Dana, Henry Watterson, Carl Schurz, E. L. Godkin, or Joseph Pulitzer, but all of these gentlemen were highly propserous members of the business upper class and put forth appropriate opinions. Their personal differences were over desirable means, not the ends or goals of the growing business system.

Another advance in business influence also started in the mid-nineteenth century when the telegraph greatly speeded the spread of news. Even the big metropolitan dailies found individual wire service too expensive and quickly formed associations for the distribution of telegraphic news. This was the beginning of a trend toward collecting and distributing all national and international news through press associations, generally owned by the cooperating papers. By the 1880s features and national advertising, largely patent medicines, were also distributed in prepared form, called boiler plate and patent insides.

As time went on, mergers between competing associations took place until, by 1915, except for a few big papers which had their own staff at key cities, all national and international news came to originate with one of three national press associations. Although there may have been little direct censoring of the news, the dominance of the press associations by a few publishers tended to influence releases on subjects such as finance, labor relations, and pending legislation.[83]

RELIGION

By 1860 there were about a hundred religious weeklies that competed with secular papers in general news coverage. Moving away from the field of general news in succeeding decades, a greatly increased number of religious weeklies constituted a major part of the reading matter of American adults, particularly in the country regions. Insofar as these papers carried a "social message," it was generally in accord with the views of the business members of the denomination.[84]

Northeastern Protestantism, as we have seen, had been close to business in its social ideas and values since the colonial period. The Reverend Theodore Parker of Boston, famous preacher and abolitionist, spoke sarcastically of the attitudes of his area: "The Saint of the nineteenth century is the Good Merchant; he is wisdom for the foolish, strength for the weak, warning to the wicked, and a blessing to all. Build him a shrine in Bank and Church, in the Market and the Exchange."[85] The clergy of eastern Massachusetts were active as writers and lecturers on the virtue of success by self-help, hard work, and moral character. The famous novelist of success, Horatio Alger, started as a Unitarian minister in Brewster, Massachusetts. There is little indication that by the late nineteenth century Protestant ministers in the less industrialized areas differed with the Easterners. In the changes that took place in the attitudes of the Protestant churches between 1850 and 1915, business leaders took an active, and often a progressive role. In 1878, the Reverend Matthew H. Smith said that "whoever wrote the history of American business would also have to write the history of religion."[86]

John G. Cawelti sees a change in emphasis in the admonitions of the Calvinist clergy. Colonial sermons stressed industry, frugality, honesty, and piety, whereas the clerical admonitions of the mid-nineteenth century added initiative, aggressiveness, competitiveness, and forcefulness.[87] He adds that it would be wrong, however, to neglect a continuing emphasis by certain clerical and lay writers such as Emerson and Parker on individual fulfilment and social progress rather than wealth or status.

Ministers continued to use business language, and businessmen in the conduct of their affairs invoked divine sanctions. Revivalist preacher Sam Jones held that God's law was "a business contract binding on you;"[88] while the pastor of a Fifth Avenue church spoke of preaching to $250 million every Sunday.[89] God's plan for America seemed clearly revealed to numerous businessmen in such matters as railroad routes left open by the "Great Architect of the Universe," or in "Divine ordination for a currency based on specie."[90]

Confidence in the understanding of economic laws increased among both ministers and business leaders. In 1866 the Reverend George W. Boardman appealed to his fellow ministers to study political economy as a branch of natural theology. In the political economy of "clerical laissez-faire," the minister would learn the impossibility of escaping from the laws of the market regulated by supply and demand. Poverty and vagrancy were "crimes and should be *prevented* or *punished*."[91] "In 1876," says Henry F. May, "Protestantism presented a massive, almost unbroken front in favor of the status quo."[92]

The leading religious periodicals carried business advertising of many types including those for patent medicines and railroad securities, together with occasional articles on the achievements of the advertiser. As editor of the *Independent*, the famous Congregational minister Henry Ward Beecher had to deny charges of accepting pay for publishing articles on the Northern Pacific Railroad.[93] The business scandals of the Grant administration produced admonitions against speculation and fraud, but no continuing criticism of the business system. As Beecher saw it, success and morality generally went hand in hand.

Urban Protestant churches had always relied heavily on wealthy parishioners, and increasingly large incomes from business made it desirable for the pastor to seek their approval. Beecher said, "Our churches are largely for the mutual insurance of prosperous families, and not for the upbuilding of the great under-class of humanity."[94] The church, of course, recognized an obligation to the poor, and as philanthropy became a way of gaining prestige from the possession of wealth, the church helped direct the flow. Evangelists and their religious revivalism, strongly individualistic and unconcerned with social problems, received financial support from business leaders. Joshua Levering, prominent Baltimore merchant, underwrote the fiery Sam Jones. John Wanamaker, of department store fame, aided evangelists Reuben Archer Torrey and the more famous Dwight L. Moody. Of the latter's work Wanamaker said, "Hundreds of men . . . out of work, and wandering about the streets have been kept in the way they chose when they embraced the religion of Jesus Christ."[95] Business contributions to save souls helped expand the Moody revivals into gatherings that filled the largest auditoriums of the big cities.

Meanwhile the Protestant churches were losing contact with the working man. As early as 1870 it was clear that he was not attending services. Partly, it was a case of physical desertion by the churches. As the middle class moved away from the center of the city, leaving slum areas behind, their churches moved with them. But in part the split was lower-class dissatisfaction with the middle-class atmosphere and economic doctrines of the Protestant church. Pastors denounced unions as contrary to natural and divine law and affirmed that wages could only be governed by supply and demand. Spectacular strikes such as those on the railroads in 1877 caused floods of clerical criticism. "Trades unions," said the *Christian Advocate*, "are despotic and revolutionary in tendency."[96]

Two different types of change took place in the Protestant churches between about 1880 and World War I. The first was a readjustment of theology to accommodate evolutionary science and historical biblical criticism, in the course of which theology and the Bible both lost their absolute authority. The second change, only indirectly related to this shift in ultimate sanctions, was an effort to make the urban churches more important as social institutions. In general, the theological changes came first, and particularly in the less intellectual denominations, produced a division between modernism and fundamentalism, between ministers who preached the perfection of man through evolution and those who stuck by the "old-fashioned religion" of original sin and damnation.

In these controversies business had no uniform role. The modernist congregations were generally in the cities and had the wealthiest parishioners, whereas the back-country areas, where industrial business had penetrated least, were strongholds of fundamentalism. The cleavage, however, was based more on geography and environment than on occupational groups or classes. Southwestern business leaders were often fundamentalist and Baptist, while those of the Northeast tended to be modernist and Episcopal. Pastors of urban churches were unsympathetic to farm movements, and rural preachers denounced the sins of cities.

The gradual transformation of Protestant churches away from being authoritarian guides to morality and belief toward serving as community and social centers had many facets. Of one of the early aspects, that of developing a greater interest in lower-class problems, May writes, "The Christian social movement . . . owed its existence more to the impact of labor conflict than to any other single cause."[97] After a virtually unanimous condemnation of militant workers and their unions in the railroad strikes of 1877, some church publications began in the 1880s to take a more inquiring attitude toward the labor movement. While each subsequent crisis, such as the Haymarket Square affair or the Homestead or Pullman strikes, provoked fresh condemnation of the action of organized labor, a few journals discussed the issues objectively. After the Homestead strike of 1892, the Congregational *Andover Review* went so far as to suggest that the worker should have an equity in his job.[98] In 1887 New York City Episcopalians formed a Church Association for Advancement of the

Interests of Labor, with bishops serving as president and vice-presidents. Like many other upper-class groups in civic or business associations, the churchmen campaigned against child labor and slums, and for the arbitration of strikes. While the Congregationalists, Episcopalians, and Presbyterians were taking an interest in social issues, the Methodists and Baptists, except for a small group of the latter led by Walter Rauschenbusch, remained passive until after 1900.

Although the labor interests of some socially minded ministers made business parishioners uneasy, they favored other aspects of the broad movement to make the churches community centers. Sunday schools, parish houses, basketball teams, dances, and other social activities were well-supported financially. The nondenominational social settlement house movement from 1886 on brought together ministers and business leaders in meetings in the slums. Jane Addams of Hull House, Chicago, drew money from local millionaires with the skill of a college president, and the settlement's buildings and welfare activities expanded accordingly.

Around 1900, as the many movements to reform society grew stronger, there was a flood of books and articles on the social teaching of Jesus. While this movement, usually called the Social Gospel, substituted ethical and humanitarian sanctions for the old theological ones, conservatives could apply the sanctions to internal rather than external social problems. Throughout the literature and sermons there was a strong note of upper middle and upper-class individualism. "Social regeneration is to come," said the Reverend Orello Cone, "through the dissemination of the spirit of reverence for personality."[99] He and other moderate clergy denied that Jesus was a social reformer.[100]

As with other aspects of Progressivism, some reformers moved well to the left of the main body, and were certainly unacceptable to business parishioners. Ironically, many if not most of the extremists were professors in seminaries made independent of denominational pressure through endowments given by businessmen; almost all were associated with religious enterprises other than parish churches. A small group formed the Christian Socialist Fellowship in 1906 and tried to win support for the American Socialist party, but the most prominent of the advanced thinkers like Congregationalist George Washington Gladden and Baptist Walter Rauschenbusch advocated reform within the individual and in human relations rather than abrupt change in the political system.*

The middle group that composed the bulk of the Social Gospel movement wanted, as did thoughtful business leaders, to prevent violent change and to produce a more efficient society by necessary reforms in attitudes and laws. Typical of this group was Congregational minister Josiah Strong, who in 1886 helped arouse the upper class to urban problems by his book *Our Country*.[101]

* This statement applies to Gladden throughout his career. Rauschenbusch did become more favorable to political socialism between 1912 and 1916.

A dozen years later he formed the League for Social Service, designed to bring business and other civic leaders in contact with the ideas of specialists in the social sciences. After four years the league became the American Institute for Social Service, among whose directors were Mrs. Andrew Carnegie, Grace H. Dodge, Walter Hines Page, Grover Cleveland, and Woodrow Wilson. The institute conducted public forums led by ministers with the aim of acquainting both business and labor leaders with up-to-date thought regarding social issues.

In such activities the Social Gospel group showed much the same faith in simple solutions to complicated problems that was manifest in the political reforms of Progressivism, the aims of scientific management, the world peace movement, and other programs for the perfection of society. But the active Social Gospelers were a small minority in the Protestant church. Most ministers found it safer and more congenial to urge humanitarian action, but to defend the politico-economic status quo. Although each major denomination had a committee or commission for social action, the influence of these bodies on their churches was not strong. They did, however, succeed in founding in 1908 an ecumenical Federal Council of Churches of Christ in America that played the role of the social conscience of American Protestantism.

A MAJOR TRANSITION

By the beginning of World War I, Americans of the urban middle class, at least, had acquired the attitudes that were to characterize twentieth-century managerial society in the Western world. As in the case of ideas regarding management, child rearing was moving from the realm of traditional practice into that of psychological science. Confused parents, reading or hearing of the new theories, were conditioning future executives by a pragmatic combination of traditional admonitions and advanced scientific reasoning.[102]

The middle-class family was aware that a high school education was necessary for success in a complex technological society, while business executives wanted to hire not only high school graduates, but a large number of specially trained men from the colleges and universities. All over the Western world, businessmen recognized the necessity of advanced public education and compulsory school laws, particularly at the end of the period, because of the deficiencies found among the men drafted to serve in World War I. Business leaders who had scoffed at early attempts to substitute study for experience in administration and related activities now valued formal instruction at both undergraduate and graduate levels. But in contrast to the mid-twentieth century, when learning came to be regarded as necessary for national survival, the men of the turn of the century saw it as useful for better business.

Business leaders, many of whom were personally devout, regarded the church as a moderating influence in the rapid social change forced by technological advance. While a few clergymen attracted attention by their radical social views, the great majority preached adjustment to the world as it was. Like other representatives of the upper strata of society, socially conscious ministers joined with their parishioners in advocating moderate social reforms that would help capitalist democracy to function more honestly and efficiently.

CHAPTER 12

A Business Bar and Bench

"The interplay of law and market," writes James Willard Hurst, "has expressed a good deal of our way of life."[1]* The complex of values that businessmen sought to protect or advance through the law—individual freedom of action, opportunity for material success, and attitudes favorable to the active local developer—have been common elements in the American national character. How the law, in a local, state, and federal system, could best serve these major values, was a continuous underlying theme of legal development. By World War I most of the ground-rules were known, most of the major conflicts apparently resolved, and the common law adjusted to serve the needs of what John P. Roche calls "entrepreneurial liberty."[2]

THE BUSINESS LAWYER

The chief sources of legal income had always come from actions concerning property and contracts, but in the period before 1850, the ambiance of a new American legal system and the excitement of creative precedents had given to leaders of the bar, like Kent, Marshall, or Story the appearance of pioneers in statecraft. In the latter part of the century, however, the essential connections of the law with the concerns of business became even more rewarding and demanding. The same kind of men now had more the appearance of technicians of the law or partisan pleaders for rich clients. "The technicians," writes legal historian Hurst, "supported the status quo with the colorless, implicable force of inertia. The partisan wielded the sword, whether in the hot blood of Guthrie, the complacent arrogance of Choate, or the reasoned ruthlessness of Cravath."[3] Some of the ablest pleading may have been for doubtful causes. It is said, for example, of Julian T. Davis' handling of 2,000 damage suits by property owners against the steam-powered, coal burning New York Elevated, "but for his brilliant efforts in restricting the amounts recovered against the company, its

---

* I am indebted to Professor Hurst and his writing for many of the ideas of this chapter.
  The men cited, William D. Guthrie, Rufus Choate, Paul D. Cravath, are all among the great businesslike leaders of the bar between 1850 and 1900.

control would have passed permanently from the owners into the hands of the judgment creditors."[4]

The very nature of the corporation as a legally created artificial entity made lawyers continual participants in its activities. As corporations grew larger and explored the possibilities of their status, the lawyers were the well-rewarded pioneers. The hard-driving first generation of great corporate capitalists put strong pressure on their lawyers for legal justification of pragmatic policy, and the lawyers responded ably and innovatively. It took legal advisors, not entrepreneurs, to develop the all-important corporate lease, the first mortgage bond, or the action by a stockholder against his corporation that could be used to attack state regulatory laws.

While the leaders of the bar perpetuated, sometimes by wealth alone, the prestige they had won in former days, and became learned specialists in the most remunerative types of practice, the average lawyer had always been and continued to be a politician, a small businessman, or both. From 1790 on, over half the members of the House and Senate of the United States were lawyers, and probably the proportion in state legislatures and city councils was even higher. The ordinary lawyer was trained by the apprenticeship system in the practical work of a law office, in organizing businesses, forming partnerships, handling credit instruments, realizing on posted security, and dealing with creditors, and the many and involved details of real property (land) titles and transfers.

The favored few who went to law school gained time to think, but may have had less useful training. Starting with the teaching of Christopher E. Langdell at Harvard and his casebook on contract law in 1871, the leading law schools introduced the case system, whereby a "logic of the law" was relentlessly applied to judicial reasoning without regard to the political and economic pressures that, in fact, bore upon the case. It took the fresh insights of the Progressive period to bring the law schools back from the ivory-tower emphasis on abstract principles to consideration of the effects of the market place for money or votes.[5] Yet, the late nineteenth-century emphasis on case law was by its very nature conservative, based, that is, on reiterating earlier precedents; this was highly satisfactory to most businessmen. Only the large corporation with its new powers and possibilities would, in general, be irked by the rigidities of *stare decises*. According to Roscoe Pound, corporations suffered as deeply as American laborers from doctrines going back to earlier, even Roman, times. He saw limitations on national companies stemming from old conceptions of them as dangerous monopolies whose freedom might be restricted by local authorities.[6]

Like other competitors, in the 1870s lawyers formed associations on the local, state, and national levels, and like business trade associations, they had no legal power and hence small influence. Even by 1915 state bar associations embraced only about one-fifth of the lawyers.[7] The National Bar Association, formed in 1878, was chiefly notable for bringing about uniform state laws on such old and important business matters as negotiable instruments (endorsed notes, etc.) from 1896 on, and on sales and warehouse receipts after 1907.

LAWYERS AS A STABILIZING FORCE

In spite of their commitment to moneymaking and their lack of interest in public welfare, lawyers were at times social heroes protecting viable customs and stability in a chaotic political and economic world. The period from 1850 to about 1890, quite apart from the disruption of Civil War, covers perhaps the poorest functioning of the federal system. It was a time when many state governments were a menace to the welfare of their societies; when most men successful at making money refused to waste their time serving the public; and when men in politics instead of serving their constituents spent their time trying to make money. That the system survived with its federal or multiple character-istics almost unchanged in structure was due to the depth of sectional jealousies and of the localism of American political horizons, but also, in part, because lawyers guided business in its relations to government, the public, and the courts. The best of the lawyers maintained a level of ability generally superior to that found in politics or on the bench, and a feeling of responsibility for public order greater, at least, than that of most of their clients.

In a country only slowly beginning to recognize the general value of higher education, lawyers were the largest group of "learned" men. While preachers may have been as numerous, few had educational training equal even to the apprenticeship or "reading" preparation required in the law, and in any case, the ministers' knowledge lacked practical utility. In an age of small, expanding, and migrating business, lawyers were constantly in demand, particularly in new areas with their many problems of land titles. In 1860 frontier Trempeleau county, Wisconsin, for example, which was selected as an agricultural area of rather normal growth, had six lawyers in a gainfully employed population of about 700 people, or perhaps six times the average for the nation.[8] Membership in the bar not only assured the able man a good independent practice, but also was an asset in most types of business and the principle stepping stone to a political career. Surveys of the United States Senate in 1860 and 1900 show that at both dates about three-quarters of the members were lawyers.[9]

Responding to the needs of businessmen involved in land, trade, and manufacturing, lawyers developed doctrines to protect the rights of their clients and persuaded judges that the new principles were sound. "The inescapable fact," writes Howard J. Graham, "is that the American legal profession and its clients, at length managed to seduce American judges and courts—and not vice versa."[10] "Seduce" is an invidious term; one may as well say that in an age when the vast majority of the nation's people wanted rapid economic develop-ment, the lawyers sought, like other men, to evolve principles that would stimulate the process.

In the course of representing more and bigger business concerns, the offices of successful lawyers became sizable business enterprises in themselves, and their senior partners were among the most ditinguished men of their communities. On the other hand, great increases in the number of practitioners reached a peak of only 704 people per lawyer in 1900, and left many who made only modest livings.[11] Consequently, it is as difficult to speak of the bar as having *an* opinion as it is in the case of business. Social reformers generally regarded the leading lawyers as a conservative group, overly close to big business. To James Bryce, writing in 1885, American lawyers were more conservative and less open to new ideas than those in England. He also thought that the willingness of big corporations to "pay vast sums for questionable services" threatened the vigor and integrity of the bar.[12]

Perhaps the members of the bar had been less influenced by business needs and more by public considerations in the midcentury years before the rise of corporate practice on a large scale. Certainly, with the spread of railroads and other utilities, many lawyers became salaried employees of big corporations. But granting the middle- to upper-class status of lawyers, and the general views of American communities, the lawyers' primary emphases on private property rights and the validity of private agreements seem normal, regardless of business connections.[13]

That part of the population which regularly patronized important lawyers, chiefly entrepreneurs of various types, continued to emphasize the need for freedom of contract and individual opportunity. Disregarding the concept of laissez-faire, which seems to have had little reality in America outside of textbooks, editorials, and public addresses, businessmen wanted protection for dispersed private decision-making based on the market. They wanted the courts to protect them through the common law doctrines of property and contract and by restraining the police power of the state. They wanted freedom to exploit economic opportunities for maximum immediate profits, and such laws as would facilitate a safe supply of credit. They saw law, if used in support of the decisions of the market, as a positive force in economic growth, and in general, although slowly at times, the law responded to their needs.[14]

POLITICS AND THE COURTS

During the mid-nineteenth century when state legislatures often operated as markets where government favors such as franchises and tax relief were for sale, and protection against adverse regulations also had to be bought, lawyers at the state capitals were indispensable to businessmen. In New York State, the commercial center of the nation, the Black Horse Cavalry, a group of corrupt legislators, bought and sold favors and demanded tribute.[15] President Ackerman of the Illinois Central Railroad said that the Illinois legislators would "Make you any amount of wild promises, but . . . they are utterly unreliable."[16] The majority group in the Wisconsin legislature in the late 1850s were variously called the "old lobby," "Monk's Hall," or the "forty thieves."[17] In spite of the appearance of corruption in aid of business, such governments were probably a deterrent to economic growth. They not only exacted costly tribute from new enterprises, but they also failed to provide the reliability and stability of legislation necessary to the financing of highly capitalized long-run ventures.

In an effort to find some firm context for lasting commitments, businessmen turned inevitably to the common law and the courts. Here the personnel, particularly in the state supreme courts, was of a somewhat higher type than in the legislature, and the common law legal traditions argued by able lawyers might prove strong enough to withstand the lapses in honesty or efficiency of state government. But the state judges, many of whom were elected officials, were still close to state politics, and in many situations they found ways of satisfying local sentiment at the expense of the interests of substantial absentee property holders. The municipal bonds floated to aid railroad construction in many states were a good example. When overoptimistic or dishonest railroad promoters dissipated the proceeds of such securities and failed to build the roads, many of the municipalities tried to repudiate the bonds. State courts, such as those of New York, upheld repudiation on formal pretexts that if regularly adhered to would have made all security financing impossible.* The federal Supreme Court, however, ruled in favor of the bondholders in all cases where the municipality had the power to make the issue.[18] *

These and other actions involving local or state interests suggest the hypothesis that the more remote a bench was from the influences of local democratic politics, the more likely it was to protect property interests by the common law doctrine of contract. Since important acts were invariably tested by legal action, the history of the law in relation to business from 1850 to at least 1900 is more concerned with the rulings of the courts than with the shifting and often unenforced acts of legislatures. It was the United States Supreme Court, for example, that by voiding a Maryland tax on out-of-state salesmen, in 1870 enforced an "open door" policy for national business.[19] Even in later years, when the Progressive movement led to new state and federal regulation, often sponsored by substantial business interests, the courts in general and particularly the Supreme Court of the United States adhered to legal doctrines protecting entrepreneurial liberties and private property rights. Thus, the courts were the final arbiters of how far the regulatory or police power of government might go and of what was in reality the law.

PROPERTY AND CONTRACTS

In the emerging world of corporate business and impersonal sealings, the bar and bench together, with the aid of the federal constitution, gave new meaning

---

* The Wisconsin Supreme Court, however, upheld the rights of the bondholders; see Hunt, *Law and the Locomotive,* 48-53.

to the common law protection of property rights and private contracts against interference by government. As we have seen more effective protection for the rights of property first evolved in relation to actions by the states to recover land for nonpayment of taxes. In 1855 Chicago lawyer Robert S. Blackwell in *Blackwell on Tax Liens* stated that "the legislature has no power by its own action to deprive any citizen of his property" without the right of appeal to the courts.[20] At this time, property was generally thought of as physical assets, but as business transactions came to be more important, lawyers and judges, within a generation, extended the concept to cover the right to carry out activities arising from use of the property. In other words, the property of a business consisted not only of its physical assets, but of the legitimate use of these for making a profit.

To most American businessmen, whose operations were on a "shoestring," a contract was a private matter between two parties and concerned no one else. It was a way of defining a bargain so that energies might be freely and safely released for its fulfillment. The law of contract did have complex ramifications in negotiable instruments, secured transactions such as mortgages and liens, types of business organization, and in connection with insurance. As generally employed in business bargains, however, the law was traditional and understandable. "By the second half of the nineteenth century, contract was a firm body of doctrine," and contract law was the "legal embodiment of the market."[21] From the 1870s on, the doctrines of the security of property and contracts came together in holding charters and private agreements to be property whose free use could only be denied to the owner through due process of law, thus placing such agreements, according to Roche, "on a higher level of legitimacy than the police power of the state."[22]

Looking at the effect of these doctrines on the development of business, Hurst points out that "the market could work only within a sturdy social context . . . it required the support of framework institutions outside it—as, for example, the law of property and contract."[23] This reenforcing effect of the privately oriented common law becomes obvious by comparison with the more complex statutory codes of other nations. In the Spanish Commercial Code of the late nineteenth century, for example, exect methods of bookkeeping were prescribed by the state, and the code warned that "books of merchants shall be evidence against themselves no proof to the contrary being admitted." In cases of discrepancy between books, correct form established legality.[24]

THE AFFIRMATION OF STATE POLICE POWER

"Police Power," as the concept is customarily used by lawyers, covers the means by which the legislative and executive powers of the state are used to regulate behavior. On the one hand, it gives the protection of stable social order necessary for any contract involving time; on the other, it is potentially the chief legal menace to freedom of contract. As we have seen, colonial governments dominated by the ideas of mercantilism frequently placed restrictions on contracts for wages, prices, and interest rates. While the new states became generally freer in these respects during the late eighteenth century, new types of proscriptions appeared against lotteries and other contracts regarded as immoral. Those essential to most types of business, however, were freed of almost all restraints as to wages, prices, and conditions of fulfillment.

The late nineteenth-century legal struggles came primarily from the application of the state police power in two areas: problems connected with public utilities, chiefly railroads; and regulation of contracts with labor. Conflicts between big business and government in the first of these areas were also contests between different types of business, the interests of carriers, for example, as against shippers. Obviously democratically elected state legislatures could not be continually controlled by a single business interest, such as the railroads, in opposition to organized groups representing much of the business of the state and thousands of aroused constituents.

Furthermore, in adjudicating regulatory laws, the courts were traditionally inclined to recognize the police power of the state as an attribute of sovereignty in areas clearly involving the public interest. Hence, while among the agencies of government, businessmen put their chief reliance in the courts, the latter would not guarantee complete freedom from interference.

Between 1871 and 1887 a number of the Northern states, including all those in the northern Mississippi Valley, established railroad commissions with power to prevent railroads, and usually grain elevators, from exceeding certain maximum rates.* In general the state courts upheld this extension of the police power on the ground that those activities involved a public interest, and the railroads ultimately appealed to the Supreme Court of the United States.

Reluctant to make itself the final authority in rate cases, the Court at first denied its authority. When *Munn* v. *Illinois*, the leading rate case, was argued before it in 1877, the Court held that there had not been deprivation of "property," which was still seen as a physical entity, and that "due process of law" in this case meant proper procedure by the Illinois legislature.[25] The decision, with only two justices dissenting, was a shock to many lawyers and railroad men. Two important legal writers, Thomas M. Cooley and John Norton Pomeroy, Jr., in books published in 1868 had extended the concept of property to cover intangible attributes, and many judges and lawyers beside the two dissenters on the Supreme Court took the same view.[26] In addition, the idea that "due process" should mean a substantive test of correctness by the Court went back to Blackwell. President Robert Harris of the Burlington Railroad only expected to "rally when the first stunning effects have been exhausted."[27]

---

* Massachusetts set up a railroad commission in 1869, but gave it no control over rates. Only Wisconsin gave its commissioners power to adjust rates, as against merely enforcing maximums.

In the light of previous decisions President Harris should not have been so surprised. *Munn* v. *Illinois* illustrated the continuing reluctance of the high court in the sixties and seventies to assume a decisive role in the struggles between business and the police power of the states. Only with changes in personnel and increasing pressure from interstate business over the course of the ensuing generation was the Court led to assume the final authority in state cases involving regulation of activities that affected business income rather than physical property.

THE ASSERTION OF NATIONAL POWER THROUGH "DUE PROCESS"

The occasion for change was the case of the *Chicago, Milwaukee and St. Paul Railway* v. *Minnesota* in 1890, again presenting the problem of whether or not the legislative power of the state was final in regulating public utilities such as railroads.[28] As in its earlier decisions, the high court did not deny that the state legally possessed such power, but it now held that the clause "due process of law" in the Fourteenth Amendment implied judicial review, that final authority could not be delegated by the state legislature to the Railroad and Warehouse Commission of Minnesota. This decision made the Supreme Court the final arbiter of just regulation at a time when the great upsurge of electrical utilities was making the issue one of growing importance. In *Smyth* v. *Ames* (1898) the court explicitly assumed the burden of determining fair valuation and return, and in *Wilcox* v. *Consolidated Gas Company* (1909) it held specifically that restriction to a rate of 6 percent did not constitute deprivation of property.[29] Commenting years later on these decisions, Justice Harlan Fiske Stone said, "In assuming the task of determining judicially the present fair replacement value of the vast properties of public utilities, courts have been projected into the most speculative undertaking imposed upon them in the entire history of English jurisprudence."[30] Fortunately for the Supreme Court justices, the cost of litigation led to the settlement of most rate controversies at lower levels.

The railroads and a few other enterprises affected with a public interest had fought the battle against state regulation of rates and with the aid of the courts achieved a considerable degree of success. These decisions implicitly affirmed that business not directly involving thy public interest was free from interference regarding rates and profits, and other decisions affirmed further freedoms from interference by the states.

THE COMMERCE POWER

While the Fourteenth Amendment thus came to be a protection for business against some extensions of the state police power, the commerce clause of the federal constitution, as interpreted by Chief Justice John Marshall, could protect interstate business absolutely from state interference. As in the case of the Amendment, it took the Supreme Court more than a generation to reaffirm the federal commerce power in Marshallian exclusiveness applied to the states and to place new limitations on Congress. The increasing pressure on the Court for clarification is shown in the number of cases arising under the commerce clause. Up to 1840 only 5 cases had required interpretation of this clause. In the next twenty years there were 15 more, with the Court generally taking a limited view of federal powers. From 1870 to 1890 there were 118 cases, including the important Wabash decision of 1886.[31]

This decision holding that a state could not regulate rates within its borders on goods that were in interstate movement, the major step in curbing state control over interstate commerce, was quickly followed by the entrance of the federal government in this field through creation of a regulatory commission (Chapter 14).[32] The ruling made it impossible for states to fix rates on a major part of their railroad traffic. In 1890 the Court revived the doctrine of John Marshall in *Brown* v. *Maryland* (1829) by holding that until the original package had been broken or the goods had been sold, commodities shipped in interstate commerce were not subject to the state police power.[33] Subsequent decisions regarding state regulation, before 1915, were mainly clarifications of the principles reaffirmed in these two leading cases.[34]

HEALTH AND WELFARE VERSUS FREEDOM OF CONTRACT

Beginning in the late 1860s, states passed laws governing the conditions of labor for groups whose health or welfare seemed threatened: child labor was prohibited or restricted; maximum hours were set for the labor of women; and in a few instances, payment of wages in company scrip was forbidden for all labor in mines or factories, as well as withholding wages for alleged imperfections in work. These acts, passed by the Northern states from Massachusetts to Oregon, obviously restricted freedom of contract between business and labor. By the mid-1880s, test cases were reaching the supreme courts of the states.

In most of the cases, the state law was held unconstitutional, as a violation of freedom of contract, and hence no appeal to the federal Supreme Court was possible.[35] One of the earliest of these state cases was the Pennsylvania action *Godcharles* v. *Wigeman* (1886) against a law prohibiting payment of wages in mining or manufacturing in other than lawful money. Judge Isaac M. Gordon set forth the doctrine that was to be generally adhered to by the courts for the next generation in clear simple terms:

> The Act is an infringement alike of the right of the employer and the employee . . . . He may sell his labor for what he thinks best . . . and any and every law that proposes to prevent him from so doing is an infringement of his constitutional privileges and consequently vicious and void.[36]

Late in this year 1886, Christopher G. Tiedeman, professor of law at the University of Missouri, said in his *A Treatise on the Limitations of Police Power in the United States*, "The unwritten law of the country is in the main against the exercise of police power, and the restrictions imposed upon persons and private property are jealously watched and scrutinized."[37]

In two decisions, separated by seven years, the Supreme Court took its stand. In *Holden* v. *Hardy* (1898) the Court upheld a law of Utah limiting workers in mines to an eight-hour day on the basis of both public health and inequality in bargaining power.[38] But employers faced with an increasing number of laws restricting hours were left uncertain as to what constituted an "unhealthy" occupation. In *Lochner* v. *New York* (1905) the Supreme Court indicated strict limitations on the use of health as a basis for regulation by disallowing a ten-hour law for bakers, who were alleged to work in unhealthy basements. To dissenting Justice Oliver Wendell Holmes, the case was decided not solely on the basis of law, but also "upon an economic theory which a large part of the country does not entertain."[39] While three years later in *Muller* v. *Oregon* the high court in accordance with *Holden* v. *Hardy* upheld an eight-hour law for women, labor in general was still free to contract for any number of hours.[40] Looking back on these decisions Roche says, "The Court implicitly made a crucial choice among social and economic values when it exalted the well-being of the investor and the liberty of the entrepreneur over both economic rationality and the police power of the state."[41]

Another extension of police power into employee-employer relations came to a climax between 1910 and 1917. Under the traditional doctrines of the common law, it was practically impossible for an employee to collect damages from his employer in cases of accidents on the job. If the employee were killed, the common law recognized no party able to take action. The old system of compensation on a paternalistic basis became unworkable in large impersonal corporations like railroads, which carried on highly dangerous operations; a more precise and substantial policy was needed.

The first step was a Georgia law of 1856 which abrogated in railroad accidents the doctrine that if a fellow employee was responsible for the mishap, the injured man's action was against him rather than the employer. The states continued to modify the common law in various ways for diverse occupations, but still left a nearly insuperable barrier to recovery for the poor man—the cost of effective legal action. By the early twentieth century, as industrial accidents of all kinds accounted for 25,000 a year killed and a million injured, various states set up commissions to study remedies. Nearly all of these commissions reported in favor of compulsory insurance taken out by the employer, providing for automatic payment of fixed amounts for various types of accidents. By 1917, when the Supreme Court validated three different types of compensation provisions, enlightened employers and their associations favored such laws.[42]

LIMITATIONS ON CONGRESS

In these critical decisions regarding property, contracts, and due process, extending over three decades, the federal Supreme Court gave business protection from arbitrary state laws, but still left open the question of regulation by

Congress through the commerce clause or the power to tax. As noted in Chapter 9, the rise of large industrial corporations in the 1880s and the use of the voting trust for unified ownership of diverse companies led Congress to pass the stringent Sherman Anti-Trust Law prohibiting agreements to control or monopolize commerce between the states.

There could be no legal question regarding the power of Congress over goods in interstate transit; but there remained the important one of when, in the processes of manufacture and distribution, goods first entered into interstate commerce. In the *United States* v. *E. C. Knight* (1895) the Supreme Court held that a monopoly of manufacture did not necessarily constitute restraint of trade, that the commerce power of Congress could not be stretched to cover the conditions of manufacturing within a state, even though the goods produced would ultimately be shipped across state lines.[43]

Within the next few years, however, the Court upheld the Sherman Act, and also the federal Interstate Commerce Commission Act in respect to agreements or regulations more directly affecting interstate trade.[44] The stage was now set for a vigorous application of the law to nationwide business. As we have seen, this resulted by 1911 in assumption by the Supreme Court of the power to pass on the reasonableness of the restraints imposed on trade by semimonopolistic companies, and then three years later, to the Clayton Act defining more specifically the character of illegal restraints.

The strict enforcement of the antitrust laws was desired by men in many small or medium-sized businesses, and the E. C. Knight case was not, in itself, a victory for the business community. In another case the same year, however, there seems little doubt that the majority of prosperous businessmen applauded the limitation placed on the taxing powers of Congress imposed by the conservative Supreme Court. In 1894 a tax on personal incomes above $4,000 a year had been inserted in the Wilson Tariff Act. This raised two constitutional questions: was this a "direct" tax and hence subject to the limitation that it could only be levied in proportion to population; and was it a "uniform" tax within the meaning of that term in the constitution. The test case was *Pollock* v. *Farmer's Loan and Trust Company*.[45] The opponents of the law argued that the tax was direct, particularly because it would be applied to income from real estate, and that it was discriminatory in taxing some 2 percent of income receivers for the benefit of the other 98 percent.

The famous attorney Joseph H. Choate, arguing against the constitutionality of the tax, told the Court, "I do not believe any member of this court has ever sat or ever will sit to hear and decide a case the consequences of which will be as far reaching as this." In some ways Choate was correct. As long as federal taxes were light and fell on consumption through tariffs and excises, saving and investment tended to be at least adequate for demand, and deflation was the chief menace to a prosperous economy. From the 1930s on, with heavy federal taxes largely raised by a progressive income tax, consumer demand tended to outrun saving and investment, and inflation became the danger to stability. Such long-run considerations were beyond the scope of business or economic thought at that time; the usual conservative opposition to the measure was that the progressive taxing of wealth was a first step toward socialism or communism.

The five-to-four decision against the constitutionality of the tax, in which it was necessary for the Court to maneuver tortuously around earlier precedents, led to a storm of protest from liberal lawyers all over the country, and coming coincidentally with the E. C. Knight decision, made the Court appear to be a reactionary body blocking progress.[46] That the Court had, in fact, gone contrary to the developing opinion of liberal business leaders was indicated by the passage of a constitutional amendment in 1913 specifically providing for a graduated income tax.

CORPORATION LAW

While the courts of the nineteenth century were trying to preserve both entrepreneurial freedom and the inviolability of contracts, the corporation as designed and manipulated by businessmen and lawyers was changing the nature of contracts themselves. A contract with a symbolic person such as a corporation that could transfer its assets to subsidiaries, that could set up other symbolic persons to take its own business away, or that could dissolve altogether only to reappear in a new form in another state was a different instrument than an agreement with a real individual. As of 1850, corporate law was only partially understood, because the railroad lawyers, the chief innovators of corporate devices, had only begun to explore the possibilities.

The corporation was involved with legislative power in respect to charters, franchises, and policies affecting social welfare, but more litigation probably arose from the relations of the corporation to its various classes of owners and creditors, or from what might be called the internal relations of the corporation. To explore these new areas of legal action with any pretense to thoroughness would require a large volume; here we can only give a few examples of the problems that troubled legislatures and courts.

When a corporation became insolvent, creditors could petition in equity for a court to appoint a receiver to take over and divide the corporate assets. Since a large number of corporations had owners and creditors living in more than one state, such actions were often argued in the federal courts. In most trade and manufacturing, the receiver wound up the operations of the firm and apportioned the proceeds to the creditors on the basis of the priority of their claims, a matter of some complexity, but one which could be brought to a reasonably rapid conclusion. In the case of public utilities, however, such as gas companies, toll bridges or railroads, the receiver had to maintain operation, and thus became a general manager as well as an agent of the court. The first case to reach the Supreme Court, in 1858, legalized the continued operation of a toll bridge with the receipts held by the receiver for the benefit of the creditors.[47]

In the depression of the 1870s, the courts were flooded with railroad receivership cases, many of which reached the United States Supreme Court. Most of the questions involved priority of claims between employees, suppliers, first, second, and chattel mortgagees, and debenture bondholders, occasionally complicated by the bankrupt line having been leased for a long period of years to another now insolvent line. Recognizing that such relationships in a going concern involved considerations new to the law, the Supreme Court in 1879 gave receivers the right to pay debts incurred for labor, supplies, and permanent improvements ahead of the claims of the first mortgage bondholders, but affirmed that the latter had first claim on the residual property.[48]

The decision encouraged one of the bizarre practices of the corporate wonderland. Since the first mortgage bondholders were generally the ones who could petition successfully for a receiver, and often with a little judicial assistance, have the received chosen from among their number, the strategic securities to own in a corporation approaching insolvency were the first mortgage bonds. The bondholder's committee with the receiver could shake off or reduce the claims of equity owners or junior creditors and run the company for an indefinite period in the interests of the owners of the first mortgage and those receiving salaries or having contracts from the road. In theory, the court should protect all classes of owners and creditors and see that the receiver acted expeditiously and in good faith. But American courts being what they were in the late nineteenth century, practice might diverge greatly from theory. Smart operators such as Jay Gould made millions from manipulating receiverships to favor certain security interests. In judging the lax corporate morals of the late nineteenth century, it should also be remembered that as Hurst says, "In this culture every presumption favored the moral worth and social contribution of the shrewd manager of men and resources."[49]

While the multiplication of types of corporate, particularly public utility, securities increased the danger of fraud, it should not be overlooked that they also drew capital not otherwise available to needed enterprises. A railroad, for example, that had exhausted the possibilities of mortgaging its fixed physical assets, could issue "debenture" bonds secured by the total value of "rolling stock" in cars and locomotives. The tendency of world and United States prices to fall from 1865 to 1896 made even these types of bonds an attractive form of investment in comparison with most common or preferred stock.

Interpretations of corporate charters and the right of the state to amend charters continued to be a source of litigation. While most states had general incorporation laws by 1860, special incorporation often remained the rule. In Wisconsin, for example, a general incorporation law was enacted in 1849, but during the next twenty-three years there were 1,130 special incorporations and only 143 charters secured under the general act. It was relatively easy to get special charters that contained just the clauses wanted by the incorporators, and no others, whereas the Wisconsin general law provided for annual reports, disclosures of stock transfer, access of stockholders to the books of the company, stockholder liability for wage debts incurred during the preceding six months, and other restrictions which many promoters preferred to avoid.[50] In 1872 an amendment to the Wisconsin constitution outlawed incorporation by special act. While the important Eastern states did not make general incorporation mandatory, the broadening or easing of the provisions of general acts, particularly in states like Delaware and New Jersey that were bidding for corporations, made special acts unnecessary.

THE AGE OF ENTERPRISE

Looking back upon these initial contests between legislators pressured to do something about increasing urban, industrial, and business problems on the one hand, and property owners anxious to avoid restrictions and develop new corporate devices on the other, it seems clear that persuasive lawyers and sympathetic judges had been able to preserve the major requisites of entrepreneurial liberty. In fact, Abrams and Levine think that much of the favorable relationship between business and government inherited from the earlier nineteenth century had been preserved by the United States Supreme Court. "Whatever the Court may have thought it was doing," they write, "it did not choose 'laissez-faire' over 'paternalism' but merely preserved a condition whereby the dominant business classes remained the protected 'wards of the state.' "[51]

To a greater degree than in the leading states of Western Europe, the courts protected freedom of contract, property rights, and freedom of business operation. Friedman calls the late nineteenth century the "golden age of contract."[52] Except for clear hazards to public health, freedom of personal contract was upheld. Only in the case of railroads, other public utilities, banks, and enterprises constituting a monopoly of trade had important concessions been made to the regulatory power of Congress, or the states and in these instances the regulations allowed probably represented the desires of a majority of the businessmen involved. But as we will see (Chapter 14), businessmen, after much talk of laissez-faire, were rediscovering the obvious fact that government could be a useful agency in stabilizing overly-competitive markets or protecting many small enterprises against a few giant corporations.

CHAPTER 13

Politics of the Free Market

In the history of American politics, the great event of the nineteenth century was the Civil War. Military coercion was resisted initially by important merchants and bankers in the Northern cities, because of a general fear of the effects of war on their immediate ties to the cotton trade.[1] In December, a meeting of leading businessmen in New York unanimously asked for reconciliation initiated by the North.[2] Peace was strongly advocated by the Northern business press up to and after the firing on Fort Sumter.[3] Yet in its long-run results, the war was, as Marx pointed out, the conquest by business of the one area of the country whose elite refused to accept the values of industrial capitalism. Gradually, in the decades after the war, the romantic, antibusiness attitudes of the planter aristocracy were submerged by the spread of nationwide values arising from the culture of industrialism. Outside the South, the Civil War had relatively little effect on the long-run shaping of social institutions by the needs of business.

Quite apart from the war, however, the mid-nineteenth century was a period of major change in the relations of business and government. It was a time when government action was still needed for charters, franchises, and grants, but when state financial participation in large enterprises was less needed or desired, and when the doctrine of strictly limiting the activities of government began to develop its greatest influence.

Private capital, as we have seen, was now strong enough to buy up most of the state-owned banks and railroads.[4] The Pennsylvania and Michigan Railroads were bought by private interests in 1846; in Indiana an excellent state bank became a private institution in 1852; Missouri largely withdrew from banking in 1857; until, in all, by 1860 there were only a few state banks and one state railroad, the Western and Atlantic of Georgia. Most of the newer states, like Wisconsin, either prohibited chartered banks or left both banks and railroads to private enterprise. Since canals and turnpikes were generally unprofitable, few were built, and the existing ones were left as government operations.

Until the decade of the sixties, some railroadmen still found it beneficial to remain active in politics. The chief executives of the New York Central, Erastus

Corning and John Pruyn, for example, were leaders of the Democratic party in Albany; Edwin D. Morgan was a New York state senator while president of the Hudson River Railroad, as was Samuel Sloan who succeeded him in both posts; Gregory Smith was a state legislator and governor of Vermont while he was receiver for the Vermont Central; Alvah Crocker, a promoter of many Massachusetts enterprises, served two terms in the legislature; and William D. Bishop, president of the Naugatuck and the New York, New Haven and Hartford Railroads served in Congress and the Connecticut state legislature.

With state works to be acquired, railroads to be projected and built, land with timber and minerals to be bought, and franchises to be allotted, it was necessary in the newer regions for many businessmen to continue to stay close to the state capitals either in the legislature or the lobby, and to be on good terms with the state administrations. In the 1850s, such activity by entrepreneurs reached its peak in heroic competitive battles in Western state legislatures for railroad charters. Each railroad interest was contending chiefly for grants of the public land given the states by the federal government. In many of these contests, the promoters, interested in too many ventures to give proper attention to any one operation, greatly underestimated the costs and difficulties of railroad construction. As a result, even where no dishonesty was involved, the original group usually failed to complete a road, and the farmers who had mortgaged their properties in order to buy railroad bonds not only lost their money, but failed for many years to secure a railroad. These and other frustrations regarding railroads made them prime targets for attack by legislators seeking public support, and produced antagonism between railroad managers and politicians.

THE DETERIORATION OF STATE GOVERNMENTS

As the business world, both East and West, grew in size and complexity, and leading entrepreneurs in most types of business became too busy to devote themselves to politics, relations with government entered a new phase. In states where the initial charters, franchises, land grants, and regulatory structure had generally been established, attendance at the state legislatures became less important. By the post-Civil War years, "Wisconsin people," writes James Willard Hurst, became "busy with private business, from which public affairs were an annoying distraction."[5] Contemporary journalist E. L. Godkin thought that "the railroad and the telegraph increased the pace of life so that it was impossible for men to pay any fruitful attention to politics without neglecting their private affairs."[6] As a consequence, a period of decline in the prestige and ability of state legislators set in that was only somewhat arrested by political regulatory and reform movements that began in the late 1880s. Viewing the process of deterioration at about its lowest depth, James Bryce could write of state legislatures: "A place is valued chiefly for its salary, or for such opportunities of obliging friends or securing commissions on contracts as it may present."[7] To find able men willing to devote their full time to state administration was even more difficult than attracting good men to the legislatures—a problem that has never been altogether solved in American state and local government. This partly explains why the practical impact of nineteenth-century government was more through judicial enforcement of the law than through continuously operative public policy.

The two-party system in the hands of poorly educated politicians in the legislatures and continually shifting and venal state administrators left a need for some men with continuing knowledge and ability to run the "government market." This need came to be supplied, almost universally, by the "boss." Usually a successful lawyer or businessman who craved power and liked people, the boss controlled the party as a business organization. He ran the informal, sub rosa machinery, and by so doing he largely directed the distribution of official positions. He decided which requests by business were politically viable or marketable and which were too extreme. In some instances, particularly in the 1870s and 1880s, he was more powerful than any other man or interest in the state. Lincoln Steffens writes of the blind boss of Rhode Island: "General [Charles R.] Brayton received in the sheriff's office the lines of visitors who had business with the State, openly. And openly he did that business. He ran the Legislature across the hall. He said so; everybody knew it; and he ran it for businessmen."[8]

There was a hierarchy of bosses. Each county had one, and the major cities had bosses who could deal on nearly equal terms with the boss of the state. Each major party had its hierarchy, but since local political power, either Democratic or Republican, tended to be traditional and relatively permanent, the bosses of the party in power made the allotments of money and jobs, and the bosses of the local minority party accepted a share and ran a small complacent organization.

The failure of government to take action to alleviate slum conditions, dependency from sickness, industrial accidents, and other causes of destitution, gave city and county bosses another type of function that accounted for much of their power. By dispensing philanthropy and employment, the local boss attached the poorest voters to his regime. The fact that the party machines profited from this philanthropic function made them as disinclined as were the larger taxpayers to have government officially enter the field. During the 1870s, most of the major cities discountinued outdoor relief, that is, support of indigent families in their own homes, and relied only on poor houses and emergency "soup kitchens."[9] Thus what Louis Hartz calls the "New American Whiggery," with its extreme emphasis on individualism, personal responsibility, and self-help, played a part in supporting bossism.[10]

THE USE OF ASSOCIATIONS

One way for businessmen to achieve continuing, long-range political pressure without sacrificing too much of their time was by forming associations to accomplish the desired ends. The growing size of the national market, legal impediments to intercompany agreements, intense city rivalries, and perhaps a high degree of cooperativeness in most Americans also stimulated a proliferation of voluntary associations, local, state, and national. Since businessmen in firms not big enough to afford continuous individual legislative influence were the mainstay of these associations, they often represented opposition of smaller firms against the big companies that, in general, refused to join the organizations. For example, the Iron and Steel Association was prior to 1912 an organization of the small firms in the industry, and the American Bankers Association did not represent the big Wall Street banks. Seen another way, associations could serve as the medium-sized businessman's protection against big companies using government regulations to squeeze out weaker competitors.

Often allied with the industry trade associations, but working for regional rather than national ends, were chambers of commerce, boards of trade, commercial clubs, and many other city organizations. Such groups formed for both business and political purposes were not wholly new. Following the New York chamber of commerce, founded in 1768, Charleston, New Haven, and Philadelphia had formed similar bodies by the early nineteenth century.[11] These early chambers of commerce were interested in providing for arbitration of commercial disputes and in enforcing honest labeling, weights, measures, and quality for the purpose of expanding local trade. Thirty or more cities, including the leading ones of the Middle West, had started chambers of commerce or boards of trade before the Civil War.[12] Some of these agencies such as the Chicago Board of Trade (established in 1848 to run the primary wheat market) were organizations for specific services; others were concerned generally with the advancement of local business and civic interests. In the late nineteenth century, such organizations appeared in nearly all American cities.

They were used continually by local business to bring needed laws or modifications of regulations to the attention of the state legislatures or Congress. In the course of one month in 1880, for example, memorials or resolutions were read in the United States Senate from the chambers of commerce of New York, Pittsburgh, St. Louis, St. Paul, and Milwaukee, and the boards of trade of Bangor and Oswego.[13] In their own states the business associations backed programs of promotive regulation, civic improvement, and helped to secure the licensing of professions and trades to protect local practitioners from out-of-state competitors.[14]

Local commercial associations were chiefly supported by the more substantial merchants, who generally outnumbered the manufacturers. Inevitably these firms had interests different from those of interstate companies, such as common carriers or manufacturers with many plants. As champions of the interests of small shippers, for example, the local associations came into violent conflict with the railroads. The venerable New York Chamber of Commerce fought with the trunk-lines during the 1870s and 1880s, sponsoring a regulatory bill which New Yorkers said was defeated because the state senate was dominated by the railroads. In these struggles the chamber was aided in the mid-1870s by a Cheap Transportation Association reputedly representing the small to medium-sized shippers of the nation.[15] In opposition to these pressures, specially favored shippers along the route of the New York Central formed a Merchants', Manufacturers', and Farmers' Union to prevent railroad regulation.[16] Similar internecine warfare went on between organized groups over every aspect of public policy that concerned business.

In the long run, the local boards and chambers became chiefly promotional agencies for their areas, publishing literature on locational advantages, working for civic improvements of economic value, and setting up plans to attract new business. The intensity of these activities varied greatly from place to place. In large old centers like the East Coast ports the chambers of commerce confined themselves chiefly to political pressures to protect business or to improve local trade, and to collecting and publishing useful information. But in cities of the West, such organizations sponsored local tax exemption for new manufacturing firms, got local capitalists or banks to set up loan or subsidy funds to assist new plants, and sent representatives around the country to attract companies to the home city. When more money was needed in loans or subsidies to secure new companies, local newspaper editors ran campaigns to aid the commercial club or chamber of commerce.

By the end of the century there were some 3,000 commercial organizations and at least 100 national bodies.[17] Obviously such a bewildering array of business pressure groups needed coordination, some association that might speak for, at least, a large number of them. A National Board of Trade, founded in Boston in 1868, offering a Washington lobby for the benefit of all business groups, tried for several decades to serve this purpose.[18] The board adopted a number of causes such as creation of a Department of Commerce, improvement of waterways, international remonetization of silver, and establishment of a federal commission as a step toward tariff reform, but its main efforts prior to 1887 were for railroad regulation.[19] By the nineties, it was working for the revival of an American merchant marine, and expansion of trade, but its influence was waning.

FEDERAL POLICIES IN LAND AND TRANSPORTATION

Prior to the 1870s, businessmen looked to the federal government chiefly for small subsidies, aid in building transportation, protection against imports, and help in the acquisition of public land. In this period, federal regulation of internal business relations was almost never an issue, chiefly because no business group saw anything to be gained by invoking the use of this power. When Congress finally undertook regulation by the Interstate Commerce Act of 1887 and the Sherman Act of 1890, the situation had so altered that a majority of businessmen undoubtedly wanted and brought about such federal action. But before 1900 neither act was interpreted by the courts in a way that would accomplish the aims of those supporting the laws or greatly bother those opposed.

In the middle of the century, expenditures that would directly aid business often ran above 10 percent of the relatively small federal expenses and in some years over a third. From 1845 to 1860, ocean-going steamships received federal grants. Railroads and ships received mail contracts that amounted to subsidies. Western rivers needed continuous federal expenditures to maintain navigation; roads and canals were aided; and the expansion of the network of military outposts brought business to their areas. Railroads frequently benefitted from government surveys and engineering advice.[20] Henry W. Broude concludes that "all these were responsible to some degree for the introduction of new money into the remoter areas, giving rise to higher expectations and subsequent investment activity."[21]

The policy of using the public lands to aid transportation ventures, either public or private, began with a grant to Ohio at the time of its admission as a state in 1803 for westward extension of the "National Road," but the policy was not actively continued. In 1823 Ohio received another federal grant for a road between Columbus and Sandusky, with the type of clause that was to become usual, and ultimately to cost transcontinental railroads many millions of dollars: "no toll shall at any time be collected . . . of any troops, or property of the United States."[22] Four years later a grant was made to Indiana for a north-south road. These two acts, disposing of 251,000 acres, were the only highway grants before the Civil War. From 1863 to 1869 seven more, totalling a little over 3,000,000 acres, were made for roads on the frontiers, and then the policy was abandoned.[23] Between 1824 and 1866 Congress granted some 4.6 million acres to canal companies, most of which were state rather than private enterprises.[24]

The most important instances of federal aid were land grants to private companies for railroad promotion. From 1835 on, Congress frequently granted railroads rights of way through the public lands and the privilege of using adjacent timber, stone, and earth. An act in 1852 made this policy general. By then the pressure of railroad interests in Congress for land grants was becoming strong enough to produce large-scale action. In 1850 Senator Douglas of Illinois skillfully organized congressional support for the passage of a land grant to the State of Illinois in aid of the Illinois Central Railroad. This act, providing for the transfer of some 7,000,000 acres of good farming land, introduced the practice of reserving alternate sections of land for government sale at no less than a minimum of $2.50 per acre. Through this system, it was argued, the land grants to private companies would cost the government nothing, as the remaining alternate sections would sell for twice as much.

For the next few years only two railroad groups were able, on a small scale, to duplicate Senator Douglas' feat of lining up the necessary votes, but in 1856 and 1857 many years of lobbying were rewarded by the granting of nearly 20,000,000 acres to the North and South Central States for railroad purposes. This largess precipitated the battles for railroad land grants in the state legislatures, referred to earlier.

By 1862, the withdrawal of Southern legislators broke a deadlock over routes, and the heightened nationalism of the war period led Congress to charter transcontinental railroads. Congressman John Pruyn of New York, who was also treasurer of the New York Central Railroad, argued that since the government was going to have to supply almost all the money, it ought to own and build the road. "I do believe," he said, "that the road could be built by the government ... not only cheaper, but better ... because they [government supervisors] would have in view all of the great elements of durability and usefulness."[25] But the day had passed when Pruyn's argument might have been seriously considered. The only real contests were over the details of the private arrangements. The easy defeat of Pruyn's plan for federal construction of a transcontinental railroad contrasts with the equally easy victory in New York half a century earlier of those who proposed state construction and ownership for the Erie Canal. The two instances mark the rise in prestige of business entrepreneurs: in the earlier case private enterprise for vast works was not trusted, even by large capitalists; by the time of the latter case the public trusted private operators and lacked confidence in political administrators.

Two companies, the Union Pacific to build from the East and the Central Pacific to start from the West, were chartered in 1862, but since the government assistance offered was not sufficient to attract private investors, more liberal charters were issued in 1864. These charters were the first granted by the federal government since the Second Bank of the United States in 1816. They provided for a large issue of government bonds on a mileage basis, which would be a second mortgage, thus allowing the company to sell first mortgage bonds to investors. In addition each road received a land grant of twenty sections per mile.

As Robert W. Fogel has pointed out, this ingenious scheme for securing private construction of a "premature" development, in which very few people could see hope of legitimate profit within any calculable time, produced paradoxical situations. While business in general and farmers along the route would gain from the railroad, the entrepreneurs of the venture believed that they would have to make their profit from construction. The result was relatively costly and poor construction, which yielded the contractors high profits and occasioned a congressional scandal. Both Fogel and the contemporary railroad pundit John Murray Forbes of Boston have concluded that considering the difficulties, the risks, and the public needs, the profits were justifiable.[26] *

---

* Charles Perkins remarked some twenty-five years later: "The Union Pacific has so far had Congress and the Courts on its side and two generations of speculators have grown rich out of it—one out of the construction and another out of the profits of operating the Road" (Cochran, *Railroad Leaders*, 189).

The policy of large land grants to private companies for transcontinental construction was continued in charters to a dozen companies between 1864 and 1871. In all, some 130,000,000 acres of public land were transferred directly by the federal government to Western roads, and some 50,000,000 additional acres through the states. Eah of the federal charters contained a provision for special rates on troops and government freight.

The federal government supervised the dispersing of both the railroad grants and others to states for various purposes, and also directed purchase, preemption, and homesteading by settlers and speculators. These duties placed a burden on the public land office for which Congress refused to provide.[27] In fact, Congress was apparently not interested in enforcing a systematic honest handling of public land questions, perhaps because too many people close to government were profiting from the general confusion in policy and administration.[28]

OTHER BUSINESS INTERESTS IN FEDERAL POWER

Congressmen and the national party leaders represented men of considerably more ability than those found in state government, but they inevitably shared the nonintellectual, pragmatic business attitudes of the day. A British observer of the 1850s said that he saw members of Congress "betraying a practical contempt for all knowledge not palpably convertible to the purposes of pecuniary profit.... In short, it strikes me that American legislators are more remarkable for acuteness than foresight; for those qualities of intellect which lead men to profit by experience than those which enable them to direct it."[29]

Successful, continuing business influence in such Congresses required more attention and consistency of purpose than the members of most trades or industries possessed. "Despite significant expenditures and efforts, from the most legitimate to the most questionable," writes David J. Rothman, "business interests could not successfully prejudice the legislative process. Their methods were too haphazard."[30] Considering the nearly mandatory force of some local pressures on congressmen the statement seems rather extreme, but there is little doubt of the intermittent haphazard character of most business lobbying.

Individual wealthy men also found national politics baffling and unrewarding. August Belmont, for example, a leading financier and the U.S. representative of the Rothschilds, was unable to influence national Democratic party politics in favor of his candidates. In 1884 he complained to his son: "I have been for 40 years an active and for more than 30 years a prominent man in the party, have been Chairman of the National Committee and have spent $500,000, if I have spent one dollar, in the service of the party. What do I get in return? ... I have not even had the recognition of being asked to speak [in the Cleveland campaign]."[31] Belmont's complaint indicates not so much the party's lack of respect for his wealth and prestige, as it does the division of business interests within it, each group working for their own ends and candidates.

Tariff legislation, while producing some of the earliest continuing pressure groups in Washington, is an excellent example of the divisions within business. Since business attitudes toward the tariff varied all the way from active demands for more protection through indifference to equally strong demands for free trade, with some of the extremes occuring within the same industry, tariff legislation produced periodic battles between opposing lobbyists.[32] The iron and steel interests and the carpet and worsted manufacturers were among the earlier groups to set up permanent Washington lobbies. John L. Hayes, one of the innovating pioneers in lobby tactics and public relations, represented both groups successively from 1850 to his death in 1887, while in his spare time he translated Latin hymns.

The excise taxes and rapid tariff increases of the Civil War period led other interests to form associations that could aid the legislative aims of business and support representatives in Washington. The United States Iron and Steel Association began the publication of a monthly protariff bulletin, edited by James M. Swank from 1873 to 1914. Swank also managed the American Industrial Associaton for which he wrote public relations pamphlets favoring the tariff with statistically backed arguments. He frequently appeared at hearings on the tariff and conducted himself so professionally that in 1882 President Arthur thought it politically safe to appoint him chairman of a congressional tariff commission. In his role as a commissioner he recommended reductions; later, in his role as a lobbyist he opposed those affecting his industry.

Because of the internecine business warfare over the tariff, some seasoned politicians came to regard it as a local issue, dependent on the interests of each congressional district. But on the whole, the interests that wanted some particular increase in rates were prepared to spend more energy and money to secure it than interests like the railroads, that were in principle opposed to all barriers to trade, were willing to spend to prevent the increase. It would not pay the railroads, for example, to work as hard to prevent an increase in the worsted schedule, as it would pay particular woolen manufacturers to work to secure it. Furthermore, coalitions of interests wanting protection where each member supported all the increases sought by the others were often unbeatable, particularly in the Senate where the numbers were small.

Thus, in spite of the periodic attacks by the low-tariff interests, and strong campaigns for reduction by President Cleveland, the tariff remained high until Woodrow Wilson threw the whole force of his newly elected administration behind the Underwood Bill of 1913. While this act reduced rates to the general levels of the 1850s, every industry was presumably given protection enough to make its products competitive on an equal footing with those from abroad.

On many other matters of economic policy, businessmen were equally divided. Some wanted a deflationary, sound money policy, others preferred controlled inflation; some wanted to Republicanize the South, others wanted government by the conservative Democrats; some wanted government help in exploiting foreign markets, others were isolationist. Speaking of the period after the Civil War, Stanley Coben says, "Actually, northeastern businessmen had no unified economic program to promote. Important business groups within the region opposed each other on almost every significant economic question."[33]

A more generalized business interest in the use of federal power was stimulated during the long depression of the 1870s by fears of radically led mass-movements and state and local regulations deemed harmful to profits. The overthrow of French government control in Paris by the National Guard for two months in 1871 was incorrectly interpreted by conservative American business-men as the victory of the socialist working class. The Second International dominated by Marxian ideas established its headquarters in New York in 1872, and in spite of its largely German membership and rapid disintegration during the depression, Americans began to fear a new kind of revolution.

The widespread and often disorderly character of the railroad strikes of 1877 and the ineffective action of the state national guard units caused further alarm. *Harper's Weekly* said, "The time has come in this country when there must be the most ample and ready supply of the organized force necessary to maintain order at all costs."[34] Just as Shays' rebellion of 1786 had led to a conservative demand for more central power, the great railroad strikes gave some businessmen a desire for more of the strong uniform order that only national government could provide. This willingness to increase federal police power did not necessarily involve a greater participation by businessmen in national politics. Yet the fact that businessmen looked to Washington for protection could not help but bring an increased interest in federal activities. Meanwhile, reform of the civil service, starting in 1883, was making national parties less able to raise money from office holders and hence more dependent on contributions from business, while close elections made it advisable for the political leaders to appease all interests.[35] In 1884 Grover Cleveland more directly represented the business interest in national politics, as did his opponent James G. Blaine, than had earlier been the rule. The Allison-Aldrich leadership in the Senate marked a return of direct participation by a few substantial businessmen, although, in general, the new business interest was to operate indirectly through contributions and other influence.

THE END OF AN ERA

By the 1890s, a decade of business troubles, the relatively disinterested attitude of most businessmen toward public policy was coming to an end. Problems of many varieties were growing up around the free market and lessening the beneficence of its operation. Overproduction and resulting discon-tent on farms; the failure of cities to provide decent housing or adequate care for their poor; the problems of absorbing Eastern European immigrants in the industrial labor force; and the expensive and poor government provided by venal politicians left to their own devices all challenged the concept of the self-regulating society.

While during this period of competitive allocation of political or business rewards, economic development had been rapid, it seemed clear to young German-educated scholars that other policies might lead to still better results.* When natural resources still seemed unlimited, wasteful methods could be tolerated, but with the end of some of these in sight, conservation seemed necessary. As machinery became more complicated and expensive, highly capitalized firms looked askance at freely competitive national markets. In addition, the rise of scientific knowledge was producing a general climate of opinion favorable to planned corrective action rather than laissez-faire.

Hence the years from 1887 to around 1900 mark a break in political attitudes and actions that makes it impossible to treat the period 1850 to 1915 as a unit. From 1850 to 1887 there had probably been less regulation of business by the central government than in any other industrial nation in the world, and many American businessmen would look back on this time as a golden age of free enterprise. Yet, while liking the system that placed politics in a secondary or degraded position, the businessmen, and much of the rest of the nation, lost respect for the men who performed the necessary government services. "When all political campaigners plead the venality of each other," writes Earl Latham, "and all businessmen argue which of them is the more virtuous, it may be supposed that stereotypes became fixed in the public consciousness (or unconsciousness) of the politician as a suspicious character and that of the businessman as a praiseworthy fellow."[36] In no other industrial nation were government officials actually looked down upon by the highest elite. Such a situation, in which the custodians of sovereign power were regarded as incompetent to exercise it, was essentially unstable and was bound to inspire efforts at correction.

---

* Japan also had a higher growth rate than the United States in some decades, but Japanese practices seem to have had little or no impact, whereas the German experience led to the rise of institutional economics that guided Progressive thinkers.

CHAPTER 14

The Age of Administration Begins

Characterizations of the twentieth century as one of managerial enterprise, labor bureaucracy, or dictatorship have one element in common: the emerging system had to operate through hierarchical administration. By the late nineteenth century, movements toward specialization and professionalism in all branches of activity, plus better technical education, led to a more systematic understanding of the importance of good administration. New concepts, applied first in large-scale business, inevitably began to generate ideas for reforming political procedures.[1] Reform, in general, meant making the locally oriented politician more responsive to administrative control from above in the interests of efficient business and social policy. This movement was noticeable in national politics as early as the 1880s, but in state and local politics scarcely before the 1890s. In a broad sense it may be seen as the reshaping of politics to fit new business ideas of efficiency in administration and regulation, both of which required that decisions be made on the basis of more expert knowledge. While much of the reforming energy was spent at the state and local levels, both Presidents Roosevelt and Taft subscribed to the need for greater administrative efficiency.[2]

Local pressures for reform in these directions were likely to originate in chambers of commerce or other business associations, while congressional regulations or reforms were usually sponsored by national business or professional associations or by informal groups of business leaders.[3] By the early 1900s the national atmosphere had been so charged by journalists and civic betterment associations with their campaigns for greater political efficiency, couched more in social than in business terms, that on occasion the aroused enthusiasm of the voters led to politicians sponsoring laws not altogether desired by business or professional organizations. The language used, not necessarily hypocritically, by inspired political leaders gave a highly deceptive coloration of democracy and the triumph of the people over the sinister forces of selfish interest or monopoly. In fact, however, the business interests were often financing the campaign for reform, and working to have efficient business practices applied to politics.[4] "When the middle class citizen who wished to wrest control from the urban boss . . . , spoke of 'the people,' " writes Robert C. Bannister, Jr., "he really meant the educated, public-spirited middle class who had organized chambers of commerce, united charities and civic improvement associations."[5]

THE UPPER CLASSES ORGANIZE

The new phase of state and local political evolution seems to have had its origins in gradual recognition of the fact that bosses, particularly municipal ones, too often represented the interests of the politicians who had to run local wards, as against the interests of the elite groups of business and professional men who were interested in the city as a growing economic unit. The famous muckraking journalist Lincoln Steffens saw the businessman as the typical urban citizen whose aim was to elect a businessman as mayor and "let him introduce business methods into politics and government."[6] Led by chambers of commerce and other business, civic, and upper-class philanthropic organizations, movements for municipal reform spread widely in the 1890s and early 1900s, temporarily replacing bosses with businesslike city managers, and electing commissions or boards of aldermen at large rather than by individual wards.[7]

In one sense "municipal reform" was another phase of the intense rivalry of urban communities for more business. In earlier decades, local merchants had been well aware of the losses being sustained from bad government, but had not been well enough organized to take control.[8] By the 1890s the business community had the trade and civic associations necessary for more effective action. In Chicago, for example, Lyman J. Gage was president of both the First National Bank and the Civic Associations, and he was supported in "cleaning up" the city by local millionaires and publishers. They not only elected a reform mayor but introduced a "business-like Civil Service."[9] In Cleveland the chamber of commerce drew up a housing code, campaigned for public health and welfare, and formed a committee to beautify the city.[10] In Rochester, New York, a leading businessman elected as mayor set forth the doctrine that "a city, like an industry, profits more by investing than by hoarding its talents." The "investment" included expanded schools, better streets, proper fire protection, and civic beautification.[11] In Boston, department store owner Edward A. Filene and a group representing the principal business and professional associations invited Lincoln Steffens to diagnose the ills of the city.[12]

These reform administrations set about trying to make the city a more efficient business organization. It was recognized that unsanitary slums, buildings that were fire hazards, child labor, poor schooling, and failure to provide for growth and traffic were detriments to the material progress of the community. Quickly the urban elite discovered that for most major reforms they needed state action, and pressures for efficiency were transferred to the state bosses and the legislators, who, often in the absence of effective counter pressures, gave way rather easily. In some instances, business leaders successfully ran for governorships.[13] Recent studies "emphasize the role of trade and business groups . . . and suggest that they were more characteristic sources of change in the Progressive era than were farm or labor organizations."[14]

Yet, because of distinguished leadership, it is easy to overestimate the rather sudden interest of businessmen in reform. On the one hand, groups of businessmen had, as we have seen, always urged various specific regulations. Even in the corrupt 1880s, for example, "in an age which is frequently remembered only for its party battles and bosses, New York began the creation of that structure of social legislation that today is among its most distinctive features."[15] On the other hand, some individual businessmen and business organizations were practically always opposed to specific instances of promotive regulation or laws for greater governmental efficiency.

Similarly, the wave of business enthusiasm for municipal reform was not shared by the beneficiaries of corruption, and had varying results in different types of cities. In the country market towns, business had always been in control, and the bosses, if one may call them that, were businessmen. Of Wisconsin, James Willard Hurst writes, "substantial mill owners controlled local government in their operating areas as a routine aspect of business."[16] In medium-sized cities the efforts of business associations had their greatest success, either replacing the bosses or forcing them to recognize the needs of the upper-class reformers. The greatest spread of the city manager plan was at this urban level. In the big cities, however, the war between the lower-class interests of the ward leaders supporting a boss and the upper-class interests of the civic associations was never over, and the largest American cities alternated between control by businesslike "reformers" and by the machines of the ward politicians (Chapter 20).

Regardless of their success in introducing efficiency in municipal government, the business organizations played an important role in competitive promotion of the city. This was a particularly important function in the developing areas of the West, as it has been on the East Coast in the early part of the century. According to the Brookfield newspaper, for example, "at least six Missouri towns, including Brookfield, obtained factories by means of subsidies."[17] In 1907 the Brookfield Commercial Club raised a $60,000 bonus to bring the Brown Shoe Company to the town and "the city also agreed to furnish free a factory site, water, and sewage disposal."[18]

The business-inspired civic associations continued to multiply in the early twentieth century. By 1912 the Department of Commerce listed 3,356 local, 183 state or territorial, and 243 interstate associations. "Commercial club" was the most popular title with 868 entries, "board of trade" next with 490 and "chamber of commerce" third with 414.[19] Since in 1910 there were only 768 American cities with populations of 8,000 or more, there must have been few or none without some such organization. These groups interested in civic welfare and promotion were added to by the so-called service clubs, designed to promote sociability, exchange of useful information, and the welfare of the business community. Rotary, the first of the new clubs, began in 1905. One outstanding man in each line of business in the particular city was invited to join. The meetings were weekly luncheons at which there were lectures and discussions. As Rotary spread rapidly, Kiwanis (1914) and Lions (1917) Clubs were formed to include more of the business community, and none of the clubs adhered strictly to having only one representative of each type of business. By 1915 service clubs were beginning to be important institutions for the formation of business opinion on community affairs and the organization of local business action.

A NATIONAL CHAMBER OF COMMERCE

Heightened federal activity, both foreign and domestic, and frequently conflicting business interests made it seem desirable to have some moderate, conservative organization that could speak for business as a whole. The National Association of Manufacturers (Chapter 11), whose membership rose from about 1,000 in 1900 to 3,500 in 1914, hoped to be such a spokesman, but its opinionated, aggressive leaders divided its ranks.[20] For example, while President Van Cleave and the Washington lobbyists of NAM tried to weaken the Food and Drugs Law of 1906, the Pure Food Committee of the association worked actively to keep the original bill intact.[21] Furthermore, although the NAM worked for such general business causes as the establishment of the Department of Commerce (1903) and vocational education, it was still an organization limited to small manufacturers, with its greatest emphasis on combatting the "closed shop." By 1907, attempts were underway to subordinate both the NAM and the old National Board of Trade to a new superorganization, the National Council of Commerce. Poorly promoted by men in the government, it failed to gain strength. The movement that finally succeeded was undertaken cooperatively in 1909 by the Boston Chamber and the Chicago Association of Commerce.

Led by moderate progressives such as the widely known pioneer of new employee relations, Edward A. Filene, the group appealed to Charles Nagel, the Secretary of Commerce, for federal aid in establishing a national organization. Seeing such a move as good Republican politics, government officials persuaded President Taft in 1911 to recommend the formation of a United States Chamber of Commerce. After a small planning conference, he issued a letter inviting some thousand business associations to send delegates to a founding convention.[22]

Prior to 1915, the United States Chamber of Commerce exerted little influence on either legislation or public opinion. Eschewing political partisanship, its first president, Chicago banker Harry A. Wheeler, said that the chamber marked "the death for all time of a lobby system."[23] The mild character of its pronouncements, based on referendums of the membership, disgusted the militant president of the NAM and also led the American Bankers' Association and the National Founders Association to resign. Meanwhile, big business as usual remained aloof. But the chamber survived, and in later years with more vigorous policies, it came closer than any other organization to being a spokesman for the majority of American businessmen.

THE REGULATION OF NATIONWIDE BUSINESS

By the 1880s a wide gap in interest was opening between small-scale business and its associations and the few large companies that monopolized or threatened to monopolize markets. Consequently many of the lobbyists sent by urban business associations to Washington urged regulation of big enterprise in order to control competition for the benefit of smaller firms. Congressmen from the farm states and lobbyists for organizations such as the Farmers Union, the Grange, and the stronger farmers' cooperatives were also among the representatives of "small business" anxious to regulate the railroads and tax or destroy the trusts. As farmers grew more prosperous in the years just before World War I, western and southern farm state Progressives became increasingly important in shaping national legislation.

Federal regulation, however, was also favored by a number of big business leaders. The influx of new competition was particularly demoralizing in industries where all companies had high capital overhead. Speaking before the Massachusetts Reform Club, to an audience that included many businessmen who felt this kind of pressure, Charles Warren said that the club was united "in a broad way on one principle, namely that the government is best whose interference is least, and least often felt . . . . But government interference may be more beneficial to the public than the present system of ruinous competition between private companies."[24]

The unsettling effects of extreme competition among highly capitalized enterprises was most obvious in the case of the railroads whose rates affected all other business firms. Here the division was really three-fold, with the big shippers who could bargain successfully for special rates on one side, the small shippers who protested discrimination on the other, and the railroads in the middle. The roads wanted protection for their heavily bonded properties against all types of low rates whether forced on them by powerful companies or state regulations. If such protection could be secured, the roads could reduce rates for most small shippers.

The competitive situation became more chaotic in the early eighties, which meant more special rebates to big shippers, and more rate cutting by roads hungry for traffic. In the boom year that commenced in 1879, parallel lines were built merely to force existing roads to buy them, and rate wars sprang up everywhere. In addition, state regulation reached new heights and interfered with any effective control of rates by private associations.

Railroad men had long advocated legalization of pooling as the solution to excessive competition (Chapter 10), but associations representing shippers were strongly opposed to giving such power to the roads.[25] On the issue of a federal commission with power to fix rates, railroad men were divided. If regulation by the federal government was to be the solution, they preferred a commission or a court, but many still felt uneasy over extensions of government power.[26] Early in 1886, however, the Senate Committee on Interstate Commerce reported that it had "found among the leading representatives of the railroad interests an increasing readiness to accept the aid of Congress in working out the solution of the railroad problem."[27]

With no interests strongly opposed, Congress was able in 1887 to pass the Interstate Commerce Act providing that all rates should be "reasonable and just," prohibiting rebates and higher charges for short hauls, establishing a five-man commission to administer the law, and providing that rulings of the commission could be appealed directly to the circuit courts. But the act also forbade pooling, which the roads preferred to rate regulation by any government agency.[28]

In spite of a commission friendly to the railroads, the system worked poorly. The courts in general failed to sustain the commission, and no one was sure of the meaning of the law.[29] Business organizations, such as the Detroit and Indianapolis Boards of Trade, angered by the prorailroad attitude of the commission, wanted repeal of the law.[30] While many railroad men agreed with President Melvin E. Ingalls of the Cincinnati, Chicago and St. Louis that the commission "could never make a rate so bad as some we have made ourselves if they tried," executives generally wanted the law amended to legalize pooling, punish shippers for extorting special rates, and allow greater flexibility in freight classification.[31] At least one bill to allow pooling was said to have been killed by the big and favored shippers.[32]

Senator Elkins of West Virginia, a railroad owner himself, framed an act in 1902 designed to give the roads what they wanted. As finally passed in 1903, it was not entirely satisfactory, but was a distinct improvement over the chaotic existing situation. Rebates were prohibited with a fine of $20,000 against the shipper for each violation. Joint rates filed with the commission "shall be deemed to be the legal rate and any departure from such rate ... shall be deemed to be an offense." This, in effect, legalized pooling.

While the railroads were now reasonably content, shippers were not. Both Southern and Western manufacturers objected to the fact that the heavier flow of manufactured goods in their direction from the East led to lower rates than those on their own products shipped the opposite way.[33] In addition, prices were advancing, and with the joint proviso railroads were in a better position to raise rates. By 1906 there was sufficient pressure by shippers on Congress to bring about a new law, the Hepburn Act, which changed the situation in minor ways. The railroads welcomed its stronger provisions regarding rebates and special rates and the prohibition of passes, but not the extension of the control of the commission to bookkeeping. Yet many railroad men thought that in view of the political strength of the millions of shippers, the roads had come out well.

Voicing such sentiment, President A. B. Stickney of the Chicago, Great Western said, "The country is indebted to Theodore Roosevelt for his courageous course in regard to legislative control of rates," and the chief executives of the New York, New Haven and Hartford and the Pennsylvania Railroads, at least, concurred.[34]

The Bureau of Labor Statistics Wholesale Price Index rose by nearly one-third between 1900 and 1910, and the railroads suffered from increasing costs, a problem accentuated by a lower volume of traffic in the aftermath of the panic of 1907. In the spring of 1908 George W. Perkins of J. P. Morgan and Co., representing the railroad investor's interests, alarmed the shippers by negotiating a general railroad agreement to increase rates. Midwestern shippers quickly organized a new association, the National Industrial Traffic League, to battle the railroads, while Taft in his campaign for the presidency talked ambiguously of regulatory action in the railroad situation.

Early in 1910 President Taft asked for enactment of a new regulatory bill, which was drawn up by advisors friendly to the railroads. The ensuing struggle initially pitted the administration, conservative congressional leaders, and the railroads against the Progressive Republicans, the Democrats, and numerous associations representing shippers. Speaking for this opposition, Senator Robert M. La Follette of Wisconsin called the original administration bill "the rankest, boldest betrayal of public interest ever proposed in any legislative body."[35] As might be expected, in view of the strength of the opposition, the bill was amended in ways adverse to the roads, particularly by eliminating legalized pooling, which forced the carriers to oppose further action.

In the final Mann-Elkins Act, the railroads secured a five-man commerce court to hear appeals from the Interstate Commerce Commission, while the shippers gained power for the commission to suspend rate changes up to ten months pending hearings. During the years that the commerce court functioned, the railroads won about 90 percent of their appeals, joint-rate associations (pools) were upheld, and state regulation set aside. But the court overreached itself. The Supreme Court decided against it in important cases, and the special tribunal survived in 1912 only because Taft vetoed an act for its abolition. Weakened still further by revelations of corruption on its bench, the commerce court was abolished by Congress late in 1913.

Thus in the long run, the shipper's associations had proven too strong and persistent for the railroads.[36] During the course of these five years of legislative warfare, the roads relearned the need for public relations men in addition to their able Washington and state lobbyists. Led initially by the Pennsylvania Railroad with the ingenious Ivy Lee, the roads set up publicity offices and strove, as in the 1880s, to present a more conciliatory image to the public.[37]

No doubt executives of other big corporations would have preferred legalized regulation of overly competitive markets through trade associations or pools, but, as in the case of the railroads, political pressure by organizations representing small business and other antimonopoly groups forced the big companies to seek protective regulation by congressional acts. In the case of markets depressed in both price and quality by cutthroat competition, demands for regulation might arise from the representatives of both buyers and sellers. The big meat packers, for example, wanted certain types of federal regulation as did the advocates of pure food, which did not mean, of course, that there were no disagreements over specific provisions. The leading companies wanted to regularize conditions of competition among a rapidly increasing number of small packers and to establish federal inspection practices that would satisfy the European import requirements.[38] Other big food and beverage companies favored regulation that would force higher standards on small competitors and protect the large national advertisers in their relations with consumers. For example, Fred Pabst, one of the biggest brewers, testified that a regulatory law "would be a very good thing."[39] As a result of these combined pressures, a Pure Food Act was passed in 1906 that appeared as a victory for consumers, but was at the same time satisfactory to many of the big producers.

Unlike the railroad situation where the majority of all businessmen secured regulations that were resisted by those in the industry involved, or unlike food and drugs where the big-business minority in the industry, by making some concessions, won regulation of small competitors, the Federal Reserve Act of 1914 is, rather, an example of regulation of market conditions designed to suit a majority of those actually operating in the particular business. Banking reform was a matter on which neither President Wilson nor Carter Glass of the House Committee on Banking and Currency had any preconceived ideas. The Owen-Glass bill that formed the basis for the system was framed by the pulling and pushing of big-city bankers who wanted a private central bank, by the pressure of part of the American Bankers Association that wanted a new system but no central bank, by the resistance of some country bankers who wanted no action at all, and by the opinions of various experts from banking and the academic world.[40] Thus, while bankers and their experts fought with each other for a year over the terms of the act, it was a quarrel within the banking fraternity and not to any important extent a struggle with politicians seeking to represent the wishes of the voters. As Carter Glass put it: "Almost everybody with whom you confer about a matter of this kind is more or less unyielding in his attitude and feels that unless he can get incorporated in the bill everything he thinks should be there he does not regard the bill with favor."[41] But the final act undoubtedly pleased a majority of the bankers and the business community.

The Clayton Act of 1914, attempting stricter definition of antitrust policies, was supported in principle by the United States Chamber of Commerce and by small blusiness. It was, however, a confusing act that ultimately pleased only some big businessmen who might have been interfered with by a more carefully worded law.

Business in general had wanted a federal trade commission for many years, and the Clayton Act now made such a commission a matter of pressing importance. The chief question was how much power the commission should be given to investigate and to prevent or punish violations of the antitrust laws. Major business organizations were divided on the desirability of a strong commission, but a majority favored the creation of such an agency.[42] The final law, like the early interstate commerce acts, gave the commission a broad range of power but left enforcement to the courts. The United States Chamber of Commerce, as usual, voiced what was perhaps the majority sentiment of business in saying, "the Commission's value would have to be judged on the basis of its future course of action."[43] Business had, at least, gained a new service and information bureau that offered much help and little threat to any legitimate interest.

The small businessmen on farms also gained from the expanding activities of government. Since practically all the work of the Department of Agriculture was directed toward better profits for the farmer, the mere fact that under the vigorous James Wilson, secretary of agriculture from 1897 to 1913, the number of employees in the department rose from 2,444 to 13,858, indicated a great increase in aid. Specifically, the department helped by advice on the formation of marketing cooperatives, which in 1915 numbered nearly 10,000, by sending "county agents" (expert advisors) to areas where producers were having trouble, and by the results of continuous research carried on at the state experiment stations and in Washington.[44]

Progressive political leaders in agricultural states, such as Robert La Follette of Wisconsin and Albert Cummins of Iowa, awakened the farmers to the fact that their interests as businessmen were not being properly represented either at the state capitals or in Washington. From about 1910 on, a farm lobby and a farm bloc in Congress became important forces in the movement to gain advantageous government regulation or aid. The farmer found many political allies, and few who wanted to be known as his enemies.[45] Business groups including railroads, mail order houses, farm equipment manufacturers, and mortgage companies, interested in increasing the purchasing power of farmers, joined the farm lobby in working for agricultural legislation. In 1914 they won the Smith-Lever Act, providing federal aid for county agents wherever the states would cooperate with matching funds. By the end of World War I, 2,435 counties had agents.[46] The needs of the Allies for American food also brought federal regulation of grain exchanges, long advocated by the Grange, and a special credit agency for the expansion of farm production.

NEW BUSINESS INTEREST OVERSEAS

While business as a whole was absorbed in winning or combatting regulation, or in checking the alarming spread of union labor, some business leaders were thinking about expanding foreign trade and markets. The idea was growing that advanced industrial nations could only avoid overproduction and unemployment by selling their surplus abroad.

At the same time, many developments favored international expansion. In 1896 Frederic Jackson Turner suggested in the *Atlantic Monthly* that with a closed farming frontier we would expand in new areas.[47] As the rate of return on prime domestic railroad bonds fell from 8 percent in the 1870s to about 4 percent in the midnineties, the higher yielding securities of Latin American governments became attractive.[48] Furthermore, the United States had a new steel navy capable of commanding respect for American interests in the Caribbean and more distant seas. Internationally, as the markets of Asia were being seized by Japan and the European powers, the situation seemed to call for action before it was too late. But perhaps most important in the immediate situation, foreign trade was seen as a relief from the deep depression that had started in 1893, thought by some to menace the stability of American society. With China in mind, Senator William Frye said, "We must have the market or we shall have revolution."[49] Some substantial manufacturing firms, particularly in textiles, seeing foreign trade as a release from overly competitive home markets, were anxious for government help in penetrating areas overseas. In 1895 an editor interested in Latin American trade and a group of Cincinnati producers formed the National Association of Manufacturers. Its early aims were to aid exporters by tariff reciprocity, reform of the consular service, revival of a subsidized merchant marine, uniform freight rates, and a Nicaraguan canal.[50] The association well illustrates the new pressure on federal government to provide helpful regulations. The preamble to its constitution stated, "United action in all matters affecting the manufacturing industries of the United States of America is essential to their conservation and Promotion."[51] In fact, almost every aim of the association prior to 1902 required federal intervention or aid.

The defeat of China by Japan in 1894 called particular attention to the great potential of Chinese trade. J. Pierpont Morgan sought to finance the Chinese indemnity loan through an American syndicate. An American China Development Company sought railroad concessions in China, and the *New York Journal of Commerce* devoted much attention to Far Eastern trade.[52] In 1899 in San Francisco the Chamber of Commerce, the Board of Trade, and the Manufacturers and Producers Association joined in forming a Bureau of Foreign Commerce and sent a representative to the Far East to investigate markets.[53] Since financial intervention in Chinese affairs was an opportunity sought by the leading imperialist powers, United States financiers working on a purely business basis achieved no success. With this same heightening of interest in the business penetration of less developed areas also taking place in the leading nations of Western Europe, businessmen familiar with international conditions felt that it took a determined effort just to maintain whatever position they managed to establish.

Probably no businessman was against the extension of foreign trade, or interested in opposing the numerous business organizations and journals that, together with Presidents Cleveland and McKinley, were actively working for it; in the beginning, however, few wanted to use war as a means of expansion. For example, in 1895 Secretary of State Richard Olney's belligerency toward Great Britain over Venezuela alarmed business, while business associations favored the abortive general arbitration treaty with Britain in 1896.[54] But by 1897, at least, some businessmen with direct or indirect foreign interests were bringing pressure on McKinley to find a way to terminate the insurrection against Spain that was going on in Cuba, both to protect American property there and to permit greater attentin to American interests elsewhere.[55]

By March of 1898, in view of the continuing insurrection and the failure to arrange negotiations, conservative Eastern business leaders of the United States were becoming reconciled to the inevitability of war over Cuba; with their backing, or at least their neutrality, McKinley was ready to appease the war party, which appeared to represent the popular majority.[56] While it is undoubtedly true that businessmen and particularly financial leaders were generally opposed to war, it is also evident that the Spanish War and its results were in harmony with a widespread belief in the necessity of greater foreign activity.

The NAM, for example, in its journal *American Trade* for June 15, 1898, while the war was still in progress, said that the Philippines seemed "assured as colonial possessions of the United States."[57] After the acquisition of the remains of the Spanish empire, President Theodore Search of the NAM said that "our business interests have been enormously the gainers by the American administration of affairs."[58] Undoubtedly some businessmen were troubled by the implications of the new imperial policy. "Though some businessmen and business journals took up the cause of annexation joyfully, it may be that many of them were also trying to keep ahead of the steam roller."[59]

The Open Door Policy, formalized by Secretary of State John Hay in 1901 through an exchange of notes with the leading colonial powers regarding China, gave explicit form to the continuing aims of American exporters of goods, life insurance, and capital.[60] In general, these firms wanted equal opportunity in the world's markets, without incurring the cost of colonial administration. On the whole, the policy succeeded.

In contrast, the policy of the State and Navy Departments was to keep the Caribbean Sea as a protected area of the United States, and to replace European with American investment in the independent islands and surrounding nations as rapidly as possible. This, in turn, involved policing the financial policies of these governments to make sure that they did not encourage intervention by powers other than the United States through defaults on government bonds or abrogation of foreign concessions.

In 1901 New York life insurance interests had chartered the International Banking Corporation (IBC) that established branches in the Far East.[61] The State Department soon persuaded IBC to open branches in the Caribbean area to give added confidence to American traders and investors. The New York banking interests were not enthusiastic about Caribbean investment, and except in Cuba and Mexico, they participated for themselves and their clients largely to support government policy.* If one includes losses to the New York banks from the collapse of sugar prices in 1920, it can be said that the program was a losing one for the investors, and the early reluctance of the banks was justified. Meanwhile, the IBC branches in the Far East had aided United States trade in cities such as Tokyo, Shanghai, Tientsin, and Singapore, even though the dreams of a vast Chinese and Indian trade had not materialized.

Another area of government activity of general concern to business was control of immigration. Beginning with the return of prosperity in 1897, immigration began to mount until in the ten years preceding 1915, it reached an average of a million people a year. Since over 80 percent of the newcomers were between fifteen and forty-five years old, and 70 percent of the total were males, they were a major addition to the labor force and a stimulant to economic growth.[62] On that basis, they were welcomed by business, particularly in interior areas short of labor, but the national origins of the immigrant masses created alarm. Of the nearly ten million who came to the United States in the years 1900 to 1910, the older types of immigrants, those from the United Kingdom, Germany, and Scandinavia, made up only about a quarter of the flood. The rest came from Russian Poland, Italy, and other parts of Central and Eastern Europe. Many of the latter spoke languages whose structures were so different from English that linguistic acculturation was slow; they were dark-complexioned; and since both Russia and the Austro-Hungarian Empire had violent radical protest movements, those who left were suspected of being anarchists or socialists.

Business was divided regarding solutions. In Eastern industrial centers that initially received the newcomers, many people wanted restriction, but there was little organized support for any particular means. The South and West wanted immigrants, but only those from Northern Europe. All wanted some basis for choosing between those regarded as desirable and undesirable. A number of organizations led by the NAM proposed modification of the laws against importation of labor under contract, that trade unions had been able to get enacted from 1882 on, but Congress was apparently afraid of the political effect of such a move. Between 1913 and 1917 Congress did pass laws for the imposition of literacy tests, which could no doubt have been administered to exclude numerous "undesirable aliens." Both Presidents Taft and Wilson vetoed

---

* I have written a history of the International Banking Corporation, but the manuscript is confidential material in the possession of the First National City Bank of New York.

the early bills as undemocratic and contrary to traditional American policy, and by 1917 when Wilson finally approved such an act, the public was ready for much more rigorous restriction.[63]

COUNTERVAILING POWERS

With the rise of more organized pressure groups such as chambers of commerce and similar associations, business not only broadened the range of its objectives to include new types of social betterment but also joined with professional groups in presenting a more united front that discouraged party or self-serving political corruption. On the national level, agricultural and urban business, working with the federal government after the 1890s, established regulations for the marketing of essential products and services.

But one should not be misled by the more socially conscious campaigns of business and civic associations, or the apparent influence of business for beneficial economic regulations, into assuming a completely changed milieu in which all forces strove for increased social efficiency. The change from former days was mainly one of degree. There were still continual conflicts between business interests themselves, where if the victory of a particular group served the public interest, it was only by chance; there were civic groups and business interests that profited from bad conditions; there were farmers who were sure that urban business exploited them; there were ineradicable differences between the masses in the cities and even the welfare-minded urban elite; and there were bitter battles between businessmen and organized labor. Since each native white group had votes, the business guidance of politics was always in dispute. The chief point made by historical investigators in recent years is that regardless of what may have gone on in a thousand smaller contests, in the most widely cited advances in urban and national reform, phalanxes of businessmen were among the leaders of the march, not only because they were against public abuses, but also because they recognized that reform was to their economic interest.

CHAPTER 15

Status and Greater Responsibility

While rapid movement of population in and out of both old cities and new had always weakened community cohesiveness, the growth of a nationwide business system brought local communities new forces of disintegration. American localism, however, also had unusual sources of strength. From colonial days there had been an attachment to local institutions and suspicion of provincial or imperial agencies. New England, the great exporter of population to the Middle West, was essentially governed by its towns, and community consensus was strongly emphasized. Across the mountains, town communities preceded well-organized territorial or state governments. During the territorial regime in any area, local people largely managed their own affairs. The intense local rivalries for county seats and other agencies were not ended by the achievement of relative maturity in population and industry. Each of the great metropolitan centers of the twentieth century still saw itself in competition with its peers.

THE NATIONAL BUSINESS ELITE

In the process of industrial growth, hundreds of local centers, each with its economic and social leaders, declined in importance in relation to a score of interlocked metropolitan areas. The economic forces producing the shift were numerous (Chapter 9), but the most obvious ones were railroad transportation, industrial mass production, and the need of larger scale business for metropolitan financing. Beneath the change, however, were important continuities. Industrial businessmen, as had commercial farmers and traders before them, were shaping a society largely unhampered by the traditional social structures of Europe. The United States could fit its society to industrialism, while to some degree the European nations tried to fit industrialism to their societies.

The South with its slave-operated plantations was the one area that had not adjusted readily to the needs of industrialism. By throwing the labor and management structure of that section into chaos, the Civil War opened the way for a new group composed of men whose wealth was based on nonagricultural business. These entrepreneurs were not necessarily "self-made" in the sense of having risen from the poor-white or small-farmer class, but they were seldom the same men who had owned the great plantations. Men like Lewis H. Blair, Richmond manufacturer, land operator, and reformer in the 1880s, came from good families but had to build fortunes in the postwar period through such sequences as retail trade, wholesale trade, and finally railroads or manufacturing.[1]

Since between 1865 and 1900 agriculture was more depressed in the South than elsewhere in the nation, the loss in status of the cotton and tobacco growers was greater than in the case of the large operators in grain or livestock of other regions. Those planters who continued as leading citizens did so by going into other businesses, and the occupations of the Southern elite in large towns and cities became similar to those of other areas. "By the time the Reconstruction experiment ended," writes Grady McWhiney, "Southerners were thoroughly Americanized. Every Southern state was controlled by businessmen or the friends of business."[2]

In the larger towns and cities of the nation the bankers continued at the top of the social pyramid. In 1850 the nation had between 800 and 900 banks; by 1900 it had 13,000 and by 1915, 28,000.[3] Such figures show that by 1915, in numbers alone, bank owners and presidents were a major elite group. If each bank had but a single owner-president, this group by 1915 would have been large, but, in fact each bank of any size had several officers and owners who shared in the social prestige of their connection so that the entire group may have approached 100,000 members.[4]

Sharing prestige with the banker, but usually a step below, were successful lawyers, some of whom might be in politics, and merchants, doctors, and manufacturers. But as manufacturing became larger scale and more concentrated in big cities, important small-city manufacturers were fewer than those in the other divisions of the highest elite. The status of newspaper editors varied from medium to high depending on their personalities and the circulation of their papers. Successful farmers were usually too remote and too busy to play much of a role in town affairs, while teachers and clergymen were too poor to keep up the level of expenditure expected of local leaders.[5]

In the American towns where land and buildings were owned by a manufacturing or mining company, there was no question as to where social prestige or authority lay. These company towns which had started with Waltham in 1814, and spread rapidly after midcentury, were populated chiefly by company managers and workers, with a very small, independent middle class. The initial reason for most such communities was attraction of labor to remote areas where churches, stores, and recreation would not have existed otherwise, or to set up a plant beyond the easy reach of union organizers. The companies or their managers often ran the stores as well as the housing, and in some instances the stores made more money than the company did from production.[6] The weakness in such situations was more psychological than economic. "Power and paternalism, however well intentioned," writes Morrill Heald, "produced exploitation and bitterness more often than they managed to create harmony."[7]

The big metropolitan areas, where even the largest firms or the wealthiest men exercised only a moderate influence, also had bankers of varying degrees of importance, as a part of their highest social and business elite. The needs of the new public utility and transportation enterprises for widespread selling of securities built those financial houses that could tap broad markets into imposing national powers. By the 1880s some large industrial companies were able to sell securities through investment bankers, adding still more to the latter's power. In other words, the crucial element in the "means of production" in this rapidly evolving industrial society continued to be capital, and the men who could control the flow of this necessity were the accepted leaders of society.

In this rapid rise in the influence of the men who controlled the financial apparatus of the major metropolitan centers, there was a surprising continuity in the social status of older business families. Most of the sons of the great merchants of the early years of the century were not playboys, scholars, or statesmen, but hard-working businessmen, many of whom moved into the new sphere of private banking.* The controllers of the old mercantile capital were in every way best suited for the rising business of finance, and a newcomer without substantial resources had relatively little chance of success. Therefore, private, or what was soon called investment, banking, had from the start an aristocratic aura. If an occasional self-made man, such as E. T. Stotesbury of Drexel and Co. in Philadelphia, rose to a partnership he was automatically invested with high social as well as economic status. About 1900 Hugo Munsterberg found the activities of New York dominated by "wholesale merchants, the banker potentates and the corporation attorneys."[8]

The family backgrounds of major executives in the large firms that produced for, or served, the national market also showed much continuation of high status from the early to the late nineteenth century. A study of the upper echelon of executives in railroads, steel, and textiles, as of 1870, indicates a group reared mainly in business or professional families.[9] These men were also of old American Protestant stock, and had the benefit of good education, in a day when higher education was rare, almost 40 percent had attended college. Aside from any direct family pressures, it made business sense to hire and promote

---

* The largest number of exceptions to the rule of continuing activity in business probably occured in Boston, but even here continued business appears to have been usual. See Gabriel Kolko, "Brahmins and Business, 1870-1914; A Hypothesis on the Social Basis of Success in American History," in Moore, *The Critical Spirit*, 343-363, for support of the idea of continuity; and Frederic Cople Jaher, "Proper Bostonians in the Era of Industrial Capitalism," in Jaher, *Industrialism*, 188-262, for a more detailed discussion of the overall failure of the original entrepreneurial families to maintain their positions.

young men who combined ability with early training in a business atmosphere and had good family connections. If, in truth, "there was always room at the top," these favored young men were the strongest candidates.

Just as the English upper class trained its members for governmental responsibility, the American upper classes trained them for success in business. The training was resisted on occasion, and in Boston, particularly, a number of Brahmins pursued careers in the arts or professions, but even these exceptions, like Henry and Brooks Adams, felt uneasy about their nonconformity.[10] James Bryce observed in the 1880s that "the practical ability which in the Old World goes to Parliamentary politics or to the civil administration of the state, goes in America into business, especially into railways and finance."[11]

A study of top executives of the largest corporations in the decade 1900 to 1910 by William Miller indicates a continuance of these trends.[12] More than a quarter of the men had inherited business status, and "most of the men in this group had taken over their father's, father-in-law's, or uncle's firms. Others had used their continuing connection with such firms, or funds available through them, to gain key positions in major outside companies."[13] Seventy-nine percent of the entire sample had fathers who were businessmen or professionals. Only 12 percent had come from farm families, and only 2 percent had working-class backgrounds.[14] Taking "upper class" to mean a family of wealth or prominence, Miller found that half of his businessmen came from such families, and another 45 percent from middle-class families.[15] As in the study by Gregory and Neu, Miller found these men had relatively high educational levels.

It appears, therefore, that the new big business of the late nineteenth century recruited much of its top personnel from the families of those successful in earlier types of enterprise. The Boston Brahmins going into banking and railroads perpetuated their social positions as did the erstwhile mercantile and landed families of New York and Philadelphia. In all these big cities, new businessmen also rose to the top, some such as Rockefeller, Carnegie, or Gould amassing far more money than was possessed by the scions of older families. In strictly "society" matters, the new families might be excluded for a generation or more, but in the world of power, business or political, there were no such barriers.

In the smaller cities of the Eastern area, from which many able young people moved to seek opportunity elsewhere, there appears to have been the same trend toward continuity of wealth and influence seen in the major metropolitan centers.[16] In the newer areas west of the Appalachians, recently built by in-migration, the controllers of economic activity and the men with social and political influence were usually first generation, although not necessarily self-made in the "rags to riches" sense. In Milwaukee, for example, whose rise as a large manufacturing center almost exactly spans the period from 1850 to 1915, the German brewers and Yankee manufacturers generally brought both know-how and some capital.[17] In the country as a whole during this period, the shifting managers of the branch plants of the largest corporations do not seem to have taken a leading part in local affairs.

By the turn of the century, acceptable social standing was beginning to be institutionalized nationally around education in certain private academies, colleges, and universities. While, in general, attendance at these schools required the help of a moderately prosperous family, the educational ladder offered opportunities for able students not initially qualified by family connections or wealth to win scholarships and gain entry to the world of the social elite. Since the Eastern metropolitan centers controlled national business and finance, the most prestigeous schools and colleges were Eastern and, particularly, New England.[18]

Emphasis on the social stratification of business leadership, needed to counter a traditional overemphasis on social mobility, should not obscure the open-class character of American society. While the young man with proper schooling and financial resources had a better chance of reaching the top, the road was not closed to any able young man who was white and spoke understandable English. Although in the two studies we have discussed, only 4 percent and 2 percent, respectively, reached the heights from a working-class start, many more self-made men achieved success in newer, smaller companies, or moderate success in larger enterprises. The great expansion in the number of enterprises provided an ever greater range of opportunities for success either in big-company careers or in profits from smaller ventures.

THE USE OF BUSINESS POWER

The number of men with enough money to influence politics or other social matters increased rapidly, alarmingly so to the people of the time. In 1850 there were probably less than a score of men with as much as a million dollars in capital and some of these, such as William Astor or the "Patroon" Van Rensselaer, probably the two richest men in New York, were primarily owners of real estate.* By 1890 the New York *Tribune* estimated that there were more than 4,000 millionaires, most of whom were manipulating their money in industry and finance.[19] James Bryce said the railroad men particularly had more power—that is, more opportunity of making their personal will prevail—than perhaps any one in political life except the president and the speaker of the House, who after all held their power only for a short span of years, while the railroad tycoon might keep his for life.[20]

The millionaires gravitated to the great metropolitan centers, particularly to Chicago or New York, but there were also powerful local elites in other major cities. Here, while commercial and investment bankers gained in importance, merchants engaged in the essential tasks of regional marketing retained much of

---

* The 1850 figure is an estimate based on a number of sources, and may be too low.

their old importance. In the larger cities, manufacturing enterprises grew, and their owners often became the wealthiest citizens, sharing prestige and power with the bankers; while in smaller cities many manufacturers moved away to locations more advantageous for national distribution, leaving merchants and bankers as the enduring wielders of local power.* In some cities, branch plants of national corporations became the largest employers, but the executives of these plants were generally less influential than the established local families.

In the small city as well as the great metropolis, sociologists see three different elites: the public-political; the private-economic; and the possessors of special knowledge.[21] The latter group, made up of engineers, lawyers, professors, physicians, and clergymen, historically had little political or economic power of its own, and its members became important only when in alliance with the political or economic elite. Engineers and lawyers, almost inevitably, formed such alliance, leaving only professors, physicians, and clergymen as a sort of unorganized and weak third force outside the two major power elites.

As indicated in the previous chapters, by 1850 the public-political elite had become separated from the private-economic, largely through the withdrawal of the latter group from time-consuming public affairs. Yet, since political fortunes waxed and waned while well-managed business wealth both increased and remained in the same hands for longer periods of time, wielders of private economic power tended to realize their own aims. In small cities where a few families had large economic power, this influence on politics might be direct and continuous, but in larger cities (as seen in Chapters 14 and 20), there could be real struggles between organizations built on political controls such as the party and the ward, and those in the form of lobbies or associations representing the strong economic groups.

To a large extent, the business leaders and their families dominated the culture of everyday life without regard to political power. They set the material goals of life, the orders of preference in consumption, and the approved attitudes and behavior. The fact that in most states the capitals were not in the largest cities removed the politicians from the main centers of economic activity and social prestige. Yet, the dominance of the economic elite over all rivals was still not thoroughly a part of the traditional literary culture. School children were taught to have soldiers, political leaders, and explorers, not businessmen, as their heroes.

In 1902 a writer for the *Review of Reviews*, after listing the "American Captains of Industry" under various headings, concludes "for the most part, these men's records are to be found in no dictionary of American biography; many are not in 'Who's Who'; they figure but little in the press; they are not the

---

* McKelvey, *Urbanization*, says that of the fifteen largest American cities in 1910 only New Orleans was primarily mercantile; see p. 48.

types that have been chosen to stand for American greatness in the Hall of Fame."[22] Not favored by established forms of literature, businessmen were often denounced by editors, writers, and clergymen who lived their everyday lifes in deference to businessmen, their customs, and their standards.

RISE OF THE MANAGERIAL MIDDLE CLASS

While the range of opportunities for self-employment was widening, the most important change in the social structure was the rapid increase in middle-class office and managerial employees. In dealing with the estimated figures in the table that give percentages of all gainful workers, it must be remembered that

OCCUPATIONAL GROUPS
AS PERCENTAGES OF LABOR FORCE

	1880	*1910*
Wage-earners	52.7	57.1
Clerical and sales	6.5	11.1
Professional employees	2.8	3.7
Managerial employees	1.1	1.8
Business enterprisers	8.0	7.7
Professional practitioners	1.1	1.0
Farmers	36.9	26.3

SOURCE: Bell, *Productivity, Wages and National Income*, 10.

urbanization, employment of women, and heavy immigration of adult males combined to increase the number of gainful workers over sixteen years of age from 32.5 percent of the total population in 1880 to 39.3 percent in 1910.[23] Therefore, the increase in professional employees from 2.8 percent to 3.7 percent, and of managerial employees from 1.1 percent to 1.8 percent of the gainful workers means that in relation to the population as a whole the combined categories rose nearly 50 percent.

As compared with the urban middle class of 1850, composed of independent professionals, mercantile proprietors, artisans, and only a few managerial employees, that of 1910, about half of whose members were business careerists, either as managers or specialists, had acquired a new dimension. This group had benefitted from high school and often college education. They were potentially business executives, but ones who had to think and work in a cooperative or bureaucratic atmosphere. These careerists favored "scientific" solutions for problems and backed the conservative social reforms which were so much features of this age.

Since the managerial employees in particular were presumably moving upward to higher positions, the size and importance of the company for which they worked gave them social prestige. Their potentiality of becoming big businessmen, as well as their education, gave them a status above that of the middle-class small proprietor. An assistant cashier at the National City Bank of New York might have a much smaller income than a successful corner grocer, but his job put him in a higher social group.

While most of the new class of managerial employees were destined to be specialists or bureaucrats all of their lives, never to rise to the level of making ultimate entrepreneurial decisions, they were trained to talk the language of free enterprise and profit. Consequently, their rise added to the size of the urban segment of the population directly responsive to business aims and values.

SOCIAL RESPONSIBILITIES

In the great period of pioneer industrial development from the 1840s to the 1880s, reinvestment of a man's earnings in expanding his business was regarded by many as more socially useful than making contributions to charity. Three of the richest men who died during this period—John Jacob Astor, Alexander F. Stewart, and Cornelius Vanderbilt—left practically nothing to charity. While some journalists criticized them for this omission, much of the press, particularly in the case of Vanderbilt, agreed with the New York *Evening Express* that "The benefits of posthumous charity are not to be compared with those of business enterprise."[24] Vanderbilt was hailed as a valuable citizen because he "gave employment to thousands of mechanics and tens of thousands of laborers by the creation of works on sea and land of great public utility."[25]

Not all successful entrepreneurs were as confident as these early millionaires in the overarching and sufficient value of their business creativity. Long before Andrew Carnegie's famous article "Wealth" in the *North American Review* of June, 1889, rich men had recognized their responsibility as stewards or trustees for the public. While in democratic America there was great emphasis on success as its own justification, many felt they had succeeded through God's grace and owed him a return in good works.

Whether from such inward promptings, or the needs of the situation, or the pressure of ambitious wives anxious to attract attention, business leaders played an increasing role in philanthropy. Since poverty in America savored of sin, local governments did relatively little to save or rehabilitate the indigent or the physically unfortunate. And such government activity was diminished between 1873 and 1900.[26] Yet the poor of the rapidly growing cities needed far more help than those in rural areas where there was more possibility of subsistence on family farms.

Faced with the increasing problem of black and white orphans, widows without employment, the halt, the lame, and the blind, many families used money from successful businesses to form societies to deal with special types of hardship. In the mid-nineteenth century, Philadelphians, as we have seen, organized some 150 such specialized charitable societies; some were denominational, but the majority secular.[27] In these good works the wives of business leaders were particularly active; because philanthropic endeavor was above criticism as a path to social distinction, it held particular appeal for the newly rich.

The social welfare activities of mid-nineteenth century businessmen, chiefly merchants, were also influenced strongly by Christian evangelism. Robert M. Hartley, a New York merchant, for example, spent his free time between religious and welfare activities. While he came to regard sanitary reform as "the basis for most other reform," he was continuously active in supporting the New York Association for Improving the Condition of the Poor.[28] His support of causes such as temperance, increasingly popular among businessmen, "though it may seem today a moral, if not moralistic, concern, drew him increasingly into an understanding of the brutal facts of slum life."[29]

Toward the end of the century, as older men who were partially retired from business came to administer private fortunes of from fifty to hundreds of millions of dollars, a new age of large-scale philanthropy began. On the whole, vastly wealthy businessmen preferred giving to education and research which advanced the able rather than subsidizing the failures. A leader among such men, Andrew Carnegie urged the "millionaire class" to "concentrate its philanthropic efforts on the side of the industrious. He wished to provide ladders upon which the aspiring can rise."[30] Accordingly, he started his major donations with gifts to libraries in the 1880s and to colleges and foundations for research and social betterment between 1890 and his death in 1917. John D. Rockefeller, who ultimately gave more than Carnegie, endowed the University of Chicago in 1890 and organized his principal foundations between 1900 and World War I. Both he and Carnegie had to set up staffs to run their philanthropies, in addition to the professional administrators of the foundations. Dozens of other men of great wealth followed these examples. By the nineties the increase in philanthropy was inspiring articles by journalists. The *Review of Reviews* in 1893 attempted an analysis of giving by millionaires in major cities. While the evidence is far from adequate, the results illustrate public attitudes toward giving.[31] Baltimore, in which 49 percent of the local millionaires were classified as active givers, headed the list, and New York was at the bottom. While different cities were said to have special philanthropic interests, such as overseas relief in Philadelphia, Harvard University and the Massachusetts General Hospital in Boston, or musical and artistic ventures in Cincinnati, aid to the local poor was not conspicuous. Not only was poverty still widely regarded as reprehensible and not to be encouraged, but donors also preferred parks, foundations, museums, or other creations that could bear the family name.

By 1900 in many types of enterp·ises, and long before this in railroading, company participation in supporting community welfare might be more important than the private contributions of executives. Before the mid-twentieth century, however, there was considerable doubt as to the legal rights of officers to donate the stockholder's money for good causes. As local development companies, railroads could justify many such donations, but most other businesses could not. R. H. Macy, for example, as a business dealing directly with urban customers could have been expected to be conscious of local obligations, yet from an operating profit of $114,000, in 1887, only $1,100 went to "charity."[32]

SUPPORT OF THE ARTS

Following the customs of the earlier merchant society, successful businessmen gave support to the arts, particularly those of architecture, music, and portrait painting. Starting with the Vanderbilt Mansion in New York in 1879, multimillionaires, with the advice of scholarly architectural firms such as McKim, Meade and White, built palaces in New York and Chicago on a far larger scale and with more scholarly attention to design than ever before in the United States. As cheap structural steel in the early eighties made skyscraper office buildings practical in the downtown sections of big cities, architects were given an additional opportunity to experiment with new forms and styles in office buildings, banks, and department stores. The early efforts at business buildings were somewhat boxlike and conventional. Neglecting the varied and ornate uptown mansions, a British visitor of the midnineties said of New York City: "Nothing is given to beauty, everything centers on hard utility." But by the early twentieth century, architects such as Ernest Flagg and Cass Gilbert were being given freedom by major business firms to build tall towers that were recognized abroad as America's chief contribution to the arts.

In addition to individual buildings, some of the leading businessmen became involved with both architects and politicians in planning for more beautiful and spacious cities. Fairmount Park in Philadelphia, Central Park in New York, and Prospect Park in Brooklyn depended for their ultimate success on continuous efforts by local businessmen and business lawyers. By the 1880s, prosperous businessmen were leading a movement to the suburbs which produced some magnificent country estates, and a new upper-middle class society was built around country clubs.[33]

As in Europe, symphony orchestras and lavish housing for opera had always depended on patronage beyond the sale of tickets to the public. As wealth increased in the 1850s, the businessmen of Boston, Chicago, New York, and Philadelphia subscribed to the building and support of opera houses or "academies of music." Intercity trade rivalry made such contributions easier to secure than those for less obvious improvements. In the 1850s all four cities had opera seasons. In the decades after the Civil War, business contributions slowly expanded chamber music societies into symphony orchestras; the Boston Symphony, in 1881, was largely the result of the contribution of a leading banker, Henry Lee Higginson. In Chicago, Charles Norman Fay, not outstanding in the business world, was able to gain backing for an enduring symphony in 1891. In New York and Philadelphia, support by the wealthy was unreliable and led to the varying success of competing groups in the 1870s and 1880s. The present New York Philharmonic, although founded in 1878, was not properly underwritten until a decade later, and the Philadelphia Orchestra not until 1900.

In supporting such ventures, no critical judgment of art was necessary. They represented efforts by the business and professional community for the greater glory of the city as well as for their pleasure at the performances. Individual patronage of painting and sculpture, on the other hand, was more strictly a matter of gaining personal pleasure and social prestige. Each wealthy patron found it best to work through a few trusted dealers who would protect the purchaser from fraud and guide his taste in accordance with the accepted standards of the day. The dealer preferred to sell the most expensive pictures, those whose future value seemed assured, and this category did not include the work of living American artists.

Consequently, although American businessmen such as Henry C. Frick, J. Pierpont Morgan, or William A. Clark probably spent more on art between 1880 and World War I than the patrons of any Western nation in earlier times, contemporary painting and sculpture in America lacked patronage. While the works of foreigners who caught the vogue of the moment sold in the late 1890s for $40,000 or $50,000, only one picture by an American, George Innes, brought as much as $10,000 and very few brought as much as $5,000.[34] American patronage was a matter of transferring a considerable portion of the art of the Western world from European to Americal walls.

AMERICA'S "IRON AGE"

There is general agreement that the years from 1850 to 1915 are the period when business interests came to be most important in American culture. There is also wide agreement that the last half of the nineteenth century had many unpleasant features. In addition to its bloodiest war, the nation developed ugly, sooty, unhealthy cities, a West given to lawlessness and violence, and a general disinterest in the arts or intellectual or spiritual concerns other than "old-fashioned" Protestant religion. It was also a time when the manipulative possibilities of the modern corporation and wasteful exploitation of easily accessible resources made business seem to many a malevolent force; it has often been called the "Iron Age," "the Age of the Robber Barons" or "The National Barbecue."

There was no question that business was largely responsible for the social structure. The thousands of millionaires at the top were the only nationally accepted upper class. Politicians, ministers, artists, scientists, or professional men, while they might on occasion attract public favor or acclaim, were on lower levels of socio-economic power. The new managerial middle class, created by business in its own image, ranked equally with the professions and above the small retailers and artisans. Technology had also created the impersonal mass of industrial labor, which had scarcely existed before 1800, and which by 1910 seemed to the higher classes to be a somewhat foreign and menacing lower half of the nation.

Although economic progess came from the business system, which also appeared to shape, or undermine, manners and morals, conversely the socio-economic situation set the conditions for doing business. The hasty extension of settlement, constant migration, and rapid exploitation of natural resources are not a formula for a beautiful society. Australia and Eastern Russia, with considerably more government direction, also showed most of the unpleasant features of the United States. The virtues of the migratory and frontier societies were also their defects. If migration led to an emphasis on equality and success by individual effort, it also bred a disregard of ceremony, tradition, and sensitivity which seem basic to civilization. If the frontier produced vigorous, self-reliant men, it also made them crude in manners and narrow in outlook. If throughout nineteenth-century America, "achievement motivation" was high, regard for the niceties of law or method was low.

At the beginning of the twentieth century, there was a revulsion against the abused freedom of the nineteenth, and a demand by the propertied classes for more rules, and safeguards. More regulations were demanded in the interest of both business and social efficiency.[35] The influx of millions of unfamiliar types of Europeans made the need for social safeguards seem still more pressing. The period ended therefore with efforts to correct the exaggerations of the late nineteenth century and to come closer to the norms of Western civilization. It was a period of reassessment by political and professional leaders, who were joined by many from business in giving thought to what constituted a good society.

Part IV

AFFLUENCE, 1915-1970

CHAPTER 16

The Rise of "Big Management"

Social change in the twentieth century challenged business executives more than in any previous period. In big companies, management became more expert and more powerful in its control of resources. At the same time, however, it was confronted by growing complexity of the economic system and expansion of governmental authority in ways that occasionally exceeded its immediate ability to respond. One might say that for nearly a century prior to 1929, entrepreneurs dominated and largely shaped the American physical and social environment, while from the Great Depression on, they were forced to adjust to changing political and social conditions. New technology and some new resources continued to present alert entrepreneurs with the old physical opportunities, but management also had to be concerned with employee's rights and welfare, with big bureaucratic labor unions, with maintaining efficiency in growing corporate bureaucracies, with needs for vast and relatively less profitable capital investments, with controlling pollution of the environment, and with the handling of government and other public relations.

Closer relations between government administrators and those of maturing capitalist industrialism led to a further reversion from the pronounced laissez-faire attitude of the late nineteenth century toward the earlier idea of government as a coordinate economic utility. The change was a gradual one starting, as we have seen, back in the 1880s; before the Great Depression, it did not seriously disrupt the business or classic economic ideal of the self-regulating economy.

In the first half of the twentieth century, the size of management grew rapidly, and the ratio of administrative to production workers in industrial enterprises increased three-fold, a rate only exceeded by industry in Sweden.[1] In big business, the shift meant an increasing emphasis on management as a profession and the treatment of plant organization and technological productivity as specialized engineering problems. The old fashioned chief executive needed to "know men" in order to staff the plant, but once the men were selected, they could be judged by tangible results. In the large corporation of the mid-twentieth century, overall results depended on a complicated structure of internal and external, personal and institutional relations. As the biggest corportations came to have as many employees as most national governments, they acquired a large number of the problems of governments, in addition to those of profit-making enterprises. A mere rerouting of the path of decision-making within a company, for example, might make a substantial difference in policy.[2] The common saying that distribution was more important than production had a corollary stating that business problems were more important than those of technology.

CONTINUITIES IN THE BUSINESS STRUCTURE

Changes in the problems and character of big management did not radically alter the relative numbers of large, medium, and small business units. While it is not possible to find exact comparative figures in the census records, it seems certain that, for the period as a whole, the number of nonagricultural business units grew somewhat faster than the population. General relations of size and number were stable enough within the business structure, so that a detailed picture of the statistics for 1965 is fairly representative of relationships for most years of the period. Excluding agriculture, forestry, and fisheries, there were some eight million proprietorships, partnerships, and corporations. Of these, four-fifths were sole proprietorships, of which about half reported having one or more employees eligible for social security. Many of the owners of the two and a half million enterprises that showed either a loss or a net profit under $5,000 a year had other sources of income.[3] These relatively unsuccessful small proprietors, however, were undoubtedly more numerous than all the policy-making executives of the 10,000 moderately and very large corporations.

The size of business units cannot be measured by any single dimension. Employees, assets, and sales are three measures commonly used. Measurement by employees makes manufacturing and transportation firms appear large; measurement by assets favors financial enterprises and public utilities; while measurement by sales gives a high ranking to companies in trade. Out of the eight million nonagricultural business units, only 63,000 had 100 employees or more and only 9,000 had over 500 employees.* Not counting a small number of large proprietorships and partnerships, 79,000 active corporations had assets of over a million dollars at the end of 1964, including 6,000 with assets of over $25 million each.

If one shifts, however, from numbers of companies to total volume of assets or receipts from operations, the picture is quite different. The corporations with over a million dollars in assets had nearly 90 percent of the total and accounted for about 75 percent of the corporate returns. Yet, in spite of this growth in the volume of production by larger business units, the degree of monopoly in

---

* Nearly half the "business units" were probably ventures carried on by entrepreneurs also engaged in some other activity.

markets increased slowly, if at all.[4] At least two factors maintained competition: (1) the Justice Department with additional antitrust powers under new laws, particularly the Cellar-Kefauver Act of 1950 defining monopoly to cover vertical as well as horizontal integration, prevented mergers of large companies supplying the same markets; and (2) partly because of this legal restraint, big companies usually expanded into new markets which they did not dominate.

In sum, the relatively stable, nonagricultural business structure of the middle third of the twentieth century was composed chiefly of small proprietorships and partnerships of which about 60 percent made over $5,000 a year in profit. Less than 6 percent of all enterprises had over 100 employees, and less than 8 percent had more than a million dollars in assets, but these larger units did about three-quarters of the dollar volume of business. The 100-employee or million-dollar asset level is, of course, far from giant enterprise. Taking $50 million in assets as a purely arbitrary measure of real bigness, giant enterprise accounted for 41 percent of corporate receipts.

Finally, an examination of business structure by type of activity also demonstrates both continuity in relationship and the wide dispersion of small enterprise. Between 1929 and 1957 the "annual average number of firms in operation" increased a total of about 50 percent.[5] The categories growing more than this in number of firms were contract construction; transportation, communication, and other public utilities; and wholesale trade. The categories of manufacturing; retail trade; finance, insurance, and real estate; and service grew by less than 50 percent in number of enterprises, but all grew about 25 percent or more. Of all the categories, only mining and quarrying grew by less than 20 percent.

The channels through which goods moved from producers to consumers also showed strong continuuities. While to win and hold a national market, big companies advertised both directly and in cooperation with their dealers, they still found it best to have such outlets operate as independent wholesalers or retailers. The intermediate steps varied with the type of product, but as we have just seen, the percentage of wholesalers in the business population increased. While supermarkets, discount houses, and chain enterprises in general checked the expansion of independent retail and service enterprises, the former grew by 45 percent and the latter by 39.

CONTINUITIES IN BUSINESS ATTITUDES

Hence the picture of American business is ambiguous. The men who represented "business opinion" have been small enterprisers struggling to make a modest living, while the men who administered the creation of mass employment and industrial goods have been a minority made up of high-salaried executives. A secondary and perhaps less significant division is that most of the small enterprisers have been in trade, service (including brokerage and real estate), and construction, while most of the salaried administrators have been in manufacturing, banking, and public utilities. As we shall see, these divisions make for very different interests and attitudes among the various segments of the business population, to say nothing of further types of diversity if one includes lawyers, professors, and other professionals (not included in any of the above calculations) who are closely related to business operations.

In spite of more organizations and more numerous public statements, the economic and social attitudes of the vast majority of businessmen, the owners or managers of small firms, did not appear to change greatly from 1915 to 1970. In the decade of the twenties, these operators joined in the movement for trade associations to control competition, a realistic endeavor, but often accompanied by public pronouncements that business was developing new social responsibilities and new ideals of service. The American Management Association, formed by a number of trade organizations in 1923, spread the new doctrines through publication of the *Management Review*. F. M. Felkner of the McGraw-Hill Company saw the associations as a force "which would set up for the guidance of each member standards of practice or codes of ethics."[6] The following year the United States Chamber of Commerce adopted a statement of "Principles of Business Conduct" which was agreed to by the chamber's 750 member associations, representing 300,000 firms.[7] These promoters of the new ideals of business in the 1920s were reenforced by statements in business publications, and by deans of business schools and other specialized spokesmen for the free enterprise system.

Yet, the small operators that constituted most of the members of the business organizations that spread the idealistic doctrines continued to be the staunchest upholders of laissez-faire, self-help, and decisions based on the market. In 1929 Dean Wallace B. Donham of the Harvard Business School commented that while the association codes dealt with serious subjects, they tended to dismiss them with "platitudes about morality and service," and the *Nation's Business* flayed "the rhetoric of service as little more than a sales device."[8] The Great Depression made these discrepancies obvious, and in the more cynical age that followed World War II, pronouncements of this type were no longer regarded as of much value to business.[9]

ALTERATION OF THE BUSINESS ENVIRONMENT

In the decades after World War I, technological change was most rapid in the industries dominated by big companies, such as automotive, chemical, and electrical, with accompanying reactions on business and social life. Problems in the automobile industry, for example, led to innovations in the managerial structure of big business, while the use of the automobile and the truck changed the locational pattern of industry, the methods of retail distributions, and the needs for social overhead capital in roads, tunnels, and bridges. In spite of some major technological advances, such as the introduction of diesel-electric power, still more rapid advances in automobiles and aircraft made the railroads a declining industry, and in 1970 the failure of the Penn Central, the nation's largest railroad, raised new problems of the relations of government to non-profitable, but still esstential, business services.

Electricity, available in all urban areas by 1930, enabled small plants with separately motorized tools to operate their machinery as efficiently from the standpoint of power as a large factory. This meant that in many manufacturing operations there were no longer what the economicst would call "economies of scale," and small businessmen flourished both as subcontractors and independent producers even in such technically advanced industries as aircraft, electronics, and motor vehicles. Meanwhile, the truck made it possible to transport small amounts of goods with a cost per unit only a little above that charged by the railroads for moving the amount needed to fill a freight car. Cheap small-scale transportation both preserved the small competitor and greatly expanded the area available for the location of plants.

This latter factor, whose effect was held back by the Great Depression, brought rapid changes from 1941 on. War plants could be built in the rural regions where there was a surplus of labor and could bring their products to major distributing points over uncongested highways. After the war, management began to calculate the savings to be effected by locating plants on cheap land in urban fringe areas where the workers could live in the country or suburbs and commute by automobile. Plants, laboratories, and offices that needed no direct contact with buyers or auxiliary services and that employed a moderate number of workers were the first to move from the central cities, but soon large manufacturing operations needing thousands of workers were locating in exurban areas, confident that a supply of labor would follow them.

The movement of people to country areas surrounding the new business operations was, of course, followed by a migration of trade and service. Led by supermarkets for food, other suppliers clustered in shopping centers. By the 1960s, planned centers with department stores, cheap discount houses, moving picture theatres, and specialty and service shops were replacing even the larger towns as ultimate distributing areas. Many of the stores were parts of chains, but independent retailers, especially in service trades, managed to prosper. The essence of the development was a place to park the automobile while all usual needs were being supplied. Meanwhile, business tended to decline in the old towns in which parking was difficult and different types of stores further apart. A result was the transformation of suburban life from town-centered to multiple-centered for different functions such as shopping, schools, clubs, and politics.

In earlier times such spread-out chains of industry or trade units would have been hard to run under one management. Here also electricity and the gasoline engine helped to solve the problems they had created. The telephone and a host of other electronic devices for communication and accounting made the grasp of management as firm over long distances as in the same building. If face-to-face contact was deemed desirable, company or commercial airplanes could accomplish it in short order. The next step in this direction appeared to be video phone connections whereby face-to-face conferences could be held with the participants hundreds of miles apart.

Aside from retailing and service, the operations that remained and grew in the downtown areas of the big cities were those in which personal relations with men in other firms, or a wide assortment of specialized abilities played important roles. Head-office financial men wanted to know the big commercial and investment bankers, the managers of advertising departments wanted to confer frequently with their outside agencies, and the men in charge of both wholesale buying and selling found it advantageous to be in a central marketplace. This was particularly true where changing patterns of style or design were involved. Firms in the ladies' garment trade, for example, found it advisable either to locate in New York City or to keep a representative there. In fact, while branch plants and chain operations were fanning out across the country, the trend to locate head offices in New York or a few other regional centers increased.

The Great Depression brought the federal government into complex supporting and regulating relationships with business that ended the possibility of a self-regulating economy, and in 1946 Congress passed the Employment Act specifically assuming responsibility for economic welfare. By guaranteeing, from 1933 on, a large percentage of the value of mortgages on small homes the federal government became an active force in the "urban explosion," but as both a customer and a regulator, it also reshaped the business environment. After World War II the government underwrote new plants for military equipment, or research and development, by subsidies, loans, or special tax allowances for depreciation, and bought enormous quantities of the products of these and other plants. Because of the size of the contracts involved, most of this trade went initially to the larger corporations which, in turn, might commission subcontracts.

About midcentury, it was thought that automation in general and the digital computer in particular might greatly alter both the structure and processes of business all over the world. Small enterprises, which could not afford such expensive equipment, would be squeezed out and larger firms would dispense with both plant and office employees through automation. Thus business would be run by fewer executives who would employ machines rather than men. No one can say that such may not become a trend in the future, but up to the end of the 1960s, few human beings had been displaced. Writing in 1965, Charles E. Silberman in a study for *Fortune* said, "no fully automated process exists for any major products in any industry in the United States."[10] And America was well in the lead in computer technology.

Since many plants were largely automated by older types of technology before the advent of the computer, in the decades of the fifties and sixties the new device did not have a strong effect on productivity per worker in manufacturing, nor did it substantially alter the nature of plant management. The assembly line, quality control, and other devices after World War I increased manufacturing productivity per worker more rapidly from 1920 to 1929 than was the case from 1955 to 1964.[11]

The computer appeared, so far, to have increased the effectiveness of management and the productivity of capital without notably diminishing the use of labor. Better and multiple systems of accounting, uneconomic when carried out by manual calculations, could give a clearer picture of the strong and weak areas of company operations. Computer-controlled inventories could safely be kept smaller than with only periodic taking of stock. This meant that fewer goods were immobilized in the pipelines between raw materials and consumption of the finished product. Forecasters seeking to predict the market could now put every conceivable factor into their equations. In all, management could adjust more quickly and effectively to its environment, but often with the employment of more, not less, skilled personnel. Put another way, while computers could do things impossibly laborious for human beings, the computer demanded a considerable labor force to program and feed it.

Meanwhile important changes were occurring in the structure of big business. With the technical problems of production securely in the hands of engineers or other specialists, top executives were able to concentrate on developing managerial skills transferable from one business situation to another. At the same time, the uncertainties of technological change made it wise for a large company to diversify its activities.[12] The increasing scale of management as a specialized activity led companies like Du Pont and General Motors in the 1920s to create systems of general "staff" officers, with no confining duties, of other staff specialists for various functions that ran all through the various operating branches, and of subsidiary corporations with their own managements to handle the problems, particularly in marketing, that were peculiar to different types of products. A net result of these developments was an increased emphasis on management as a profession, and the expansion of higher education for business, both to fulfill the need for such men, and by research to suggest innovations in theory and practice.

Through research and development departments, large corporations, particularly in the period after World War II, also sought to increase their control over technological change. In this way the management of large corporations took on innovation as a recognized function. Even though many of the devices that led to significant changes in technology or management still came from individual inventors in small enterprises, successful exploitation of the innovation often required entering into a contract with a big company. "Freewheeling" entrepreneurs bought patents from inventors either outright or on a partnership basis, established pilot runs to prove practicality, and then licensed big companies to produce and market the device.

In the late 1950s new problems in dealing with strange and confusing environments came to big business from ownership of foreign subsidiaries. In scores of the largest corporations, foreign activities came to produce 20 to 25 percent of total net revenue. In 1965, total revenue from all foreign investments, about two-thirds the value of which was in direct holdings of corporations, was some $7 billion. By way of an indirect comparison, the total net profit of the 500 largest manufacturing companies, the ones chiefly interested in overseas investment, was $20 billion.[13] Sixty percent of the migratory capital was invested in Canada and Western Europe, where the relations of labor, management, and consumers were not strikingly different from those that executives were familiar with at home. But even here, there were divided sovereignties, contradictory foreign policies, national traditions, customs, and personality types that posted major challenges. On the one hand, American management practices had a powerful impact on those of the other nations, and on the other, some middle and top corporate executives joined the ranks of Americans educated in the ways of other cultures.

In 1961 business investment in less industrially advanced areas was encouraged by federal insurance of the capital involved. But aside from continuing interests in foreign oil, the unique problems of most less developed countries made Americans hesitant about undertaking such risks. Even if the economic enterprise succeeded, local governments were prone to raise arbitrarily the exactions for taxes or franchises in order to keep money from leaving their country.

In many foreign operations Americans were repeating, in considerable part, the earlier experiences of English, French, and German businessmen, with, one suspects, too little attention to "the lessons of history." Regardless of occasional errors in management or human relations, however, these companies, abetted by moving pictures and television tapes, were spreading American goods and customs throughout the world. It may appear to later historians that the most pervasive single influence on world cultures from 1945 to 1970 was that of American business and its products.

THE DYNAMICS OF BIG MANAGEMENT

The temporary difficulties faced by management from 1930 to 1945 will be noted in Chapter 20. From World War II on, business operated in an expanding economy in which most firms could grow without necessarily squeezing each other, eliminating small enterprise, or greatly increasing their control over markets. But big companies grew the most in both products and size. If, because of the reduced value of the dollar, one equates assets of $50 million and over in 1940 with $100 million and over in 1964, the increase is from the 1,032 firms of 1940 to 1,758 in 1964, or about a 73 percent increase in numbers, during a period when population increased slightly less than 50 percent. Estimating the rise in the number of professional managers is far more difficult. Before World War I many more medium-sized firms and even some large ones were family managed. Managerial hierarchies even in the giants were smaller and less specialized. Perhaps 200,000 would include all men who consciously saw themselves as career or professional executives. By 1970 the number may have risen to over 1,000,000, but any such figure might be 50 percent too high or too low.

The leading role of the big company in American business, however, depended not on numbers of firms, assets, or employees, but on the intellectual, political, and economic influence that could be exerted by executives having great resources in brains and money at their disposal. The size of the managerial staff gave them much flexibility in interpreting and pursuing company interests. For example, during the National Recovery Administration (1933 to 1935), the small proprietor could not afford the time to attend hearings and bring pressure on the code authority that administered his industry, whereas the big company could assign a full-time lawyer or even a department to such duties.

In 1926, Herbert Bayard Swope of General Electric said that management was in a position "to define its own responsibilities."[14] While management determined its influence in a wide variety of ways, they were all expected to relate directly or indirectly to the welfare and survival of the company. Aside from actual production, the broadest fronts of planned contact with the environment were public relations and advertising.

Prior to World War I, public relations, usually called "publicity" at this time, was only partially recognized as a continuing need of big business (Chapter 10). When a regulatory bill was pending in Congress or some crisis arose in labor relations, one of the few experts such as Ivy L. Lee might be called upon. Big advertising agencies had departments that would advise companies concerning their public image, but the companies themselves entrusted such work to their advertising departments.[15]

During World War I, a federal Committee on Public Information, headed by journalist George Creel, was influential in building patriotism and anti-German feeling to a high pitch. After the war, people who had worked for the committee gravitated to public relations work. One of these, Edward L. Bernays, who claims credit for first using the title Counsel on Public Relations in 1920, became the most articulate expounder of the new profession.[16] In the 1920s the distinction between public relations and advertising was still vague, and perhaps always will be. If a cigarette company argued the superiority of its brand over those of its competitors, it was advertising; if the message was "reach for a Lucky instead of a sweet," it was essentially public relations for all cigarettes. This particular campaign produced a counter move from the sellers of sugar and candy, each side enlisting the medical profession. "The competition of ideas in the American market place" says Bernays, "is an essential democratic process, for then the public can make its own choice. Even when ideas conflict and confuse, public debate clarifies issues and makes for a sounder choice, in the long run."[17]

No matter how skillfully contrived to arouse emotional or intellectual reactions, this older style of public relations was in the realm of words and pious exhortation. When the Great Depression came in 1930, the words had a hollow ring. The Packard slogan of "a dollar for a job not a dole," for example, appeared meaningless to all but the preconvinced, because the alternative was unrealistic. Such real social issues as security or better industrial relations were passed over. From the failure of words alone in the 1930s there emerged a more substantial type of public relations.

The new form was in part a reaction to the challenge of greater problems. The New Deal had, as we shall see, put management on the defensive; businessmen felt challenged to prove their worth to American society. As large companies grew by merger, and many plants which had once been independent local enterprises became branches, more communities had some or all of their manufacturing controlled by absentee companies. At best, a transitory executive moving up in a corporate complex had less local influence or social value than a native proprietor; at worst, he and his company might come to be resented the way foreign companies are in less developed areas.

The Du Pont company's "precinct" plan represented one type of effort to meet this alienation. Each of nearly 100 plant managers was made responsible for community relations within his precinct. He was to become a good citizen of the community, supporting civic causes with company money and cooperating in general with movements for local welfare. Wages were to be as high as the best prevailing levels, but no higher, so that Du Pont would not draw labor away from established local firms. Such enlightened companies accepted Bernays' definition that public relations was a two-way street along which ideas traveled from the public to the company as well as in the reverse direction.

The problem of the local relations of the big company, however, was inherent in the situation and could not be met completely. No executive present for only a few years could become a true member of the continuing community, and no ambitious executive could devote more than a limited amount of his time to local affairs. Furthermore, he could not, in general, involve his company in partisan politics. From the companies' standpoint there were also limitations. Norton E. Long writes, "It is good business to get on with and be liked by the natives, but it is bad business for the management to go native . . . costs are incurred for other than good business reasons, and the mobility on which competitive success depends is sacrificed."[18] The most that could or should be expected in the relations of absentee-companies and local communities appeared to be mutual recognition of rational limits to expectations.

While public relations expenditures improved the public image of a company and its types of products, often in rather intangible ways, advertising was aimed at selling specific goods or services. From about 1910 on, this operation was performed with increasing efficiency primarily because of new techniques of communication. Few would question the twentieth-century growth in the force of advertising in creating markets, yet the efforts took a smaller percentage of the national income. In 1910 and 1920 the cost of advertising was over 4 percent of the national income, whereas in the 1950s and 1960s it ran about 2.5 to 2.7 percent. Such a relative calculation, of course, conceals a very big increase in current dollars, and also is not corrected for the growing government expenditures included in the figures for national income. Yet no matter how one reckons, television and radio represented an increasingly effective way of persuading people to buy the advertised products.

Within the advertising profession, Merle E. Curti thinks that "by 1930 the majority had come to believe that human nature is essentially non-rational and emotional and that the social sciences, especially psychology, offer effective aid in persuading the reader of ads and in manipulating his buying behavior."[19] Certainly, Western world advertising came to represent a high degree of sophistication and, frequently, close correlation with research to discover the effects of the campaign.

The steady and massive pressure of public relations and advertising on the consumer led to economic theorizing that big management controlled its markets as to both type and quantity of products. The history of the postwar years casts doubt on the effectiveness of such control. As illustrated by the history of the automobile industry, in spite of large advertising outlays, some companies lost competitive positions. Innovations by smaller rivals could change the type of product consumers wanted regardless of the efforts of the biggest advertiser. It appears that the new methods of market research and the resulting outlays for public relations and advertising were more adjustments to the influence of wars, tax policies, the business cycle, and social fashions on national markets than they were controls of such markets by management.

At all events, the managers of large corporations saw it that way. Having to consider the effects of policies on relations with labor, competitors, government, consumers, and various communities, chief executives were more worried about the limitations on their activity than they were reassured by a presumed power to control the flow of goods in the economy. W. H. Ferry, vice-president of the Fund for the Republic, observes that "much of the manifold public-relations activity . . . aims at invisibility," or, in other words, keeping the corporation out of trouble.[20] This discussion does not deny that collectively the executives of the 1,000 largest manufacturing corporations were responsible for most of the industrial product, but "power" or "control" has to be in the hands of discrete individuals, not an anonymous collectivity, and has to be viable for the achievement of desired ends.

THE CORPORATE EXECUTIVE

Before World War I the executives of the big corporations had become a recognized group deeply affecting the character of American society. The change over the next half century was both in the quality and pervasiveness of this influence. If our earlier estimate of a 400 percent increase in numbers is roughly correct, this group was growing over twice as fast as the national population, and it was, on the whole, the most prestigious elite. Barring change brought about by military coups or conquests, such rapid growth of a "power elite" had probably never taken place in history. The characteristics of this group were, therefore, of great, if not overriding importance to the society.

Those members of the group who reached positions of high authority in the years after 1940 had been affected to some degree by the newer elementary and secondary education, as well as the newer "scientific" ideas of child rearing. All of which joined with the atmosphere of the society around them in weakening traditional values and emphasizing pragmatic decisions (Chapter 18). These forces also reenforced the adaptibility to changing environment which came from high rates of geographical mobility. All of these were characteristics well suited to the large corporation operating in a rapidly changing world of business. Journalist William H. Whyte called these executives "organization men" and sociologist David Riesman saw them as conforming to the expectations of other men, or "other-directed."

Top executives were becoming a highly educated group. Of roughly 7,500 such men examined in 1928, 45 percent had been to college, and 32 percent had graduated. In a carefully replicated sample taken in 1952, the figures were 76 percent and 56 percent respectively.[21] A sample of 1,000 young executives assembled by *Fortune* in 1964 showed 85 percent college graduates and 40 percent with graduate work.[22]

The shift from family connections to education and specialized ability as qualifications for success in corporate business was accompanied by an increase in the number in the 1952 group who came from families of low occupational status. In 1928, only 11 percent of the executives had fathers who were laborers, while in 1952 the figure was 15 percent. In 1928, 64 percent had fathers who were professional men, owners of a business, or major executives; in 1952 this favored group was only 55 percent of the total.[23]

According to their own statements the primary qualification that these men had in common was the ability to make business decisions. Therefore, a major part of the study of how the big corporation was affecting these members of the social elite must be centered around the social conditions of the decision-making process.

One factor was a high and perhaps increasing uniformity in the type of man recruited for executive positions. As we have seen, he was generally a college graduate and obviously able to thrive in the culture of the middle-management business office, a place where intense seriousness and ambitious drive to succeed were combined with, at least, a superficial gregariousness, cooperation, and conformity. Half of a considerable group of companies polled in 1951 also practiced "wife screening" for similar qualities.[24] A writer for *Fortune* characterized the 1964 group of 1,000 young executives as "highly intelligent though culturally limited, competitive, pragmatic, totally committed to meeting the challenge and responsibility of their jobs."[25] This is perhaps equivalent to saying that these men were representative of most Americans, yet in a long view it also meant that the culture of the managerial office was emphasizing the value of having such characteristics.

The ends or goals of managerial decisions were also important both for their immediate social effect and for the attitudes they engendered in executives. The most generally agreed upon formulation of a common goal was the long-run welfare of the organization.* This had, however, quite varying corollaries in the minds of different chief executives. For example, Frank Abrams, chairman of the board of the mammoth Standard Oil of New Jersey, said, "The job of professional management is to conduct the affairs of the enterprise in such a way as to maintain an equitable and workable balance among the claims of various interested groups—stockholders, employees, customers and the public at large."[26] Yet, since for such balancing there were no accepted theoretical guides, it was probable that managers in less exalted positions would fall back on the classic doctrine of long-run maximization of profits. Even if some business executives really believed that they were acting to equalize these varied social interests, they were nevertheless likely to use a protective language of enlightened self-interest.[27] The consideration, "I have to live with him, don't I," could make good morals sound like good economics.[28]

Looked at externally, the chief executives of large corporations were likely to have long-time horizons and be sensitive to the potential effects of numerous political and social forces. It was not clear, however, that any new ultimate goals, theories of action, or moral justifications had been substituted for the long-run material welfare of the organization. For example, when a number of executives of electrical companies supplying switchgear were convicted of violation of the antitrust laws in 1960, the attitude of all the companies except one was that the needs of the organization were more justifiable than the letter of the law—an attitude little changed since the nineteenth century.[29]

Looked at another way, corporate executives as a whole were becoming more farsighted, sophisticated, and in spite of the preceding example, more ready to work with government in their decisions. In the large company with a relatively secure position in its market, decisions were said to be made on a judicial or objective basis. In the middle ranks of management, a professional engrossment in their specialty was said to make the profit motive a remote consideration. Wilbert E. Moore speaks of the "two faced" expert, the man who inevitably represented the findings of men in his specialty, or outside clients, to the general management of the corporation.[30] At the advice of "experts," corporations tended to take on many staff functions in training and research that were hard

---

* Cyert and March in *The Firm*, 115 ff., categorize variables operating on decision-making into those affecting organizational goals, expectations, and choices.

to evaluate on an accounting basis. In spite of a language couched in terms of profit, and the hard fact that in the long run profit was essential, Moore thinks that a "fair case can be made for the view that large corporations set their competitive strategy in terms of position (rank) in the market, which may not accord with optimal profit-producing strategies." Corporate management was free to do this because of "its freedom from detailed accountability to investors."[31]

The rise of the conglomerate in the late 1960s was to some extent a move to impose on management a stricter and more expert accounting based solely on profits. The top executives of the conglomerate were divorced from the organizational and human problems in the various corporations composing the group. James J. Ling, spectacular organizer of the conglomerate Ling-Temco-Vought, explained to an interviewer from *Fortune* that "a corporation is a bundle of assets subject to 'redeployment,' i.e., corporate structures are simply one of the means of managing assets."[32] He and the other operators in corporate securities, who saw nothing sacrosanct in the continued life of a particular corporation, represented a reaction against the judicial or sociological view of institutional decision-making. Ling wanted men around him who were "absolutely financially oriented."[33] Only time would tell whether the new attitude was in truth a return to the fundamentals of business which would pay off in higher long-run profits.

The danger seen by many critics of the conglomerate movement was that it led to purchasing competitors rather than developing internal means for successfully competing with them. If, for example, an oil company went into the fertilizer business by creating its own manufacturing division, it increased competition. If, however, it entered the field by purchasing an established company, it did not add to the number of competitors, and it reduced the total number of business firms. The critics proposed that in federal antitrust actions "the burden of proof should be on the large purchaser to show that he could not enter this industry by internal means."[34]

AN INSTITUTIONAL CAPITALISM

To finance mergers or the formation of conglomerates, corporations often secured long-term loans from banks and sold securities to mutual and other funds. In the general corporate prosperity from 1958 to 1968, many big companies were able to provide capital for routine expansion from profits. Thus large-scale American financing became increasingly a matter of institutional arrangements rather than of marketing securities to the general public. In the decade 1947-1957 Adolph Berle estimates that 60 percent of new corporate capital came from internal saving by the companies involved, 20 percent from bank credit, and 20 percent from capital markets. Of this latter, individual investors directly supplied no more than a quarter, or 5 percent of the total, and this amount no doubt dropped still further between 1957 and 1970, as pension funds, building and loan associations, and mutual funds all grew rapidly.[35]

Of the estimated 24,000,000 stockholders of 1968, a large part, probably a majority, owned the shares of mutual funds. In this way the influence of leaders of the financial sector of the economy, greatly weakened by the Great Depression and the legislation of the New Deal, had been revived. Instead of the earlier echelon of investment bankers led by the House of Morgan, there was now a large coalition of financial interests made up of the officers of funds, the partners of investment houses, and the executives of the big banks, insurance companies, and conglomerates. It seems more proper to call this fraternity an influence, rather than a concentrated power, because mobilization of its forces was difficult. But it meant that coalitions of these financial interests could buy the stock necessary to overthrow the management, or gain control of companies by "over-head" tenders made directly to the institutional and individual stockholders. Such tactics were usually less connected with whether management was doing well or poorly, than with larger plans, often built on tax considerations, for building conglomerate empires.

While the financial community was the strongest force in the society against inflation, it could not prevail against higher wages and government spending. Between the two World Wars, stagnation and deflation had been the greatest menaces to a stable economy; from 1941 on, inflation and too rapid expansion were the twin dangers. The space program and the costly technology of war could absorb unlimited amounts of money, and a Congress largely representative of local entrepreneurs and free-enterprising professional men was not deeply interested in governmental economy or stable prices. As a consequence, institutionally directed capitalism did not always behave in a way that satisfied its financial directors.

THE OTHER-DIRECTED WORLD OF BUSINESS

Inflation was only one of a complex of environmental problems that challenged management in the mid-twentieth century. In earlier periods unusual American advantages, such as extra labor supplied by immigrants, abundant natural resources, and few fears of disturbing influences from war or government had shaped the attitudes of businessmen. After World War II the national situation became less unique and more like that of the nations of Western Europe. Entrepreneurs were confronted with living in a complex society where success depended more on knowledge and influence than the old-time frugality and hard work.

Attention had to be given to many regulations, state and federal, to complicated tax laws, to the problems of bureaucracy and to unpredictable international relations. For all of these purposes, education was necessary, and big business recruited its executives largely from among college graduates. Consequently, while many old-style "seat of the pants" or empirical entrepreneurs still flourished, particularly in small business, alongside them was developing a larger and larger group of highly educated specialists, whom Arthur H. Cole has called "cognitive" entrepreneurs.[36] While still in middle management, many of the rising men in big companies appeared to be more professionals than profit-oriented businessmen, but when they reached the top, they became, at least, verbally insistent on maximizing long-run returns.*

An increasingly urban society with less firmly held values, more permissive child-rearing, and education for adjustment, tended to produce a man who "was concerned with the attainment of status rather than success. He preferred fitting in to standing out."[37] Such men moved easily into big companies, but the society as a whole rather than business may have been the shaping force. It should also be remembered that this corporate elite with relatively secure careers and the expectations of comfortable pensions was only a minority of the business population. The great majority of the group categorized in the census as "managers, officials, and proprietors" were men working directly for uncertain profits.

While it is very difficult to generalize about values or characteristics of a population as diverse as American businessmen, a group of social scientists at Harvard, studying the "American Business Creed" in 1955, thought that it differed only in some emphases from the values of other major groups in the society such as farmers, professional men, politicians, and workers. Americans were seen as believing in the values that had, in fact, arisen from three centuries of a business environment, beliefs in individualism, involving freedom and moral responsibility, material productivity, practicality, progress, competition, and democracy.[38] There were rebellions by the young and differences in emphasis between the small businessmen and the large, as well as between the other groups, but there seemed abundant evidence that advertising, high geographical mobility, use of leisure time, and mass communication were making American cultural values more uniform around the core supplied and emphasized by the needs of business.

---

* E. E. Hagen believes that business executives think that profit maximization is more important in their thinking than it really is: "The Internal Functions of Capitalist Organizations," *Journal of Economic History*, 30 (March, 1970), 227.

CHAPTER 17

The Rise of "Big Labor"

Big corporations employed only a small minority of Americans, yet, as in other business matters, their executives exercised leadership in determining salaries, wages, and working conditions. Before World War I they based their decisions on estimates of the free market price of labor and the types of ability needed; by 1970 the large corporation found it necessary to compromise with wage rates and conditions of work set by national unions and to adjust prices accordingly. All over the Western world the altered relationship between management and labor constituted one of the major changes in the history of business and must be examined in some detail.

CHANGING CHARACTERISTICS OF THE LABOR FORCE

In addition to altered conditions of wage bargaining in the United States, there was a significant change in the character and supply of workers. Up to World War I, immigrants had been a rapidly increasing part of the working population. In 1910 men of foreign birth or with at least one foreign parent made up about half the white male population; by 1960 the fraction had dropped to one-fifth. Some world readjustments contributed to this decrease, but it resulted chiefly from the restriction of immigration by federal laws.

While large employers of labor had always been opposed in principle to restriction of immigration (Chapter 14), many had been worried by the large influx of workers from Southern and Eastern Europe. The Bolshevik revolution added greatly to these fears, while the depression of the early 1920s temporarily eliminated the need for additional labor. A coal company president, for example, complained that "We have enough immigrants from Southern Europe to last us for the next fifty years if we are to maintain Americanism."[1] Consequently, while the majority of employers may still have opposed the Quota Act of 1921, their protests were mild, and the combination of organized labor with nativist and patriotic societies won the restriction they had long been seeking.[2] From 1924 on, immigration was restricted by a series of laws to a maximum of about 150,000 a year, not counting citizens of the Western hemisphere who were allowed relatively free access. Fifteen years of depression and war from 1930 to 1945, which effectively checked all European immigration also speeded the shift toward a native-born labor force. During periods of heavy demand for labor, migration of Negroes from the rural South substituted for immigration, and the urban population became increasingly black.

Another important long-run change was in the direction of well-paid union labor becoming more conservative and middle class rather than radical and proletarian. This was part of a worldwide change taking place in each of the foremost industrial nations and in the United States more than elsewhere. It involved the gradual shift of the nation from a class toward a mass society, from one of capitalists and proletarians separated by a relatively thin middle class toward a pattern based on occupations that from top to bottom formed a scale of social status with closely graduated and often indistinct differences. To designate wide bands of similarity in such a society it is still convenient to neglect ambiguities and use a three-class terminology.[3] In the course of increasing affluence, many union members became relatively conservative in outlook and anxious to protect their special status against social and technological change.

SHOULD THE CLOSED SHOP EXIST IN AMERICA?

For the two decades following World War I, the struggles between union organizers and highly resistant management continued. In considering these contests it should be remembered that they were largely confined to management and blue-collar or "operative" workers in manufacturing, construction, mining, and transportation. Finance, trade, and service, involving many more businessmen and almost as many employees, were never effectively organized. Therefore, the ups and downs of organized labor frequently failed to arouse much positive response among the majority of employees, and occasionally success for unionists caused a powerful wave of resentment among other workers.

The attitudes of large employers toward labor were collected in hearings before a Congressional Commission on Industrial Relations in 1913 and 1914. In general, the leading businessmen did not deny the abstract right of labor to organize. John D. Rockefeller, Jr., involved in labor troubles in his Colorado Fuel and Iron Company, said that workingmen "should be equally free to organize or not organize as they see fit."[4] The manager of the California Moline Plow Company presented the advanced idea that "labor unions are a necessity, not only for a protection to the employee, but also as a protection to the employer against himself."[5] But when it came to actually dealing with union representatives, these statements of principle tended to give way. Percy Straus of Macy's, whose sales force was unorganized, said frankly, "Theoretically, I am in favor of trade unions. Practically, I would be rather opposed to them."[6] His equally unorganized competitor John Wanamaker expressed the practical approach in phrases that were already becoming clichés, "It is a private concern . . . In one word, it is a great family . . . . We deal with everyone individually."[7]

To the president of the Women's Trade Union League, a benevolent organization for the education of working women, the prevailing attitude demonstrated that "The theory of industrial autocracy is still very much with us. Man after man will do everything under heaven for his workers except give them the right to decide for themselves."[8] The rejoinder of men like Wanamaker was that employers had responsibility while organized labor had none.[9] The operational attitudes of employers and unions according to business analyst Roger Babson made their relations "simply warfare."[10]

World War I brought a partial truce in the contests over the closed shop and union bargaining. The American Federation of Labor, led by Samuel Gompers, increased its membership by agreeing not to strike in return for government support of collective bargaining in the plants of war contractors. While this agreement also gave rise to company unions in the plants of some 200 large enterprises, it helped to add about a million members to the A.F. of L. In the two-year period of postwar scarcity, with excessive demand built up by large "reconstruction" loans to foreign nations, organized labor was able to wield unprecedented power. A record number of strikes led to inflationary settlements and rising real wages. By early 1920 there were 5,000,000 organized workers, four-fifths of them in the A.F. of L.

Even in these boom conditions of labor scarcity there were obvious signs of weakness in the structure of American unionism. The A.F. of L. had failed to penetrate large-scale mass production industry. In the prolonged steel strike of 1919, the internal rivalries of the twenty-four different A.F. of L. craft unions involved had gone far to prevent success. The "skilled workers feared the semi-skilled, the semi-skilled feared the common labor; in the vast hierarchy of steel jobs each feared being put in a lower rank even if the strike were won."[11]

Employers who studied the situation had reason to hope that continued opposition would eliminate effective unionism from all but a few areas of American activity, and preserve or restore the management-run shop instead of the union shop. When one considers that union organization had secured a place only in medium-sized or small plants in manufacturing, a tenuous hold in mining, and real strength only in railroad transportation and building construction, the managerial goal of the universal open shop does not seem unrealistic.

The depression of late 1920 set the stage for a vigorous national campaign against unions and the closed shop. Playing on the fear of the middle and upper classes that the Bolshevik Revolution might engulf the world, many politicians and journalists created the impression that leaders of organized labor were pink, if not red. Although neither had important relations with organized labor, both the National Grange, representing conservative farmers, and the American Bankers Association endorsed the open shop.[12] Open Shop Associations sprang up all over the country and the business clubs such as Kiwanis and Rotary helped to further the campaign.[13] In January of 1921, state manufacturing associations, meeting in Chicago, adopted the slogan "American plan" for the open shop.[14]

After the unsuccessful steel strike, the unions largely abandoned efforts to organize production workers in big plants. The businessmen most involved in resisting the closed shop in the 1920s were the small to medium-sized employers in the types of activity in which the A.F. of L. crafts had strength. This was also the group represented in the National Association of Manufacturers, which took a leading part in promoting the "American plan." To militant spokesmen of the employer view, neither unions nor the closed shop were legitimate social institutions, and both should be prevented by law.[15]

The campaign centered on persuading employers to refuse to sign closed shop contracts with unions, and to give them help from various associations in case of ensuing trouble. Newspapers and magazines, themselves medium-sized employers, spread hostility to unions and their leaders. To prevent secret efforts of union organizers, employers turned increasingly to their associations for reliable "intelligence" or espionage agents. Private detectives, largely from the Burns or Pinkerton agencies, took jobs in the plants and were able to spot the union organizers and report employee opinion in advance of trouble. Lists of known organizers and men discharged for union activity were exchanged between regional employers associations. In some industries employees were asked to sign a so-called yellow-dog contract stating that they would not join a union.[16] Nonunion employers brought pressure against those firms that had union contracts. The Industrial Association of San Francisco, for example, claimed by 1923 that through boycotting union employers, denial of bank credit, and other means, it had changed the city from a closed to an open shop town. In 1926, the Employers Association of Detroit advertised in a local paper, "The Open Shop has made Detroit a great industrial center ... buy only from Open Shop producers .... Think Open Shop!"[17]

To a degree, the militant employers succeeded. They were helped by federal and state courts, which were ready to grant injunctions in case of strikes, by a fair margin of unemployment in most years, by the disruptive efforts of Communists to form rival unions, and by the spread of welfare policies within companies. The membership of the A.F. of L. was reduced a million between 1919 and 1922, 100,000 between 1923 and 1929, and nearly 700,000 more by the spring of 1933. Even where a union structure existed, its power over wages and working conditions was weakened during the prosperous years and nearly eliminated in the Depression. Had the nation returned to prosperity without federal labor legislation, unionism might well have remained confined to building construction, the garment trades, and some other small manufacturing shops. Even in mining its strength was largely gone.

GOVERNMENT AIDS LABOR

At this low ebb in union strength, in 1933, Section 7A of the National Industrial Recovery Act (NIRA) suddenly posed a new threat to the open shop. It stated "That employees shall have the right to organize and bargain collectively through representatives of their own choosing, and shall be free from the interference, restraint, or coercion of employers of labor."[18] But in practice this clause proved inoperative. In some cases the provision was included in the industry code only in a meaningless form, or was disregarded (Chapter 20). In many large companies, unions supported and controlled by the corporation were recognized as bargaining agents, and the A.F. of L. was excluded.

In all, the Bureau of Labor Statistics records a growth in national union strength from 2.7 million in 1933 to 3.1 million in 1934, while a research team of the Twentieth Century Fund estimated an increase in company union strength from about 1.3 million before NIRA to 2.5 million in November 1934.[19] Although there was a further increase in national union strength of 500,000 from 1934 to 1935, NIRA still had a greater effect on company union strength. It is also worth remembering that the national union strength of 3.6 million in 1935 was only about 100,000 higher than the relatively low levels of the middle and late 1920s and no higher as a percentage of total nonfarm population. Employers could well hope that the growth of national trade unions might still be reversed and the closed shop completely eliminated by concerted managerial action.

During the two years of disputes regarding Section 7A, the National Association of Manufacturers came to be the most active spokesman for the militant business opposition to legally enforced collective bargaining. In earlier decades the NAM had been supported by a minority group of small to medium-sized employers, but now, as the struggle between autonomous and government regulated labor policy became critical, the association was reorganized and received the support of many of the largest corporations. Although it had only from 1,500 to 3,000 member firms from 1933 to 1937, through its affiliated National Industrial Council, an organization of employers associations, it was said by 1937 to represent 35,000 to 40,000 manufacturing firms with 4,500,000 to 5,000,000 employees. While these figures amounted to only a small minority of all firms in manufacturing, they represented employers of nearly half of industrial labor.[20]

The NAM and other employer organizations operated under difficult circumstances. Public opinion had been alienated from business both by the very fact of depression and mass unemployment, and by revelations of dishonesty in high financial circles. Labor leaders elicited unusual sympathy because through them the distressed public could attack business. As a result, the campaign of the NAM and other business organizations for company representation plans and the attack on Section 7A as unconstitutional (which involved refusal to cooperate with the National Labor Relations Board) aroused considerable public hostility. In the midst of the campgain, the election of 1934 returned a House and Senate with overwhelming liberal and Democratic majorities.

The crucial bill in the history of American labor relations was introduced in February, 1935, by Senator Robert F. Wagner of New York. The new proposal would prevent employers from trying to influence their employees in any way that might interfere with organization by outsiders, prohibit support of company unions, and force firms to bargain with whatever union could, at a time of its own choosing, secure a majority vote of the employees. This union could then speak for all the workers and enforce a closed shop. No one on either side doubted the effect of enforcing such a law. Senator Wagner had had a year's experience as chairman of the NRA Labor Board, and he knew government support was needed for the success of organizers from national unions. Large employers also knew that with the prevailing national sentiment they could probably not avoid loss of control over the conditions of work if the bill became established law.

In view of the great historic importance of the bill, the struggle in Congress appears very mild. The NAM put on a major campaign, first to influence the form of the bill in the hearings, then to amend it, and finally to defeat it—all without avail. A three-day meeting in Washington to bring senators face to face with important constituents just before the final vote on the bill seems to have had a negligible effect.[21] All of this is hard to explain. The bill was an extreme measure, and most senators have been business lawyers or business owners. Senator Wagner, to be sure, had light industry constituents who were largely unionized and who probably favored a law that would extend an equal degree of organization to other areas, but widespread legal belief that the bill was unconstitutional may explain most of the sixty-two other affirmative votes in the Senate. An added reason is that the general opposition of business, and particularly big companies, to the reform legislation of the spring of 1935 had created a public sentiment that made few politicians want to appear as enemies of labor and friends of business. Only a dozen senators voted against the National Labor Relations Act.

Up to the time of its passage, the NAM had predicted the dire effects of the bill on prosperity and productivity; now its legal office switched rather abruptly to the line that the law was unconstitutional. Judged by the Supreme Court decisions of the previous twenty years, there was much strength in the NAM contention. The principal provisions of the act could only be effective if workers in manufacturing were regarded as involved in the flow of the goods they made in interstate commerce. This required a broad interpretation of the commerce power which the recent decisions of the Supreme Court made highly unlikely.

During the nearly two years between the passage of the Wagner Act and its test by the Supreme Court, labor relations were chaotic. These same months cover the one period of strong economic upswing in the 1930s. Prices and employment rose, and workers demanded higher pay. Encouraged by the law, a group of associated national unions, later to form the Congress of Industrial Organizations, started organizing drives in the large manufacturing industries —the chief defenders of the open shop.

The organizing drives were met with many types of employer resistance. Ford and some other companies had their own espionage system for detecting organizers and their own police for expelling them. Smaller companies received advice from their employer's associations and the NAM, and hired labor spies from private detective agencies.[22] Still more manufacturing companies worked with employer's associations that advised compliance with the law, and preservation of the open shop by granting wages and conditions of work equal or superior to those demanded by the unions. The leaders in resistance to enforced collective bargaining were the employers in motors, steel, and the metal trades, some regional organizations, such as the Associated Industries of Cleveland, and the NAM. Motors and steel became the spectacular battlegrounds between militant labor and resistant employers.

Under pressure from Governor Frank Murphy of Michigan and President Roosevelt, who had just won a landslide reelection, General Motors, followed by the other car manufacturers except Ford, gave way and compromised with the union.[23] United States Steel surprised everyone by ignoring the advice of the Iron and Steel Institute and entering into a contract in the spring of 1937, but the other large producers, known as "little steel," decided to resist. At Ford and the many plants of the "little steel," companies a labor war continued fitfully until 1940.

Meanwhile, President Roosevelt had introduced his bill to alter the composition of the Supreme Court, a turn of events that resistant employer organizations could scarcely have foreseen. In the beginning, when the NAM and other associations counseled resistance on the grounds of unconstitutionality, most business leaders appear to have thought that Roosevelt would be defeated in the election of 1936. In the congressional session of 1937, the administration's effort to increase the number of Supreme Court justices failed, but either the threat, or the manifestation, of overwhelming popular support for the president in the election, changed the opinion of the Court. On April 12, at a time when the decision could undermine support for the president's bill, the Court held, 5 to 4, that the Wagner Act was constitutional.

The National Labor Relations Board (NLRB), now able effectively to order elections and collective bargaining, ended resistance at Ford and the "little steel" companies. Handling nearly 30,000 cases by 1940, the board issued orders against yellow-dog contracts, blacklists, labor espionage, and antiunion propaganda. It made company unions as independent as outside unions and supported all types of peaceful picketing. In these rulings the NLRB was continuously supported by the Supreme Court, which now expanded the commerce power of

Congress to the greatest extent in American history. The labor shortages of World War II and the patriotic need for continuous production also worked to maintain and entrench the rulings of the NLRB and the temporary War Labor Board.

Employers who sincerely believed with W. Gibson Carey of Yale, Towne Manufacturing Company, "that any trend toward the abolition of fair company unions or individual relationships between employees and employers is decidedly not in the public interest nor in the interest of the employees themselves,"[24] had been defeated by what amounted to a revolution in labor relations. As important as employers loss of control of organization and meetings in their plants, was the fact that labor relations were now governed by federal laws and agencies. From this time forward, changes in practice would be a matter of politics and congressional lobbying.

THE POLITICS OF INDUSTRIAL RELATIONS

Looking back on the political warfare of the 1930s, businessmen could well feel that they had been defeated by a temporary wave of hostility not representative of normal American opinion. The Wagner Act and its support by the Supreme Court were products of that wave at its very crest, and while it seemed that the federal government could never be removed from its new position in labor relations, the rules for the exercise of its power might gradually be altered. Even during the war a relatively unimportant modification of the labor laws in 1943 had indicated the existence of a strong antilabor coalition in Congress.

The first opportunity for a major change came shortly after the close of the war. Inflation from pent-up demand, as in 1919, produced a series of strikes. The unorganized majority of American workers, blue- and white-collar, resented the relative success of organized labor in keeping up with inflation and swung to the right politically, although this was the side that had opposed continued price regulation. As a result, in the fall of 1946, the Republicans won control of both houses of Congress, which, with the support of Southern Democrats on most economic measures, constituted a very large majority in favor of stricter regulation of labor.

Since 1940, state laws controlling union activity had been on the increase. In 1947 there was a bumper crop of such acts, prohibiting the closed shop and secondary boycotts and regulating union finances. Clearly, business had Congress and public opinion behind it, but the lasting effect of the labor revolution of the 1930s was shown by the fact that instead of sweeping aside the guarantees of collective bargaining, Congress merely modified them to increase the power of employers. From the latter's standpoint, perhaps the most important provisions of the Taft-Hartley Act of 1947 were the banning of the closed shop and sympathetic strikes or secondary boycotts, and making unions, for the first time, liable for damages for breach of contract or violation of the law. Employers were now able to argue with their employees regarding matters of organization. President Truman vetoed the bill, and it was speedily repassed by the two-thirds majorities necessary to override.

Labor held that the law marked a return to pre-New Deal conditions, and also objected strongly, on principle, to a provision requiring labor leaders to take anti-Communist oaths. Polls taken shortly after the passage of the law indicated that about one-third of the leaders thought that business wanted to break the unions, and a large majority believed that businessmen only tolerated unions.[25] Well over two-thirds of the labor officials thought that in their contests business was stronger than labor.[26] At each congressional and presidential election from 1948 on, labor backed candidates in favor of repeal of the Taft-Hartley Law.

In these political skirmishes labor demonstrated some strength at the polls. Congress for example was only Republican from 1953 to 1955, but business demonstrated its strength in Congress time and again. Congressmen, at home in the world of business, had little first-hand knowledge of the problems of workers or union leaders. The mass media were also sympathetic to the employer view. Except for the middle years of the New Deal, there seemed little likelihood of much prolabor legislation in either the states or Congress.

A dozen years after the Taft-Hartley Act, another showdown developed between the political forces of labor and business that well illustrated the continuing balance of forces in Washington. In the congressional election of 1958, the Democrats won a victory of landslide proportions. In the new Senate there were 64 Democrats and only 34 Republicans; in the House the division was 283 to 153. Republican Postmaster General Arthur Summerfield held that "union bosses" were responsible for the Democratic sweep, and warned that "America teeters on the precipice of a labor-bossed Congress."[27] The "professed friends of labor" also controlled the necessary congressional committees. Surely, a move back toward the Wagner Act seemed irresistable.

Yet other short- and long-run forces favored the resistance of business. Senator McClelland of Arkansas had been holding hearings before a Senate committee that gave widespread publicity to corruption and the use of violence by labor leaders such as Dave Beck and Jimmy Hoffa of the Teamsters. The Southern Democrats were as strongly opposed to organized labor as in earlier years, and the presidential administration, while outwardly liberal, had important members working with the business interests.

In the complex campaign for amendments and substitute bills that takes place when a controversial law is being put through Congress, the labor lobbyists were ubiquitous, confident, and outspoken. In the early stages of committee work, they seemed unbeatable. The employer interests lacked the necessary votes. To redress the balance, business organizations conducted an extensive educational campaign through the press, television, and movies, keynoting labor violence and the fight of the people against labor bosses.[28] Soon Congressmen began receiving the type of mail in favor of a "strong" labor bill that they recognized as indicating a trend in voter opinion.

At the proper time the Landrum-Griffin Bill, with the provisions business wanted, was introduced. Edward McCabe, the White House liaison with the Senate, advised a group of the representatives of the largest companies meeting in Washington to leave the congressional work to the professionals and not to try to dictate minor provisions. The principal business interests should continue to create the kind of national opinion that would feed back to Washington, and they themselves should keep away from the halls of Congress. He also assured those present that the administration would do its part.[29] A few days later, labor lobbyists suddenly found that their favorite, the Shelley Bill, had no chance of passage, that the moderate Elliott Bill that they hoped could be amended was also out, and that the Landrum-Griffin Bill which had only appeared late in the proceedings now had the necessary votes. After a number of amendments in both houses and in conference committee, the administration substitute became the Labor-Management Reporting and Disclosure Act of 1959.

The provisions of the law were involved and dealt with a number of special situations. The internal procedures for governing unions were strictly regulated, and union officers were required to post $500,000 bonds. Jurisdictional and various other special types of picketing were permitted under certain conditions. The states were specifically allowed to regulate labor matters not covered by federal law. In general, the provisions made it more difficult to organize new unions and helped to check the spread of organization in the South. As a whole, the bill represented a moderate victory for employers, but a considerable addition to the rising mountain of labor law. The days when employers could reach decisions on the basis of their own judgment were even more remote than under Taft-Hartley.

THE MANY WORLDS OF BUSINESS AND LABOR

The handful of big industrial unions that had lobbyists in Washington and negotiated three-year nationwide contracts with the management of the largest corporations were but one small part of the world of labor and a still smaller part of the world of business. Fringe benefits, pension funds, guaranteed annual wage, and continually mounting rates of pay for this segment of factory labor led many other workers, as well as members of the white-collar and professional groups, to regard them as a favored elite and a dangerous inflationary force in the economy. In 1959 the widely publicized gains in wages and conditions won in bargains between "big labor" and "big management" led George Romney of American Motors to attack the concentration of union and industrial power.[30] Certainly in the period of rapid inflation that began in 1965, three-year contracts based on estimates of continuing inflation became in themselves major causes of inflation. Yet, management in the leading companies found it more expedient to compromise generously with the union demands and then raise prices than to risk a long and costly strike.

Another world of industrial relations was that in which many small or medium-sized employers had to deal with big nationwide unions, as in the building trades and trucking. After World War II, bargaining was usually conducted by the unions with employer organizations. The latter often lacked cohesiveness, and as in the case of big company management, found settlement safer than a prolonged strike. The balance of power was indicated by continually higher wages that, on an hourly basis, surpassed factory rates.

These unions, in particular, sought to maintain their bargaining power by strict enforcement of apprenticeship regulations. Frequently new members were accepted only on a quota basis, and until the late 1960s Negroes were generally excluded. Restrictive building codes, supported by both unions and contractors, contributed to a vicious circle of high costs, retarded building, and less employment.

Another world of business and labor was in the service and retail trades. Except for some supermarkets and other chain stores, the small numbers of employees in each establishment made organization extremely difficult. In 1962 the A.F. of L. C.I.O. began a special campaign to unionize workers of every type in selected major cities. While gains were reported, after two years the campaign in Los Angeles, at least, was abandoned because of "meagre results," and, as a whole, the membership of the unions continued to decrease.[31]

Small cities with no important industrial activity were likely to remain nonunion. In many farm-market centers there were neither unions nor any businesses employing many workers.[32] The upward pressure on wages in these places, after 1945, came from chronic inflation and the need to keep men from leaving the small city to seek better pay in some metropolitan area.

As technological change increased the proportion of white-collar workers, from a quarter of the total in 1920 to half in 1970, more employees came to have a feeling of "belonging" to the company for which they worked. Probably this came mainly from a middle-class desire for security and stability on the part of the worker, but in the 1950s and 1960s many companies became more acutely aware of the cost of labor turnover, with its attendant need for new training. To hold its work force, which was three-quarter white-collar or technical, International Business Machines, for example, put all employees on a steady salary basis. Such developments might presage a move in large companies toward the Japanese system of high job-security, but this could affect, at the most, only a small part of the American work force.

The concept of all levels of employees as part of the company community undoubtedly added to the disinclination of "big management" to risk crippling strikes. Ideally, at least, wage difficulties should be settled around a conference table on the basis of what was possible policy for the welfare of the firm. Large employers had given up fighting against unions, and even strikes tended to be orderly and according to rules.

For the great majority of American employers, whose workers were not organized, wages and conditions of work were still on the old, uncertain basis of what "others" were paying and what would attract and hold employees. The rise of many blue-collar wages from 1940 on to a level as high or higher than those for clerical work had undoubtedly improved the status of manual labor. Perhaps employer-employee relations, disturbed by the great influx of immigrants from 1880 to 1914, had returned to the more democratic state of the earlier nineteenth century.

CHAPTER 18

Conditioning in a More
Scientific Society

To the prosperous American of the 1920s, business and science seemed demonstrably to be the guides for a good life. Businessmen had not planned or worked for such ascendancy; it happened from the combination of American economic progress, its traditional culture, and world events. With American business as apparently the strongest force in the world, and science thought to offer the clue to the mysteries of life, parents sought guidance from psychological precepts in bringing up their children; they favored a utilitarian education that would fit them for a place in the affluent society. Meanwhile, in the 1920s, affluence itself had important effects on childhood conditioning.

The Great Depression injured the image of American business. Success in business became, perhaps, less often the exclusive aim of upbringing, and other careers in government or the learned professions gained in attractiveness. But since such careers depended on specialized knowledge, the change probably reenforced scientific, as against humanistic or religious, attitudes and strengthened a pragmatic, utilitarian approach to social problems. Consequently, scientific child rearing and "community-oriented" education for good social adjustment continued to gain in strength until, at least, the 1950s. Again, without planning by businessmen, the new conditioning fitted people for easy and effective participation in an impersonal corporate society where individual eccentricities were suppressed in the interest of harmonious action by the group.

THE RISE OF PERMISSIVENESS IN CHILD REARING

The new ideas that deeply affected child rearing and schooling were a part of the general scientific attack upon existing religious and moral sanctions that, as we have seen, began a little before the turn of the century and had carried most of the citadels of educated belief by the 1920s. Late nineteenth-century experimental psychology and other scientific approaches such as historical analysis of the Bible and anthropological study of human behavior cast doubt on the authority of many older moral values. William James' *The Principles of Psychology*, published in 1890, was one of the earliest books to spread the new scientific ideas. "The human being who appears in James' psychology," wrote

Edna Heidbreder, "bears little resemblance to the rational man of earlier years."[1] Later in the decade, John Dewey began applying the new psychology to child reading and education.

During the next generation, academic psychologists were effectively undermining the religious ideas of will power and rationally controlled activity, but for the educated, urban, upper middle class, which appears to have been the source of most future business leaders, the theories of Sigmund Freud were more dramatic and exciting.[2] The popularity of his ideas in the United States fitted the social trends arising from urban industrialism as well as from the whole complex of experimental attitudes. The initial Freudian emphasis on sexual repression as a primary cause of neurosis fitted well with postwar ideas regarding elimination of the double standard of morality and more freedom for women. Bringing sex "into the open" went with short skirts and equality with men in smoking, drinking, language, and voting. But the more important and lasting effect of Freudianism, one that later revisions scarcely weakened, was to cast further doubt on the objectivity of all reason. Rational processes according to Freud were guided by unconscious urges. Given the same situation, two "reasonable" men would, because of different infantile sexual repressions, select facts that led by logical processes to different conclusions. While later clinical experience has broadened the scope of what is repressed, included external social pressures, and lengthened the period over which the unconscious is conditioned, these later scholars have not restored nineteenth-century confidence in reason and conscious "will power" as guides to conduct. Ideas have remained ideologies, and truth relative to its context.

In the United States, particularly, the attack on reason was carried to an extreme. Experiments with the conditioned reflex in animals led the University of Chicago psychologist, and later advertising man, John B. Watson, to advance a system called Behaviorism in which all "thought" was merely the verbalizing of conditioned reflexes.[3] The existence of consciousness was held to be a delusion akin to religion, myths, and other superstitions. In 1928, Watson wrote, "No one knows enough today to raise a child."[4] While too extreme in his break with tradition to convince the majority of experimental psychologists, a few big university departments were won over to Watson's views. Easier to understand that Freud, and more concerned with normal psychology, Watson converted many middle-class parents into Behaviorists, and also influenced writers on child rearing. Behaviorism was specifically incorporated in *Infant and Child Care*, a booklet widely distributed by the U.S. Department of Labor in the mid-1920s.[5]

While Watson made all morality a matter of conditioning rather than thought or will, Freud, in effect, turned old-fashioned American morality upside down. Repression of self-indulgence by the use of will power in order to abide by divine precepts was now seen as psychologically dangerous in the case of the young and probably futile in the case of adults. The repressed desire would find some alternate and perhaps more subtly dangerous form of expression. As in the case of Freudian ideas regarding sex, the new morality, or amorality, of indulgence suited other social trends. Businessmen in the 1920s were emphasizing greater consumption. Since from 1923 to 1939 lower-class purchasing power per capita was scarcely increasing, greater consumption had to come from luxury spending by the upper income groups—those who were most influenced by the new psychological ideas. So the older American morality of abstinence, frugality, and saving was for many replaced by an acceptance of indulgence, high consumption, and living on credit.

Later attitudes have modified some of the extreme ideas of the 1920s, but the general acceptance of the view of mental processes generated by Freud's theories remained the rule in medicine and the social sciences. Invading the old-time religious preserves of child rearing and education, the experimental psychologists, psychoanalysts, and educational specialists insured the perpetuation of their influence through inevitably altering the personality of many members of the ensuing generation.

Even before World War I the effects of the new scientific attitudes were beginning to be apparent. There was more emphasis on introspection by parents, and original sin and depravity were generally rejected. The effect of scientific questioning is reflected in Ernest H. Abbott's note that in religious training our ancestors had an advantage: "They knew very definitely what they wished their children to do and to believe . . . . Now, although they wish to give their children a full complement of doctrines, they either do not possess the full complement themselves, or do not believe that their children are mature enough to receive it."[6] On the whole, however, Geoffrey H. Steere has found that the admonitions of the early century were still in terms of divine will and recognized principles.[7]

By the 1920s the revolution in child-rearing texts had occurred. "The predominately religiously oriented text . . . was an anomaly."[8] The measures advanced were generally in terms of psychology or physiology. Writing in 1920, the editor of *Mothers' Magazine and Home Life* came out squarely for experimentation. The child "cannot learn it by looking at it simply or listening to words that adults use to describe it."[9] He warned the mother that "the more she limits her child, the more she handicaps him in his struggle to learn the world in which he must live."[10] Parents were urged to be friends with their children rather than disciplinarians.[11] In contrast to the clergymen and laymen of the earlier periods, the authors were mainly doctors. While there was an emphasis on permissiveness for the child and self-study for the parent, no principles were stated with the unquestioning confidence of the Christian precepts of earlier times. Authoritarian parents of the old religious type could find little support in the textbooks. Freudian or Watsonian attitudes toward moral training were usually present, either explicitly or implicitly. Chidren were being trained not for the hereafter, but for pragmatic adjustment to a changing present.

David Potter finds the same influences on children, as well as additional ones, arising from the "abundance" of maturing American industrialism. Among the additional results of affluence were bottle feeding, with its inevitable emphasis on individual separateness; a room for each child, working in the same direction; physical freedom of movement in warm rooms, as against swaddling or heavy clothing; more permissive toilet training resulting from washing machines, fewer children, and paper diapers; more permissive general training thought to develop independence of judgment; and a more intense emotional relationship between the child and mothers who had leisure.[12]

Subscribing to mid-twentieth century theories that the society and its projective systems bear strongly on childhood conditioning, Potter emphasizes the greatly increased effect of advertising. It trained the child, and for that matter continued to condition the adult, for "the role of consumer—and it profoundly modifies the system of values, for it articulates the rationale of material values for him in the same way in which the church articulates a rationale of spiritual values."[13] The real change in personality, however, may have been less than has been assumed. In the people subjected to the new forces of education and the business environment, there also remained many of the old attitudes of Protestant morality. The offhand admonitions of parents and teachers had changed less and may have had more force than pediatric or educational theory.

The continued questioning of formerly accepted principles and values decade after decade, contributed to the suffering of educated middle-class parents from what Max Lerner has called "child panic." In spite of such confusion, however, he notes that the rapid growth of the middle class led many families, particularly those of immigrant origin, to train the child, as in earlier generations, to try to surpass the achievements of the parents. Coupled with the new psychological ideas, this led to a muting of the parental ego, parental assumption of the role of advisor rather than disciplinarian, and left a family with no center of authority. "In the already child-oriented American family," Lerner writes, "this deference vacuum often brings the family close to child-centered anarchy."[14]

The early extremes of scientism in child rearing were producing a reaction by the 1950s. Leading child psychologists then began advising parents to follow their "instincts" and their common sense, but meanwhile a large percentage of the business leaders of the period from 1945 to, at least, 1970 had been brought up in relatively affluent families by the "scientific" ideas of child rearing. These were the widely discussed, "other directed" or "organization men." Many other forces undoubtedly joined in demolishing older mores and producing men with relatively few fixed values and a desire to find happiness through adjustment to and conformity with their environment, while cooperation, for example, had always been a major aspect of American culture, among factors promoting it such as altered schooling, a more corporate society, and geographical mobility, the new child rearing must take an important place.

What did the whole complex of forces mean from the standpoint of the characteristics of American entrepreneurship? A penetrating and subtle effect on business thought and process may have come from the doubts cast by psychologists on "objective" decisions. If no man's judgment was to be trusted as unbiased, it might be best to average out personal idiosyncracies by working through committees. The same approach applied to business ethics. If there was no divinely revealed right or wrong, but only pragmatic relationships to be considered, it again might be safest to poll the opinion of a number of interested people. Thus the forces of psychology joined in shifting decision-making from the old strong-willed individualists toward more bureaucratic concensus. "Child-centered anarchy" in the home may have generated committee-centered anarchy in some big companies.

Perhaps the retreat from certainty and religious authority did not greatly alter the underlying values of the business society. The new influences were to a considerable degree emphasizing values or attitudes already present in American upbringing. There is, for example, no reason to suppose that there was a sharp diminution of emphasis on success and efficiency, although, as we have seen, success might be redefined. The changes in business attitudes, the longer and broader views of corporate executives, and the readier acceptance of government aid can be seen as reactions to a different business situation rather than to basically different social or personal values held by entrepreneurs. Yet one hesitates to segment such intangible complexes. All forces seemed working in common directions, submerging the old self-assured authoritative middle-class culture, built on success in business, in what theologian Paul Tillich has called a "heteronomy" of contending values and ideas.

EDUCATION FOR SOCIAL ADJUSTMENT

The conditioning of children by the public education system from World War I until the late 1950s had much the same aims, and perhaps the same results, as the new child rearing. Applying the scientific-utilitarian calculus to education produced a breakdown of the old ideas regarding mind training and disciplinary studies, and spread an uncertain pragmatic approach through the school system. John Dewey's precepts of progressive education (Chapter 9), which revolved around study of the needs of the child, gradually became the orthodox language of educators, with a resulting displacement of the traditional subject matter of education that Dewey, himself, had not expected.

In discussing these trends and their substantial reversal in recent years, it is easier to assess the changes in their relation to business philosophies or needs than to trace business influence in bringing them about. Aside from members of school boards, it appears that only a few business leaders before the 1950s gave serious thought to general, as distinct from vocational, elementary and secondary education. There was apparently little effort, for example, to indoctrinate children with reverence for business leaders. Taking surveys of the types chosen as people that school children would like to emulate, businessmen started at 1.6 percent in a survey of 1902, declined to 1 percent in 1910, the same in 1928, and .6 percent in 1958. It is worth noting that in the same surveys nonserious entertainers gradually replaced national heroes such as George Washington as the top category.[15] Reinforcing the lack of direct efforts at indoctrinating for business success is an observed decline in achievement motivation in school readers from the high 1900 level to about that of 1850.[16] Content analysis of the *4-H Club News*, a rural youth magazine from 1924 to 1958, also indicates a decline in achievement values. An analysis of third-grade readers made in 1956 indicated that the theme of "winning friends" had increased from 4 percent of total content in the 1900-1920 period to over a third by midcentury. Adjusting to one's group had also become a major theme.[17] John G. Cawelti finds a change in juvenile fiction from emphasis upon habits of industry, economy, temperance, and piety, practiced because of their aid to personal achievement, to a greater stress on play, creative activity, and "getting along" with associates.[18]

Such evidence lends additional support to the conclusion that the influence of business on general public education was more the effect of a business-like culture than of planned business pressures. In making the schools more businesslike, the administrators were responding to the ideas of important people in their communities and to what was valued in their society. "In the great number of American cities that have between 25,000 and 1,000,000 population," wrote Howard K. Beale, "religious forces have much less power over teachers than do businessmen or politicians. In suburbs of great cities religious groups and politicians are alike unimportant in comparison with business interests."[19] Yet the net results were not necessarily favorable to traditional business ideals.

The most sensitive level of the educational system, the stage on which most of the strife centered, was secondary education. By 1920, practically all children were compelled by law to enter the high school, and here the critical economic choices had to be made: (1) to drop out at the minimum age level permitted; (2) to choose a vocational course; (3) to continue a general course without future educational plans; and (4) to prepare for college. Of these choices many would no doubt select the third, partly from inertia and partly from a middle-class stigma attached to dropping out or going to a "manual training" school.

Recognizing the revolutionary alteration in the high school situation brought about by compulsory school laws, the 1911 Reports of the Committee of Nine of the National Education Association (Chapter 11) became the starting point for forty-odd years of curricular change. The report held that the task of the high school was "to lay the foundations of good citizenship and to help in the wise choice of a vocation," aims that all cognizant business groups must have applauded. Proper choice of a career, the report noted, required an early exposure to vocational training. For this, girls might substitute "household science." Proceeding in more detail, the commission saw seven main objectives of education: health; command of fundamental processes; worthy home membership; a vocation; good citizenship; worthy use of leisure time; and proper ethical character.[20] Of the seven, only "command of fundamental processes" required the traditional type of subject matter, and the discussion brought out that this should be mainly continuing instruction in the three Rs. According to the report, schools should be designed to take care of varying needs with "agricultural, business, clerical, industrial, fine-arts and household arts curriculums. Provision should be made also for those having distinctively academic interests and needs." As Richard Hofstadter notes, the relegation of the old learning to the last sentence is revealing.[21] Clearly the supposed "needs" of the child and the desire of the school to hold the child's interest had triumphed over the mastery of subject matter.

The report or its publication as a pamphlet *The Cardinal Principles of Secondary Education* does not appear to have attracted major comment by businessmen. But the committee's message was clearly in support of emerging managerial attitudes: "Preference for vocationalism is linked with preference for character—or personality—over mind, for conformity and manipulative facility over individuality and talent."[22] These were the qualities wanted, at least, in lower and middle management, the kinds of traits the personnel officer was instructed to have in mind when hiring.[23]

As we have seen (Chapter 11), businessmen had always supported the movement for vocational education, or what was often called manual training. As technology became more complex, engineer Charles R. Allen and school superintendent Charles A. Prosser became convinced that the conventional high school education did not fit students for the better paid manual jobs. In 1906 they helped to organize a National Society for the Promotion of Industrial Education that worked for the Smith-Hughes Act of 1917, granting money to states for vocational high schools. The ideal of Allen and Prosser was to concentrate entirely on utilitarian or applied knowledge and to avoid all discussion of controversial economic or social questions.[24] Soon, medium-sized or large cities had at least one manual training high school.

Private industrial schools also continued to spread. In 1916, Henry Ford, for example, started his own trade school, in which the instructors were skilled employees already on the payroll and the textbook was the Ford plant. "It offers," he contended, "more resources for practical education than most universities."[25] A boy completing the course had no obligations and might go elsewhere to work. By 1920 company schools were so numerous that their directors formed the National Association of Corporation Training, comprising trade apprenticeship, office work, advertising and selling, and various other types of special training schools. After World War II, General Electric ran a school with 250 teachers and many of its own textbooks.[26]

In addition, the private business "colleges" with their six-weeks to six-months commercial courses continued to flourish, with an increasing emphasis on secretarial training for girls. The number and variety of correspondence schools also grew, some offering work in higher professional fields such as law and engineering. As Frank A. Vanderlip, president of the biggest American bank, saw the situation at the end of World War I, "There has been introduced such complexity into modern business . . . that the young man who begins without the foundation of an exceptional training is in danger of remaining a mere clerk or bookkeeper."[27]

During the price inflation of World War I, the idea of more businesslike and efficient public school administration gained ground rapidly.[28] The new-style administrators tended to "view the school as an organization devoted to dispensing ready-made knowledge much as a wholesale establishment prepares and assorts packages for distribution, grading them according to the needs of the different types of customers."[29] Never had the elementary and secondary school been closer in spirit to the aims of business than after World War I. As a National Education Association pamphlet said, "The free public school and American business are partners, each supplementing and strengthening the other . . . . Setting aside all the important cultural, civic and social values of education the schools can easily justify themselves in their contribution to business."[30] In this partnership, the school boards, controlled by businessmen, inevitably regarded the administrators as more important than the teachers.

As local and state expenditures for elementary and secondary education rose from $764 thousand in 1918 to $2.3 billion in 1930, boards and legislatures inevitably took a hard, businesslike look at mounting costs.[31] But there seems to have been little conflict in aims between businessmen, school administrators, teachers, and students. Urban businessmen recognized the need for secondary education in a complex industrial system, but some farmers mounted a steady opposition. All groups, except a few academic scholars, had been won over to the idea of immediately practical education. In addition, writers on education saw as desirable the "inculcation of certain attitudes toward property and government, of certain theories concerning relations between employers and workers, a certain scheme of values."[32] John Dewey's plea for concentrating on the needs of the child had become the orthodoxy, but the needs were interpreted in a way that Dewey had not foreseen. He had hoped to make difficult subject matter interesting, the public schools were progressively eliminating such subjects; he had hoped to educate for an ideal social democracy, the educational system was moving toward support of the status quo.

There was, to be sure, a wide rift between school board members, and other representatives of business, and the social views of some leading progressive educators, but the latter were chiefly in the colleges of education. To scholars such as George Counts and Harold Rugg of Teachers College, "education for democracy" meant schooling that would teach the need for more equality of income and rights and more social security, but this was not the thrust of the movement either in the public schools or in the National Education Association.*

When it came to educating their own children, the leaders of national business were less sure of the virtue of a strongly practical utilitarian curriculum. The leading private schools remained the stronghold of traditional academic subjects. Here the bright student would be better educated for the demands of college, and less indoctrinated in community relations.

The 1930s produced the same financial stresses and strains in the world of public education as in the realm of business. Unable to collect the full quota of taxes, by 1932 some municipalities were unable to pay their educational bills. Schools were shut down, 85 percent of those in Alabama; teachers lost their jobs, 11,000 in New York City alone; others went unpaid, including those in Chicago. As in most cases of hardship, business was blamed. Even the NEA, which spoke for administrators and superintendents as well as teachers, complained that "greedy bankers, manufacturers and politicians try to save themselves, forgetting that in a time like this, he who would save his life must lose it to the common good." Such people were "debasing the currency of American culture in the mad scramble of the super-salesman."[33] For protection against pay cuts and firing, teachers joined unions and associations, including one for teachers of business, formed in 1934.[34]

Increased support for public education in the late thirties was followed by serious troubles during and after World War II. In a period of full employment, inflation and rising wages, average salaries, including those of principals and superintendents, rose only from $1,441 a year in 1940 to $1,995 in 1946.[35] At such levels it was impossible to hold able young people in the school system or to recruit sufficient replacements. Yet district school boards were unwilling to incur taxes for realistic increases. One is reminded of Cubberley's statement in 1916 that "any marked educational progress was impossible under the district system."[36]

While the caliber of teaching was declining, professional educators in the teachers colleges moved still further away from academic subject matter. The aggressive push toward the new practical subjects was heralded by Dr. Prosser, the pioneer of vocational education, in the Inglis Lecture at Harvard in 1939. "The important thing," he held, "is not to teach pupils how to generalize but to supply them directly with the information they need for daily living."[37] In the late 1940s Commissioner John W. Studebaker put the influence of the United States Office of Education behind the movement for "life adjustment."

---

* The NEA had a kind of professional progressivism, even in the 1920s, but did little to resist the utilitarian trend.

The life adjustment enthusiasts merely put the finishing touches on the long-run decline in high school learning as against training. Between 1910 and 1950 academic subjects in the public high school curricula fell from four-fifths to one-fifth. While the fall of registration for Latin from 49 percent of all students enrolled to 8 was not surprising, the fall of all mathematics enrollment from 90 to 55 percent in a world that was rapidly making mathematics a universal language was arresting.[38] A similar decrease in physical science enrollments also seemed a trend away from the real needs of both business and the nation. In place of taking the old academic subjects, students were offered nearly 200 new subjects ranging from "home and family problems" to automobile driving and hairdressing. Although the movement was toward practicality, proponents of business training thought that their subjects were neglected by the United States Office of Education.[39]

Together with an emphasis on subjects immediately applicable to life experience went an emphasis on the 60 percent of the students who might finish high school, but could not be expected to go on to college. The 20 percent classed as bright students were regarded as capable of educating themselves and needed no special attention. This was a new conception of equalitarian democracy, one in which all were made more equal by penalizing those above the norm. Had the United States lived in a world of static technology and international relations, the concept might have prevailed, but in the 1950s this was far from the case.

THE SWING TOWARD LEARNING

More complex technology and resulting business and college pressures for more adequate schooling, alone, might have brought about a change in educational trends, but awareness of a race against Russia in physical science, and the protests of leading university educators such as President Conant of Harvard and Killian of M.I.T. produced a crisis in education. As the latter put it, "The Russian satellite did not initiate it, but it added immensely to its momentum. Educational innovators who were struggling for support—financial support and moral support—found themselves at last commanding attention."[40] Business leaders quickly joined academic scholars in demanding a return to disciplinary schooling. In 1956 the president of the Los Angeles Chamber of Commerce complained that

> Students are getting fewer and fewer courses that train them to think clearly . . . modern schools are so geared to mediocracy that bright students are discouraged . . . . Our public education system has a responsibility to anticipate the needs for its product—trained students—in the quantities required and with the skills necessary to meet the needs . . . . The job has not been well done.[41]

In 1955 the Progressive Education Association quietly passed away, and by the time Sputnik appeared in the fall of 1957, the United States was moving rapidly toward more adequate public secondary schools. But the apparent Russian superiority in, at least, one branch of technology produced a strong reaction. In March, 1958, *Life* magazine began a series of articles on the "Crisis in Education." "The geniuses of the next decade," warned *Life*, "are even now being allowed to slip back into mediocrity . . . . We must recapture an honest respect for learning and for learned people."[42] Even local school boards, encouraged by prosperity, were raising teachers' salaries to levels where able women, if not able men, could be recruited.

The basic weakness in the fifty-year rise of progressive education was that ideas put forward by John Dewey for the primary education of young children were seized upon by school administrators wishing to comply with utilitarian needs and expanded into a system of secondary education. The business-oriented culture of the nation was no doubt a major factor in the growth of the system, while American businessmen, operating under new conditions, were a force in restoring respect for scholarly learning. In assessing the trends since 1950, it is also necessary to note the force of a new emphasis on professionalism and research that arose from the Depression and World War II, one that made learned careers more prestigious, and both business and the military more dependent upon specialized advanced knowledge.

HIGHER EDUCATION FOR BUSINESS

From 1920 on, the United States led the world in offering higher education to a large and increasing proportion of the school population. In this vast upsurge, however, older patterns were preserved. Local pride and economic interests still led each urban community to want its own college, and its founding or maintenance was encouraged by chambers of commerce and other business groups. Even in the Great Depression the Lynds wrote that the teachers' college in Muncie, Indiana was said to bring in "a million dollars worth of business a year."[43] The business community, of course, valued private colleges more highly than public. Some members would doubtless agree with Curti and Nash that "Capitalism and free enterprise owe their survival in no small degree to the existence of our private independent universities."[44] In agreement with these sentiments, foundations such as Carnegie and Ford put substantial funds into the support of small, private colleges.

As a result of both business and pollitical suport, small colleges and "universities" increased rapidly. In 1920 there were 1,000 institutions of higher learning in the United States as compared with less than 50 in any of the leading nations of Western Europe. By the 1960s the number in America had doubled. Meanwhile enrollment had risen from 600,000 to nearly 5,000,000, or 40 percent of the age group eighteen to twenty-one years old.[45]

Since the spread of state teachers colleges was a significant part of the increase, about one-third of the institutions of 1960, enrolling a majority of the students, were government controlled. While businessmen had subsidized, and to a large degree had established, the major policies of the private sector, they had not strongly resisted the spread of state higher education. In fact, there was no great difference in the type of men who sat on the public boards of regents for higher education and the private boards of trustees. Except for a few professional educators or politicians on the public boards, the members were successful professional and businessmen. Their policies were, almost invariably, to fit higher education to the needs of economic development and an advanced industrial society, rather than to any traditional concepts of learning or theology.

Following World War I "a veritable craze" for business education swept over the country. Between 1919 and 1924, 117 colleges and universities developed business curricula of some type.[46] This rapid increase in courses and also in specialized collegiate schools of business led a general movement toward more specialized higher education. In 1920 there were forty-five university business schools with 36,000 students; in 1928, eighty-nine business schools enrolled 67,000 students, but in addition, about half of all American institutions of higher learning offered some business courses.[47] In spite of the hostility toward business created by the Depression, enrollment in colleges of commerce, finance, or business continued to increase. In 1936 there were 79,430 men and 17,306 women in such undergraduate schools, and 3,110 men and 542 women pursuing graduate business education. The G.I. Bill of Rights, by which the federal government financed higher education for veterans following World War II, and again after the Korean War, increased the number in business as well as all other kinds of education. In 1954, over 14 percent of all bachelors degrees (or 41,655) were granted in business or commerce; nearly 6 percent (3,336) of masters degrees, and more than 1.5 percent (144) of doctors degrees.[48]

On the undergraduate level, business schools in both day and evening courses taught subjects such as banking or business law, useful for the general or small businessman. On the graduate level, particularly after World War II, there was a tendency to concentrate on problems of administration and decision-making, to apply the social sciences to a better understanding of the functioning of large bureaucratic hierarchies. Such education fitted the student for big business with its specialization of functions, and its emphasis on general principles of management. It was also useful education for public administration. While small business generally recruited its hundreds of thousands of new entrepreneurs and managers from the ranks of men with practical experience, big business came to depend more and more on a supply of management personnel from graduating classes of the universities.

The trend toward specialization on business problems was deplored by some educational leaders such as Abraham Flexner of the Rockefeller Foundation, who objected to "draping the ugly practicalities of life in academic finery," and held that only medicine and law were worthy of university attention.[49] But many others credited business education with the presumed superiority in practice of American over foreign management. A group of Englishmen representing the Anglo-American Council on Productivity reported in the late 1950s that

> the steps taken by American business to educate, train and develop its future business leaders . . . have had . . . a vital bearing upon American productivity.
> There is a quality in management stimulated by the American system of higher education in general, and, in particular, by that part of it which is devoted to administrative studies.[50]

A BASIS FOR CULTURAL CHANGE

The growing conviction among business leaders and social scientists in the 1960s that education was one of the most important factors in economic growth had far-reaching consequences. Since the beginning of the colonies, some education had been regarded as necessary for certain types of activity, but the general level of education of the public had not been seen as a cause of economic growth. Also, while economic growth and the higher standard of living had always been American goals, competition with international Communism now made them appear necessary for survival. It seems improbable that any earlier big businessman would have asked, as did Frank Pace, Jr., president of General Dynamics

> How do we as a nation assure ourselves that the bright young minds that graduate are going to be well enough taught, well enough motivated and well enough educated to be sure that democracy in a complicated world is carried on successfully?[51]

The changing society produced new types of rebellion among the highly educated young against the pressures of conformity to older business expectations. Sociologist David Riesman, studying interviews with college seniors of the class of 1955, found that few of them contemplated even modest capital accumulation "the capital is, as it were, society's built into the schools and suburban developments and Blue Cross plans and corporate reserves. A floor is under these men, a low ceiling over them (analogous to the high-ceilinged Victorian home), and they provide a narrow and constant level of happiness."[52]

Undoubtedly the growing number of careers in large organizations, under the conditions discussed in Chapter 16, increased the historic American tendency toward conformity to the opinions of the group, or what has been called a high vulnerability "to the impersonal and unorganized authority of their social environment."[53] Riesman sees a shift toward "other-directed" rather than "inner-directed" personality, while some analysts see more outward conformity as a protective mechanism for inner individuality. Whatever change there was, and there is a basic disagreement about the matter, it may have been caused by child rearing and schooling that indoctrinated the young with fewer absolute values rather than by life in large organizations.[54] This latter assumption involves a feedback from the nineteenth-century rise of science and secularism that was associated with industrial business. The problem of causation is, in any case, highly complex. As anthropologist Clyde Kluckhohn wrote, "Perhaps the changes . . . are the product of still deeper processes not yet satisfactorily analyzed or named. At any rate, all of the shifts are inter-connected and mutually reenforcing."[55]

CHAPTER 19

Efforts to Restore Community

History scholars have emphasized the relative weakness of the feeling of community in the United States because of continual migration, and its further weakening as much of the population came to live in large, impersonal cities. Countering these trends, and testifying to the strength of the human desire for some type of community relationship, were the creation of neighborhood groups, ethnic and fraternal associations, emphasis on face-to-face recognition in the urban areas, and an increasing reliance on the church as agency for absorbing newcomers into a meaningful group.

Alongside this old community of physical proximity, mass media and communication were seeking, for business reasons, to build a national community in which all might share vicariously in the lives and actions of real or fictional characters. One need not agree with the extreme views of Marshall McLuhan to affirm that Franklin D. Roosevelt became a friend to millions of Americans by radio, as no president could have done earlier, or that the cast of a television show could become intimates, who entered the home once a week, and whose vicarious acquaintance was shared with other friends and neighbors.

In addition to creating a new type of community built around the national advertising efforts of business, the mass media of the twentieth century came to be powerful conditioning forces for a uniform national culture. This culture was not specifically planned to satisfy business needs, but one subject to subtle business influences, surveillance, and censorship. In the nineteenth century, children probably received most of their impressions of remote people, places, and events from books and schooling, and had little contact with newspapers beyond reading the comic strips. The new media of the twentieth century, however, reached children as much as, if not more than, adults. Hence in the period since the rise of the moving picture, nontextual media have gained enormously as social conditioning forces. As moving pictures, radio, and television came to have a powerful influence from childhood on, contributions of the older media, such as newspapers, magazines, and books probably tended to decline, although against such a conclusion must be balanced the increase in the amount of schooling and literacy. Undoubtedly all people caught up, willy-nilly, in the national community of advertising and entertainment became more conditioned by all types of mass media in comparison to personal contacts and direct experience. But theorists of communications still regarded personal influence as more important in guiding ultimate decisions.

THE OLDER MASS MEDIA

While in the late nineteenth century, metropolitan newspapers and popular magazines had already become substantial businesses in themselves, deriving their chief revenue from selling space to advertisers, their immersion in the interests of business continued to increase. In the twenties, as advertising rose to three times the revenue from sales of papers, public relations releases from advertising agencies were regularly printed in the news columns. In the Great Depression, advertising fell back to about double the revenue from purchasers and public relations efforts declined. As radio had become a strong competitor, newspapers moved into that field and by 1940 had bought a third of the broadcasting stations.

Spread of this business web controlling the collection and marketing of news was accompanied by a diminution in the number of daily newspapers and an increase in the size of the successful ones. Morris Ernst, a legal authority on freedom of speech, has estimated that the American newspaper press reached its peak of diversity in 1909. From then on until World War I, the number of dailies ran over 2,400. During the twenties, the last great decade of undisputed newspaper supremacy as a medium for communicating news, daily circulation rose by a third while the number of dailies dropped 10 percent.

In addition, previously independent dailies were being gathered into chains, most rapidly by William Randolph Hearst, Frank Munsey, and E. W. Scripps. By 1929, fifty-four chains owned 280 dailies, among which the Scripps-Howard chain, with twenty-five papers, controlled the largest number. That the chains influenced the character of the news is illustrated in Roy Howard's perceptive statement: "I do not subscribe to the general idea that news and opinion are two easily separable elements."[1] There were readily detectable biases running through the various chains, but very little disagreement on what was sound business policy.

The spread of uniform editorial policies established by the holding companies for their chains was perhaps less frustrating to the citizens of a community used to what had once appeared to be editorial individualism, than was the gradual disappearance of local competition. In 1930 only one American city in five had two or more competing English language dailies; by 1950 only about half of the cities over 100,000 population still had such competition. Yet, in spite of radio and television, newspaper circulation continued to increase, and the size of papers grew alarmingly. Newsprint paper consumption was 3.5 million tons in 1945 and 8.5 million in 1965.

Regardless of diminishing competition, a newspaper had to be a local community organ. About four-fifths of its advertising was local, and to hold its mass reading public, it had to be interested in community welfare. The paper also had an interest in "creating a good climate for business," which involved boosting community enterprise and improvement and playing down or omitting material that showed the city in a bad light.[2]

In contrast, magazines and their advertisers were nationally oriented. They spread an increasingly uniform national business culture which served as a basis for the vicarious community-building effects of the electronic media. In 1923 the lively and opinionated weekly *Time*, which was eventually to reach a very broad middle-class national audience, was started by Britten Hadden and Henry R. Luce. In competition with the stodgy *Literary Digest*, it won immediate success, and soon its general format was copied by *Newsweek* and by the more specialized *Business Week*. *Fortune*, a high-priced monthly for corporate executives, started by the Luce organization in 1930, served to channelize business opinion, just as the weeklies gave a new uniformity to general middle-class views.

In the twenties the weekly *Saturday Evening Post*, with at that time the nation's largest magazine circulation, became a leading reporter of the successes of American business leaders. In the thirties the upper-income business character of all of these weekly publicaitons was illustrated by their opposition to most of the New Deal. With the eclipse of left-wing liberalism after 1945, the weeklies became less strongly partisan in domestic affairs, and fairly united behind a strong anti-Communist foreign policy.

One effect of filtering printed news through a structure of business organizations was to keep it in tune with American business interests. "Objective news" came from men whose views were in the mainstream of cultural beliefs, covering those elements of a situation that were the traditional interests of the business of journalism. For example, before 1930 news of the Italian communities in cities was usually crime news; the social and political activities in ethnic ghettos were not within the normal range of "news."[3] This, in turn, built a distorted public image of these ethnic groups.

How such norms became established is, of course, an extremely complicated study, and one to which this book has been largely devoted. Basically, the norms mirror how elite groups, fairly unified in morals and beliefs see their culture. The range of social interests was middle to upper class, businesslike, and religious in the Judeo-Christian tradition. Objectivity consisted in keeping within the anticipated norms of expression; to go beyond them, particularly in ways derogatory to the major ideals of the culture, was controversial. Or still more simply, competitive views could be strong and colorful, but they should be of interest to advertisers and readers and be within the rules of the game.

MOVING PICTURES: A BUSINESS ART

Newspapers and magazines were published to make revenue from advertising while supplying "objective" information; moving pictures, in contrast, could be deliberately fabricated by the studios to please consumers. In the first case, there was a certain inevitability in the material that had to be carried; any events, though unfavorable to the publishers, that would not be suppressed by all journals, had to be noted by all. There were, however, no demands on movie content other than its legality and saleability. Hence as soon as moving pictures came to be produced by a few large theatre-owning corporations, the product became standardized around certain recognized trends in public taste. The process, while it involved the arts as an essential ingredient, was from the business standpoint much like automobile design or other industrial art forms, created primarily to sell goods.

The industry, like automobile production, began with a number of competing small enterprises. In 1908, at the time that W. C. Durant was putting automobile companies together to form General Motors, Jeremiah J. Kennedy was moving in on the many small producers through the Motion Picture Patents Company and the General Film Company. By 1910 these licensing and distributing corporations controlled the output of ten large producers and were collectively referred to as the Biograph Trust. As in the case of General Motors, there were still powerful outsiders such as the nickelodeon owners Fox and Laemmle, but unlike General Motors' competitive position which depended largely on the reputation of its cars, Biograph's practices involved restraints of trade and were successfully attacked by Fox in an antitrust suit. From 1930 to about 1950 the industry was dominated by a few combinations such as Fox, Paramount, Loew, Radio-Keith-Orpheum, Metro-Goldwyn-Mayer and Warner Brothers, that both produced films and owned the first-run theatres where the films would be shown. In 1948 federal antitrust action led to a United States Supreme Court decision that divorced theatre-owning from production, forbade block booking, that is compulsary taking of all of a line of pictures from a given producer, and left it to the lower courts to work out details. As a result of the court decisions, the industry came to have a rather confusing business set-up in which for tax purposes each of the major producers often established a special subsidiary corporation for an important picture. In this way, stars could be paid partly in stock that would give a return subject to capital gains rather than income taxes.

But no matter how the business end of production was organized, it still controlled what was to be produced. The relation of the management of the production studio to writers, directors, and actors was much the same as that of the sponsors of radio or television programs. With the cost of full-length features running from hundreds of thousands of dollars to many millions, the production manager could not afford to indulge any idle interest in art or education at the possible expense of revenue from sales. He was accountable to a board of directors, which often included Eastern bankers who felt responsible for the financial welfare of the firm. Only by chance would important members of the board of directors or stockholders have an interest in moving pictures as a form of art. As the famous director Rouben Mamoulian remarked in the 1930s, "The picture industry is no different from the underwear business, for example. It is completely governed by the law of supply and demand."[4]

As registered by box-office returns, demand appeared to be for romantic plots representing oversimplified solutions to human problems, usually worked out by people with a very high standard of living. The support of materialistic or businesslike values was a circular process. The audiences of a culture oriented toward material success created a demand for pictures that showed the life of the rich, and such pictures, in turn, reenforced the desire to achieve such a standard of living. For those who knew they no longer had a chance to acquire wealth, pictures could provide vicarious enjoyment. The element continually slighted in this fairly stable adjustment to the market was the serious exploration of human personality or complex social problems. The Hollywood slogan "This is an entertainment industry, if you have a message send it by Western Union" continued to state the rule.[5]

In addition to their major effect as a force for indoctrination with the values of a business culture, moving pictures were of use to business in a number of other ways. Until after World War II, American films were the principal type seen in the underdeveloped areas and were popular in all nations. Consequently they created a foreign demand for the American products displayed. Short films explaining the operation and problems of a firm or an industry might be shown in commercial motion picture theatres. In some companies, films were used as a part of training programs or to familiarize new employees with different aspects of the firm.

THE NEW MEDIA OF COMMUNITY

Although moving pictures were produced by large business firms, their content, good or bad, was supplied by authors, directors, and actors, who might be influenced by personal views on religion, romance, agriculture, partisan politics, or a number of other social interests. In the new media of radio and television, however, there was a much closer tie between content and the business reasons for production than existed between either authors and publishers, or directors, artists, and motion picture producers. Each single production using an hour of prime radio or television time cost a great deal of money, and the businessmen paying the physical costs wanted to be as sure as possible that the content would create a favorable image for their company and its products.

Another aspect of the electronic media also gave advertising a new social importance. One could read media in print without paying attention to the surrounding advertising; but to avoid absorbing the sponsor's message on radio or television required more special equipment and effort than the great majority would bother with. Hence, from the 1930s on, advertising reached a new maturity as a social institution, one that David Potter sees as the major institution produced by American "abundance," and one ranking with education or religion as an agency of social control.[6]

This new institution differed fundamentally from those of learning or religion in that it lacked social goals and responsibilities other than maintenance of orderly and profitably markets. "It is this lack of institutional responsibility," writes Potter, "this lack of inherent social purpose to balance social power, which . . . is a basic cause for concern about the role of advertising."[7] "To fix the attention but not to engage the mind" is a precise statement of the advertiser's formula.[8] The sponsor wanted the program to attract as wide an audience as possible, which usually meant that programs would play upon easily aroused emotions, but would not produce any "controversial" or divisive ideas.

The viewer, or listener, had some feeling of physical contact with the speaker or actor. While still at home, he was nevertheless in a live show, a part of ongoing events, vicariously running the risks of unforeseen happenings and sharing the triumphs of a successful performance. The man on the electronic waves was, after all, addressing each one of his audience personally, and they might reply by letter or phone in such a way as to influence subsequent performances. In addition, Marshall McLuhan thinks it important that sensory apparatus different from those used in reading were called into play in receiving radio or television.[9]

The "electronic revolution" occurred rapidly. Between August of 1920 when a radio station owned by the Detroit *News*, a daily paper, began broadcasting special features, and the beginning of 1923, nearly 600 transmission stations were set up. About 40 percent were owned by radio or electrical dealers or manufacturers, over 10 percent each by educational institutions and news publications, and about 5 percent by department stores.[10] While in 1920 American Telephone and Telegraph, General Electric, and Westinghouse had entered into a cross-licensing agreement, A.T. & T. with its exclusive rights in wire transmission was really in control. The telephone company thought of establishing a national system of broadcasting stations, but business resistance to such a monopoly was strong, and A.T. & T.'s station WEAF in New York was not making money. Consequently the company, in 1924, offered licenses to use wires to the hundreds of local stations, already guilty of patent infringement, and two years later sold WEAF to Radio Corporation of America, a subsidiary of General Electric, which organized the National Broadcasting Company with twenty-four stations.[11]

In the beginning Secretary of Commerce Hoover, Vice-President Walter A. Gifford of A.T. & T., and many others saw radio more as a public service than an advertising medium. It was thought that expenses might be met from a tax on sales of equipment. At a conference called by Hoover in 1922 (because by an act of 1912 his department had the right to assign broadcasting frequencies), he said: "It is inconceivable that we should allow so great a possibility for service . . . to be drowned in advertising chatter."[12] But neither A.T. & T. nor any public authority took the action necessary to establish a workable system of control. The telephone company's deicision to open the field to local commercial stations and provide transmission wires paved the way for national networks and advertising. By 1929, three major networks, that were to dominate national broadcasting from then on, were competing for the big advertising accounts and agencies were advising a moderate investment in radio time.

Up to this point, radio programs had been primarily news, sports, and popular music, and many stations, maintained in order to hold a position in the broadcasting field, had been losing money. The profits had been in the sale of equipment. Now, in spite of the deepening Depression, broadcasting became profitable. Advertising agencies offered sponsors programs by the stars of the night clubs, theatres, and movies, and the station rates for prime evening time shot upward. A prediction made by two writers in 1925 that "more attention will be given to the contents of political speeches which will be heard in the calm of the fireside" was fulfilled by Franklin Roosevelt both as governor of New York (1929-1933) and as president.[13]

BUSINESS CONTROL OF THE NEW MEDIA

Radio assumed the major entertainment role that it was to play, largely on the basis of market forces that no one planned for or attempted to control. To make a profit, stations had to sell time to advertisers at high rates. By the mid-1940s prime evening time on a national radio network was worth $10,000 an hour, which meant, first, that only a few large companies could afford this form of advertising, and second, the advertiser wanted to be sure his program attracted the right listeners. The advertising agencies were very careful, therefore, to find programs that would attract the maximum number of potential customers, such as sports broadcasts and variety shows. On the low-valued time, much of which was unsaleable in the 1930s, stations would run music, drama, or educational programs that were available free through use of records or the services of educational institutions.

The desires of the network, the agency, and the sponsor both to sell a product and hold an audience in competition with other shows had important results. It meant that, in reality, the networks such as ABC, CBS, or NBC surrendered control of programming to the advertising agencies and the big business sponsors, an arrangement which, as we shall see, both the networks and many directors and artists would resent in later years. In the liberal climate of the 1930s, censorship by the stations was chiefly directed against offensive language or opinions that were not within the range normally expected in the society. The agency wanted the program to be entertaining and appealing, and not weighed down by any excess baggage of serious or dull discussion. The sponsor had similar interests, but, in addition, wanted nothing said that might, even indirectly, reflect adversely on his product or his industry. A cigarette company, for example, censored the use of Jerome Kern's great song hit "Smoke Gets in Your Eyes," and a milk company found a menace to sales in the song "The Old Oaken Bucket."[14] Selectivity based on popularity with listeners was made more rigorous by the rise of program rating services from 1929 on; these services estimated the size of the audience, first on the basis of recall by listeners and later through sampling by "coincidental" telephone.[15] In 1956, such testing developed the interesting fact that adults and teenagers on Iowa farms that had television spent more time watching it than city dwellers.[16]

The net effect of censorship and selection in the interest of sales was to limit network broadcasting on the early evening time to features that could be counted on to possess wide appeal: news and comment; well-known bands; serial melodramas; and variety shows with nationally recognized stars. In local broadcasting and at off-hours this market-oriented selectivity was less exacting, but the aim of the station was always to find shows popular enough to attract sponsors.

Radio, and after World War II television, grew steadily in relation to other advertising media. While total expenditures for national advertising in relation to national income were declining, slowly in the 1920s and rapidly in the 1930s, to reach by 1943 the lowest point in the twentieth century, national advertising over radio was growing in dollar expenditures, and in percentage of both national income and total advertising outlays. It reached its peak in the late forties, and then lost revenue to television. By 1966, advertising expenditures were divided: 17 percent for television, 6 percent for radio, 8 percent for magazines, 15 percent for direct mail, 30 percent for newspaper, and the remaining 24 percent in miscellaneous special forms. A large part of all but magazine and television advertising was local. Only 30 percent of television advertising was on networks, and about one-third of this came from a dozen big companies.[19] This fact led a critic to complain that network advertising "is operated in the specific interest of certain patent medicine makers, soap chemists and tobacco curers."[18]

The rise of television as the most effective medium for national advertising in the 1950s raised the total costs for a one-hour show into the hundreds of thousands of dollars, with corresponding pressure on the agencies to develop popular programs. And while the advertisers were, in general, giant corporations, the agencies by comparison were much smaller, highly competitive businesses, each of which had only a few big accounts. "The calamitous effects of a change of agency by any one of the ten leading advertisers," writes Gilbert Seldes, "haunts the hucksters' dreams. In these conditions, everyone concerned looks for insurance against failure and this means they must be guaranteed of instantaneous success."[19] Such an attitude necessarily restricted innovation by artistic effects whose appreciation required some conditioning, or by the use of material that was unfamiliar to the average viewer.

Commercial requirements have not necessarily prevented occasional good programs, but they have held the subject matter of the national electronic community to the accepted norms of a business society. Both the usual programs and the advertising tend to produce satisfaction with American products and strongly to sanction efforts to acquire more of them. As one analyst observes: "What is familiar has a good chance to being liked."[20]

THE PROBLEM OF CONTROL

The scholarly analysts of television have tended to be interested either in marketing, education, or audience reactions, rather than in abstract problems of influence and control. Social scientists are particularly interested in the impact of programming on the viewers, among whom they find "the protesting attitude is a limited one." Most viewers are reasonably satisfied with the general content and want merely better programs of the same type.[21] Perhaps because of the amount of private scholarly investigation, the networks have neglected research on the subtler or lasting effects of programs on their audiences.

The types of control over television content, exercised solely for advertising reasons, were superficially apolitical and amoral. But the great anti-Communist scare from 1947 to 1953 demonstrated that the business controls could also be manipulated by organized minority groups working for personal or political ends. In these instances, as usual, the decisive influence was exercised under the rubric of "the demands of the market," but this did not lessen the force of the decisions as an example of effective social control.

In 1947 some ex-FBI men sought to profit from the rising fear of Communism by forming American Business Consultants and by publishing a paper *Counterattack*, both designed to expose subversive activities in the United States. As the Red Scare waxed, half a dozen major companies employed American Business Consultants to ferret out Communists, and in 1951 the consultants published *Red Channels*, a compendious listing of 151 alleged subversives. The bases for inclusion in the list were fantastic, such as having attended a single meeting at which Communists were present, and the reports were often completely erroneous.

The effects on the moving picture, radio, and television industries, however, were amazing and tragic. In 1949, well before the height of the panic, Ed Sullivan, for example, was pressured by his sponsor to drop a dancer from his show because of his alleged subversive ideas, and thereafter Sullivan consulted the editor of *Counterattack* about "questionable" performers.[22] As Senator Joseph McCarthy of Wisconsin skillfully built the Red Scare by lies and innuendos, other men found it profitable to get on the bandwagon. Lawrence A. Johnson, owner of a chain of supermarkets, mounted a campaign based largely on material from *Counterattack* and aimed directly at sponsors, agencies, and networks to prevent them from employing "Stalin's little creatures."[23]

Since about 60 percent of television advertising revenue came from goods sold in supermarkets, the Johnson campaign, coupled with the fears aroused by Senator McCarthy, had strong effects. Agency and network executives came to the conclusion that "controversial people are bad for business."[24] Sponsors took the position that they must protect the interest of their stockholders. As is so often the case, those that had earlier allowed the greatest freedom of expression now had to do the most to reassure their clients. CBS, for example, in 1951 appointed an executive to specialize in security; performers soon called him the "vice-president in charge of treason." Other networks and large agencies took similar precautions, either through their legal departments or special executives. Producers submitted the names of writers, directors, and actors to the agencies for investigation and were subsequently informed by phone with a simple yes or no for each name. A banned actor was said to be "unavailable," and of 5,000 names submitted in one year to the security staff of a large advertising agency, over 1,500 were rejected. The persecution, which was largely over by the middle fifties, drove most black-listed artists to other ways of earning a living, and a few to alcoholism, drugs, or suicide.

The whole episode presents an arresting example of the tenuous place of freedom of opinion in electronic media. A few businessmen were either conscientious fanatics or publicity seekers, but the great majority were simply trying to adjust their policies to what seemed to be required by the market. Yet, when such a policy led to questioning appearances by Eleanor Roosevelt or Pearl Buck, or eliminating the word "peace" because it sounded communistic, adjustment to the market seemed dangerous in an industry "affected with a public interest."

With the ending of the Korean War and the discrediting of Senator McCarthy, the Red Scare passed away. In the calmer atmosphere of the late 1950s, network executives sought, under the banner of social responsibility, to gain greater control over the personnel and content of broadcasting. On the surface they appeared to make progress. In this they were also aided by the rise of multiple sponsoring which made no single company responsible for the entire program. But the network executives are themselves running profit-making operations, and no realignment of the authorities that respond to the needs of the market can alter the basic situation of control in the interests of business.

In fact, much has still to be learned about both the control and long-run effects of these electronic media, which are not only a powerful influence on adolescents and adults, but probably the strongest nonfamilial forces on child socialization that have ever existed. Because of the capital equipment involved and the cost of production, the media seem bound to be controlled by some financially strong agency, and any such group inevitably has special interests to serve. Hundreds of business firms may, in fact, exercise a safer type of control in some respects than government, because on many issues the business group represents differing viewpoints. To be effective, power has to be exercised by individuals, not by vaguely defined groups. Thus, although the degree of control in the common interest of profit and the sale of products is practically absolute, in matters of method and content there is considerable leeway.

In spite of the fact that all the companies involved with national television media are very large, they are also highly competitive for public favor. Hence, while they may be unduly sensitive to well-organized minorities, they are also responsive to broad shifts in social attitudes. Corporate executives may not have much emotional involvement with civil rights, for example, but they know it is good business to have some blacks on the shows they sponsor. Looked at another way, if actual events influence the majority of people in a certain direction, sponsors are loath to offer opposition unless the movement is directly menacing to the business system.

BUSINESS GUIDES THE CHURCHES

Religion continued to supply a feeling of community in two ways, first by providing local churches which were discrete communities in the larger impersonal society, and second by providing a feeling of belonging to a great group of religious communities dedicated to the American way of life. Both of these functions seemed valuable to businessmen, even if they were not themselves devout churchgoers.

Faced with stronger agnosticism in the twentieth century, writers saw more clearly the powerful role played by religion as a binding force in American culture. "The period of dominant individualism in America has taken the cohesive forces of society so much for granted, and lived so unconsciously on the borrowed capital of Christian values and the largess of American natural resources," writes Walter G. Muelder, "that its theory neglected the power of the invisible value structure for which religious rootage supplied the culture."[25] By the midcentury, with both Christian values and natural resources diminished, it seemed as though business could no longer rely so heavily upon them for maintenance of the old values. Yet much of the religious, and by inference the social spirit, of the earlier periods remained. Writing as late as 1967, an eminent theologian saw "the obligation both collective and individual to carry out God's will on earth" as a theme lying "very deep in American Tradition."[26] Such belief could still lend an aura of divine sanction to material success, and inspire a crusading desire to spread God's American way to other nations.

The Progressive movement before World War I had generated in the churches a missionary spirit aimed at social abuses and permeated by a spirit of optimism regarding human perfectability. In contrast, the twenties was a decade of complacency or frustration. Social reform was no longer a popular topic in Protestant churches with wealthy congregations.[27] The group of clergymen associated with the advanced social gospel, always a minority, were largely restricted to editors or seminarians.

In the suspicious fear-ridden atmosphere that enveloped the United States after World War I, reform activities by clergymen seemed subversive and dangerous. In 1919 a group of Catholic bishops, led by Father John A. Ryan, published a manifesto entitled "Social Reconstruction: A General Review of the Problems and a Survey of the Remedies."[28] It urged wages based on family needs, unemployment, health and old-age insurance, abolition of child labor, legal protection of the right of labor to organize, and public housing. This statement was labeled by President Stephen C. Mason of the National Association of Manufacturers as "pro-labor union, socialistic propaganda under the official insignia of the Roman Catholic Church in America."[29] The following year *Industry* magazine attacked clergymen for intimating, in connection with the steel strike of 1919, that the teachings of Christ should be brought into the industrial field. Even in the calmer and prosperous atmosphere of 1926, the Detroit Board of Commerce got most of the churches to withdraw invitations to A.F. of L. leaders to speak while in town for their national convention.

While the general disinterest or hostility of business toward a revival of social reform could not control the national church organizations or publications, such disapproval was quite effective in its influence at the parish level.[30] The Lynds reported in the 1920s that the business leaders of the community adopted a condescending tone toward clergymen and had little communication with them.[31] In a discussion with half a dozen influential businessmen, "the general opinion of the group was that the ministry is 'played out.' " The Lynds regarded the omission of clergymen from the Rotary Club as a conspicuous example of their loss of influence in community leadership.[32] There was little drive for social reform in the churches or their periodicals, perhaps signifying a realistic recognition that religious authority would not be respected when it went contrary to the opinions of community business leaders. The minister of the largest Protestant church in Middletown (Muncie, Indiana) who preached "If God has given you wealth, be happy; if he has given you poverty, be happy," was perhaps close to the norm of the Protestant social message of the 1920s.[33]

Close conformity of the Protestant church to changing social attitudes was not altogether a product of the inner revolution that had undermined religious authority. American religion had always had an essentially secular character and an aura of social morality rather than theological proscription.[34] But in the twenties, leaders both clerical and lay recognized business as a shaper of ethics more explicitly than ever before. Dean Shaler Mathews of the University of Chicago Divinity School wrote in an article entitled "Business, Maker of Morals," that "Business does more than wait for others to make its moralities. It evolves its own for . . . it is not a machine, but a social operation . . . . There is no greater influence in human relations than our economic life."[35]

Reversing the age-old relationship, popular writers went a step further and suggested that the church should conform to business. "The sanest religion is business," wrote Edward E. Purrinton. "I have seen more Christianity to the square inch as a regular part of the office equipment of famous corporation presidents than may ordinarily be found on Sunday in a verbalized but not vitalized church congregation . . . I would make every business house a consultation bureau for the guidance of the church whose members were employees of the house."[36] Bruce Barton, an ingenious advertising executive, showed in detail how the Bible had been misinterpreted by weak Christian traditions; read properly, the testaments revealed Christ as demonstrating aggressive, fair, and intelligent sales practices, a revelation which businessmen would do well to study and copy.[37] Other advertising agents also tried to make religious or moral duty an aid to selling: "The use of religion or semi-religion as a sales weapon" was hailed by a journalist as a "distinct American innovation . . . . People would buy more freely if convinced that buying was a moral duty."[38]

Clerical prestige was further undermined by the failure of salaries to keep pace with inflation. A survey of 1922 placed the average Protestant ministerial stipend at $937.[39] The result was undoubtedly a decline in the ability of men recruited for the church. In a society where material success was the main criterion of status, a vocation dependent on charity for a decent living could hardly command prestige. The clergy tended to become a group apart, patronized by the well-to-do and listened to as interpreters of the gospel, but not to be trusted with important social responsibilities. A successful but frustrated minister complained in 1930 that it was "a fairly safe generalization to say that no profession of men is so thoroughly empty of dignity and grace as that of the Protestant ministry today."[40]

Loss of clerical prestige did not necessarily indicate a loss of religious belief on the part of businessmen. In 1926, Roger Babson, the well-known business analyst, sent the following six questions to fifty major business leaders:

(1) Did you have a praying father, a praying mother, or both?
(2) Do you believe there is some Power higher than human power?
(3) Do you feel we are responsible to this Higher Power?
(4) Do you feel we need help from it?
(5) Do you ever pray?
(6) Has this feeling of responsibility influenced your life?

Thirty answers were yes to all questions; only one reply was generally negative. Babson thought his results demonstrated that "almost without exception men who are leaders in business are religious."[41] J. Edward Baker said: "I have yet to see a point of conflict between good business principles and Christian principles. I have always found that a good society judged by the best business tests will meet the highest requirements of Christian ethics."[42] The Lynds found that "men usually accept the religious beliefs . . . but as one listens to their conversation . . . one gets a distinct impression that religion wears a film of unreality to many of them."[43] If diminishing religion or pietism was a fact, it might well produce greater emphasis on the church as an answer to the need for community.

THE CHURCHES SUPPORT BUSINESS

The Great Depression made many of the nonparochial clergy, the teachers, administrators, and editors, more critical of business and its leaders. Liberals within the clerical group moved from a tacit acceptance of business leadership in the late twenties to belief in the necessity of a partially socialized society. But taken as a whole, neither the ministry nor the church periodicals turned against American business.[44] *

One great element of stability was that partly because of the continuous influence of business values in the culture, the Christian doctrine of the holiness of the poor had never taken root. Ministers with pulpits were inclined toward the business views that the Depression was an inevitable working of economic laws, or possibly a heavenly retribution for sinful extravagance. Through the election of 1932, Hoover's stand in favor of prohibition prevented active support of Roosevelt by any important church journal. In 1936 only the *Christian Century* openly supported the president.

Suffering from a 50 percent decline in church attendance by 1932, Protestant ministers were generally careful not to alienate their wealthy parishioners by needless political or sociological observations. "The pulpit on Sunday morning," says an historian of the 1930s, "was the least likely source of radical social pronouncements."[45]

Among all varieties of pastoral clergymen, the professed socialists were few and the Communists a negligible number, and many of these had been critics of capitalsim even in the prosperous twenties. The prominence of a few able religious intellectuals gave a false impression of liberalism or even radicalism in the pulpit. Harry Emerson Fosdick, a Baptist, Bishop Francis J. McConnell, a Methodist, and John Haynes Holmes, a Unitarian, were among the few leading liberals who had parishes, and their congregations were drawn from the big cities. Liberal clergymen from welfare organizations, periodicals, or seminaries were occasionally able to get church conferences to pass resolutions condemning the capitalist system, and to establish committees for social action. In the severely depressed year of 1933, the Federal Council of Churches of Christ, an association supported by a number of large Protestant denominations, resolved that "the Christian conscience can be satisfied with nothing less than the complete substitution of motives of mutual helpfulness and good will for the motive of private gain." The same year, in rather ambiguous terms, the Presbyterian General Assembly called for planning and government control.[46] As in the case of a number of other antibusiness resolutions, the religious groups passing them launched no program of political action, nor was there any reason to believe that their views represented those of the majority of the clergy.

The Methodist Federation for Social Service was the continuing leader of anticapitalist religious opinion. During the Spanish Civil War it entered into joint

---

* Most religious journals had endorsed Hoover in 1928; see Miller, *American Protestantism*, 116.

activities with the American League Against War and Facism, an organization regarded by the FBI as a Communist front. But in general the sustained attitudes of the clerical liberals were only slightly to the left of the New Deal. Early in 1934, the periodical *World Tomorrow* polled 100,000 Protestant clergymen regarding their political opinions. Only 21 percent replied. Of this group 28 percent were socialist, with Methodists highest at 34 percent and Presbyterians lowest at 19.[47] In 1936 a *Literary Digest* poll of 15,000 Protestant clergy indicated that 70 percent disapproved of the New Deal, presumably because it was too liberal.[48]

Within the Catholic church the same type of divisions occurred. Most parish priests were little touched by radical economic doctrines. The *Commonweal*, the principle liberal Catholic journal, endorsed the New Deal and its National Industrial Recovery Act, and editorialized: "From anarchy in the business world we are advancing rapidly toward the formation of covenants for business."[49] Some nonparish clergymen such as Monsignor John A. Ryan moved to a position just short of socialism. In New York City, Dorothy Day organized a Catholic Worker Movement and published the *Catholic Daily Worker*, which if not openly socialist was clearly antibusiness.[50] The association of Catholic Trade Unionists, formed in New York early in 1937, published a magazine *Labor Leader*, and established worker's schools. The effort to build Catholic labor strength was pursued in other large cities, most strongly in Detroit, where about forty parish labor schools were opened in connection with an Archdiocesan Labor Institute.[51]

The Depression also emphasized economic issues in the Jewish denominations, but in a different way. Trouble in Germany as well as in the United States brought Orthodox, Conservative, and Reform Jews together in relief associations. In 1940 the United Jewish Appeal became the central organization, and from these interdenominational contacts, the middle of the road Conservatives were gaining. This coincided with the ending of the radical ideas of the Jewish immigrant generations and the development of the suburban synagogue as a religious community strongly influenced by its leading businessmen and their values.

RELIGION JOINS BUSINESS IN THE AMERICAN WAY OF LIFE

World War II, with its emotional tensions and increases in migration, started a rapid upswing in Church membership and support. From 1910 to 1940, membership in religious bodies by those over thirteen years of age had declined from 55 to 50.7 percent of that portion of the population, by 1950 the figure was 63.7 percent.[52] Suburban churches were social centers where a rapidly shifting population formed their community ties, and as the suburbs grew to include by 1970 a majority of the people of the United States, church units became larger and wealthier social centers. This brought the clergy more respect and social status. In 1942 an Elmo Roper poll had indicated that only 17.5 percent of the sample thought religious leaders were "doing the most good for the country," whereas 18.5 percent thought business leaders were. Five years later the vote for religious leaders had risen to 32.6 percent, while business leaders remained about the same. A similar poll in 1953 showed religious leaders favored by 40 percent.[53] These figures probably registered an abstract or ideal respect for religious activity. In 1948 the majority of another sample held that their religious beliefs had no real effect on their business or political conduct.[54] Sociologists of the 1960s joined with the economists in recognizing that economic (or business) institutions were the most powerful in American society; they regarded religious institutions as among the least able to make their values dominant.[55]

The affluent suburban churches tended, particularly, to emphasize community organization within the folkways of the American business society. By 1962 Lutheran theologian Loren Halvorsen complained of "innumerable meetings, immersion in 'churchness', the not-a-minute-to-spare crowding of the temple calendar and the pursuit of statistical success."[56] In a sense, the folkways had absorbed religion, and what middle-class Americans believed in was their type of society. Writing in 1955, Will Herberg said, "By every realistic criterion the American Way of Life is the operative faith of the American people."[57]

In the postwar Congregational, Episcopal, Jewish, and Presbyterian churches, business and professional men averaged about a third of the male membership. These churches were also the ones likely to be strong in community influence.[58] The upper economic group assumed the prerogatives of leadership. "Why shouldn't the Board of Trustees be made up of prominent community leaders?" asked a bank president. "They're the ones most aware of what's going on . . . and can help the church do the things that are best for the community."[59] An unwanted result of such church communities was said to be that "the majority of Protestant laymen . . . dwell in a middle-class ghetto and remain so effectively isolated from the world that they readily accept the myth that they alone possess every true virtue and protect all significant values."[60]

Regardless of their own religious views there was a widespread opinion among businessmen that churches, in general, were important preservers of social stability. In 1957, for example, the Junior Chamber of Commerce of the United States organized an "Attend a Church or Synagogue of Your Choice Month." Each week a prominent businessman contributed a statement on "What Religion Means to Me."[61] A gradual change had taken place as a result of which religion was now regarded as good because it was useful in furthering other desirable values.

Such business and middle-class support should not obscure the fact that some clergymen favored labor rather than management in industrial disputes. Even more than in earlier decades, when theological beliefs were stronger, ministers sought to please their congregations. One might say that churches operated in a strong buyers' market and had to be ever alert at pleasing the customers. Hence in a working-class parish the church was for the workers, and the factor that attached most churches to business was the increasingly middle-class, suburban character of American life. In his prosperous suburban church the conscientious businessman wanted to be reminded of his ethical and religious responsibilities, but he did not want the minister making rules for business conduct.

As in the 1930s, if advanced liberal views were put forward in a denomination, they usually originated with editors, seminarians, or central administrators not with the local clergy. While in the thirties these advanced views had often been fundamental attacks on the capitalist system, by the 1960s capitalism appeared to be taken for granted and Leftist liberalism dealt with civil rights, urban improvement, and antiimperialism.

BUSINESS AND THE NEW TYPES OF COMMUNITY

Clearly the characteristics of metropolitan urbanism were major forces in the breakdown of the personal or community relationships mankind had known in earlier centuries; capitalist business had supplied organizing principles generally followed in creating new types of communities. "Conformity is not, of course, a characteristic peculiar to business," wrote Crawford Greenwalt, then president of the Du Pont Company; "It may be found to some degree in all organization of whatever nature or size."[62] But since business was the dynamic factor in forming new associations, its institutional trends and values inevitably were conformed to in some degree.

Both mass media and religious types of community were examples of how the advance of industrialism, administered by businessmen, was producing a more uniform culture, centered around the values of business. The process obviously had a number of aspects, such as the trend toward cultural uniformity through continuously high rates of interstate migration and uniform content in education and the mass media; an increasing emphasis on the values of business through increasingly utilitarian education (to the mid-1950s at least); and through the merging of religion with a business oriented "American way of life."

Thus a considerable degree of conformity by ministers and rabbis to the views of their congregations was a necessary condition for the church serving as a form of community within the city or suburban area. Few scholars would question the fact that cities are composed of such subcommunities; the point here is that those built around the Protestant and Jewish churches, at least, tended to be in harmony with the values of business and were usually led by businessmen.[63] The other type of community, the vicarious one of the mass media, McLuhan's "global sized village," while it had within it unpredictable social effects, was nevertheless created in accordance with business values.[64]

CHAPTER 20

Business in Political Administration

In his second book on American society, Frenchman Andre Siegfried remarked, "The whole of American business forms a closely bound bundle of interests, which express themselves in a way of life, of administration and government, and a certain attitude toward society, production and exchange of goods, men's ways of dealing with each other, and international relations."[1] Granting the truth of Siegfried's observation, there are two different levels on which to explore business influence in twentieth-century American politics. On the fundamental level the goals and values of a business-oriented culture established the rules of the game: how men were expected to act, what they strove for, and what qualities or achievements were rewarded. On this level the business culture and its politics were indivisible, and they can only be discussed in terms of long-run change that affects the basic social situation. But since modern culture is organized diversity, on the more superficial level of year to year events there was always leeway and rivalry between occupational groups. Business groups had varying interests, each represented by politicians who battled each other, and the roles of democratic politician or government administrator in turn involved occupational interests that might superficially conflict with the aims of any or all business groups.

James Bryce's observations of the 1880s on the low ability and prestige of state and most federal administrators continued to hold true until the Great Depression. From that time on, a number of factors, such as welfare, war, and world affairs, increased the importance and probably the ability of political administrators, particularly in the federal government. From the standpoint of businessmen's relations with government, the rising importance of administration was welcome. There was a closer occupational bond and easier communication between the business executive and the government administrator than between businessmen and elected politicians. From 1953 on, this friendliness between big businessmen and top civil and military officials became so obvious that social scientists began to worry about rule by a power elite, or an establishment, composed of all three groups.

LAW AND THE RISE OF ADMINISTRATION

Much of the business influence in earlier American law and politics had been negative: defeat of unwanted restrictions or regulations, or prevention of the enforcement of some laws that reached the statute books. But, as we have seen (Chapter 14), in the Progressive period laws were passed that many businessmen wanted to have enforced, and to do this often required giving power to a special commission. Government and law enforcement by administrative commission became increasingly the rule as the century progressed, and lawyers, congressmen, and state legislators came to spend much of their time representing their business constituents before commissions. By the 1930s new government regulations, state or federal, almost routinely involved either a new or an existing commission. An allied and necessary legal development of the middle years of the century was a broadening of constitutional interpretations to uphold the new regulatory statutes.

Licensing of occupations, one of the oldest types of regulation, grew rapidly from the 1870s on without producing important legal crises. Such regulations might arise either to protect the public, as in a public utility commission, or to protect the operators in a business from excessive competition, as with licensed barbers. In the nineteenth and early twentieth centuries, enforcement of many such restrictions was left to the courts; as time went on, judicial processes proved too slow and costly, and administrative commissions were established to police the laws. Commissions might appear to businessmen to be hostile, when participants in the regulated business were barred from seats, or friendly when staffed by members selected from the industry, but in either case they lessened competition. They moved away, that is, from the free market and legality purely by contract, leaving the courts to deal only with "residual marginal details . . . and with questions of performance and breach."[2] "The inner history of the Progressive Era," says L. M. Friedman, "might be written in terms of which groups succeeded in what ways in achieving legal or extra legal support for their competitive position, and why."[3] By 1970 the economy was a honeycomb of such protected positions, necessary to safeguard both the honest businessman and the consumer in an impersonal society.

A less obvious change had also been taking place. The effects of regulatory legislation in an advanced and highly varied industrial society, and the work of commissions, had become so complex that only insiders, or "experts," could foresee the incidence of new legal provisions and their judicial interpretation. Except for a few laws of sweeping character, such as the Hawley-Smoot tariff of 1930, the Securities Exchange Commission Act of 1934, or the National Labor Relations Act of 1935, it was difficult directly to inform legislators or to arouse the general public about the potential effects of a law.[4]

The need for expert specialization in legal matters led to a steady growth in the number of registered lobbyists in state capitals and in Washington. There were more than a thousand at the national capital by midcentury, representing all types of interests and organizations from patriotic societies to trade associations and large companies. In addition, there were the legions of lawyers practicing at a state or the national capital who could quickly summon experts to support their clients' causes. Most of these lawyers and experts had at one time held some legislative or administrative office which had acquainted them with part of the legislative process. In Washington, and to a lesser extent in the states, the executive departments and the standing legislative committees also had staffs of specialists to give advice on policy, interpretation, or the framing of laws. For example, leading professors held that by brilliant phrasing supplied by three expert drafters, the corporate income tax law of 1918 had "created a new body of doctrine, 'income tax accounting.' " The important clauses were that income should be computed "in accordance with the method of accounting regularly employed" or "in such a manner as in the opinion of the Commissioner does clearly reflect the income."[5] Yet, it was probable that when the law was in Congress, few legislators and almost none of the informed public saw anything striking in this language that gave wide power to the firms accountants.

On the whole, the growing complexity of laws and regulations probably increased business influence in politics, because the firms specifically interested were likely to know more and be better represented than the usually dispersed opposition. But since on most issues there were business interests directly involved on both sides, such a generalization has only limited applicability. The continuing conflicts of interest emphasized the necessity of commissions to understand and administer the intricacies of important laws, and the need for specialized lawyers to present the cases of business clients.

The confusions between the desires of some businessmen for uniform national regulation, and fear of expanding regulatory power as a matter of principle continued. With the exception of a handful of Progressive decisions between 1910 and 1917, ones that can be regarded as somewhat exceptional even at the time they were rendered, the Supreme Court of the United States maintained strict limitations on the regulatory power of both Congress and the states until 1937. The return, in 1917, to stricter construction was dramatically affirmed by *Hammer* v. *Daggenhart*, which declared the national child labor law of the year before to be an unconstitutional extension of congressional power over interstate commerce.[6] While in individual cases, members of the business involved may have favored regulation, on the whole, businessmen appeared to applaud the strong restrictive stance of the Court. When this judicial attitude led to overruling New Deal Laws such as the National Industry Recovery Act (NIRA) and Agricultural Adjustment Act (AAA), the court won even greater approval from business.

But in holding the line against the New Deal, the Court had dangerously weakened the federal commerce power essential to national business, and judicial reaction was probably inevitable. It came in the spring of 1937 when the

Roosevelt administration sponsored the bill to increase the number of Supreme Court justices. By a shift in attitude on the part of Chief Justice Charles Evans Hughes and Associate Justice Owen J. Roberts, the Court began to uphold the use of the commerce power for regulating the conditions of manufacture of products sold in interstate trade. This broad or nationalist construction on the part of the Supreme Court, favorable on the whole, to all big companies, continued in the three ensuing decades.

The quantity of federal and state statutes directly affecting business, particularly after 1933, was vast. The regulations of public utilities and common carrier transportation increased decade by decade. Collective bargaining and the organization of unions were protected by federal law. Federal corporate and private income tax law became major elements in determining business policy. The Sherman and Clayton Antitrust laws were amended to protect small business and preserve competition.[7] Yet the total structure of business and its relations with American society changed less than one might expect.

BUSINESS AND THE WARS

Twice within a generation business leaders and spokesmen were faced with the problems of neutrality and major wars. In both instances, as in earlier international crises, the reaction was much the same: businessmen were happy to expand trade on any peaceful basis, but anxious to avoid legally declared war. The desire to expand foreign sales was strengthened in both 1914 and 1939 by deep domestic depression. In 1915 and 1916, selling based on mounting foreign loans continued, partly because of fear of depression if it were cut back; in 1941 exports rose on a government-financed, lend-lease basis, prompted by fear of British collapse. In both instances leading business spokesmen dreaded controls on prices and profits that would follow a declaration of war.[8]

While business journalists in the earlier period were more openly pro-Ally than President Wilson and condemned his foreign policy as weak, they did not propose intervention. Of thirty business periodicals examined for this period by Harold Syrett, only the *Bankers Magazine* opposed allied loans.[9] When the German announcement of unlimited submarine warfare, at the end of January, 1917, led Wilson to abandon neutrality, these business journals, with the exception of the *Commercial and Financial Chronicle*, swung to his support.[10]

The situation in 1940 was complicated by the widespread distrust of the president among businessmen.[11] While ready to prepare the country for possible attack, some feared that militarism might facilitate a Roosevelt dictatorship. They did not like the idea of giving the president power to allocate production, and they feared rising debt and taxes. Furthermore, many Americans, particularly in the Middle West, blamed all the European nations equally for failure to keep the peace. When Russia became involved as an ally of England, many businessmen could see little to choose between the two sides.

Meanwhile, to combat the pro-English campaign being waged by the administration, R. Douglas Stuart, Jr., son of a vice-president of Quaker Oats, Robert E. Wood of Sears Roebuck, Henry Ford, and other important Middle Western businessmen had formed the strictly neutral "America First." Eastern journalists and other Anglophiles countered with a national association to give all aid to the Allies short of war. The two sides fought each other right down to the attack on Pearl Harbor, with businessmen divided between them probably more Easterners for aid and more Westerners, led by Senator Robert Taft, for neutrality and strong national defense. *Fortune* reported that between January 1940 (before the fall of France and the unsuccessful Wilkie campaign) and November of that year, the number of businessmen anticipating war had risen from one-third to nearly half of the total replying to its poll.[12] Since aid to England and Russia was financed by the government, there was no private financial involvement, as in 1917, that could be blamed for bringing the nation into war.

The Korean and Vietnam Wars bore a quite different relationship to business than any of the earlier ones, and will be discussed later in the context of world economic dominance, and the efforts at its preservation.

BUSINESS IN THE LOCAL POLITICAL STRUCTURE

In the national identification with business that characterized much of America following World War I, it might be expected that local politics would be run in the interests of businessmen. But because of the needs for specialization in a complex industrial society, businessmen and local politicians remained distinct from each other and sometimes hostile. The division was rendered more striking by the fact that most men came to politics from law or business, and in order to meet the high risks of political unemployment, often remained active in their previous callings. But, because the politician of necessity played his role as a professional party man, differences in aims and attitudes developed at an early date. These differences were emphasized by successful businessmen when considering the lower levels of men in party or government. From the mid-nineteenth century on, the attitude scarcely changed. As a business leader of the 1920s expressed it: "Politics is dirty, I wouldn't mix in it here."[13]

Edward C. Banfield and James Q. Wilson see a half dozen different types of balances between business and local political leaders that developed from varying histories and the resulting strength of business interests. Community groups generally agreed that "the principal criterion for becoming a top level decision-maker is that a man must play a senior role in business financial or industrial life."[14] Conversely, to be effective, such business leaders needed to be actively interested, united in aims, and in "control of resources valued by politicians."[15] The gradual disappearance of family companies lessened continuing semiaristocratic business leadership in many communities. Even if the local executives of absentee companies took some part in civic affairs, they lacked the prestige and influences of established local wealth.

In a broad view, the chief changes in the nature of local government and its power structure in the second and third quarters of the twentieth century came from growth in the relative size of the middle class and further loss of local economic and political autonomy. Communities of small to moderate size, where the direct influence of business in politics had been greatest, declined in economic and political power in the "mass society." The regional market towns of the nineteenth century had been individual units of political power run indirectly by real estate operators ("large farmers"), bankers, merchants, lawyers, and newspaper publishers.[16] As industrial business and necessary public services advanced in size and complexity, the town of a few thousand people came, in most areas, to be too small a unit for autonomous action. By the end of the Great Depression of the 1930s, there had been a "rural surrender."[17] Medium-sized enterprises had moved to more central locations or been absorbed by bigger companies; state and federal grants for highways, schools, and public buildings left only routine chores for local politicians. The politically prestigious group were "those with contacts in and knowledge of the outer world."[18] Even this group in the small city had little power, but they could, at least, know what to expect from above. In the society of the mid-twentieth century, places with populations up to 10,000 or even 25,000 were still voting units of importance to state and national politics, but they were neither independent sources for forming public policy nor good bases for broader political influence.*

Larger cities that were still centers for industry sought to maintain their importance by using the old devices of the nineteenth century, such as tax exemptions, municipal loans, donations of land, and the advantages of the locality in educational or research facilities to attract new business. In August, 1964, *Fortune* estimated "11,000 public and private organizations were trying to attract business to particular areas."[19]

While city power structures varied on the basis of ethnic groups, and other social differences, the influence of resident businessmen probably reached a maximum in those just big enough to contain sizable independent firms, declined in varying degrees through the level of half a million or more population, and became lost in diversity somewhere around the million mark.[20] In Atlanta, Georgia, for example, with an in-city population of about 500,000 Floyd Hunter found in 1950 a power structure in which the chief local decision-makers were 80 percent businessmen or business lawyers, but were divided into several "crowds" that did not always work together.[21]

In the largest cities boss rule formerly based on political control of immigrant and other poor wards gradually gave way to city administrations that rested insecurely on a mixture of middle-class and slum votes, and the support of

---

* Norristown, Pa., for example, with a population of 40,000 in 1950, was still an unimportant political power unit. See Sidney Goldstein, *The Norristown Study*, 55-56.

various organized groups.[22] On the one hand, this made local politicians more responsive to the general values of middle-class business culture, but on the other hand less capable of rendering special favors to certain businesses. In cities as large as Philadelphia, Los Angeles, or Chicago, where power was thus dispersed, strong, well-run political machines could exercise considerable autonomy. Robert A. Dahl, however, also found a diverse and unorganized pluralism in New Haven, Connecticut, with a population of only 150,000.[23]

By 1970 a majority of the people of the United States lived near urban areas, outside the limits of the central city. In the larger metropolitan complexes, these "outside" areas often contained centers with more than 100,000 people, but mainly they were composed of medium-sized townships or cities. The latter were usually fairly homogeneous middle-class communities, made up of property owners, many of whom, particularly the more important businessmen, commuted to the central city. The lively participation by commuters in suburban political affairs illustrated the strength of the American middle-class feeling, perhaps self-protective, of a duty to work for community welfare. Township commissions and borough councils were made up of businessmen, and occasionally their wives, who served for nominal salaries.[24] School budgets and building funds were the big business of most suburban communities, and hence the school boards were also staffed by fairly prestigious businessmen and women. Professional county politicians, generally Republicans, filled the patronage posts, but were subservient on most policy issues to the business amateurs. Since, except for land zoning, there were relatively few devisive issues, there was a good deal of concensus on local policy between the amateurs and professionals, and also the major parties.

In both cities and suburbs, the organizations for shaping and expressing business opinion continued to increase in size and number. The service clubs, Rotary, Kiwanis, and Lions, representing selected cross sections of local businessmen, had over 9,000 local chapters by 1940, with about 400,000 members. In addition, more than a dozen somewhat similar national business clubs had appeared. These clubs plus the chambers of commerce and manufacturers associations created a well-knit business community in which information could travel rapidly. The Lynds held that local newspapers "echo the sentiments heard at Rotary and the Chamber of Commerce."[25]

Although the business elite had the advantage of a continuing basis of power through their personal wealth or their powerful companies, while individual politicians came and went, the local business community as a whole usually had few positive political aims.[26] Business leaders interested themselves in local political issues either to serve the community and perhaps gain personal prestige and satisfaction, or to serve the interests of their firm. "To be a civic statesman," write Banfield and Wilson, "may be one of the fringe benefits that a large corporation gives its head."[27] Businessmen were also consulted by political leaders as a precaution and to gain their valuable public support. Business leaders with a program learned that the various civic associations such as the chamber of commerce or the service clubs were useful for developing means of procedure and testing opposition, but were not very likely to achieve much through their own cautious efforts.

To accomplish concrete results, small groups of top business leaders formed ad hoc combinations. Since 1945 a popular aim for such activity has been urban redevelopment, usually centered around improvement of the central business district. Since most of the money came from the federal government, this was a popular cause with local politicians, unless the upsetting effect on local slum populations was too severe.

If the latter was the case, the big-city businessmen were at a disadvantage in a contest with the local political machine. They were usually Republicans, the machine was usually Democratic; the slum dwellers had thousands of votes, while most of the business leaders and their staffs lived in the suburbs.[28] Consequently, many city machines opposed redevelopment, as for example that of Mayor James F. Tate in Philadelphia in 1968,* although the lure of state or federal money that would benefit local labor and contractors was hard to resist.[29]

Since, aside from redevelopment, there were relatively few chances to benefit urban business as a whole, ad hoc action by businessmen was usually defensive, aimed at preventing increases in assessments, taxes, or other financial burdens. For most big companies, property taxes were not highly important, and therefore local political action might be quite infrequent. There were, however, some types of enterprise such as department stores, real estate operation, newspapers, utilities, transportation, and banking that had rather continuous involvement with local government. Partners in leading law firms were also likely to be involved in political decision-making because of the interests of their clients.[30] Since bankers were financially interested in many types of enterprise, they were often the leaders in organizing ad hoc action.

The fact that American local government had been strictly limited in its economic and welfare functions by more than a hundred years of business watchfulness, left to voluntary associations much of the civic activity performed by local governments in other nations. In organizing and administering the care of the indigent, the poor, and the sick, in supporting the performing arts, and in establishing museums, leading members of the business community played major roles (Chapter 21). But such activities, while highly prestigious, should be clearly distinguished from organizing for political pressure. In the large cities, business leaders tended to specialize in one or another type of good work and to know little about what was happening in other fields of civic betterment.

At the state level the enterprises most in need of favorable government treatment continued to be those whose operations were both monopolistic in local areas and essential to public welfare. In the early twentieth century,

* Mayor Tate refused to take the action necessary to condemn land for a central-city expressway through a Negro home area.

electric street railways, telephone, and power and light companies became new subjects of regulation as local monopolies. By the 1920s the rapidly expanding telephone and power companies were in the forefront of business relations with government.

Government regulation has as its necessary and proper counterpart representation of the regulated companies before government. Indirect means of influencing political actions through favors to editors and press associations, pressures on textbook publishers, and news releases from the agents of important advertisers were both pursued and vigorously criticized in the 1920s and 1930s. Save in some added elaborations, such as campaigns to spread stockholding or distribution of free motion pictures, such activities were not essentially new.[31] In all such efforts to shape policy, it should be remembered that nearly everyone involved, publishers, politicians, and commercial organizations, was interested in the welfare of business, and the real issue was whether or not a particular interest was asking too much.

As in federal politics, influence at the state administrative level was generally easier and more useful than lobbying in the legislature. Hunter says of Georgia, "All candidates are financed largely by the big business interests who control the elected governors."[32] The actual exercise of political influence was usually through groups of business leaders who had among them someone friendly with the governor. This man acted as a liaison agent without formality or obvious pressure. Such representatives of prestigious business coprorations were considered to be far more effective than paid lobbyists, whose personal influence might have been worn down by overuse. In smaller matters where the individual company wanted a favor, the old-style lobbying still persisted. An influential corporate leader in Georgia said that some unscrupulous legislators went on year after year "milking gullible businessmen—and very reputable ones sometimes at that."[33]

OPEN DOMINANCE IN NATIONAL POLITICS

In national politics the period since 1915 breaks clearly into three parts: (1) a period up to 1932, in which, aside from the war years, essential business-government relations continued under much the same conditions as in previous decades, but with a stronger and more open business influence in federal administration; (2) the period of the Great Depression when a large number of liberal politicians reluctantly gave up faith in the self-regulating economy and followed their constituents in brief periods of opposition to business influence and opinion; and finally (3) a period since 1941 in which the old relations have been largely resumed, but one in which continuing regulation, war, and international tensions have built up the power of administration and given some businessmen a greater stake in national political decisions.

The "drafting" of businessmen into government administration in World War I and the expansion of federal activities speeded the transfer of business systems of administration to government, while the use of trade associations by War Industries Board Chairman Bernard Baruch to mobilize production brought businessmen together for political pressure. But neither businessmen nor most of the federal political leaders wanted these intimate relations perpetuated. In fact, social scientists familiar with the national government in later years saw a cultural resistance to effective bureaucracy in government that was hard to overcome. Writing in the late 1950s, Walt W. Rostow believed that the "national style" had hindered the solution of bureaucratic problems in both business and government. Among the parts of the "style" or national character responsible he noted,

> An empirical approach that tends to discount the reality of problems" until they have become acute; "a related tendency to organize staff work on highly specialized lines which make difficult the development of an overall view . . . the tendency to accord all units in an organization a voice in major decisions. . . . As a result, fundamental policy decisions take the form of compromise among responsible operators. [34]

While in American political bureaucracy these characteristics may be fairly universal, whether they have been operative to the same degree in business bureaucracy seems doubtful. In any case, they appeared increasingly to characterize large-scale government organization in the decades after World War I.

Following the Republican landslide in the election of 1920, Elbert H. Gary, the famous leader of United States Steel, said, "We have every reason to believe that hereafter there will be close cooperation between the business world and those adminstering the affairs of government."[35] In the decade that followed, the political desires of the American middle class and the leaders of business coincided as never before. The great majority of these overlapping groups wanted to return to an earlier and somewhat mythical laissez-faire, in which government was frugal and limited and business successfully regulated itself. More specifically, business leaders wanted the rapid liquidation of wartime federal agencies, a friendly attitude on the part of those that remained, no new economic ventures by the federal government, and reduction of taxes.[36] On the question of tariff protection, business was as usual divided, with the transportation, finance, and export industries for low rates, and thousands of manufacturers and their friends for rates high enough to check importation; and as was so often the case when small and medium-sized business politically opposed big business, the more numerous smaller enterprisers had their way.

Despite the pressures of continuing technological change, national politicians were able to live up to the ideals of frugality and laissez-faire to a surprising degree. In the cities and states, adherence to these ideals was impossible. As we have seen, more education was a general middle-class goal, and it cost money. Street and highway expenditures were also needed beyond the sums that could be recovered from gasoline taxes. As a result, state and local taxes and also debts mounted rapidly, rising by around 100 percent in real dollars, and government employees problably rose by a nearly equal percentage.* In these state contests, the back-country people were usually opposed to increasing expenditures; the urban business interests, standing for the added sums deemed necessary for maintaining economic progress in the area, generally won.[37]

Thus the demands of the growing industrial system were being met by the accumulation of eight to ten billion dollars of debt at the state and local level, while the gross federal debt was falling some seven billion. For contemporary businessmen this transfer of indebtedness from federal to local authorities had several advantages. First, the taxes necessary to service and repay the debt would fall more heavily on land and consumption and less on business or personal income. Second, most of the new debt was in tax-exempt bonds, whereas the income from federal bonds was taxable. In a period of remarkably stable prices, 1922-1929, tax exempt bonds were excellent investments for anyone with an income above the lowest tax brackets. Third, the local debt and tax policies were in the hands of authorities more easily influenced by coalitions of property owners than were the legislators of the remote federal government. One might say that this was an unformalized business-inspired theory for the proper lines of development in essential public services. Who, in 1929, could have predicted that the city of Chicago would be bankrupt in 1932?

To the surprise of many liberals, the wartime federal agencies and operations were liquidated with a minimum of protest. Federal operation of the railroads, and also wire communication, necessitated early in 1918, by short-sighted government prohibitions on private joint operations, coupled with an unusually severe winter, had not pleased the shippers. Whereas fear of the political power of this large and varied group had often led private management to give way to shippers' demands, the wartime federal administrators, temporarily free from outside interference, did what they thought best for efficient transportation.[38] As a result, at the end of the war, shippers joined with railroad stockholders in demanding prompt return of the roads to private operation, and only railroad labor opposed such action. When the federal leases of the railroads were terminated in 1920, the Interstate Commerce Commission was given still broader powers over rates and finance; on the other hand, pooling, the major desire of the roads, was legalized, and consolidation plans were invited. The same lame-duck session of the wartime Congress set up a Federal Power Commission, but restricted it to regulating the use of water power on the public domain. Telephone and telegraph administration was also ended. The Shipping Board was retained, however, to administer millions of tons of slow ships built during the war and now fit for only limited uses. This board was, in fact, a service agency to aid American shipping, rather than a regulatory commission.

---

* Unfortunately state and local figures for the nation were prepared only at five-year intervals, 1922, 1927, 1932 (*Historical Statistics,* 726). There are no consolidated employment figures before 1929.

The Federal Trade Commission (FTC) was the most important new regulatory body whose normal functioning had been postponed by the exigencies of war. When it swung into action in 1919 with a report condemning five meat-packing firms for activities in restraint of trade, conservative leaders in Congress attacked the findings and stalled action. In 1921, the new Republican Congress moved regulation of the meat industry to the Department of Agriculture, outside the jurisdiction of FTC. The federal courts also adopted a severely questioning attitude toward the findings of the commission.[39] These evidences of legislative and judicial support encouraged more businessmen to resist the efforts of the commission to gain information, so that even before its membership could be remade by Republican appointments, the FTC had become a relatively unimportant body.

The presidents of this period, Harding, Coolidge, and Hoover, were generally more sympathetic than Congress to what businessmen regarded as sound policy. In the legislature, organizations representing farmers, organized labor, or other groups could, on occasion, overcome the representatives of business, but bills such as those for government operation of the Muscle Shoals Nitrate plants, aid to the farmers, and a soldiers' bonus all met presidential vetoes. The latter measure, however, was finally passed after vetoes by Harding and Coolidge.

Active repression of legal change adverse to business was usually unnecessary. With few notable exceptions, political apathy increased during the decade. A student of Massachusetts politics, for example, finds "that through the 1920's, at least to 1928, not one major reform measure appeared on the statute books."[40] The famed slogan of "normalcy" seemed to mean not only business activity and political quiescence, but a real fear of departing from the status quo.

With the scope of federal government strictly limited and substantial budgetary surpluses, there was a continuing demand by businessmen for tax reduction. One must remember that in 1920 corporate income taxes were only ten years old and personal only six. Big businessmen wanted to return to the situation during the first decade of the century when customs and excise taxes, borne by all consumers, paid for the costs of central government. In the early twenties, a congressional coalition of Democrats and insurgent Republicans, presumably representing farmers and small business, were able to prevent sweeping tax reductions on large incomes, corporations, and inheritance. But the Republican landslide of 1924, accumulating annual surpluses and the pressure of Secretary of the Treasury Andrew Mellon and other important businessmen made reduction politically irresistible. In the law of 1926 the top personal rate was cut from 40 to 20 percent, and the estate tax was also halved. In 1928 Congress reduced the corporate income tax to 11 percent.

Because of the low federal tax rates, a change in the oil depletion allowance lacked the importance that it was to assume for heavily taxed later generations. Up to 1924, American oil reserves seemed inadequate for the long run, and new prospecting appeared to be of the highest importance. Actually, new discoveries started coming in rapidly during the following years, but under the old psychology of scarcity, Congress was induced in 1926 to raise the amount deductible, before taxes, from each year's income from an oil well to 27.5 percent. Ironically, at the very time Congress was offering this incentive, the Texas and Oklahoma regions were entering on a period of serious overproduction.[41]

BUSINESS-GOVERNMENT PARTNERSHIP FOR SURVIVAL

By 1932 the Great Depression had produced conditions of bankruptcy, economic stagnation, and mass unemployment that plunged business from the crest of the wave of popular and political approval to the lowest ebb of its public prestige in all of American history. If such conditions were allowed to continue, they would lead to radical solutions. Both business and government were challenged to devise remedies. For a time in 1933 they cooperated in a number of remedial measures, but soon cooperation broke down over issues of labor, monetary, and financial policy. Public demands led government to the creation of what, to most businessmen, was a state which aided labor and the underprivileged to an extent that might discourage free enterprise.

But the phase of strong antagonism, from 1934 to 1938, between business leaders and the administration proved to be a passing one. Politicians, made uncertain by the traditions of the culture, were unsuccessful in promoting lasting prosperity, basic social attitudes regained their strength, and high productivity in World War II reestablished the prestige of business. The enduring results of what had seemed like a minor revolution were a series of welfare and regulatory acts, quite similar to those of other Western industrial nations, stronger labor unions, and a higher prestige for government and military administration. All of these elements contributed to a stronger capitalism.

Such is the paradox of the New Deal. Seen from one angle, it is the great watershed of American history, separating the culture of the self-regulating economy and its individualistic society from that of the welfare state and its mass society; separating a simpler small group society from one based on impersonal bureaucratic procedures.[42] But from another angle, all that had happened was that the United States had caught up with European practices for the preservation of social stability, as it always had in the past.

In spite of unemployment that reduced hours actually worked in 1932 to about 40 percent of 1929, all of the leading candidates for the presidency and vice-presidency in the two major parties had what appeared to be orthodox or classic economic attitudes. Franklin D. Roosevelt was distinguished from the rest only by a reputation for being willing to consider change, or perhaps by having slightly weaker orthodox convictions. Commenting on the campaign of 1932, the *Christian Century* noted that Roosevelt "said practically nothing—nothing except that he wants to be President."[43] Some other liberal journals were equally severe. Orthodoxy demanded government economy and a balanced budget, and both Hoover and Roosevelt continuously promised these. Only one speech of the campaign, in San Francisco late in August, indicated that Roosevelt might be open to economic experimentation.

The first hundred days of the new administration has been called the Honeymoon, because moderate liberals liked the new president, and conservative business and political leaders found only a few causes for dispute. The National Industrial Recovery Act (NIRA), the most important attempt to fuse governmental and private industrial controls in American history, framed by liberal Senator Robert F. Wagner of New York, Hugh Johnson, a protege of financier Bernard Baruch, and John Dickinson, Assistant Secretary of Commerce, was endorsed by the United States Chamber of Commerce and accepted, in principle at least, by a large number of trade associations.

Passed by Congress in June, the act provided for regulation of prices and conditions of production, including wages and hours, through codes drawn up and submitted for President Roosevelt's approval by representatives of each industry.

Trade associations were the logical agencies to draw up the codes, and they generally provided the necessary leadership. In industries where cutthroat competition was producing losses, such as cotton textiles, producers were so anxious to get the protection of the price-fixing parts of the act that they were willing to take a chance on the effects of the labor provisions. In business where natural monopolies or well-established price leadership softened competitive pressure, such as automobiles, the major producers were more inclined to resist the labor provisions.[44] In the code of the automobile industry, Section 7A, which concerned labor relations, was modified to prevent enforcement, and even then, Ford refused to sign.

General Hugh S. Johnson, a former manufacturer of agricultural machinery, who was made administrator of the regulatory part of the act, won the confidence of businessmen. But with the benefit of hindsight, one can see that from the start there were too many difficulties to be overcome in this hasty effort to bring all types of business into a single regulatory system. Essentially it was a move en masse to the kind of cartelization that many American manufacturers held responsible for inefficient production in Europe. Effective regulation would require uniformity in processes that each businessman had formerly run to suit himself. By late July it was clear that the carrot of price-fixing was not going to lure a majority of industries into drawing up voluntary codes.

The government now took up a campaign of persuasion. Producers who had signed a code were allowed to display, on labels, flags, or in windows, a blue eagle with wings spread against a white circular space on a red background. In advertisements, articles, and speeches, consumers were urged to patronize only those who could display the eagle. President Roosevelt reviewed NRA parades in the major cities and proclaimed the unity of the nation in support of codes. If no code was agreed to in an industry, firms could gain the right to display the eagle by signing a President's Reemployment Agreement (PRA). This form, provided for in the original law, bound the firm to the wage and hour provisions, but could not, of course, do anything about general prices or trade practices. Faced with signing PRA, many firms reluctantly worked for a general code as the lesser of evils. By early 1934 nearly 600 types of business activity were covered by NRA codes, but individual firms, of which Ford was by far the most important, refused to come into the system.

In the late summer of 1934 the great experiment in regulation was faltering. The Recovery Administration was swamped with arguments and complaints; organized labor was disgusted with the operation of Section 7A; General Johnson was under strong attack from liberal Democrats because of his support of business management; but, most important of all, NIRA had not brought recovery. At this time the dollar volume of business activity was only a little above that of the desperate spring of 1933. In September General Johnson, by now driven toward alcoholism, was forced to retire, and administration of NIRA was put in the hands of a board. As opinion in the presidential administration turned against price-fixing, many businessmen felt that the government had failed to carry out its share of the partnership, that they "had been betrayed."[45]

Johnson and his deputy administator, Donald Richberg, had had doubts about the constitutionality of NIRA from the beginning, and had tried to find a good test case. Most of the codes were so hastily drawn that legal problems were obvious. Before the administrators found their ideal case, an extremely weak one was on its way through the courts. In *A. L. Schechter* v. *United States* (decided in May, 1935), a unanimous Supreme Court held NIRA unconstitutional, chiefly on the grounds that power which could only be exercised directly by the president was delegated to the local code authorities. By this time, few people in business, labor, or government wanted to prolong the system. About as conclusively as is ever possible in real life, complete and uniform government regulation of business activity to insure fair competition had proved unsatisfactory to all concerned.

BUSINESS FIGHTS THE NEW DEAL

While many businessmen were far from happy with the monetary policies of the New Deal, which restricted the use of gold to foreign exchange and ultimately reduced the dollar to 59.06 percent of its former value in gold, there was no clear breakdown of the politics of concensus during 1933. Meanwhile, financial leaders, harrassed by a prolonged Senate investigation in 1932 and 1933, had accepted the divorce of investment from commercial banking, and legal requirements for public information regarding new security issues, with only moderate complaints.

In the spring of 1934, however, the Securities and Exchange Commission Act, which regulated stock market practices and ordered the disclosure of large amounts of information regarding all securities traded, aroused the financial community and its influential friends. Furthermore, the bill indicated an ominous swing of the administration beyond measures thought necessary for recovery toward more fundamental changes in the nature of American capitalism. Such fears, plus increasing expenditures for relief and "made" work, an unbalanced budget, and the growing bureaucracy of departments such as Agriculture or agencies like NRA all entered into a general indictment of the New Deal by spokesmen for business and other members of the upper-income group.[46] In the fall of 1934, conservative Republican and Democratic leaders moved to organize opposition to Roosevelt. Financed by such businessmen as R. M. H. Carpenter of Du Pont and John J. Raskob of General Motors, and supported by some Democrat political leaders such as Alfred E. Smith, the American Liberty League was formed to present the conservative case to the voters.

The National Association of Manufacturers, which had lost membership in the political calm of the 1920s, also became a rallying point for business opposition to the liberal Democrats. Large companies which had not bothered with the NAM in earlier years now brought their contributions. During the entire New Deal period from 1933 to 1938, Alfred S. Cleveland finds that the NAM opposed thirty-one of what he regards as the thirty-eight important laws.[47] After its initial sponsorship of NIRA, the Chamber of Commerce of the United States also joined in the opposition to continuing New Deal legislation.

In spite of the mounting opposition of business organizations, in 1934 the Democrats added greatly to their majority in Congress. Consequently, the political representatives of business suffered a devastating defeat in the congressional session of 1935. By the end of August the large liberal majority had raised income taxes, begun social security, passed a "death sentence" for large, multilevel public utility holding companies, enlarged the powers of the central Federal Reserve Board, and assured labor of preferred treatment in bargaining with employers. While the Reconstruction Finance Corporation Act of 1932 may symbolize the end of faith in the self-regulating economy and the advent of the welfare state, the legislation of 1935 made the latter a reality.

Beaten in Congress, business leaders nevertheless persuaded themselves that the New Deal program was unpopular with the voter, and that Roosevelt could be defeated in 1936. It is highly unlikely that there was ever a time between 1932 and 1936 when Roosevelt could not have swept the country, but the fall of 1936 was a particularly unfortunate time for the conservative businessmen to have to make their challenge. The economy was in a substantial upswing, jobs were gradually increasing, the soldiers' bonus of World War I had just been paid in full, and there seemed to be no reason for the average citizen to complain of the Roosevelt leadership.

The crushing electoral defeat of 1936 left only remnants of the Republican party in the House and Senate. The Liberty League was abandoned as useless. The business effort to preserve the old tradition of limited central government had failed, and could not be successfully revived. Businessmen had now to learn how to get among with "big government," and a system of high federal taxation.

THE RISE OF FEDERAL ADMINISTRATION

During the depressed period from 1930 to 1935 there was relatively little recruitment of new managerial personnel by business, while the federal government increased its civilian employees by about one-third. Clearly the opportunity for smart young men was in Washington. To staff the new boards, commissions, and agencies able young college graduates, particularly lawyers, were drawn away from junior executive positions or corporate legal practice. For perhaps the first time in American history, capable young men found promise and excitement in the federal bureaucracy. Since the peace-time staff of the civilian wing of the federal government was to grow about 200 percent during the next generation, the new opportunity became a continuing one.

Within government there was also a drift of power to Washington. In many regions during the depression the finance of local government broke down, and states and cities sought federal grants. Using federal money for local purposes meant a shift from real property taxes toward corporate and personal income taxes. This was at the core of much of the opposition to the centralizing tendencies of the New Deal. The big and expert Washington bureaucracy also came to constitute a fourth branch of government, alongside the executive, legislative, and judicial branches, and one that because of its specialized knowledge and relatively nonpolitical character constituted a new type of influence on policy, and as we will see, both a new challenge and a new political opportunity for business.

The economic failure of the New Deal in the depression from 1937 to 1939 and the consequent loss of both power and prestige by the president was only a brief interlude, ended by World War II, before many lasting effects were noticeable. With the coming of war both regulation and bureaucracy advanced, as business pundits had feared, but patriotic enthusiasm and high-level prosperity made cooperation easier.

Having become accustomed to the new laws and made friends in the new commissions, men seemed to go about their business as in earlier periods. Yet, there was a fundamental difference. Both business and the public had been unwilling to endure the first major old-style "free market" depression of the twentieth century. The breakdown of the voluntary National Credit Association, made up of leading bankers, led Herbert Hoover in 1932 to remark, "Its members—and the business world—threw up their hands and asked for government action."[48] Thus ended the era in which thoughtful men could stoutly affirm "that government is best which governs least." The Employment Act of 1946, passed by a Congress with a conservative majority, explicitly reaffirmed the responsibility of the federal government for policies that would maintain employment, gave the president a Council of Economic Advisors, and required him to report annually on the economic welfare of the nation.*

BUSINESS AND GOVERNMENT IN WORLD POWER

The prosperous years after World War II and increased big business interest in military and foreign policies led to even closer relations between business and the federal government than had existed in the years just before the Great Depression. High corporate taxes, of course, constituted one of the unwelcome differences in the relationship. As Lammot Du Pont Copeland of the Du Pont company, said, "One thing is perfectly apparent. Whether we like it or not, the Federal government is a partner in every business in the country. For most of us here today, it has been a majority partner, for let me point out that the government has been taking 52 per cent of the earnings of the Du Pont Company before anything has been available for our 233,000 stockholders who have invested their savings in our enterprise, and who are, at least, its nominal owners."[49] But there were many compensating factors that pleased business leaders with federal policy.

Ironically, the continuation of New Deal agricultural policy plus great advances in agricultural knowledge and technology built business strength in Washington. An informal coalition developed between prosperous commercial farmers, who received large federal payments for restricting acreage, although often expanding production, and many other business interests willing to pay this price in order to have such influential friends in Congress. This bipartisan coalition of agricultural and industrial conservatives, with Southern agriculturalists in many key positions on congressional committes, was able to outmaneuver or outvote labor and liberal reformers. Consequently, in spite of mildly liberal or progressive presidents, including Eisenhower, the structure of legislation affecting domestic matters, other than the problems of Negroes and the poor, did not change greatly. In these two exceptional matters, urban business, guided by both conscience and public relations, was inclined to break with conservative Southerners, and the latter could not make reprisals against Northern business for fear of a general attack on agricultural subsidies.

Following World War II top-level government administrators and big business leaders were united in their views on American world policies. Control of sources of raw material and open areas for safe investment were the positive incentives, international containment of Communism and exclusion of unwanted products and people from the United States were the negative aims. Frequently the positive and negative policies went hand in hand, as in supporting conservative governments in areas of American investment. Up to 1967, at least, when

* The wording of the law posed a basic problem: regulation of the economy in the interest of free enterprise. The council did not exert much influence during the first fifteen years of its existence. See Canterbery, *Council of Economic Advisors.*

support of a conservative government in South Vietnam began to be extremely expensive, there appears to have been practically no difference between the interests of big business companies and the foreign policies of either Democratic or Republican administrations.

As always, business was likely to be divided on specific policies. Foreign aid, while expressed in dollars, went in the form of American goods, and favored the manufacturers, who were often able to penetrate new markets, while other businessmen might object to the added tax burden. In the mid-1950s J. P. Sprang, Jr., president of the Gillette Razor Company, a firm with old foreign market positions, advocated helping nations by buying their products. He said, "What we are now doing in our foreign aid program is taxing ourselves for the privilege of excluding foreign merchandise."[50] But the influential private Committee on Economic Development, supported by businessmen, advocated continued foreign aid. While friendly to the principle of aid both *Fortune* and the *Wall Street Journal* criticized the strings attached. These ties to the purchase of American goods, and prohibition on trade with Communist nations, they said, prevented the building of normal economic relations between the recipients and other countries, and discouraged local enterprise competitive with United States supplies.[51] In all such foreign policy discussion, there seems to have been a doubt that business enterprise through trade alone could be a major force to weaken Communism. By the late 1960s the drain on dollar exchange led increasing numbers of businessmen, both in and out of Congress, to advocate cutting down on all but the military programs for free distribution of goods.

Because of the large difference in wages between other countries and the United States, American firms, from the late 1950s on, invested heavily in foreign plants to supply overseas markets. While most of this direct investment, totaling $55 billion in 1968, was in Canada and Western Europe, areas with which the United States had relatively free and friendly relations, it necessarily involved the parent companies in American foreign policy. Aside from oil in the Middle East, the big United States companies had only small investments in trouble spots such as Africa or South Asia, but businessmen in general supported the State and Defense Departments in asserting the power of the United States in any part of the world.

Entrance into the Korean War in 1950 was an emergency government decision in which business leadership had no part. While the Vietnam situation gradually developed into a large-scale war, it progressed so gradually that business opinion went through different phases. On the whole, the business magazines, and presumably their readers, supported, in principle, an aggressive anti-Communist foreign policy. When this policy led to escalation of the civil war in Vietnam, the magazines, *Fortune* in particular, strongly supported action on a scale that would lead to victory.[52]

When the Johnson administration produced rapid inflation by overspending in support of a "war on poverty" as well as one in Vietnam, business spokesmen blamed the president chiefly for not abandoning the former. But in 1968, as the cost of the war rose to a height that was producing dangerous inflation coupled with lack of progress on the battlefield, there was a rise of some business opinion in favor of ending the war. By July of 1970 a group of advertising executives had joined twenty-four United States Senators in paying for a series of nationwide television commercials demanding the withdrawal of troops from South Vietnam by June, 1971.[53]

From the Korean War on, the country remained on what by earlier standards would be called a war footing, with the annual budget for military operation running from $40 billion to over $100 billion. Military equipment, demanding continual research and new designs, kept appropriate sectors of industry continuously on the alert for contracts. About two-thirds to three-quarters of these went to some 150 corporations, big enough to organize massive projects. Partly to facilitate relations with the Defense Department, these companies, in the early 1960s, had some 1,500 retired military officers on their payrolls.* Inevitably the lobbyists sent to Washington by these companies spent most of their time fighting each other, but the top officers of the big contractors could not avoid a close involvement in policy decisions at the Pentagon and in the Defense Department.[54]

While the demands of the military led to an expansion of business interests in politics, the demands of technology produced a civilian invasion of the Pentagon by experts of many types, unavailable from among the military officers. Secretary of Defense McNamara in the 1960s reenforced this trend toward civilian preeminence.[55] At all events, a few big companies such as airframe manufacturers became so completely tied to military supply that it was hard to say whether their executive decisions and policies originated in government or private conclaves. The chief executives of the principal Defense Department contractors, the nation's most important business leaders, were also the men on whom presidents were likely to call for advice. Some commentators saw these men as part of a "power-elite" that possessed the resources for manipulating public opinion through advertising, and stood in the way of any substantial reduction in military spending.

BUSINESS AND THE ROUTINES OF FEDERAL GOVERNMENT

While in the areas of defense and foreign expansion, business had close, cordial, and effective relations with administrative government, in the area of federal regulation the relations varied over the years, depending on the agency and business involved and on the political climate. After extensive interviewing, in 1952, Robert E. Lane came to the conclusion that "since 1935 there has been

---

* It should be remembered that, in any case, a large employer would have a number of retired military officers on the payroll, because of the number of such men seeking new employment.

a long term and steady decline in business hostility to government."[56] In contrast, John Kenneth Galbraith believed in the 1960s that "the widespread suspicion and even hostility of businessmen to government, even when as in the case of the Eisenhower Administration it was presumptively sympathetic to business, is one of the great constants of our political life."[57] At about the same time, G. William Domhoff held that there was a group of liberal business leaders that was not opposed, in principle, to government action, and that these men were coming to be "the dominant influence within the upper class."[58] Whatever view is correct, the leaders of big business learned, perforce, to work intimately with the federal regulatory officials.

In the post-New Deal era there were seven major agencies involved in regulating business. To the older Interstate Commerce, Federal Trade, and Federal Power Commissions, the New Deal had added the Civil Aeronautics Board, the Securities and Exchange Commission, the National Labor Relations Board, and the Federal Communications Commission. By 1950 all of these agencies were old enough to appreciate the views and interests of those they regulated, although they all suffered from confusions regarding the nature of administrative government. The laws defining the functions of the agencies were usually unclear, and congressmen continually badgered the board to favor companies in which the legislator or his important constituents had an interest.[59] Moderate government salaries and terms of only five to seven years made it hard to find men with the high ability needed to staff the commissions, and in addition, both parties used such jobs as payment for political obligations. It was not surprising, therefore, that many commissioners retired to take better paying jobs in the industry they had regulated.[60]

The Federal Trade Commission, with its duties of administering the antitrust and fair trade practice laws, was, along with the NLRB (Chapter 17), the agency with which business in general was involved. The FTC was overloaded with thousands of small complaints, 7,000 in the year 1962 alone, that took up most of the time of a staff of little over 1,000 men. The time consumed in preventing dishonest advertising, discriminatory sales promotion, and unfair discounts led Commissioner Philip Edman to write: "There operates a kind of Gresham's law. The trivial and the inconsequential cases leave little room, and tend to drive out, the substantial and significant."[61] In consequence, interpretation of the statutes for maintaining competition remained a cloudy area.

On the other side of the picture, a commission was generally an audience more friendly to and understanding of the specific needs of business than was a congressional committee. As one analyst put it, the commision gave the regulated firms a "beachhead within government."[62] In addition, a gradual process of replacing lawyers on their staffs by economists and other social scientists made the agencies more useful to business as sources for information and planning.

Relations with such federal agencies affected chiefly the few thousand medium to large-sized businesses. For the vast majority of American businessmen, primarily involved with state or local action, the federal government was principally an expensive nuisance that required extra bookkeeping for tax purposes. They neither gained nor lost through any personal relations with federal regulatory commissions, they merely paid a share of the overhead.

THE NEW BUSINESS INFLUENCE

The change in business relations with government since 1945 has also to be seen against a background of change in both the formal and informal structure of government itself. In these years the federal government reached through the state level to deal directly with municipalities. Within the federal and state governments, administrative departments took over the originating and framing of important bills, and often left legislators only the functions of modification, approval, or rejection. Since presidential administrations had large powers for both patronage and spending in the legislator's home district, rejection of administrative policy involved substantial political risks.[63]

Contemporaneous with the decline in congressional initiative was the increasing importance of grants and contracts given out by federal administrative agencies. Most of the big company representatives in Washington were "contract men" rather than all-purpose legislative lobbyists. In most congressional lobbying, general business opinion was represented only by such organizations as the Chamber of Commerce, the National Association of Manufacturers, or appropriate trade associations. This often left the legislators themselves, who would look after their own personal interests, as the strongest force representing business.

Congressmen were, by profession, expert in gauging the probable influence of various individuals or groups. Hearings on bills were useful for pressure groups in making personal contacts, but since they introduced little of which the congressmen were not already aware, the lobbyists were not thought to change many votes. This is not to say that legislators were impervious to pressure. Members of the House, particularly, needed campaign funds every other year, and much of the money came from sums secreted in business expense accounts. They were naturally responsive to men representing the legislator's own type of business, or one important in his particular congressional district, or to reliable information regarding how a bill would affect financially important constituents. A few members of both houses were susceptible to bribes aimed usually at modifying important details of bills.[64] In other words, Congress was an agency for trimming, modifying, or blocking policies that might affect some important group adversely.

A NEW BUSINESS POWER ELITE?

The limitations on congressional policy formation did not necessarily lead to policy by administrative concensus, but it did mean that the most important areas for direct business pressure were in the administration rather than the legislature. The costs of primary and other preconvention campaigning were so high that all nominees for the presidency needed the support of wealthy backers.

Since the administrative atmosphere of well-educated public servants with expert knowledge was a congenial one to the leaders of big business, at least, a considerable number of executives were frequently consulted by federal administrators, which no doubt gave the businessmen an enjoyable feeling of importance as national pundits as well as helping them to represent the interests of their companies.

On the basis of questionnaires and interviews in 1956 Hunter concluded that there were about 100 top level executives who consulted with each other and with federal authorities so often that they constituted an informal business "power structure."[65] Certainly consultation between politicians and leading businessmen was as old as representative government, but the deliberate canvassing of business opinion by the administration in Washington had greatly increased during World War I. The war also helped to make many executives of big companies more aware of their social and political problems.[66] The system of discussions between business and government, however, probably failed until World War II to achieve the influence with which Hunter credits it.

Both he and C. Wright Mills did their writing about the strength of business power elites during the Eisenhower years, when Secretary of the Interior Douglas McKay said he was part of "an administration representing business and industry," and when at least two-thirds of the top government administrators had business rather than political backgrounds.[67] This had not been the case during the Roosevelt and Truman years, and was true to a lesser extent in the two succeeding Democratic administrations.[68]

The facts that each major party was merely a collection of state parties with no effective national organization or continuing leadership, and that the civil service did not in general provide enough top-level policy makers, however, left a vacuum that business leaders felt constrained to occupy in the interest of national stability. As a result, informal groups of important corporate leaders, or men of great wealth, no doubt exercised considerable influence on national policy and, at times, on the appointment of government administrators. Probably, Hunter concludes, the advisory activities in Washington of executives of the largest "corporations give a continuity and comprehensiveness to power pressures not furnished by any other institutional grouping in American life."[69] Since the American way of life was a business way of life, it does not seem surprising that the leading businessmen should be a major force in shaping policy.

Other social scientists see the elitist influence on government as emanating from an American "governing class," generally defined as the corporate and hereditary rich. Members of this relatively large group appear in undue proportion in desirable administrative posts both public and private. Although there are some ethnic, religious, and educational qualifications made in constituting the group, the argument comes close to saying that social and governmental institutions in American society are strongly influenced by the most prestigious members of the society, who, in the American case, owe their status to success in business, past or present. It would appear that the proposition in its general form should hold true in most nations.[70]

CHAPTER 21

A Mature Business Society

In the years following World War I, Americans realized as never before that theirs was a business society. It seems unlikely that a mature journalist in any other nation or in any other time would have been inspired to write:

> Among the nations of the earth today America stands for one idea, business. National opprobrium? National opportunity. For in this fact lies, potentially, the salvation of the world . . . .
> What is the finest game? Business. The soundest science? Business. The truest art? Business. The fullest education? Business. The fairest opportunity? Business. The cleanest philanthropy? Business. The sanest religion? Business.[1]

By 1920 the rival elites of the land, politics, or the church had been submerged in the business society. The remaining rivalry for major influence in elite groups was between the local families of wealth and business importance, and the executives of national corporations; between those with status based on regional influence and those with status arising from organizational position. Had the peaceful and prosperous days of the 1920s continued, these might have remained the only groups with a valid claim to superior status.

To the temporary weakening effect of the Great Depression on the prestige of both of these groups, and the rise in influence of national political administrators, World War II added, for the first time in America, a substantial military elite, that by world traditions as well as by power in Washington had a strong claim to prestigious status. In the postwar world of high government expenditures and tense foreign relations, the balance of elites, therefore, moved toward the conventional Western world pattern; the difference was that in the United States, local eminence almost always came from wealth acquired through business rather than from the status of aristocratic landlord. Whether the two business elites were still relatively stronger in America than in, for example, England or Germany was difficult to judge. In all three nations there was a trend toward fusion between elite groups, and only on rare occasions a real conflict.

THE BUSINESS ELITES

While the substantial local businessmen and the executives of national corporations might have nearly common aims in the affairs of the nation, in local communities they tended to form discrete groups. A *Fortune* study of the Atlanta, Georgia, business elite in 1961, for example, indicated that in this major metropolitan area the two groups were distinct. The local owners, called Big Mules, had larger incomes than the nomadic corporate executives of absentee firms, lived in a different section, belonged to different clubs, and were judged by the research team to be "different species of men."[2] The fact, which one might not expect, that the Big Mules were better educated and more cosmopolitan than the Nomads was undoubtedly due to more wealth, control of leisure, and higher average age. More predictable was the greater interest of the forty-odd Big Mules in local government, for which purpose they cooperated with a dozen Negro business leaders, who, in general, also represented inherited status.[3]

The conclusions of the *Fortune* study reaffirm those of a broader, but less intensive study, made by the author in 1950. In six major metropolitan areas west of the Mississippi River the local business leaders, in each case, saw themselves as a group apart from the representatives of the national corporations. They were critical of the latter for not taking a proper interest in civic affairs or local philanthropy. Asked to support the local symphony, for example, a nomadic vice-president merely said no, he and his wife were not interested in music.[4] Such a negative response would be less likely in the 1960s, but it would have been even more likely in earlier decades. In fact, the strong emphasis on improving the community relations of national corporate executives only began with World War II, and could never, through artificial stimulation, make up for the fact that the Nomad's world was his company, not the town in which he found himself at the moment.

The wealth of the Big Mules of Atlanta was a characteristic of the local owners in the large metropolitan areas. In smaller cities the reverse may have been true, if the Nomads were well up in the hierarchy of their corporations, but this did not necessarily alter the feelings of the local elite. They still felt responsibility for the community; they were held together by many family relationships and realized that corporate Nomads would not generally take a long view of future civic development.*

Save for some community studies, usually in small cities, there is not much information on the education and social mobility of elites based on local ownership, while the national corporate executive has been the subject of

---

* Information in interviews in the Norristown files, University of Pennsylvania. There was in Norristown a double distinction. The wealthiest local elite generally lived in suburbs not immediately attached to Norristown or its surrounding boroughs.

extensive research. One of the most interesting of these studies is that already referred to (Chapter 16), in which W. Lloyd Warner and James C. Abegglen compared practically similar groups of about 7,500 executives in 1927 and 1952.[5] The findings, as noted earlier, indicated a substantial increase in those with some college education, from less than half to 76 percent, and also in those who rose from working-class backgrounds, although in 1952 the latter were still only 15 percent of the total.

Except for times of violent social revolution, this corporate group was perhaps as mobile an elite both socially and geographically as the world had ever known. The high rate of geographical mobility which had resulted from the conditions of American immigration and settlement was deliberately fostered by most large national companies. They moved rising young men frequently in order to familiarize them with the corporate "empire," and to stimulate the new ideas and innovations that were so frequently inspired by migration. Corporate policy was reflected, in part, in the national census figures that showed mobility increasing sharply with both education and income. A study in 1955 indicated that in the twenty-five to thirty-four year old group, only 27 percent of high school graduates were interstate migrants, whereas among those with at least one year of college the figure was 46 percent.[6]

These well-educated, careerist migrants spread a uniform business culture to communities across the nation. Any nonconforming folkways of the local elite were gradually altered. Family pride, local customs, and confidence in a familiar continuing status were assailed, not only by nomadic young executives but by national mass media which were, in turn, run by major national corporations.

While the locally based elite was not diminishing in size, as the big companies came to have proportionately larger and larger administrative staffs, the nomadic elite was increasing.[7] On the upper social levels of the owners of relatively large local brokerage, distributing, and manufacturing enterprises, there was usually a ready association with the national executives. In fact, the latter added to the local upper-middle class that had traditionally held aloof from associating with men in retail trade or service. In addition, the movement of college graduates into the security of the big corporation, and of the high school graduate to the more immediate opportunities of smaller enterprise, tended to widen the social distance between the local small businessman and the national company executive.

The continuous movement of the national corporate executives made local loyalties or deep friendships unlikely. As we have seen, the executive compensated for this through loyalty to his company and friendships with others in his national organization. Prestige in the company seemed more important than in outside society. These substitutions were largely denied to wives, who had to live for the day when the ultimate reward of a position in the head office would bring the family to settled residence in a big metropolitan area.

RESPONSIBILITY FOR WELFARE

Continuous movement also removed the rising executive from the traditional burden of responsibilities for community needs, save as he represented his company. This meant that in a city with a number of branch plants and stores, a considerable section of the business elite was only mildly interested in local social welfare. As already noted in regard to general public relations (Chapter 16), a partial solution was for the company itself to become a donor. Thus from World War I on, business giving has two distinct aspects: gifts by prosperous individuals and gifts by companies.[8]

Both types of donors were reluctant to give money to help those who might have helped themselves. Aid to the able-bodied poor continued to be regarded as a drain upon the society, that according to traditional American thinking had a demoralizing effect on the recipients and should not be encouraged. On the whole, therefore, the business community was reluctant to assume the increasing costs of welfare that rose with urban industrialism. Up to the New Deal period, at least, poverty and unemployment were looked upon as the results of improvidence, and adequate help was seen as encouraging willful dependency. In the major cities the voluntary associations, coordinated by Charity Organization Societies or Social Service Bureaus continued, through World War I, the type of minimum aid to disaster cases only that had characterized the nineteenth century.

To the inadequate welfare legislation of the early years of the century, the states in the 1920s added laws to regularize aid to special groups such as unsupported children, the blind, the aged, and the incapacitated. Partly to stem the advance of such public welfare legislation, and partly because of some improved techniques for private fund raising, the leading businessmen of urban communities took over the task of raising funds for annual giving.

Wartime drives suggested that a concentrated campaign of speakers and door-to-door solicitation could raise far more money than would ever be given to an agency soliciting by mail. One result was a spread of the annual Community Chest drives which had first been tried in 1913.[9] The business leaders of a city assumed executive direction of the drive and used their prestige to secure both campaign workers and contributions. The funds collected were then apportioned among the various charities in proportion to their needs.

The results of this concerted charitable effort by business were spectacular. In 1919, forty cities had Community Chests, a decade later there were 350. In "Middletown" by 1924 only 350 people had contributed to the central Social Service Bureau and only about 200 more to various other charities out of a population of 38,000. The following year the Rotary Club group took the lead in organizing a Community Chest. They appointed a "colonel" in charge, divided the city into districts headed by "captains" with teams of "sergeants" and "privates" and "whooped it up." The ensuing campaign produced 6,402 contributors, or gifts from about half the households in the city. In 1924, the Social Service Bureau had distributed $10,000; in 1925 the Community Chest was able to allot four times this sum.[10]

As a means of raising funds the Community Chest had two weaknesses: there was a tax and legal problem as to whether corporate officers could give stockholders' money for purposes that would not directly benefit a national company, and the fact that in the years of greatest unemployment and need, the donors might also be short of funds. The tax problem was resolved in the Revenue Act of 1935 (the "soak the rich" tax bill) by granting companies a tax-free allowance of 5 percent of income for gifts. Meanwhile, in 1934 the United States Supreme Court held that relatable benefits must be shown from gifts.[11] The improbability of stockholder action led many managements to a broad view of what was "relatable." In 1953 an arranged case produced a decision by the Superior Court of New Jersey that a gift to Princeton University was beneficial to the stockholders of a manufacturing company.[12] Apparently corporate giving never reached a point before 1970 that prompted stockholders to seek legal redress.

The second type of weakness in all private charity was shown in the Great Depression. Despite soaring needs, it was impossible to increase substantially the contributions of companies earning only small profits or none. Herbert B. Swope of General Electric Company became chairman of a Mobilization for Human Needs in 1935, but had little success in raising funds.[13] Giving to the Community Chests from 1929 to 1939 increased only moderately, the ten top corporate givers providing 13.5 percent more in fifty-three cities. In 1940 there were still companies, including some chain stores, that regarded local giving as illegal use of the stockholders' money.[14]

The Community Chest, renamed the United Fund, continued to operate as the major collector of private donations in the years after World War II. The principal charities of a city, with a few exceptions, raised their money through the fund. A prominent business executive was elected by the self-perpetuating board of the fund to organize and lead the annual campaign. Large business and other organizations were assigned quotas, and contributions by employees were deductible from pay checks in installments. Suburbanites were solicited at both office and home. In 1925 the chests had raised $58 million, which was 94 percent of their goals; in 1966 the Funds raised $626 million which was 101 percent of the anticipated total.[15] In this way, much of the welfare that in England, for example, was taken care of by County Councils or National Health agents was kept in the hands of voluntary private charity.

While business was chiefly responsible for this achievement it failed to act vigorously enough to prevent the ultimate dominance of government in the area of "social," or job and old-age, security. Around the turn of the century, when several states began to pass welfare laws, there were a few businessmen who visualized the possibilities of private insurance. Haley Fiske, president of the

Metropolitan Life Insurance Company, urged not only industrial insurance at reasonable rates, but also unemployment compensation.[16] In some states, compensation laws allowed insurance with private companies, but Fiske was never able to get the state legislature of New York to allow his company to write unemployment insurance. The last defeat of his bill in 1928 was largely due to the political belief that such insurance would be unnecessary in the prosperous future.

A principal cause of poverty in industrial society was, and continued to be, old age. In the society of the nineteenth century, where most enterprises were small companies run by their owners, the able-bodied were allowed to continue working well into old age, after which those still alive went to live with relatives on farms or were taken care of informally by the proprietor of the firm. Large impersonal companies in an urbanized environment, however, set up uniform rules for retirement, usually at sixty-five years of age, and it was highly unlikely that the workers had saved enough to provide a living income. Hence it became necessary either to provide a pension or to pass a law for state pensions. With very few exceptions, only railroads and public utilities adopted pension plans before 1900. The Carnegie Steel Company, with a plan in 1901, was a leader among large industrial companies. The more general movement after 1910 coincided with the enactment of weak and unsatisfactory laws by the states. In 1930, twenty-nine states had such laws, but Don D. Lescohier found "all of them crude and unsatisfactory."[17]

By this time practically all employees of Class I railroads were covered by company pensions, as were a small number of those in public utilities, banks, and insurance companies. In manufacturing, plans were largely confined to firms in steel, machinery, and chemicals, including oil.[18] Noncontributory plans were the nearly universal rule, since these left complete power to alter or suspend in the hands of the employers. Such plans in 1929 covered a total of 3.6 million employees, or about 10 percent of the nonagricultural labor force, of whom 43.5 percent were in railroads and 34.2 percent in manufacturing.

Continuous inflation from the beginning of the century to 1920 tended to make the incomes set in state laws inadequate and to place an unexpected burden on companies that raised pensions to adequate levels. As a result, many companies were led by financial difficulties to abandon or modify plans. The Great Depression produced two contradictory movements: from 1929 to 1932, 69 new plans were added to the 300-odd already in existence, but about 10 percent of the latter were discontinued.[19]

The number of workers in companies with pension plans is a somewhat misleading figure, as many workers failed to qualify for pensions. An employee usually had to be continuously in the service of the company for ten to twenty or more years before the age of retirement, and because of the ups and downs of business, many lacked this continuity. In 1930 there were more than 6.5 million people in the United States over sixty-five years of age, of whom 150,000 received private, and 179,500 state, pensions. As means of support disappeared in the depression, there was urgent need for a national social security law.

The federal act of 1935, based on employer and employee contributions, collected as a tax, was narrow in its coverage, exempting many categories of workers, and relatively low in its levels of old-age pensions. In respect to workers covered, the law was gradually amended to include almost everyone by the 1950s, but inflation from 1940 on made benefits increasingly inadequate. As a consequence, starting in 1947, labor unions, led by John L. Lewis' United Mine Workers, started asking in their contracts for employer contributions to pension funds. Forced to give way to the demands of nationally organized labor, management extended similar benefits to salaried clerical and administrative personnel, generally through noncontributory plans. In 1950, four million employees were covered by private pension plans of all types, while by 1965 the number had risen to twenty-five million. Plans covering about a quarter of these employees were insured against financial failure of the institution involved.[20]

This shift of providing security for old age from the individual worker or employer to a pension fund was another aspect of the shift away from individualistic capitalism, noted in Chapter 16. Instead of the rising administrator saving continuously for old age by investing in land, mortgages, stocks, and bonds, he now left this function, in part at least, to the company for which he worked and perhaps also to an insurance company to which he contributed. These institutions then became the chief investors and manipulators of accumulated savings, and even a successful executive might not be an individual capitalist.

In spite of such arrangements for union or company supplements to government payments, business had failed for many reasons to preserve the "voluntaristic" society in which welfare was a private responsibility. As noted in the case of the Community Chest, the law made it difficult or impossible for a company to give large amounts, and the business cycle worked against meeting fluctuating needs. In addition, many business leaders opposed large-scale corporate welfare activity. In the early part of the period, both Herbert B. Swope and Edward A. Filene agreed that the best public service was an efficiently run business.[21] Speaking for important business interests, the more recent Committee on Economic Development has supported the same view. Hampered by these differences of opinion within companies, corporate giving from 1938 to 1960 averaged only about 1 percent a year.[22] In 1968 this same general average produced a sum of a billion dollars, compared to a total for all philanthropic gifts of $15 billion.[23]

In spite of this total for private charity, individual gifts for general social welfare were not large. The whole tradition of individual free enterprise in America had been contrary to a general doctrine of total social responsibility (Chapter 13). The stewardship of wealth was a doctrine for private support, but it involved the administration of accumulated fortunes, not a day-to-day responsibility while the fortunes were being made. Private donors usually preferred giving to some particular cause or project rather than having their money "dissipated" for public relief. Many still agreed with Andrew Carnegie who combined the stewardship of wealth with belief that "nine hundred and fifty out of every thousand dollars bestowed to-day on so called charity had better be thrown into the sea."[24] Corporation executives administering other people's money might develop liberal ideas of social statesmanship, but wealthy individuals still clung to much of the Calvinist belief in self-help and personal responsibility for one's condition.

SOCIAL RESPONSIBILITY FOR THE ARTS AND LEARNING

In supporting the arts and learning, regarded as wholly different from aiding the needy, individual donors had always played important roles. The free enterprise system, with its minimization of governmental action, transferred a greater burden to private patronage than in other advanced nations. In 1916, Otto H. Kahn, a leading international banker, exhorted American businessmen, in language they would understand, to occupy themselves with the arts in addition to business. "A man going along day to day doing his daily acts will weaken his efficiency and mar his life," Kahn said, "if he gives no thought to the welfare of others."[25]

Businessmen were generally more willing to assume this function of traditional upper classes than they were to become involved in the endlessly ramifying problems of poverty. Furthermore, while the relief of the poor was professionalized through institutions for social service, promotion and advancement of the arts other than music had almost no organization.

Symphonies, as in an earlier day, were still a mark of civic importance and were supported by the local business elite whether or not the contributors personally liked music. This is not to belittle the tremendous personal efforts put into the advancement of symphonies by dedicated business leaders and their wives and widows, but rather to note that the appeal for funds to the general community also involved maintenance of the national prestige of the city which, in turn, was assumed to have economic value. Opera performed somewhat the same function, but opera was so costly that only the major cities could afford it. In these centers the opera boxes served as a prestigious meeting place for the wealthy sponsors, or as novelist Henry James remarked earlier, "some place to go after dinner." By midcentury the support of all forms of serious music and opera in the United States, with almost all of the money derived ultimately from business, was becoming proportionately equal to the mixed government and private support of the leading European nations. But many companies did not regard such gifts as a legitimate use of the stockholders' money.

Painting continued to do well in the United States on the basis of private patronage, which became wider as real income levels rose. Since many able artists divided their time between commercial and more creative work, they were in this way directly supported by business. In 1965 the New York Board of Trade formed the Arts Advisory Council to work for more use of art for commercial purposes. While its main interest was industrial design, it also supported music in order to attract more young people to its work.

Drama, a self-supporting or profitable art in the years before World War I, survived the competition of moving pictures and television only in a few major metropolitan areas. In the 1950s, however, business and professional leaders raised money for the support of local repertory theatres, while increasing general prosperity made it possible in New York, at least, to support not only a few expensive "Broadway" productions, but also a number of small inexpensive ventures elsewhere in the city. Here again, almost exclusive private support by individuals and foundations in the United States contrasted with government subsidy in the rest of the world.

Individuals or families wishing to give continuous support to the arts, education, or charity found it best to establish foundations. While a few wealthy men or families such as Carnegie, the Rockefellers, Fords, or Rosenwalds gave large sums to support research, the great majority of family foundations were set up primarily for tax purposes and assisted research or learning only frugally. Yet up to the rise of company and then government research from World War II on, foundation support had been a large portion of a very moderate total.

As taxes rose in the thirties and forties many companies, both large and small, also found it desirable to set up nonprofit foundations. By making contributions to worthy causes through such an institution, the company could transfer funds when convenient. The money given annually could be a uniform amount; experts could be hired by the foundation to direct its largess; and in some cases the foundation could be used to insure family control of the business corporation by avoiding inheritance taxes on large amounts of stock. The excess profits tax of the Korean War period, with an 82 percent maximum, also gave a boost to transferring as much as legally possible to tax-free foundations. By 1965 there were 6,800 such nonprofit private organizations, as distinct from charitable or research associations that raised funds from the general public. These foundations had about $20 billion in capital and dispensed over a billion dollars a year in grants, but government support of research, rising above $10 billion dollars a year in the early sixties, made private contributions seem minor.[26]

The Ford Foundation, established in 1936, was by far the largest private donor. Ford Motor Company stock was divided in advance into 95 percent class A nonvoting stock, and 5 percent class B voting stock. Then Henry and his son Edsel Ford willed all of their class A stock to the foundation. In this way the family could meet the inheritance taxes and still keep control of the company. With Edsel and Henry both dead by 1947 the foundation became the leader in private support of education and social research.

In spite of foundation and direct corporate contributions, however, private interests, personal or business, did not try in a vigorous organized way to check or compete with the spread of state-sponsored higher education (Chapter 15). In 1969, Neil W. Chamberlin of Harvard Business School knew of no major firm that had approached the 5 percent tax-exempt limit on gifts allowed by the internal revenue law.[27] By the 1960s many state universities were able to pay generally higher salaries to leading scholars than any but a few private institutions, and the drift seemed unquestionably toward greater state and federal responsibility for the support of learning.

BUSINESS IN AN AFFLUENT SOCIETY

Seen in the perspective of American history, business practices and aims had perhaps been the most influential on behavior and the culture, but there had always been some conflict with values stemming from landed aristocracy, democratic government, or religion. In addition, business was not a hierarchical institution like government or the military that could direct concerted power in national affairs. In spite of the apparent controls of a J. Pierpont Morgan, a "Money Trust" or a "power elite," no one could speak or act for American business. Consequently, the great influence and prestige of business in American culture of the twentieth century was not a usable or manipulable power. Although business influence was the product of 300 years of subconscious striving for both means and ends that would be called businesslike, action favorable to business might be thwarted on specific issues by any powerful, directed cultural pressure such as the needs of war or the appeal of a charismatic leader.

Social scientists who find little change in the values of American culture during the nineteenth century (Chapter 11) see major changes, in embryo at least, since World War I. These scholars are quick to admit that the evidence is fragmentary and unsystematic and that the social sciences are not mature enough to interpret the data with authority. Consequently, conclusions can vary between extremes: on the one hand is the belief that the strength of the values of the old Puritanical and business culture, such as self-help and thrift, came to an end somewhere in the wastes of the Great Depression and World War II; and on the other are such statements as that of Robin M. Williams that America has continued to support "the same main values—only more so."[28]

Granting that no equal dominance of business values existed elsewhere, one could argue that sooner or later the United States would become like the rest of the Western world. And, as the higher learning developed and politics acquired new vigor, there were portents, before 1914, of a readjustment in values. But the concerted questioning of the older values began, logically enough, when business failed to perform satisfactorily during the Great Depression. Until then, business had offered the major—one could almost say the only—normal road to success. Now the younger generation, particularly those from prosperous families, appeared less interested in acquiring wealth, and more interested in careers that promised a good life with security and adequate income. Business success ceased to be the general goal or *end* of American aspiration, and a business income became only a *means* for some to achieve a satisfactory life.

The rebellion of some well-educated young people in the 1960s against the values of a materialistic culture might be interpreted as an indirect manifestation of a general weakening of "industrial discipline" or the "work ethic" in the most advanced and affluent societies. Poor assembly-line performance and weak, careless management might be other aspects of a rebellion against business productivity as a major goal in life. But concurrent factors such as the unpopular South Asian war and fears about man's biological environment made it impossible to sort out or weigh the forces of frustration operating on youth.

Thus the primacy of business as a means of self-fulfillment seemed challenged by the social effects of the high living standards that had been its major aim and achievement. By 1970, with a median family income of $9,000 a year, and with a majority of its population living in more or less affluent urban suburbs, the United States was the first large nation in history to become economically and emotionally middle class. Furthermore, the middle-class values were shared by groups formerly opposed. A large section of organized labor, for example, held these values as firmly as did white-collar and managerial employees.

On the one hand, the creation of this great "middle class block" was a force for security and conformity, and a barrier to social change. Yet, on the other, its demands for stability and order, evident as early as the Progressive period, could only be met by the reform of dangerous social abuses. Urban and suburban ghettos, juvenile delinquency, and militant blacks menaced its security. The majority felt that in America everyone should be prosperous, and something should be done about those who were not. In a society so affluent economically, air pollution, poor transportation, inadequate hospital and educational facilities should not be tolerated.

Business was confronted with either curing these evils itself or allowing the state to expand its sphere of activity. As an editor of *Business Week* observed, "A failure of business to help solve the outstanding social issues of our time would, indeed, bring about the demise of business power."[29] In cooperating with the state in confronting these problems, business would no doubt have to "internalize" a number of costs that had previously been passed on to society. This was perhaps a distinction without much difference. Elimination of smoke, for example, could only be handled internally, and insofar as such profitless or money-losing functions were taken on, the large companies could readjust prices. The real issue, as raised in Chapter 16, was who could do what most efficiently.

Optimistic spokesmen for business, fascinated by the giant companies, wrote of a declining value placed on profit, balanced by higher values on rationality and creativity. They saw the corporate leader joining with the intellectual in building a society based on efficiency and reason.[30] But the relations of other types of businessmen with society made such developments seem remote. "Society was held together," according to Walter Lippman, "by a slightly antiquated formulation of the balance of power among the active interests of the community."[31] In any community, big-corporation executives were still only a small fraction of the total businessmen, and up to 1970 they were the fraction most concerned with the internal affairs of their companies and generally least interested in community affairs and politics. The active group that manned the chambers of commerce, trade associations, and other such societies, and brought pressure on politicians and voters were usually medium-sized operators with local interests. To most of these men, profit was far from a declining value, and the post-Keynesian ideas of big-company economists were seen as only one step away from socialism.[32] To a large degree the countervailing power against progressive action by big business was neither organized labor nor the state, but rather the rest of the business community.

The same problem afflicted the professional-intellectual world. Like the prophets of the future role of enlightened big business, some academic intellectuals predicted a takeover by the advanced men of knowledge. Sociologist Daniel Bell wrote "if the business firm was the key institution of the past hundred years, because of its role in organizing production ... the university will become the central institution of the next hundred years because of its role as the new source of innovation and knowledge."[33] Bell may be proven correct within the next century, but as of 1970 there were strong countervailing forces inside the ranks of the elite of knowledge. Conservative economists such as Milton Friedman of Chicago predicted a return to the calculus of the market place; 400,000 doctors and dentists were not notably progressive in political or social outlooks; and the same could be said of the more than 200,000 lawyers in private practice. Among the half million teachers in institutions of higher learning, there seemed little cohesion. A power strategy might develop, but as of the 1960s the intellectual's influence seemed largely confined to changing moods and styles of thought rather than altering power structures.

Business to be sure, was attracting only about 20 percent of college graduates, and probably not the ablest fifth.[34] But the great majority of the ten million proprietors or managers of agriculture and industry had never depended for their social influence on higher education. Business as a social institution was unquestionably in stronger competition with other occupational institutions than ever before, but it had on its side the traditional mores of the culture, the implicit beliefs of the middle-class population, the machinery for doing things, and last, but by no means least, the power of wealth.

Bibliographical Guide

to editions referred to in the Notes

Abbott, Ernest H., *On the Training of Parents* (Boston: Houghton Mifflin Company, 1908).

Abbott, Jacob, *Gentle Measures in the Management and Training of the Young* (New York: Harper Brothers, 1871).

Abbott, John S. C., "Parental Neglect," *Parent's Magazine*, 2 (March, 1842).

Abell, Aaron I., *American Catholicism and Social Action: A Search for Social Justice, 1865-1950* (Garden City, N.Y.: Doubleday & Company, Inc., 1960).

Abrams, Richard M., *Conservatism in a Progressive Era* (Cambridge: Harvard University Press, 1964).

————, and Lawrence W. Levine, eds., *The Shaping of Twentieth Century America* (Boston: Little, Brown and Company, 1965).

Adams, Henry, ed., *The Writings of Albert Gallatin*, vol. I (Philadelphia: J. B. Lippincott Co., 1879).

Adler, Selig, *The Isolationist Impulse: Its Twentieth Century Reaction* (New York: P. F. Collier, Inc., 1961).

Agriculture, U.S. Department of, *After One Hundred Years* (Washington, D.C.: Government Printing Office, 1962).

Agriculture, U.S. Department of, *Yearbook of Agriculture 1940: Farmers in a Changing World* (Washington, D.C.: Government Printing Office, 1940).

Aitken, Hugh G. J., ed., *The State and Economic Growth* (New York: Social Science Research Council, 1959).

Alvord, C. W., "Virginia and the West," *Mississippi Valley Historical Review*, 3 (June, 1916).

Ames, Ellis, and Abner Goodall, eds., *Acts and Resolves of the Province of Massachusetts Bay*, vol. I (Boston, 1889).

Andrews, Charles M., *The Colonial Period of American History*, vol. I (New Haven, Conn.: Yale University Press, 1934).

Andrews, F. Emerson, *Corporation Giving* (New York: Russell Sage Foundation, 1952).

Andrews, Wayne, *A Social History of American Architecture: Architecture, Ambition and Americans* (New York: The Free Press, 1964).

Appleton, Nathan, *The American Mind* (New York: Harcourt, Brace, 1927).

———, *Remarks on Currency and Banking* (Boston, 1841).

Atherton, Lewis E., *Main Street on the Middle Border* (Bloomington: Indiana University Press, 1954).

———, *The Pioneer Merchant in Mid-America* (Columbia: University of Missouri Press, 1939).

———, *The Southern Country Store, 1800-1860* (Baton Rouge: Louisiana State University Press, 1949).

Aumann, Francis R., *The Changing American Legal System: Some Selected Phases* (Columbus: Ohio State University Press, 1940).

Bailyn, Bernard, *Education in the Forming of American Society: Needs and Opportunities for Study* (Chapel Hill: University of North Carolina Press, 1960).

———, *New England Merchants in the Seventeenth Century* (Cambridge: Harvard University Press, 1955).

———, and Lotte Bailyn, *Massachusetts Shipping, 1696-1714: A Statistical Study* (Cambridge: Harvard University Press, 1959).

Baltzell, E. Digby, *The Protestant Establishment: Aristocracy and Caste in America* (New York: Random House, Inc., 1964).

———, ed., *The Search for Community in Modern America* (New York: Harper & Row, Publishers, 1968).

Banfield, Edward C., and James Q. Wilson, *City Politics,* Publications of the Joint Center for Urban Studies of Massachusetts Institute of Technology and Harvard University (Cambridge: Harvard University Press, 1963).

Banning, William Peck, *Commerical·Broadcasting Pioneer* (Cambridge: Harvard University Press, 1946).

Bannister, Robert C., Jr., *Ray Stannard Baker: The Mind and Thought of a Progressive* (New Haven, Conn.: Yale University Press, 1966).

Barclay, R. E., *Ducktown: Back in Raht's Time* (Chapel Hill: University of North Carolina Press, 1946).

Barnard, John, *A Present for an Apprentice or a Sure Guide to Esteem and Estate,* reprint of a London edition (Boston, 1747).

Barnes, David, *A Discourse on Education* (Boston, 1803).

Barnett, H. G., *Innovation: The Basis of Cultural Change* (New York: McGraw-Hill Book Company, 1950).

Barnouw, Eric, *The Golden Web: A History of Broadcasting in the United States,* vol. II, *1933-1953* (New York: Oxford University Press, Inc., 1968).

Barton, Bruce, *The Man Nobody Knows: A Discovery of the Real Jesus* (Indianapolis, Ind.: The Bobbs-Merrill Co., Inc., 1925).

Battis, Emery, *Saints and Sectaries: Anne Hutchinson and the Antinomian Controversy in Massachusetts Bay Colony* (Chapel Hill: University of North Carolina Press, 1962).

Baxter, W. T., *The House of Hancock: Business in Boston, 1724-1775* (Cambridge: Harvard University Press, 1945).

Beale, Howard K., *A History of Freedom of Teaching in American Schools,* American Historical Association Investigation of Social Studies in the Schools: Report, Part XVI (New York: Charles Scribner's Sons, 1941).

Beard, Charles A., and Mary Beard, *America in Mid-Passage* (New York: The Macmillan Company, 1938).

Beckman, Arnold O., "A Businessman's View on the Failure of Education," *U.S. News and World Report* (Nov. 30, 1956).

Bedell, Gregory T., *Sermons,* vol. I (Philadelphia, 1835).

Beecher, Henry Ward, *Sermons,* vol. I (New York: J. B. Ford & Co., 1869).

Beecher, Lyman, *Addresses to Young Men* (Philadelphia: Henry Artemus Co., 1895; original edition, 1849).

Belcher, Wyatt Winton, *The Economic Rivalry Between St. Louis and Chicago, 1850-1880* (New York: Columbia University Press, 1947).

Bell, Spurgeon, *Productivity, Wages and National Income* (Washington, D.C.: The Brookings Institution, 1940).

Bellah, Robert N., "Civil Religion in America," *Daedalus* (Winter, 1967).

Bendix, Reinhard, *Work and Authority in Industry: Ideologies of Management in the Course of Industrialization* (New York: John Wiley & Sons, Inc., 1956).

Benson, Lee, *The Concept of Jacksonian Democracy* (Princeton, N.J.: Princeton University Press, 1961).

———, *Merchants, Farmers and Railroads: Railroad Regulation and New York Politics, 1850-1887* (Cambridge: Harvard University Press, 1955).

———, *Turner and Beard: American Historical Writing Reconsidered* (Glencoe, Ill.: The Free Press, 1960).

Berghorn, Forrest J., and Geoffrey H. Steere, "Are American Values Changing? The Problem of Inner—or Other—Direction," *American Quarterly,* 18 (Spring, 1966).

Bernays, Edward L., *Biography of an Idea: Memoirs of Public Relations Counsel Edward L. Bernays* (New York: Simon and Schuster, Inc., 1965).

Bernheim, N. L., and others, *Labor and Government* (New York: Twentieth Century Fund, 1935).

Bethune, George W., *Sermons* (Philadelphia: Mentz & Rovoudt, 1846).

Beveridge, Albert J., *Abraham Lincoln, 1809-1858* (Boston: Houghton Mifflin Company, 1928).

Biddle, Bruce J., and Edwin J. Thomas, eds., *Role Theory: Concepts and Research* (New York: John Wiley & Sons, Inc., 1966).

Billias, George A., ed., *Law and Authority in Colonial America* (Barre, Mass.: Barre Publishers, 1965).

Birney, Mrs. Theodore W., *Childhood* (New York: Frederick A. Stokes Company, 1905).

Blair, Hugh, *The American Classbook or a Collection of Instructive Reading Lessons adapted to use in the Schools*, 2nd ed. (Philadelphia, 1815).

Bodo, John R., *The Protestant Clergy and Public Issues, 1812-1848* (Princeton, N. J.: Princeton University Press, 1954).

Bogart, Leo, *The Age of Television: A Study of Viewing Habits and the Impact of Television on American Life*, 2nd ed. (New York: Frederick Ungar Publishing Co., Inc., 1958).

Bogue, Allan G., *From Prairie to Corn Belt: Farming on the Illinois and Iowa Frontier in the Nineteenth Century* (Chicago: University of Chicago Press, 1963).

Bond, Carroll T., *Proceedings of the Maryland Court of Appeals, 1695-1729* (Washington, D.C.: American Historical Association, 1933).

Bonnett, Clarence E., *Employers' Associations in the United States: A Study of Typical Associations* (New York: The Macmillan Company, 1922).

Boorstin, Daniel J., *The Americans: The Colonial Experience* (New York: Random House, Inc., 1958).

———, *The Americans: The National Experience* (New York: Random House, Inc., 1965).

Bossard, James H. S., and J. Frederick Dewhurst, *University Education for Business* (Philadelphia: University of Pennsylvania Press, 1931).

Boudin, Louis B., *Government by Judiciary*, vol. II (New York: William Godwin, Inc., 1932).

Bowe, Charles, ed., *Prairie Albion* (Carbondale: University of Southern Illinois Press, 1962).

Bradlee, Francis C. B., *The Eastern Railroad: A Historical Account of Early Railroading in Eastern New England* (Salem, Mass.: The Essex Institute, 1922).

Bremner, Robert H., *American Philanthropy* (Chicago: University of Chicago Press, 1960).

Bridenbaugh, Carl, *Cities in Revolt: Urban Life in America, 1743-1776* (New York: Alfred A. Knopf, Inc., 1955).

———, *Cities in the Wilderness: Urban Life in America, 1625-1742* (New York: Capricorn Books, 1964).

———, *The Colonial Craftsman* (New York: New York University Press, 1950).

———, *Myths and Realities: Societies Of the Colonial South* (Baton Rouge: Louisiana State University Press, 1952).

Bridges, William E., "Family Patterns and Social Values in America, 1825-1875," *American Quarterly*, 17 (Spring, 1965).

Brim, Orville, G. Jr., "Socialization Through the Life Cycle," *Items*, 18 (March, 1964).

Bronner, Edwin B., *William Penn's "Holy Experiment"* (New York: Columbia University Press, 1962).

Brown, Linda Keller, "The Rise of Business Opposition to Roosevelt," Ph.D. thesis, University of Pennsylvania (1972).

Brown, Robert E., *Middle-Class Democracy and the Revolution in Massachusetts, 1691-1780* (Ithaca, N. Y.: Cornell University Press, 1955).

Bruchey, Stuart, *The Roots of American Economic Growth, 1607-1861: An Essay in Social Causation* (New York: Harper & Row, Publishers, 1965).

———— , ed., *The American Commonwealth*, vols. I, II (London and New York: The Macmillan Company, 1891).

Bryce, James, *The American Commonwealth*, vols. I, II (London and New York: The Macmillan Company, 1891).

————, *The American Commonwealth*, Louis M. Hacker, ed., (New York: G. P. Putnam's Sons, 1959).

Burrell, Caroline Benedict, *The Mother's Book: Suggestions Regarding the Mental and Moral Development of Children* (New York: The University Society, 1916).

Cadman, John W. Jr., *The Corporation in New Jersey* (Cambridge: Harvard University Press, 1949).

Calhoun, Arthur W., *A Social History of the American Family*, vols. I, II, III (New York: Barnes & Noble, Inc., 1945, 1946).

Callahan, Daniel, *The New Church: Essays in Catholic Reform* (New York: Charles Scribner's Sons, 1966).

Callahan, Raymond E., *Education and the Cult of Efficiency* (Chicago: University of Chicago Press, 1962).

Callender, Guy S., "The Early Transportation and Banking Enterprises of the States in Relation to the Growth of Corporations," *Quarterly Journal of Economics*, 17 (1902).

Canby, Henry Seidel, *Alma Mater: The Gothic Age of the American Colleges* (New York: Farrar and Rinehart, 1936).

Canterbery, E. Ray, *The President's Council of Economic Advisors* (New York: Exposition Press, 1961).

Carman, Harry J., *Social and Economic History of the United States*, vol. II (Boston: D. C. Heath & Company, 1930).

Carnegie, Andrew, *Autobiography* (Boston: Houghton Mifflin Company, 1920).

————, The *Empire of Business* (New York: Doubleday, Page & Co., 1902).

Carpenter, Charles, *History of American Schoolbooks* (Philadelphia: University of Pennsylvania Press, 1963).

Carter, Paul A., *The Decline and Revival of the Social Gospel* (Ithaca, N. Y.: Cornell University Press, 1954).

Cashdollar, Charles, "Religion and the Panic of 1873," doctoral thesis, University of Pennsylvania (1969).

Cassidy, James H., *Demography in Early America: Beginning of the Statistical Mind, 1600-1800* (Cambridge: Harvard University Press, 1970).

Cater, Douglass, *Power in Washington: A Critical Look at Today's Struggle to Govern in the Nation's Capitol* (New York: Random House, Inc., 1964).

Cawelti, John G., *Apostles of the Self-Made Man: Changing Concepts of Success in America* (Chicago: University of Chicago Press, 1965).

Census, U.S. Department of, Bureau of Census, *Fifteenth Census of the United States: 1930*; vol. 1, *Population* (Washington, D.C.: Government Printing Office, 1931).

Cesari, Eugene, "Technology in the American Arms Industry, 1790-1860," doctoral thesis, University of Pennsylvania (1970).

Chamberlin, Neil W., "The Life of the Mind of the Firm," *Daedalus* (Winter, 1969).

Chandler, Alfred D., *Giant Enterprise* (New York: Harcourt, Brace & World, Inc., 1964).

_____, *Strategy and Structure* (Cambridge: Harvard University Press, 1962).

Change and the Entrepreneur, Research Center in Entrepreneurial History, Harvard University, (Cambridge: Harvard University Press, 1949).

Channing, William E., *Works,* vol. VI (Boston, 1849).

Chappell, Matthew N., and C. E. Hooper, *Radio Audience Measurement* (New York: Stephen Day, 1944).

Cherington, Paul W., and Ralph L. Gillen, "The Company Representative in Washington," *Harvard Business Review,* 39 (May-June, 1961).

Cheyney, Edward Potts, *History of the University of Pennsylvania, 1740-1940* (Philadelphia: University of Pennsylvania Press, 1940).

Cleveland, Alfred S., "N.A.M.: Spokesman for Industry?" *Harvard Business Review,* 26 (May, 1948).

Coben, Stanley, "Northeastern Business and Radical Reconstruction: A Reexamination," *Mississippi Valley Historical Review,* 46 (1960).

Cochran, Thomas C., *American Business System: A Historical Perspective, 1900-1955* (Cambridge: Harvard University Press, 1955; Harper Torchbooks, 1962).

_____, The *Inner Revolution* (New York: Harper & Row, Publishers, 1965).

_____, *New York in the Confederation* (Philadelphia: University of Pennsylvania Press, 1932).

_____, *The Pabst Brewing Company* (New York: New York University Press, 1948).

_____, "The Presidential Synthesis," *American Historical Review,* 53, 4 (July, 1948).

_____, *The Puerto Rican Businessman* (Philadelphia: University of Pennsylvania Press, 1959).

_____, *Railroad Leaders, 1845-1890: The Business Mind in Action* (Cambridge: Harvard University Press, 1953).

_____, *Social Change in Twentieth Century America* (New York: Harper & Row, Publishers, 1971).

_____, and Ruben E. Reina, *Entrepreneurship in Argentine Culture* (Philadelphia: University of Pennsylvania Press, 1962).

————, and others, "Historical Aspects of Imperfect Competition," *The Journal of Economic History*, 3, Supplement (1943).

Cogley, John, *Report of Blacklisting in Radio and Television*, vol. II (Santa Barbara, Calif.: Fund for the Republic, 1956).

Cole, Arthur H., *The American Wool Manufacture*, vol. I (Cambridge: Harvard University Press, 1926).

————, "An Approach to the Study of Entrepreneurship," *The Journal of Economic History*, 6, Supplement, "The Tasks" (1946).

Coleman, Benjamin, *The Merchandize of a People* (Boston, 1736).

Coleman, Peter J., *The Transformation of Rhode Island* (Providence, R. I.: Brown University Press, 1963).

Commager, Henry Steele, *Theodore Parker* (Boston: Little, Brown and Company, 1936).

Commons, John R., and associates, *History of Labor in the United States, 1896-1935*, vol. III (New York: The Macmillan Company, 1935).

Cooke, George W., *Unitarianism in America* (Boston: American Unitarian Association, 1902).

Copeland, Lammot Du Pont, *It Takes Two to Make a Partnership Work*, unpaged pamphlet (Du Pont Company, 1964).

Cremin, Lawrence A., *The Wonderful World of Elwood Patterson Cubberley* (New York: Teachers College Press, 1965).

Cubberley, Ellwood P., *Public Education in the United States* (Boston: Houghton Mifflin Company, 1919).

————, ed. *Readings in the History of American Education* (Boston: Houghton Mifflin, Company, 1934).

Curti, Merle E., "The Changing Concept of 'Human Nature' in the Literature of American Advertising," *Business History Review*, 41.(Winter, 1967).

————, *The Growth of American Thought*, 3rd ed. (New York: Harper & Row, Publishers, 1964).

————, *The Social Ideas of American Educators* (New York: Charles Scribner's Sons, 1935).

————, and Peter Karsten, "Man and Businessman: Changing Concepts of Human Nature as Reflected in the Writing of American Business History," *Journal of the History of the Behavioral Sciences*, 4 (Jan., 1968).

————, and Roderick Nash, *Philanthropy in the Shaping of Higher Education* (New Brunswick, N. J.: Rutgers University Press, 1965).

————, and associates, *The Making of an American Community* (Stanford, Calif.: Stanford University Press, 1959).

Cyert, Richard M., and James G. March, *A Behavioral Theory of the Firm* (Englewood Cliffs, N. J.: Prentice-Hall, Inc., 1963).

Dahl, Robert A., *Who Governs* (New Haven, Conn.: Yale University Press, 1962).

Danhof, Clarence H., *Change in Agriculture: The Northern United States, 1820-1870* (Cambridge: Harvard University Press, 1969).

Danielian, N. R., *A.T. & T.* (New York: Vanguard Press, Inc., 1939).

Davis, Allan, "A Course of Study for Business in High Schools," *Proceedings, National Education Association* (Chicago: University of Chicago Press, 1896).

Davis, G. Cullom, "The Transformation of the Federal Trade Commission, 1914-1929," *Mississippi Valley Historical Review*, 49 (Dec., 1962).

de Charms, Richard, and Gerald B. Moeller, "Values Expressed in American Children's Readers, 1800-1950," *Washington University Journal of Abnormal and Social Psychology*, 64 (1962).

Decker, Leslie F., "The Railroads and the Land Office," *Mississippi Valley Historical Review*, 46 (March, 1960).

Degler, Carl N., "Slavery and the Genesis of American Race Prejudice," *Comparative Studies in History and Society*, 2 (Oct., 1959).

de Tocqueville, Alexis, *Democracy in America*, vol. I (New York: The Century Company, 1898).

Dewey, John, *Experience and Education* (New York: The Macmillan Company, 1938).

Dexter, E. G., *History of Education in the United States* (New York: The Macmillan Company, 1922).

Diamond, Sigmund, *The Reputation of the American Businessman* (Cambridge: Harvard University Press, 1955).

DiBacco, Thomas V., "American Business and Foreign Aid: The Eisenhower Years," *Business History Review*, 41 (Spring, 1967).

————, "The Business Press and Vietnam: Ecstasy or Agony," *Journalism Quarterly*, 45 (Autumn, 1968).

————, "The Political Ideas of American Business: Recent Interpretations," *The Review of Politics*, 30 (Jan., 1968).

Dickens, Charles, *American Notes and Reprinted Pieces* (London: Chapman & Hall, n.d.).

Domett, Henry W., *A History of the Bank of New York* (New York: G. P. Putnam's Sons, 1884).

Domhoff, G. William, *Who Rules America* (Englewood Cliffs, N. J.: Prentice-Hall, Inc., 1967).

Dorfman, Joseph, *Economic Mind in American Civilization*, vols. I, II (New York: The Viking Press, Inc., 1946-1959).

Douglas, Paul, *American Apprenticeship and Industrial Education* (New York: Columbia University Press, 1931).

Downs, Jacques M., "American Merchants and the China Opium Trade, 1800-1843," *Business History Review*, 42 (Winter, 1968).

Dubois, Cora, "The Dominant Value Profile of American Culture," *American Anthropologist*, 57 (Dec., 1955).

Dudden, Arthur P., "The Organization Man as Student," *Personnel Journal*, 38 (Jan., 1960).

Dulles, Foster Rhea, *America Learns to Play: A History of Popular Recreation, 1607-1640* (New York: Appleton-Century, 1940).

Dunlap, Orrin E. Jr., *Radio and Television Almanac* (New York: Harper & Row, Publishers, 1951).

Dunn, Richard S., *Puritans and Yankees* (Princeton, N. J.: Princeton University Press, 1962).

Early New England Sermons 1729-1794 (San Francisco: Sutro Branch, California State Library, occasional papers, reprint series no. 2, 1939).

Eaton, Clement, *The Mind of the Old South* (Baton Rouge: Louisiana State University Press, 1964).

Education, U.S. Commissioner of, *Report,* 1892-1893 (Washington, D.C.: Government Printing Office, 1895).

Education and Labor, Report of the Committee on, Pursuant to Senate Res. 266, Seventy-fourth Congress, *Labor Policies of Employers Associations,* Part III, The National Association of Manufacturers (Washington, D.C.: Government Printing Office, 1939).

Edwards, George W., *The Evolution of Finance Capitalism* (London and New York: Longmans, Green and Co., 1938).

Edwards, Newton, and Herman G. Richey, *The School in the American Social Order* (Boston: Houghton Mifflin Company, 1947).

Eliot, Andrew, *An Indirect Love of the World* (Boston, 1744).

Elkins, Stanley, and Eric McKittrick, "A Meaning for Turner's Frontier, Part I: Democracy in the Old Northwest," *Political Science Quarterly,* 69 (1954).

Ellis, David M., James A. Frost, Harold G. Syrett, and Harry J. Carmen, *A Short History of New York State* (Ithaca, N. Y.: Cornell University Press, 1957).

———, ed., *Essays in Honor of Paul Wallace Gates* (Ithaca, N. Y.: Cornell University Press, 1969).

Ellis, John Tracy, *American Catholicism* (Chicago: University of Chicago Press, 1955).

———, ed., *Documents of American Catholic History* (Milwaukee, Wisc.: The Bruce Publishing Co., 1950).

Elson, Ruth Miller, *Guardians of Tradition: American Schoolbooks of the Nineteenth Century* (Lincoln: University of Nebraska Press, 1964).

Emerson, Ralph Waldo, *English Traits, Representative Men and Other Essays* (New York: Everyman's Library, 1908).

Ernst, Morris L., *The First Freedom* (New York: The Macmillan Company, 1946).

Evans, G. Herberton, *Business Incorporation in the United States, 1800-1943* (New York: National Bureau of Economics, 1948).

Fayerweather, John, *The Executive Overseas* (Syracuse, N. Y.: Syracuse University Press, 1959).

Ferry, W. H., "Forms of Responsibility," *Annals: American Academy of Political and Social Science,* 343 (Sept. 1962).

Fine, Sidney, *The Automobile Under the Blue Eagle: Labor, Management and the Automobile Manufacturing Code* (Ann Arbor: University of Michigan Press, 1963).

———, *Sit-Down: The General Motors Strike of 1936-1937* (Ann Arbor: University of Michigan Press, 1969).

Finney, Charles G., *Lectures on Revivals of Religion,* William G. McLoughlin, ed. (Cambridge: Harvard University Press, 1960; 1st ed., 1835).

———, *Sermons on Important Subjects,* 3rd ed. (New York, 1836).

Fish, Carl Russell, *The American Civil War* (New York: Longmans, and Green Co., 1937).

Fisher, George, *American Instructor or Young Man's Best Companion* (Philadelphia, 1748).

Fishlow, Albert, "Levels of Nineteenth-Century American Investment in Education," *The Journal of Economic History,* 26, "The Tasks" (Dec., 1966).

Flaherty, David, ed., *Essays in the History of Early American Law* (Chapel Hill: University of North Carolina Press, 1969).

Fogel, Robert W., *The Union Pacific Railroad* (Baltimore, Md.: The Johns Hopkins Press, 1960).

Foner, Philip S., *Business and Slavery* (Chapel Hill: University of North Carolina Press, 1941).

Ford, Henry, *My Life and Work* (Garden City, N. Y.: Doubleday, Page & Co., 1926).

Forna, William H., and Delbert C. Miller, *Industry, Labor and Community* (New York: Harper & Row, Publishers, 1960).

Foulke, Roy A., *The Sinews of American Commerce* (New York: Dun and Bradstreet, 1941).

Fox, Dixon R., *Caleb Heathcote: Gentleman Colonist* (New York: Charles Scribner's Sons, 1926).

Franklin, Benjamin, *Autobiography* (New York: Everyman's Library, 1908).

———, *The Value of a Child* (Philadelphia, 1753).

Friedgood, Seymour, "Life in Buckhead," *Fortune* (Sept., 1961).

Friedman, Lawrence M., *Contract Law in America: A Social and Economic Case Study* (Madison: University of Wisconsin Press, 1965).

Frothingham, Octavius B., *Boston Unitarianism, 1820-1850 (New York: G. P. Putnam's Sons, 1890).*

Fund-Raising Counsel, Inc., American Association of, *Giving USA* (New York, 1968).

Gabler, Louis Richard, "The Advance and Equalization: State Government Expenditures for Public Education and Public Highways in New York, South Dakota, Pennsylvania and Tennessee, 1910-1930," Ph.D. thesis, University of Pennsylvania (1966).

Galambos, Louis, *Competition and Cooperation* (Baltimore, Md.: The Johns Hopkins Press, 1966).

Gates, William B., *Michigan Copper and Boston Dollars* (Cambridge: Harvard University Press, 1951).

Gibb, George S., *The Whitesmiths of Taunton: A History of Reed and Barton* (Cambridge: Harvard University Press, 1943).

Gilkey, Langdon, "Sources of Protestant Theology In America," *Daedalus* (Winter, 1967).

Gilman, Daniel C., "Notes on European Scientific Education," *American Journal of Education*, I, 3 (March, 1856).

Glaab, Charles N., *Kansas City and the Railroads: Community Policy in the Growth of a Regional Metropolis* (Madison: State Historical Society of Wisconsin, 1962).

Glick, Ira O., and Sidney V. Levy, *Living with Television* (Chicago: Aldine Publishing Company, 1962).

Goen, C. C., *Revivalism and Separatism in New England* (New Haven, Conn.: Yale University Press, 1962).

Goldstein, Sidney, *Patterns of Mobility, 1910-1950: The Norristown Survey* (Philadelphia: University of Pennsylvania Press, 1954).

———, ed., *The Norristown Study* (Philadelphia: University of Pennsylvania Press, 1961).

Good, H. G., *A History of Western Education* (New York: The Macmillan Company, 1960).

Good, William J., *The Family* (New York: Prentice-Hall, Inc., 1964).

Goodman, Paul, "Ethics and Enterprise: The Values of a Boston Elite, 1800-1860," *American Quarterly*, 18 (Fall, 1966).

Goldstein, Anita, *Biography of a Businessman: Henry W. Sage* (Ithaca, N. Y.: Cornell University Press, 1962).

Gordon, George, "Business Facilities in New York and London Compared," *Merchant's Magazine and Commercial Advertiser*, 15 (1846).

Graham, Howard J., *Everyman's Constitution: Historical Essays on the Fourteenth Amendment, the "Conspiracy Theory," and American Constitutionalism* (Madison: State Historical Society of Wisconsin, 1968).

Gras, N. S. B., *The Massachusetts First National Bank of Boston, 1784-1934* (Cambridge: Harvard University Press, 1937).

Green, Constance Mc. L., *American Cities in the Growth of the Nation* (Tuckahoe, N.Y.: John de Graff, Inc., 1957).

Greenstein, Fred I., "New Light on Changing American Values: A Forgotten Body of Survey Data," *Social Forces*, 42 (1964).

Greenwalt, Crawford, *The Uncommon Man: The Individual in the Organization* (New York: McGraw-Hill Book Company, 1959).

Greer, Scott, *The Emerging City* (New York: The Free Press, 1962).

Grizzell, Edith G., *Origin and Development of the High School in New England Before 1865* (New York: The Macmillan Company, 1923).

Gruening, Ernest, *The Public Pays: A Study of Power Propaganda* (New York: Vanguard Press, Inc., 1954).

Gusfield, Joseph R., *Symbolic Crusade: Status Politics and the American Temperance Movement* (Urbana: University of Illinois Press, 1963).

Gutman, Herbert G., "Protestantism and the American Labor Movement: The Christian Spirit in the Gilded Age," *American Historical Review*, 72 (Oct., 1966).

Guzzardi, Walter, Jr., "The Young Executives," *Fortune* (June, 1964).

Habakkuk, H. J., *American and British Technology in the Nineteenth Century* (Cambridge, Eng.: Cambridge University Press, 1962).

Haber, Samuel, *Efficiency and Uplift: Scientific Management in the Progressive Era, 1890-1920* (Chicago: University of Chicago Press, 1964).

Hacker, Louis M., ed., *Major Documents in American Economic History*, vols. I, II (New York: D. Van Nostrand Co., Inc., 1961).

Hale, Nathaniel C., *Pelts and Palisades: The Story of Fur and the Rivalry for Pelts in Colonial America* (Richmond, Va.: The Dietz Press, 1959).

Hall, G. Stanely, *Adolescence* (New York: Appleton, 1906).

————, *Youth* (New York: Appleton, 1906).

Hamilton, Thomas, *Men and Manners in America* (London, 1853).

Hammond, Bray, *Banks and Policits in America from the Revolution to the Civil War* (Princeton, N. J.: Princeton University Press, 1957).

Handlin, Oscar, ed., *This Was America* (Cambridge: Harvard University Press, 1949).

————, and Mary Handlin, *Commonwealth: A Study of the Role of Government in the American Economy: Massachusetts, 1774-1861* (New York: New York University Press, 1947).

————, and Mary Handlin, "Origins of the American Business Corporation," *The Journal of Economic History*, 5 (May, 1945).

————, and Mary Handlin, "The Origins of the American Business Corporation," *The Journal of Economic History*, 10 (March, 1951).

————, and Mary Handlin, "The Origins of the Southern Labor System," *William and Mary Quarterly*, 3rd series, 7 (April, 1950).

Hanna, Paul R., *Education: An Instrument of National Goals* (New York: McGraw-Hill Book Company, 1962).

Harrington, Virginia D., *New York Merchants on the Eve of the Revolution* (New York: Columbia University Press, 1935).

Harris, Seymour, et al., *The American Business Creed* (Cambridge: Harvard University Press, 1956).

Harrison, Paul M., "Church and Laity Among Protestants," *Annals: American Academy of Political and Social Science*, 332 (Nov., 1960).

Hartz, Louis, *Economic Policy and Democratic Thought* (Cambridge: Harvard University Press, 1948).

————, *The Liberal Tradition in America* (New York: Harcourt, Brace &

World, Inc., 1955).

Haskins, George L., *Law and Authority in Early Massachusetts: A Study of Tradition and Design* (New York: The Macmillan Company, 1960).

Hauser, Philip N., and Leo F. Schnore, eds., *The Study of Urbanization* (New York: John Wiley & Sons, Inc., 1965).

Hawk, Emery R., *Economic History of the South* (New York: Prentice-Hall, Inc., 1934).

Hawkins, Layton S., Charles A. Prosser, and John C. Wright, *Development of Vocational Education* (Chicago: American Technical Society, 1951).

Haynes, Benjamin R., and Harry P. Jackson, *A History of Business Education in the United States* (Cincinnati, Ohio: South-Western Publishing Co., 1935).

Hays, Samuel P., "The Politics of Reform in Municipal Government in the Progressive Era," *Pacific Northwest Quarterly* (Oct., 1964).

———, "Social Analysis of American Political History, 1880-1920," *Political Science Quarterly*, 70 (Spring, 1965).

Heald, Morrell, *The Social Responsibilities of Business: Company and Community, 1900-1960* (Cleveland, Ohio: The Press of Case Western Reserve University, 1970).

Heath, Milton Sydney, *Constructive Liberalism: The Role of the State in Economic Development in Georgia to 1850* (Cambridge: Harvard University Press, 1954).

Hedges, James B., *The Browns of Providence Plantation: Colonial Years* (Cambridge: Harvard University Press, 1952).

Heidbreder, Edna, *Seven Psychologies* (New York: The Century Company, 1933).

Henderson, Archibald, *The Conquest of the Old Southwest* (New York: The Century Company, 1920).

Henretta, James A., "Economic Development and the Social Structure of Colonial Boston," *William and Mary Quarterly*, 3rd series, 22 (Jan., 1965).

Herberg, Will, *Protestant, Catholic, Jew: An Essay in American Religious Sociology* (Garden City, N. Y.: Doubleday &Company, Inc., 1955).

Hero, Alfred O., *Opinion Leaders in American Communities* (Boston: World Peace Foundation, 1959).

Hersey, John, *Advice to Christian Parents* (Baltimore, Md., 1839).

———, "End of Subordination," *Parent's Magazine*, 2 (Jan., 1842).

Hibbard, Benjamin H., *A History of the Public Land Policies* (New York: The Macmillan Company, 1924).

Hidy, Ralph W., *The House of Baring in American Trade and Finance* (Cambridge: Harvard University Press, 1949).

———, and Muriel E. Hidy, *Pioneering in Big Business: History of Standard Oil Company (New Jersey) 1882-1911* (New York: Harper & Row, Publishers, 1955).

Higham, John, ed., *The Reconstruction of American History* (London: Hutchinson and Co., 1962).

Hill, Forest G., "Government Engineering Aid to Railroads Before the Civil War," *The Journal of Economic History*, 11 (1951).

Hirschman, Albert, *The Strategy of Economic Development* (New Haven, Conn.: Yale University Press, 1958).

Historical Statistics of the United States from Colonial Times to 1957 (Washington, D.C.: U.S. Department of Commerce, Bureau of Census, 1960).

Hitchcock, Enos, *Memoirs of the Bloomsgrove Family* (Boston, 1790).

Hoadly, Charles, ed., *Public Records of the Colony of Connecticut* (Hartford, 1868).

Hofstadter, Richard, *The Age of Reform: From Bryan to F.D.R.* (New York: Alfred A. Knopf, Inc., 1955).

————, *Anti-Intellectualism in American Life* (New York: Alfred A. Knopf, Inc., 1963).

————, and Wilson Smith, eds., *American Higher Education*, vol. I (Chicago: University of Chicago Press, 1961).

The Holmes Reader (New York: Oceana Publications, 1955).

Hoover, Herbert, *Memoirs, 1920-1933: The Cabinet and the Presidency* (New York: The Macmillan Company, 1952).

————, *Memoirs, 1929-1941: The Great Depression* (New York: The Macmillan Company, 1952).

Hopkins, Charles Edward, *The Rise of the Social Gospel* (New Haven, Conn: Yale University Press, 1940).

Hower, Ralph M., *History of Macy's of New York, 1858-1919* (Cambridge: Harvard University Press, 1943).

Hunt, Robert S., *Law and the Locomotive* (Madison: State Historical Society of Wisconsin, 1948).

Hunter, Floyd, *Community Power Structure: A Study of Decision Makers* (Chapel Hill: University of North Carolina Press, 1953).

————, *Top Leadership, U.S.A.* (Chapel Hill: University of North Carolina Press, 1957).

Hurst, James Willard, *The Growth of American Law: The Law Makers* (Boston: Little, Brown and Company, 1950).

————, *Law and Economic Growth: The Legal History of the Lumber Industry in Wisconsin, 1836-1915* (Cambridge: Harvard University Press, 1964).

————, *Law and Social Progess in United States History* (Ann Arbor: University of Michigan Law School, 1960).

Huthmacher, J. Joseph, *Massachusetts People and Politics* (Cambridge: Harvard University Press, 1959).

————, *Twentieth Century America: An Interpretation with Readings* (Boston: Allyn & Bacon, Inc., 1966).

Industrial Commission on Relations of Capital and Labor Employed in Manufacturing and General Business, Report, 19 vols. (Washington, D.C.: Government Printing Office, 1961).

Industrial Relations: Final Report and Testimony Submitted to Congress by the Commission on Industrial Relations Created by Act of Congress August 23, 1912, vols. 1, 3, 5, 8 (Washington, D.C.: Government Printing Office, 1916).

Interchurch World Movement, Commission of Inquiry of the, *Report on the Steel Strike of 1919* (New York: Harcourt, Brace, 1920).

Jackson, George L., "The Development of School Support in Colonial Massachusetts," Ph.D. thesis, Columbia University (1909).

Jackson, John, *Sermons* (Philadelphia, 1851).

Jackson, Sidney L., *America's Struggle for Schools: Social Tension and Education in New England and New York, 1827-1842* (Washington, D.C.: American Council on Public Affairs, 1941).

Jacoby, George W., *Child Training, an Exact Science* (New York: Funk & Wagnalls, 1914).

Jaher, Frederic Cople, ed., *The Age of Industrialism in America: Essays in Social Structure and Cultural Analysis* (New York: The Free Press, 1968).

James, Marquis, *The Metropolitan Life: A Study in Business Growth* (New York: The Viking Press, Inc., 1947).

James, William, *Essays in Pragmatism* (New York: Hafner Publishing Co., Inc., 1948).

Johnson, Arthur M., and Barry E. Supple, *Boston Capitalists and Western Railroads* (Cambridge: Harvard University Press, 1967).

Johnson, Herbert Alan, *The Law Merchant and Negotiable Instruments in Colonial New York, 1664-1730* (Chicago: Loyola University Press, 1963).

Jones, Fred Mitchell, *Middlemen in the Domestic Trade of the United States, 1800-1860* (Urbana: University of Illinois Press, 1937).

Joseph, Samuel, *Jewish Immigration to the United States from 1881-1910* (New York: Columbia University Press, 1914).

Josephson, Hannah, *The Golden Threads* (New York: Duell, Sloan & Pearce, 1949).

Josephson, Matthew, *The Politicos, 1865-1896* (New York: Harcourt, Brace, 1938).

————, *The Robber Barons: The Great American Capitalists, 1861-1901* (New York: Harcourt, Brace, 1934).

Katz, Irving, *August Belmont: A Political Biography* (New York: Columbia University Press, 1968).

Katz, Michael B., *The Irony of Early School Reform: Educational Innovation in Mid Nineteenth Century Massachusetts* (Cambridge: Harvard University Press, 1968).

Keller, Morton, *The Life Insurance Enterprise, 1885-1910* (Cambridge: Harvard University Press, 1963).

Kerr, K. Austin, *American Railroad Politics, 1914-1920: Rates, Wages, and Efficiency* (Pittsburgh, Pa.: University of Pittsburgh Press, 1968).

Kiefer, Monica, *American Children Through Their Books, 1700-1835* (Philadelphia: University of Pennsylvania Press, 1948).

Kirkendall, Richard S., "The New Deal as a Watershed," *Journal of American History*, 54 (March, 1968).

Kirkland, Edward C., *Men, Cities and Transportation: A Study in New England History, 1820-1900*, vols. I, II (Cambridge: Harvard University Press, 1948).

————, *Thought and Dream in the Business Community, 1860-1900* (Ithaca, N. Y.: Cornell University Press, 1956).

Kirkpatrick, Edwin A., *The Use of Money: How to Save and How to Spend* (Indianapolis, Ind.: The Bobbs-Merrill Co., Inc., 1915).

Klein, Maury, *The Great Richmond Terminal: A Study in Businessmen and Business Strategy* (Charlotte: University of Virginia Press, for the Eleutherian Mills-Hagley Foundation, 1970).

Kolko, Gabriel, *Railroads and Regulation, 1877-1916* (Princeton, N. J.: Princeton University Press, 1965).

————, *The Roots of American Foreign Policy: An Analysis of Power and Purpose* (Boston: Beacon Press, 1961).

————, The Triumph of *Conservatism* (Free Press of Glencoe, 1963).

Kuhn, Anne, *The Mother's Role in Childhood Education: New England Concepts, 1830-1860* (New Haven, Conn.: Yale University Press, 1947).

Labaree, Benjamin W., *Patriots and Partisans: The Merchants of Newburyport, 1764-1815* (Cambridge: Harvard University Press, 1962).

Labaree, Leonard W., ed., *The Papers of Benjamin Frankklin*, vols. II, III (New Haven, Conn.: Yale University Press, 1960).

La Feber, Walter, *The New Empire: An Interpretation of American Expansion, 1860-1898* (Ithaca, N. Y.: Cornell University Press, 1963).

Land, Aubrey C., "Economic Base and Social Structure: The Northern Chesapeake in the Eighteenth Century," *The Journal of Economic History*, 25 (Dec., 1965).

Lane, Robert E., "Law and Opinion in the Business Community," *Public Opinion Quarterly* (Summer, 1953).

Larkin, Oliver W., *Art and Life in America* (New York: Rinehart, 1949).

Larson, Henrietta M., *A Guide to Business History* (Cambridge: Harvard University Press, 1948).

Laslett, Peter, *The World We Have Lost* (London: Methuen & Co., 1965).

Latham, Earl, *The Communist Conspiracy in Washington: From the New Deal to McCarthy* (Cambridge: Harvard University Press, 1966).

Latimer, Murray W., *Industrial Pensions Systems in the United States and Cannada,* vol. I (New York: Industrial Relations Counselors, 1932).

Lee, Alfred M., *The Daily Newspaper in America* (New York: The Macmillan Company, 1937).

Lee, Everett S., "The Turner Thesis Reexamined," *American Quarterly,* 13 (Spring, 1961).

————, et al., *Population Redristribution and Economic Growth in the United States, 1870-1950* (Philadelphia: American Philosophical Society, 1957).

Leonard, J. Paul, *Developing the Secondary School Curriculum,* rev. ed. (New York: Rinehart, 1953).

Leonard, William N., "Towards a New Policy on Mergers," New York State Economic Association, *Proceedings,* 1968.

Lerner, Max, *America as a Civilization: Life and Thought in the United States Today* (New York: Simon and Schuster, Inc., 1957).

Lester, Richard A., *Economics of Labor* (New York: The Macmillan Company, 1941).

Leuchtenburg, William E., *Perils of Prosperity* (Chicago: University of Chicago Press, 1958).

Lipset, Seymour, *The First New Nation* (Garden City, N. Y.: Doubleday & Company, Inc., 1967).

Littlefield, George E., *Early Schools and Schoolbooks of New England* (Boston: The Club of Old Volumes, printed at University Press, Cambridge, Mass., 1904).

Littleton, A. C., *Accounting Evolution to 1900* (New York: American Institute Publishing Co., 1933).

Livermore, Shaw, *Early American Land Companies: Their Influence on Corporate Development* (New York: Commonwealth Fund, 1939).

Lloyd, Henry Demarest, *Wealth Against Commonwealth,* Thomas C. Cochran, ed. (Englewood Cliffs, N. J.: Prentice-Hall, Inc., 1963).

Long, Norton E., "The Corporation and the Local Community," *Annals: American Academy of Political and Social Science* 343 (Sept., 1962).

Lynd, Robert S., and Helen M. Lynd, *Middletown in Transition* (New York: Harcourt, Brace, 1937).

Lyon, Leverett S., *Education for Business* (Chicago: University of Chicago Press, 1922).

McAdams, Alan K., *Power and Politics in Labor Legislation* (New York: Columbia University Press, 1964).

McCadden, Joseph J., *Education in Pennsylvania 1801-1835 and Its Debt to Roberts Vaux* (Philadelphia: University of Pennsylvania Press, 1937).

McConnell, Donald, "Economic Virtues in the United States: A History and Interpretation," Ph.D. thesis, Columbia University, privately printed, 1930.

McConnell, Grant, *The Decline of Agrarian Democracy* (Berkeley: University of California Press, 1953).

McDonald, Forrest, *We the People* (Chicago: University of Chicago Press, 1958).

McGrane, Reginald C., *Foreign Bondholders and American State Debts* (New York: The Macmillan Company, 1935).

MacGregor, John, *Statistical Account of the United States* (London, 1846).

McKelvey, Blake, *Rochester: The Quest for Quality, 1890-1925* (Cambridge: Harvard University Press, 1956).

————, *The Urbanization of America, 1860-1915* (New Brunswick, N. J.: Rutgers University Press, 1963).

McKinley, Donald G., *Social Class and Family Life* (London: Collier Macmillan Ltd., 1964).

McLear, Patrick E., "Speculation, Promotion, and the Panic of 1837 in Chicago," *Journal of the Illinois Historical Society*, 62 (Summer, 1969).

McLoughlin, William G. Jr., *Modern Revivalism: Charles Grandison Finney to Billy Graham* (New York: The Ronald Press Company, 1959).

McLuhan, Marshall, *Understanding Media: The Extensions of Man* (New York: McGraw-Hill Book Company, 1964; 2nd ed., Signet Books).

McMaster, John B., *A History of the People of the United States*, vol. II (New York: Appleton, 1883-1903).

Main, Jackson Turner, *The Social Structure of Revolutionary America* (Princeton, N. J.: Princeton University Press, 1965).

Mandelbaum, Seymour I., *Boss Tweed's New York* (New York: John Wiley & Sons, Inc., 1965).

Mann, Henry G., "Corporate Responsibility," *Annals: American Academy of Political and Social Science*, 343 (Sept., 1962).

Marshall, P. G., and others, The *Collegiate School of Business* (Chicago: University of Chicago Press, 1928).

Martin, Margaret, *Merchants and Trade of the Connecticut River Valley, 1750-1820* (Smith College Studies in History, Northampton, Mass., 1939).

Mather, Cotton, *Essays to do Good* (Boston, 1710).

————, *Fair Dealing Between Debtor and Creditor* (Boston, 1715).

————, *Two Brief Discourses, One Directing a Christian in his General Calling; Another Directing him in his Personal Calling* (Boston, 1701).

Mathews, Shailer, "Business, Maker of Morals," *System, Magazine of Business* (March, 1927).

May, Ernest R., *Imperial Democracy* (New York: Harcourt, Brace & World, Inc., 1961).

Mazlish, Bruce, ed., *The Railroad and the Space Program* (Cambridge: The M.I.T. Press, 1965).

Mead, Margaret, and W. Wolfenstein, eds., *Childhood in Contemporary Culture* (Chicago: University of Chicago Press, 1955).

Mead, Sidney E., "American Protestantism since the Civil War," *Journal of Religious Philosophy*, 36.

Messerli, Jonathan, "Localism and State Control in Horace Mann's Reform of Public Schools," *American Quarterly,* 17 (Spring, 1965).

Meyer, Donald B., *The Protestant Search for Political Realism, 1919-1941* (Berkeley: University of California Press, 1960).

Miller, Arthur Selwyn, "Business Morality," *Annals: American Academy of Political and Social Science,* 363 (Jan., 1966).

Miller, Nathan, *The Enterprise of a Free People* (Ithaca, N. Y.: Cornell University Press, 1962).

Miller, Perry, *American Character: A Conversion* (Santa Barbara: University of California Press, 1962).

————, *The New England Mind from Colony to Province* (Cambridge: Harvard University Press, 1953).

————, and Thomas H. Johnson, eds., *The Puritans: A Sourcebook of Their Writing* (New York: Harper Brothers, 1938).

Miller, Robert Moats, *American Protestantism and Social Issues, 1919-1939* (Chapel Hill: University of North Carolina Press, 1950).

Miller, William, "American Historians and the Business Elite," *The Journal of Economic History,* 9 (Nov., 1949).

————, ed., *Men in Business: Essays in the History of Entrepreneurship* (Cambridge: Harvard University Press, 1952).

Mills, C. Wright, "The American Business Elite: A Collective Portrait," *The Journal of Economic History,* 5, Supplement, (1945).

————, *The New Men of Power: America's Labor Leaders* (New York: Harcourt, Brace, 1948).

————, *The Power Elite* (New York: Oxford University Press, Incorporated, 1957).

Minnich, Marvey C., ed., *Old Favorites from the McGuffey Readers, 1836-1936* (New York: American Book Company, 1936).

Moody, Samuel, *The Debtor's Monitor: The Way to Get and Keep out of Debt* (Boston, 1715).

Moore, Wilbert E., *Conduct of the Corporation* (New York: Random House, Inc., 1962).

Morgan, Edmund S., *The Gentle Puritan: A Life of Ezra Stiles, 1727-1795* (New Haven, Conn.: Yale University Press, 1962).

————, *The Puritan Family* (New York: Harper & Row, Publishers, 1966).

————, *Virginians at Home: Family Life in the Eighteenth Century* (Charlottesville: University Press of Virginia, 1963).

Morgan, Joseph, *The Nature of Riches* (Boston, 1732).

Morison, Elting E., ed., *The American Style* (New York: Harper & Row, Publishers, 1958).

Morison, Samuel E., *Maritime History of Massachusetts, 1783-1860* (Boston: Houghton Mifflin Company, 1921).

Morris, Richard B., *Government and Labor in Early America* (New York: Columbia University Press, 1946).

————, *Studies in the History of American Law: With Special Reference to the Seventeenth and Eighteenth Centuries* (New York: Columbia University Press, 1930).

————, ed., *Select Cases of the Mayor's Court of New York City, 1674-1784* (Washington, D.C.: American Historical Association, 1935).

Morton, Louis, *Robert Carter of Nomini Hall: A Virginia Tobacco Planter of the Eighteenth Century* (Williamsburg, Va.: Colonial Williamsburg, Inc., 1941).

Muelder, Walter, G., *Religion and Economic Responsibility* (New York: Charles Scribner's Sons, 1953).

Murray, David, *History of Education in New Jersey*, United States Bureau of Education Circular of Information, No. 1 (Washington, D.C.: Government Printing Office, 1899).

Nadworny, Milton, J., *Scientific Management and the Unions, 1900-1932* (Cambridge: Harvard University Press, 1955).

Nash, Gary B., "The Free Society of Traders and the Early Politics of Pennsylvania," *Pennsylvania Magazine of History and Biography*, 89 (April, 1965).

Nash, Gerald D., *State Government and Economic Development: A History of Administrative Policies in California, 1849-1933* (Berkeley: University of California Press, 1964).

————, *United States Oil Policy, 1890-1964: Business and Government in Twentieth Century America* (Pittsburgh, Pa.: University of Pittsburgh Press, 1968).

Nettels, Curtis, P., "Mercantilism and the Thirteen Colonies," *The Journal of Economic History*, 5-12 (Spring, 1952).

————, *Roots of American Civilization: A History of Colonial Life* (New York: F. S. Crofts, 1938).

Nevins, Allan, *Abram S. Hewitt, with Some Accounts of Peter Cooper* (New York: Harper Brothers, 1935).

————, *The American States During and After the Revolution, 1775-1789* (New York: The Macmillan Company, 1927).

————, comp., *Americans Through British Eyes* (New York: Oxford University Press, Inc., 1948).

Nietz, John A., *Old Textbooks* (Pittsburgh, Pa.: University of Pittsburgh Press, 1961).

North, Douglass C., *The Economic Growth of the United States, 1790-1860* (Englewood Cliffs, N. J.: Prentice-Hall, Inc., 1961).

Nye, Russell B., *The Cultural Life of the New Nation, 1776-1830* (New York: Harper Brothers, 1960).

Oak, Vishnu V., *The Negro's Adventure in General Business* (Yellow Springs, Ohio: Antioch Press, 1949).

Oberholtzer, Ellis P., *Jay Cooke, Financier of the Civil War*, vol. I (Philadelphia: George W. Jacobs & Co., 1907).

Onderdonk, Henry A., *Sermons and Episcopal Charges*, vol. 1 (Philadelphia, 1851).

O'Shea, M. V., *First Steps in Child Training* (Chicago: Frederick Drake, 1920).

Parker, Theodore, *Ten Sermons* (Boston and New York, 1853).

Paul, Arnold M., *Conservative Crisis and the Rule of Law: Attitudes of Bar and Bench, 1887-1895* (Ithaca, N.Y.: Cornell University Press, 1960).

————, "Legal Progressivism, The Courts and the Crisis of the 1890's," *The Business History Review*, 33 (Winter, 1959).

Pease, Otis, *The Responsibilities of American Advertising* (New Haven, Conn.: Yale University Press, 1958).

Penn, William, *A Collection of Works*, vol. 1 (London, 1776).

————, *Fruits of a Father's Love Being the Advice of William Penn to His Children Relating to Their Civil and Religious Conduct* (Dublin, 1728).

Perlman, Selig and Philip Taft, *History of Labor in the U.S., 1896-1932*, vol. IV., *Labor Movements* (New York: The Macmillan Company, 1935).

Perry, Bliss, *Life and Letters of Henry Lee Higginson* (Boston: Brown and Co., 1921).

Perry, Ralph Barton, *Characteristically American* (New York: Alfred A. Knopf, Inc., 1949).

Pierce, Harry H., *Railroads of New York* (Cambridge: Harvard University Press, 1953).

Pike, Stephan, *The Teacher's Assistant or a System of Practical Arithmetic wherein the several rules of that useful science are illustrated by a variety of examples, a large portion of which are in Federal money* (Philadelphia, 1813).

Porter, Kenneth W., *John Jacob Astor: Business Man*, vol. II (Cambridge: Harvard University Press, 1931).

Potter, David, *People of Plenty: Economic Abundance and the American Character* (Chicago: University of Chicago Press, 1954).

Pound, Roscoe, *Interpretations of Legal History* (New York: The Macmillan Company, 1923).

Presthus, Robert, *Men at the Top: A Study in Community Power* (New York: Oxford University Press, Inc., 1964).

Primm, James N., *Economic Policy in the Development of a Western State: Missouri, 1820-1860* (Cambridge: Harvard University Press, 1954).

Prothero, James W., *Dollar Decade: Business Ideas in the 1920's* (Baton Rouge: Louisiana State University Press, 1954).

Purrinton, Edward E., "Big Ideas from Big Business," *Independent* (April, 16, 1921).

Qualey, Carlton C., ed., *Thorstein Veblen* (New York: Columbia University Press, 1968).

Rabb, Theodore K., *Merchant and Gentry Investments in the Expansion of England, 1575-1630* (Cambridge: Harvard University Press, 1967).

Ratner, Sidney, ed., *New Light on the History of Great American Fortunes: American Millionaires of 1892- and 1902* (New York: Augustus M. Kelley, Publishers, 1953).

Raucher, Alan R., *Public Relations and Business 1900-1929* (Baltimore, Md.: The Johns Hopkins Press, 1968).

Rayback, Joseph G., *A History of American Labor* (New York: The Free Press, 1966).

Reed, Henry Hope Jr., "The Vision Spurned: The Story of City Planning in New York," manuscript (227 East 50th St., New York, N. Y.).

Reeder, Rudolph R., *The Historical Development of School Readers,* Studies VIII, No. 2 (New York: Columbia University Press, 1900).

Rezneck, Samuel, "The Rise and Early Development of Industrial Consciousness in the United States, 1760-1830," *The Journal of Economic and Business History,* 4, Supplement (Aug., 1932).

Ripley, William Z., *Railroads, Rates and Regulation* (New York: Longmans, Green and Co., 1915).

Robinson, R. R., *Two Centuries of Change in the Content of School Readers* (Nashville, Tenn.: George Peabody College for Teachers, 1936).

Rogers, George C. Jr., *Evolution of a Federalist: William Loughton Smith of Charleston, 1758-1812* (Columbia: University of South Carolina Press, 1962).

Rosenberg, Carroll S., *Religion and the Rise of the American City: The New York City Mission Movement, 1812-1870* (Ithaca, N.Y.: Cornell University Press, 1971).

Rosenberg, Charles E., and Carroll S. Rosenberg, "Pietism and the Origins of the American Public Health Movement," *Journal of the History of Medicine and Allied Sciences,* 31, 1 (1968).

Rothafel, Samuel A., and Raymond Yates, *Broadcasting, Its New Day* (New York: The Century Company, 1925).

Rothman, David J., *Politics and Power: The United States Senate, 1869-1901* (Cambridge: Harvard University Press, 1966).

Rumbarger, John, "The Social Origins and Function of the Political Temperance Movement in the Reconstruction of American Society, 1825-1917," Ph.D. thesis, University of Pennsylvania (1968).

Rush, Benjamin, *Plan for the Establishment of Public Schools and the Diffusion of Knowledge in Pennsylvania* (Philadelphia, 1786).

Ryan, Daniel J., *History of Ohio: The Rise and Progesss of an American State,* vol. IV (New York: Century History Co., 1912).

Ryon, Roderick N., "Public Sponsorship of Special Education in Pennsylvania from 1818 to 1834," *Pennsylvania History,* 34 (July, 1967).

Sachs, William S., and Ari Hoogenboom, *The Enterprising Colonials: Society on the Eve of the Revolution* (Chicago: Argonaut, Inc., Publishers, 1965).

Sawyer, John E., "The American System of Manufacturing," *The Journal of Economic History*, 14 (1954).

Scharf, J. Thomas, and Thompson Westcott, *History of Philadelphia, 1609-1884*, vol. II (Philadelphia: L. H. Everts and Co., 1884).

Schmidt, Hubert G., *Rural Hunterdon: An Agricultural History* (New Brunswick, N. J.: Rutgers University Press, 1946).

Seager, Henry R., and Charles A. Gulick, Jr., *Trust and Corporation Problems* (New York: Harper Brothers, 1929).

Seldes, Gilbert, *The Public Arts* (New York: Simon and Schuster, Inc., 1956).

Sellers, Charles Grier Jr., ed., *The Southerner as American* (New York: E. P. Dutton & Co., Inc., 1966).

Sellers, Leila, *The Charleston Businessman on the Eve of the Revolution* (Chapel Hill: University of North Carolina Press, 1934).

Sewell, Samuel, *Diary* (Massachusetts Historical Society, *Collections*, fifth series, vols. V, VI, VII).

Seybolt, Robert F., *Apprenticeship and Apprenticeship Education in Colonial New England and New York* (New York: Teachers College Press, 1917).

―――――, *The Evening School in Colonial America* (Urbana: University of Illinois Press, 1925).

―――――, *Source Studies in American Colonial Education* (Urbana: University of Illinois Press, 1925).

Shannon, Fred A., *The Farmer's Last Frontier* (New York: Farrar & Rinehart, 1945).

Shaw Co., A. W., comp., *Handling Men* (Chicago: A. W. Shaw Co., 1917).

Sherrill, Robert, "We Can't Depend on Congress to Keep Congress Honest," *New York Times* (July 19, 1970).

Shlakman, Vera, *Economic History of a Factory Town* (Northampton, Mass.: Smith College, 1935).

Siegfried, André, *America at Mid-Century* (New York: Harcourt, Brace & World, Inc., 1955).

Silberman, Charles E., and *Fortune* Editors, *What Managers Should Know About Automation* (New York: Harper & Row, Publishers, 1966).

Silk, Leonard S., "Business Power, Today and Tomorrow," *Daedalus* (Winter, 1969).

Skornia, Harry J., *Television and Society* (New York: McGraw-Hill Book Company, 1965).

Smith, Abbot E., *Colonists in Bondage: White Servitude and Convict Labor in America* (Chapel Hill: University of North Carolina Press, 1947).

Smith, Dan Throop, and J. Keith Butters, *Taxable and Business Income* (New York: National Bureau of Economic Research, 1949).

Smith, James Morton, ed., *Seventeenth Century America: Essays in Colonial History* (Chapel Hill: University of North Carolina Press, 1959).

Smith, M. Brewster, "Socialization for Competence," *Items,* 19 (June, 1965).

Social Sciences, International Encyclopedia of the, vol. VI (New York: The Free Press, 1968).

Solomon, Lewis C., *Estimates of the Cost of Schooling in 1880 and 1890* (Lafayette, Inc.: Graduate School of Industrial Administration, Purdue University, Paper 223, 1968).

Spero, Milford, ed., *Meaning and Content in Cultural Anthropology* (New York: The Free Press, 1965).

Stampp, Kenneth M., *And the War Came* (Baton Rouge: Louisiana State University Press, 1950).

————, *The Peculiar Institution* (New York: Alfred A. Knopf, Inc., 1956).

Statistical Abstract of the United States, 88th ed. (Washington, D.C.: U.S. Government Printing Office, 1967).

Stead, W. I., "The Uncrowned Queen of American Democracy," *Review of Reviews,* 6 (Nov., 1892).

Steere, Geoffrey H., "Changing Values in Child Socialization: A Study of United States Child-Rearing Literature, 1865-1929," Ph.D. thesis, University of Pennsylvania (1964).

Steffens, Lincoln, *Autobiography of Lincoln Steffens,* 2 vols. (New York: Harcourt, Brace, 1931).

————, *The Shame of the Cities* (New York: Hill & Wang, Inc., 1957).

Steigerwalt, Albert K., *The National Association of Manufacturers, 1895-1914: A Study in Business Leadership* (Ann Arbor: University of Michigan Press, 1964).

Steinman, Martin, ed., *Film and Society* (New York: Charles Scribner's Sons, 1964).

Still, Bayrd, *Milwaukee, the History of a City* (Madison: State Historical Society of Wisconsin, 1948).

————, ed., *Mirror for Gotham: New York as Seen by Contemporaries from Dutch Days to the Present* (New York: New York University Press, 1956).

Strassman, W. Paul, *Risk and Technological Innovation: American Manufacturing Methods During the Nineteenth Century* (Ithaca, N. Y.: Cornell University Press, 1959).

Strong, Josiah, *Our Country: Its Possible Future and Its Present Crisis* (New York: American Home Missionary Society, Bible House, 1886).

Sturges, Kenneth, *American Chambers of Commerce* (New York: Moffat Bard and Company, 1915).

Sullivan, Mark, *Our Times,* vol. II (New York: Charles Scribner's Sons, 1927).

Sutton, F. X., S. E. Harris, Carl Kaysen, and James Tobin, *The American Business Creed* (Cambridge: Harvard University Press, 1956).

Sweet, William Warren, *The Story of Religions in America* (New York: Harper Brothers, 1930).

Swierenga, Robert T., *Pioneers and Profits: Land Speculation on the Iowa Frontier* (Ames: Iowa State University Press, 1968).

Syrett, Harold, "The Business Press and American Neutrality," *Mississippi Valley Historical Review*, 31 (Sept., 1945).

Taussig, F. W., *Tariff History of the United States* (New York: G. P. Putnam's Sons, 1903).

Thacher, Peter, *The Fear of God Restraining Men from Unmercifulness and Iniquity in Commerce* (Boston, 1729).

Thayer, Theodore, "The Land Bank System in the American Colonies," *The Journal of Economic History*, 13 (Spring, 1953).

Thernstrom, Stephen, *Poverty and Progress: Social Mobility in a Nineteenth Century City* (Cambridge: Harvard University Press, 1964).

Thorelli, Hans B., *The Federal Antitrust Policy* (Baltimore, Md.: The Johns Hopkins Press, 1955).

Tiedeman, Christopher G., *A Treatise on the Limitations of Police Power in the United States* (St. Louis, 1886).

Timberlake, James H., *Prohibition and the Progressive Moveement, 1900-1920* (Cambridge: Harvard University Press, 1963).

Tolles, Frederic B., *Meeting House and Counting House: The Quaker Merchants of Colonial Philadelphia, 1682-1763* (Chapel Hill: University of North Carolina Press, 1948).

Trends in the American Economy in the Nineteenth Century, Studies in Income and Wealth 24, by the Conference on Research in Income and Wealth, National Bureau of Economic Research (Princeton, N.J.: Princeton University Press, 1960).

Trollope, Anthony, *North America* (New York: Harper Brothers, 1962).

Trollope, Frances, *Domestic Manners of the Americans* (New York: Dodd, Mead & Co., 1927).

Trumbell, C. Clay, *Hints on Child Training* (Philadelphia: John D. Wattles, 1891).

Tunnard, Christopher, and Henry Hope Reed, Jr., *American Skyline: The Growth and Form of Our Cities and Towns* (Boston: Houghton Mifflin Company, 1953).

Turner, Frederic Jackson, "The Problem of the West," *Atlantic Monthly*, 78 (Sept., 1896).

Tyack, David, "Bureaucracy and the Common School," *American Quarterly*, 19 (Feb., 1967).

Vatter, Harold G., *The U.S. Economy in the 1950's* (New York: W. W. Norton & Company, Inc., 1963).

Veblen, Thorstein, *Theory of Business Enterprise* New York: Charles Scribner's Sons, 1932).

Vidich, A. J., and Joseph Bensman, *Small Town in Mass Society: Power and Religion in a Rural Community* (Princeton, N. J.: Princeton University Press, 1958).

Wade, Richard C., *The Urban Frontier: The Rise of Western Cities, 1790-1830* (Cambridge: Harvard University Press, 1959).

Wallace, Anthony F. C., *Culture and Personality* (New York: Random House, Inc., 1962).

Warner, Sam Bass Jr., *The Private City: Philadelphia in Three Periods of Its Growth* (Philadelphia: University of Pennsylvania Press, 1968).

Warner, W. Lloyd, and James C. Abegglen, *Occupational Mobility in American Business and Industry* (Minneapolis: University of Minnesota Press, 1955).

Warren, Charles, *Bankruptcy in United States History* (Cambridge: Harvard University Press, 1935).

————, *The Supreme Court in United States History*, vol. II (Boston: Little, Brown and Company, 1928).

Watson, John B., *Psychological Care of Infant and Child* (New York: W. W. Norton & Company, Inc., 1928).

————, "Psychology as the Behaviorist Views it," *Psychological Review*, 20 (1913).

————, *Psychology from the Standpoint of a Behaviorist* (Philadelphia: J. B. Lippincott Co., 1919).

Watts, Isaac, *Plain Discourse for Little Children* (Boston, 1765).

Wayland, Francis, *Elements of Political Economy* (Boston: Gould, Kendall, and Lincoln, 1945, abridged from 1837 ed.).

————, *University Sermons* (Boston and New York, 1854).

Wecter, Dixon, *The Sage of American Society* (New York: Charles Scribner's Sons, 1937).

Weinstein, Allen, and Frank Otto Gatell, eds., *American Negro Slavery: A Modern Reader* (New York: Oxford University Press, Inc., 1968).

Wesley, Edgar B., *NEA: The First Hundred Years* (New York: Harper & Row, Publishers, 1957).

White, Philip L., *The Beekmans of New York in Politics and Commerce, 1647-1877* (New York: New York Historical Society, 1956).

Whiting, John W. M., and Irwin L. Child, *Child Training and Personality* (New Haven, Conn.: Yale University Press, 1953).

Whyte, William H., *Is Anybody Listening: How and Why U.S. Business Fumbles When It Talks with Human Beings* (New York: Simon and Schuster, Inc., 1952).

————, *The Organization Man* (New York: Simon and Schuster, Inc., 1956; Doubleday Anchor Books, 1957).

Wickersham, James P., *Education in Pennsylvania* (Lancaster, Pa.: Inquirer Publishing Co., 1886).

Wiebe, Robert H., *Businessmen and Reform* (Cambridge: Harvard University Press, 1962).

————, *The Search for Order, 1877-1920* (New York: Hill & Wang, Inc., 1967).

Wilkinson, Norman B., "Land Policy and Speculation in Pennsylvania, 1779-1800," Ph.D. thesis, University of Pennsylvania (1958).

Willard, Samuel, *An Exposition on the Assembly's Shorter Catechism in Two Hundred and Fifty Lectures* (Boston, 1726).

————, *Heavenly Merchandise; or The Purchasing of Truth Recommended and the Selling of it Disuaded* (Boston, 1686).

Williams, Albert N., *Listening* (Denver, Colo.: University of Denver Press, 1948).

Williams, Richard Hayes, ed., *Human Factors in Military Operations* (Baltimore, Md.: Operations Research Office, The Johns Hopkins University, 1954).

Williams, Robin M. Jr., *American Society: A Sociological Interpretation*, 2nd ed. (New York: Alfred A. Knopf, Inc., 1960).

————, "Individual and Group Values," *Annals: American Academy of Political and Social Science*, 371(May, 1967).

Williams, William Appelman, *The Tragedy of American Diplomacy*, (New York: Dell Publishing Co., Inc., 1962).

Wilson, Woodrow, *The New Freedom* (Englewood Cliffs, N. J.: Prentice-Hall, Inc., 1961).

Winterburn, Florence H., *Nursery Ethics* (New York: Baker and Taylor, 1895).

Wolff, Kurt, H., and Barrington Moore, Jr., eds., *The Critical Spirit: Essays in Honor of Herbert Marcuse* (Boston: Boston Press, 1967).

Woodward, C. Vann, *A Southern Prophecy* (Boston: Little, Brown and Company, 1964).

Woolfolk, George Ruble, *The Cotton Regency: The Northern Merchants and Reconstruction, 1865-1880* (New York: Bookman Associates, Inc., 1958).

Worcester, Dean A. Jr., *Monopoly, Big Business and Welfare in the Postwar United States* (Seattle: University of Washington Press, 1967).

Wright, Louis B., *The Cultural Life of the American Colonies, 1607-1763* (New York: Harper Brothers, 1927).

————, ed., *The Letters of Robert Carter, 1720-1727* (San Marino, Calif.: The Huntington Library, 1940).

Wyllie, Irvin G., *The Self-Made Man in America: The Myth from Rags to Riches* (New Brunswick, N. J.: Rutgers University Press, 1954).

Zemsky, Robert M., *Merchants, Farmers and River Gods: An Essay on Eighteenth-Century American Politics* (Boston: Gambit, 1971).

————, "Power, Influence and Status: Leadership Patterns in the Massachusetts Assembly, 1740-1755," *William and Mary Quarterly*, 34 series, 26 (Oct., 1969).

Ziegler, Harmon, *Interest Groups in American Society* (Englewood Cliffs, N. J.: Prentice-Hall, Inc., 1964).

Zuckerman, Michael, *Peaceable Kingdoms: New England Towns in the Eighteenth Century* (New York: Alfred A. Knopf, Inc., 1970).

Notes

INTRODUCTION

1. Nevins, *Americans Through British Eyes*, 356.
2. *Ibid.*, 385-386.
3. Wilson, *The New Freedom*, 10.
4. See Cochran, "The Presidential Synthesis."
5. Hidy, "Business History," in *International Encyclopedia of the Social Sciences*, VI, 474.
6. Biddle and Thomas, *Role Theory*.
7. For an early but extensive discussion of such roles, see Leland H. Jenks, "The Role Structure of Entrepreneurial Personality," in *Change and the Entrepreneur*, 108-152.
8. For more detail, see Cochran, *Social Change*, chap. I.
9. See Barnett, *Innovation*, 87-93.

CHAPTER 1

1. As quoted in Andrews, *The Colonial Period*, I, 73; see also Rabb, *Merchant and Gentry Investments*.
2. Andrews, *The Colonial Period*, I, 77.
3. Morison, *Maritime History*, 13.
4. Barnett, *Innovation*, 378ff.
5. Oscar Handlin, "The Significance of the Seventeenth Century," in Smith, *Seventeenth Century America*, 9.
6. Bridenbaugh, *Cities in the Wilderness*, 476.
7. Mildred Campbell, "Social Origins of Early Americans," in Smith, *Seventeenth Century America*, 86. See also Laslett, *World*, 31-34.
8. Mildred Campbell, "Social Origins of Early Americans," in Smith, *Seventeenth Century America*, 71, 73, 76.
9. *Ibid.*, 69-71.
10. Laslett, *World*, 83.
11. Smith, *Colonists in Bondage*, 311-312; Morris, *Government and Labor*, 319, 321.

12. Lee, "The Turner Thesis Reexamined," 77-84; see also Cassidy, *Demography in Early America*.
13. Franklin, *Autobiography*, 7.
14. Everett E. Edwards, "American Agriculture—the First 300 Years," in *Yearbook of Agriculture 1940*, 173.
15. Schmidt, *Rural Hunterdon*, 53ff.
16. *Ibid.*, 55-56.
17. *Ibid.*, 55.
18. Review of Forrest McDonald, *Democracy in the Connecticut Frontier Town of Kent*, by Charles S. Grant, *American Historical Review*, (Oct. 1963), 164. See also Sachs and Hoogenboom, *The Enterprising Colonials*, 57.
19. Brown, *Middle-Class Democracy*, 15.
20. *Ibid.*, 13-14.
21. *Ibid.*, 18.
22. Alvord, "Virginia and the West," 21.
23. Wright, *Letters of Robert Carter*, vi. See also Morton, *Robert Carter*, 40, who says that Robert Carter was "essentially a man of business."
24. Bridenbaugh, *Myths and Realities*, 17, 69-70.
25. Land, "Economic Base and Social Structure," 646-647.
26. Sellers, *The Charleston Businessman*, 17-18.
27. For 1763, Henderson, *The Conquest of the Old Southwest* 106; for 1767, Boorstin, *The Americans*, 120.
28. *Historical Statistics*, 756.
29. See Degler, "Slavery and the Genesis of American Race Prejudice," 49-66; and Handlin and Handlin, "The Origins of the Southern Labor System," 199-222.
30. Bridenbaugh, *Myths and Realities*, 58.
31. Herbert S. Klein, "The Slave Economics of Cuba and Virginia," in Weinstein and Gatell, *American Negro Slavery*, 124.
32. Bridenbaugh, *Cities in Revolt*, 85-86.
33. Bridenbaugh, *Cities in the Wilderness*, 200.
34. Morris, *Government and Labor*, 31.

35. Bridenbaugh, *Cities in the Wilderness*, 49.
36. See Hale, *Pelts and Palisades.*
37. Morris, *Government and Labor*, 40.
38. Henretta, "Economic Development," 79.
39. Labaree, *Patriots and Partisans*, 4-5. The exact date is 1773. For a Philadelphia example, see Warner, *The Private City*, 18.
40. Morison, *Maritime History*, 25.
41. Warner, *The Private City*, 4.
42. Morgan, *The Gentle Puritan*, 62.
43. Sachs and Hoogenboom, *The Enterprising Colonials*, 52.
44. Miller and Johnson, *The Puritans* 182-183; and Zuckerman, *Peaceable Kingdom*, 8-9, 140-141.
45. Zemsky, *Merchants*, 230.
46. *Ibid.*, 236-237.
47. Morison, *Maritime History*, 112.
48. Baxter, *Hancock*, 185.
49. *Ibid.*, 224.
50. *Ibid.*, 69, 76.
51. See, for example, White, *The Beekmans.*
52. Morris, *Government and Labor*, 325.
53. Hedges, *The Browns*, 86-122, 174.

CHAPTER 2

1. Oscar Handlin, "The Significance of the Seventeenth Century," in Smith, *Seventeenth Century America*, 6.
2. Bailyn, *Education in the Forming of American Society*, 22.
3. For the English situation, see Laslett, *World*, 89ff.
4. Calhoun, *American Family*, I, 172.
5. Morgan, *The Puritan Family*, 76-77; *Virginians at Home*, 23.
6. Watts, *Plain Discourse*, 27.
7. Franklin, *The Value of a Child*, 16.
8. "Poor Richard's Almanac," 1741, in Labaree, *Papers of Benjamin Franklin*, II, 294.
9. Willard, *An Exposition on the Assembly's Shorter Catechism*, 604.
10. Wright, *Cultural Life*, 24.
11. Calhoun, *American Family*, II, 124-125.
12. See Barnard, *A Present for an Apprentice*, 2.
13. Littlefield, *Early Schools and Schoolbooks*, 114.
14. James, *Essays in Pragmatism*, x.
15. Bailyn, *Education in the Forming of American Society*, 18.
16. Edwards and Richey, *The School in the American Social Order*, 153.
17. Sewell, *Diary*, V, 421.
18. Boston City Record II, 157, in Seybolt, *Apprenticeship*, 26.
19. *Ibid.*
20. Seybolt, *The Evening School*, 11.
21. Bridenbaugh, *Cities in the Wilderness*, 289.
22. Seybolt, *Evening School* 11.
23. Fisher, *American Instructor*, Preface.
24. Coates-Reynell Papers, "Reynell Letter Book" (1741-1744), June 22, 1743 (Historical Society of Pennsylvania).
25. Studies of later Latin American cultures support this surmise. See Cochran, *The Puerto Rican Businessman;* and Cochran and Reina, *Entrepreneurship in Argentine Culture.*
26. Bailyn, *Education in the Forming of American Society*, 18.
27. Ames and Goodall, *Acts and Resolves*, I, 62-63.
28. Hoadly, *Public Records*, 30, 375.
29. Jackson, "The Development of School Support," 78.
30. See Bronner, *William Penn's "Holy Experiment,"* 57ff. Also see "Minutes of the Provincial Council of Pennsylvania," vol. I (Historical Society of Pennsylvania), 91.
31. Edwards and Richey, *The School in the American Social Order*, 190.
32. Bronner, *William Penn's "Holy Experiment,"* 115-123.
33. Bridenbaugh, *Cities in the Wilderness*, 282.
34. *Ibid.*, 289.
35. *Ibid.*, 126.
36. Seybolt, *Source Studies*, 35.
37. Edwards and Richey, *The School in American Social Order*, 125, 146.
38. Morgan, *Virginians at Home*, 12.
39. Bridenbaugh, *Cities in the Wilderness*, 282.
40. Bailyn, *Education in the Forming of American Society*, 19.
41. Seybolt, *Source Studies*, 44, 45.
42. Labaree, *Papers of Benjamin Franklin*, III, 404.
43. *Ibid.*, 405.
44. *Ibid.*, 412.
45. *Ibid.*, 413.
46. *Ibid.*, 430.
47. Hedges, *The Browns*, 195.
48. William H. Seller, "The Anglican Parish

in Virginia," in Smith, *Seventeenth Century America*, 127.
49. *Ibid.*, 128, 134.
50. See, for example: Battis, *Saints and Sectaries*, 254-260.
51. Bailyn, *New England Merchants*, 23.
52. *Ibid.*, 21.
53. See Bruchey, *The Colonial Merchant*, 103-111.
54. Connecticut was moving in the same direction: see Goen, *Revivalism and Separatism*, 4; Dunn, *Puritans and Yankees*, 105; and Bailyn, *New England Merchants, passim*.
55. Miller, *The New England Mind*, 40.
56. *Ibid.*, 40.
57. Mather, *Two Brief Discourses*, 7.
58. *Ibid.*, 38.
59. *Ibid.*, 48.
60. Bailyn, *New England Merchants*, 176-177.
61. Willard, *Heavenly Merchandise*, 40, 50, and 5.
62. Thacher, *The Fear of God*, 18.
63. Eliot, *An Indirect Love of the World*, 7.
64. Charles Chauncy, *The Idle Poor secluded from the bread of Charity by the Christian Law* (Boston, 1752) in *Early New England Sermons 1729-1794*, 24.
65. Mather, *Essays to do Good*, 89-90.
66. Morgan, *The Nature of Riches*, 6.
67. Coleman, *The Merchandize of a People*, 10, 11.
68. Baxter, *Hancock*, 192.
69. Research by William H. Kenney III, 1963. The only known bias in selection was the availability of the sermons in Philadelphia libraries.
70. Mather, *Fair Dealing*, 2, 8.
71. Moody, *The Debtors Monitor*, 18.
72. *Ibid.*, 28.
73. *Ibid.*, 36.
74. Nettels, *American Civilization*, 483.
75. Goen, *Revivalism and Separatism*, 195.
76. Baxter, *Hancock* 82.
77. Eliot, *An Indirect Love of the World*, 25.
78. Penn, "No Cross No Crown," in *Works*, I, 296.
79. Penn, *Fruits of a Father's Love*, 74. Cotton Mather also used this quotation in his *Two Brief Discourses* in 1701.
80. Nash, "The True Society of Traders," 149.
81. *Ibid.*, 157.
82. *Ibid.*, 152.
83. Tolles, *Meeting House and Counting House*, 80.
84. *Minutes of the Philadelphia Yearly Meeting* vol. I, 15, 21, 319.
85. *Extracts from the Yearly Meeting: Epistles, 1688.*
86. *Ibid.*, 1692.
87. *Ibid.*, 1735, 13.
88. Tolles, *Meeting House and Counting House*, 49.

CHAPTER 3

1. See Haskins, *Law and Authority*, 114-118.
2. Zechariah Chafee, Jr., "Delaware Cases, 1782-1800," in Flaherty, *Essays*, 495.
3. Quoted in Morris, *Studies*, 47.
4. Haskins, *Law and Authority*, 15-16, 39-44.
5. Morris, *Studies*, 43-44.
6. Haskins, *Law and Authority*, 136-137.
7. George L. Haskins, "The Beginnings of Partible Inheritance in the American Colonies," in Flaherty, *Essays*, 222.
8. Billias, *Law and Authority*, 18.
9. Morris, *Select Cases*, 52.56. Morris estimates that up to 1750 about a dozen Americans had studied at the English Inns of Court, 52.
10. Labaree, *Patriots and Partisans*, 11.
11. Julius Goebel, Jr., "The Courts and the Law in Colonial New York," in Flaherty, *Essays*, 272.
12. Zechariah Chafee, Jr., "Delaware Cases, 1782-1800," in Flaherty, *Essays*, 506.
13. Bridenbaugh, *Cities in Revolt*, 95-96.
14. Quoted in Morris, *Studies*, 12-13.
15. See Johnson, *The Law Merchant*, 15ff.
16. See references to it in Bond, *Proceedings*, 500, 504.
17. *Ibid.*, 35. In 1751 Parliament extended the "Bubble Act" against joint stock companies to the colonies, but it was not observed.
18. Zechariah Chafee, Jr., "Delaware Cases, 1782-1800," in Flaherty, *Essays*, 509.
19. Sachs and Hoogenboom, *The Enterprising Colonials*, 119.
20. Labaree, *Patriots and Partisans*, 11.
21. *Ibid.*, 20.
22. Morris, *Government and Labor*, 140ff. Also see Bridenbaugh, *Craftsman*, 144ff.
23. *Public Records of Connecticut, 1689-1706*, 524, quoted in Fox, *Caleb Heathcote*, 145.

24. Baxter, *Hancock* 213.
25. Bridenbaugh, *Craftsman*, 144-45.
26. Hedges, *The Browns* 95.
27. Bridenbaugh, *Cities in Revolt*, 9.
28. Martin, *Merchants and Trade*, 221.
29. Robert M. Zemsky, "Power, Influence and Status," 508-510; Bailyn, *New England Merchants*, 96-97; and Labaree, *Patriots and Partisans*, 1ff.
30. Fox, *Caleb Heathcote*, 16.
31. Tolles, *Meeting House and Counting House*, 43.
32. Nettels, *American Civilization*, 312.
33. Quoted in *Ibid.*, 349.
34. Fox, *Caleb Heathcote*, 19, 31-33.
35. Zemsky, *Merchants*, 143.
36. *Ibid.*, 214-215.
37. Thayer, "The Land Bank System," 13, 148.
38. *Ibid.*, 51.
39. Nettels, *American Civilization*, 534-535.
40. Zemsky, *Merchants*, 118-119, 130-131.
41. Hedges, *The Browns*, 25.
42. Thayer, "The Land Bank System," 149.
43. *Ibid.*, 149.
44. *Ibid.*, 146.
45. Nettels, "Mercantilism," 112.
46. Williams, *American Society*, 98.
47. Bridenbaugh, *Cities in the Wilderness*, 411-415.
48. Bridenbaugh, *Craftsman*, 157.
49. Bridenbaugh, *Cities in the Wilderness*, 411-415.
50. Bruchey, *Roots*, 57-67.
51. See Main, *Social Structure*.
52. Labaree, *Patriots and Partisans*, 4-5.
53. Bridenbaugh, *Craftsman*, 162.
54. Bailyn and Bailyn, *Massachusetts Shipping*, 57, 68.
55. For Philadelphia, see Tolles, *Meeting House and Counting House*, 45ff.; for New York, Harrington, *New York Merchants*, 32ff.; and for Boston and Charleston, as well as an overall view, see Bridenbaugh, *Cities in Revolt*, 332ff.
56. Nash, "The Free Society of Traders," 150.
57. *Norris Letter Book, 1716-1730* (Historical Society of Pennsylvania), 183-184.
58. Franklin, *Autobiography*, 121.
59. Harrington, *New York Merchants*, 360.
60. Sachs and Hoogenboom, *The Enterprising Colonials*, 123-131.
61. Larkin, *Art and Life in America*, 11. See also Andrews, *Social History of American Architecture*, 34ff.
62. Zemsky, "Power, Influence and Status," 513-520.
63. Boorstin, *Colonial Experience*, 187.

CHAPTER 4

1. Adams, *Albert Gallatin*, I, 653.
2. Downs, "American Merchants," 437.
3. Gras, *The Massachusetts First National Bank*, 77, 143.
4. For the general history, see Hidy, *House of Baring.*
5. Atherton, *The Pioneer Merchant*, 9. See also Curti and associates, *American Community*, 13-18.
6. Atherton, *Southern Country Store*, 193.
7. *Bankers Magazine*, 12 (1857-1858), 521-524.
8. *Hunt's Merchants' Magazine and Commercial Advertiser* 15 (1846), 477.
9. Gordon, "Business Facilities," 339-348.
10. Dickens, *American Notes and Reprinted Pieces*, 144-145; Trollope, *Domestic Manners of the Americans*, 36.
11. Cochran, *Railroad Leadeers, passim.*
12. See Johnson and Supple, *Boston Capitalists*; and Gates, *Michigan Copper.*
13. Quoted from Boorstin, *National Experience*, 172. Boorstin has written a penetrating account of these promotional activities.
14. This quotation and other details are from McLear, "Speculation," 135-146.
15. *Ibid.*, 144.
16. Bogue, *Prairie to Corn Belt*, 171.
17. Boorstin, *National Experience*, 53.
18. Quoted from Danhof, *Change in Agriculture*, 21-22.
19. *Ibid.*, 22.
20. Stampp, *The Peculiar Institution*, 385.
21. *Ibid.*, 414.
22. Herbert S. Klein, "The Slave Economies of Cuba and Virginia," in Weinstein and Gatell, *American Negro Slavery*, 126.
23. Robert Starobin, "Race Relations in Old Southern Industries," in Weinstein and Gatell, *American Negro Slavery*, 300.
24. Stampp, *The Particular Institution*, 397-398.
25. *Ibid.*, 256.
26. *Ibid.*, 261.
27. Jones, *Middlemen* 16. Also Atherton, *The Pioneer Merchant* 61.
28. Foulke, *Sinews of American Commerce* 274ff.
29. Larson, *Business History*, 300.

30. Littleton, *Accounting Evolution* 178.

CHAPTER 5

1. *Historical Statistics* 139.
2. Robert E. Gallman, "Commodity Output 1839-1899," in *Trends in the American Economy*, 40.
3. Census of 1930, *Population*, 9.
4. *Ibid.*, 14.
5. See North, *Economic Growth.*
6. Perry, *Characteristically American*, 9.
7. Habakkuk, *Technology.*
8. Butler, *Why We Should Change Our Form of Government* (New York: Charles Scribner's Sons, 1912), 82, as quoted in Handlin and Handlin, "The Origins of the American Business Corporation," I.
9. See Livermore, *Early American Land Companies*, 297-298 and *passim.*
10. Cadman, *The Corporation in New Jersey*, 5-6.
11. *Ibid.*
12. See Handlin and Handlin, "Origins of the American Business Corporation," 16.
13. Domett, *Bank of New York*, 122-130.
14. See Shlakman, *Factory Town.*
15. Boorstin, *National Experience*, 22-23.
16. See Cesari, "Technology in the American Arms Industry."
17. Gibb's *Whitesmiths of Taunton* illustrates these problems very well.
18. Bendix, *Work and Authority in Industry*, 204, 209.
19. See Boorstin, *National Experience*, 47-48, for further discussion.
20. Cochran, *Railroad Leaders*, 79-80.
21. Appleton, *Currency and Banking*, 37.
22. Hurst, *Law and Economic Growth*, 121.
23. *The Holmes Reader*, 240.

CHAPTER 6

1. Miller, *American Character*, 23.
2. Hurst, *American Laws* 441.
3. See Bailyn, *Education in the Froming of American Society.*
4. McKinley, *Social Class and Family Life*, 38.
5. *Hunt's Merchants' Magazine and Commercial Advertiser*, 2 (1840), 250.
6. Calhoun, *American Family*, II, 133.
7. Abbott, "Parental Neglect."
8. Murray G. Murphey, "An Approach to the Study of National Character," in Spero, *Cultural Anthropology*, 144ff.
9. *Ibid.*

10. *Ibid.*, 150.
11. Hersey, *Advice to Parents*, 23. See also "End of Subordination," 105-106.
12. Hersey, *Advice to Parents*, 73, 67.
13. Hitchcock, *Bloomsgrove Family*, 147.
14. Beecher, *Addresses to Young Men*, 17.
15. *Ibid.*, 17-19.
16. Hersey, *Advice to Parents* 68. See also Kuhn, *Mother's Role* 92.
17. Kuhn, *Mother's Role*, 28.
18. R. Sunley, "Early Nineteenth Century American Literature on Child Rearing," in Mead and Wolfenstein, *Childhood*, 152-153.
19. Hitchcock, *Bloomsgrove Family*, 147.
20. Wyllie, *Self-Made Man* chap. 1.
21. A. N. Mussey, *The Fireside* (Boston, 1856), as quoted in Kuhn, *Mother's Role*, 94.
22. "The Worth of Money," *Ladies Magazine* (Feb., 1830), as quoted in Kuhn, *Mother's Role*, 94.
23. Bridges, "Family Patterns and Social Values," 10.
24. Carroll S. Rosenberg, *Religion and the Rise of the American City.*
25. Hersey, *Advice to Parents*, 159, 162, 70-72.
26. *Ibid.*, 105.
27. Beecher, *Addresses to Young Men*, 24.
28. As quoted in Kuhn, *Mother's Role*, 92.
29. As quoted in Nevins, *America Through British Eyes*, 137.
30. See Cochran, *Railroad Leaders*, 165, 214-211.
31. Cubberley, *Public Education*, 51.
32. Edwards and Richey, *The School in the American Social Order*, 240-247.
33. Rush, *Establishment of Public Schools*, 5-6.
34. James G. Carter, *Essays on Popular Education*, quoted from Edwards and Richey, *The School in American Social Order*, 273.
35. Douglas, *American Apprenticeship*, 54.
36. Edwards and Richey, *The School in American Social Order*, 270.
37. Grizzell, *High School in New England*, 31.
38. Murray, *History of Education in New Jersey*, 30.
39. Trollope, *Domestic Manners of the Americans* 4th ed., (London, 1932), 262.
40. See Ryon, "Public Sponsorship of Special Education," 241.

41. Curti, *Social Ideas*, 77.
42. *Ibid.*, 78.
43. *Ibid.*, 68-69.
44. Jackson, *America's Struggle for Schools*; see also Katz, *Early School Reform*.
45. Hartz, *Economic Policy*, 199; see also Wickersham, *Education in Pennsylvania*.
46. Good, *Western Education*, 416.
47. McCadden, *Education in Pennsylvania 1801-1835*, 236-237. The committee's lobbyist in Harrisburg, James R. Eckard, was a lawyer who shortly became a Presbyterian missionary. *Ibid.*, 255.
48. Quoted in Edwards and Richey, *The School in American Social Order*, 341.
49. Cubberley, *Public Education*, 164; Sidney Jackson, in *America's Struggle for Schools*, passim, does not indicate quite this degree of excitement.
50. Curti, *Social Ideas*, 712. See also Jonathan Messerli, "Mann's Reform of Public Schools," 107-117.
51. John D. Philbrick, quoted in *Ibid.*, 113. It is worth nothing that Mann favored state rather than private support.
52. *Ibid.*, 77.
53. Edwards and Richey, *The School in the American Social Order*, 323.
54. Grizzell, *High School in New England*, 77.
55. *Ibid.*, 125.
56. Rush, *Establishment of Public Schools*, 29-30.
57. Leonard, *Secondary School Curriculum*, 14.
58. Cubberley, *Readings*, 377.
59. Barnes, *A Discourse on Education*, 8-9.
60. Grizzell, *Origin of the High School*, 33.
61. Leonard, *Secondary School Curriculum*, 20; see also Cubberley, *Readings*, 583.
62. Leonard, *Secondary School Curriculum*, 15.
63. Robinson, *Content of School Readers*; table reproduced in Nietz, *Old Textbooks*, 52.
64. Kiefer, *American Children*, 15, 120.
65. McMaster, *A History*, II, 569.
66. Curti, *Social Ideas*, 33.
67. Blair, *American Classbook*, 187ff.
68. See for example Pike, *Teacher's Assistant*.
69. Carpenter, *American Schoolbooks*, 79ff.; Nietz, *Old Textbooks*, 74ff.
70. Reeder, *School Readers*, 19.
71. Minnick, *McGuffey Readers*, 34, 79.
72. Haynes and Jackson, *Business Education*, 16-18.
73. *Ibid.*, 26.
74. See Katz, *Early School Refoorm*, passim, for worker indifference to conventional education.
75. Hawkins, Prosser, and Wright, *Vocational Education*, 11.
76. Gilman, "Notes on European Scientific Education," 315.
77. See Strassman, *Risk and Technological Innovation*, 59.
78. Dexter, *History of Education*, 346.
79. Good, *Western Education*, 406.
80. Abbott Lawrence to Samuel A. Eliot, June 7, 1847, *American Journal of Education*, 2 (1856), 216.
81. See Boorstin, *National Experience*, 152ff.
82. *Ibid.*, 158.
83. See Hofstadter and Smith, *American Higher Education*, I, 188-189.
84. Edwards and Richey, *The School in the American Social Order*, 274.
85. Dorfman, *Economic Mind*, II, 503.
86. *Ibid.*, 707.
87. Wayland, *Political Economy*, 14, 73-76, 246.
88. Channing, *Works*, VI, 168.
89. Emerson, *English Traits*, 371.
90. Commager, *Theodore Parker*, 182.
91. Bethune, *Sermons*, 222
92. Mills, "The American Business Elite," 220.
93. Hamilton, *Men and Manners in America*, 74.
94. Atherton, *Southern Country Store*, 88.
95. *Ibid.*, 167.
96. Atherton, *The Pioneer Merchannt*, passim.
97. See Beveridge, *Abraham Lincoln*, I, 42ff.
98. *Ibid.*, 86.
99. Atherton, *Main Street*, 1.
100. Sweet, *Religions in America*, 322.
101. Bodo, *Protestant Clergy*, 13.
102. Nye, *Cultural Life*, 208.
103. *Ibid.*, 214.
104. *Ibid.*, 13.
105. As quoted in Cooke, *Unitarianism in America*, 384.
106. Appleton, *The American Mind*, II, 328.
107. As quoted in Cooke, *Unitarianism in America*, 386n.
108. Frothingham, *Boston Unitarianism*, 193.
109. McConnell, "Economic Virtues in the United States," 26-28.
110. Bodo, *Protestant Clergy*, 14.
111. *Ibid.*, 3-11.

112. *Ibid.*, 178.
113. *Ibid.*, 20-30.
114. Quoted from McConnell, "Economic Virtues in the United States," 47.
115. For the difficulties of Ohio Valley settlement before 1820, see Bowe, *Prairie Albion.*
116. See Atherton, *Main Street,* 76-88. Atherton's data came from the period 1850-1880, but seems equally applicable to the earlier years.
117. Bodo, *Protestant Clergy,* 7.
118. de Tocqueville, *Democracy in America,* I, 388, 390.
119. Boorstin, *Colonial Experience,* 187.
120. Bedell, *Sermons,* I, 152.
121. Finney, *Lectures on Revivals,* 209.
122. Finney, *Sermons,* 213-214.
123. Bedell, *Sermons,* 298-299.
124. Frothingham, *Boston Unitarianism,* 51.
125. Bethune, *Sermons,* 221.
126. Jackson, *Sermons,* 74.
127. Beecher, *Sermons,* I, 145-146.
128. Onderdonk, *Sermons and Episcopal Charges,* I, 146.
129. Parker, *Ten Sermons,* 359.
130. Finney, *Lectures on Revivals,* 434-435.
131. Bedell, *Sermons,* 225.
132. Finney, "Sermon on Stewardship," *Sermons,* 212.
133. Finney, *Sermons,* 257-267.
134. Finney, *Lectures on Revivals,* 435.
135. Frothingham, *Boston Unitarianism,* 110.
136. Channing, "The Present Age," *Works,* VI, 165.
137. *Ibid.*, 168.
138. Parker, *Ten Sermons,* 368.
139. Wayland, *University Sermons,* 65.
140. Lipset, *The New Nation,* 118.
141. Hurst, *American Law,* 357.
142. *Congressional Globe, Twenty-ninth Congress, First Session,* Blair and Ives, eds., vol. 15 (Washington, 1846), Appendix, 1013.
143. Trollope, *North America,* 263.
144. Cawelti, *Self-Made Man,* 5.

CHAPTER 7

1. Dorfman, *Economic Mind,* I, 243-257.
2. See Wesley Frank Craven, "The Revolutionary Era" in Higham, *American History,* 46-63.
3. Cochran, *Confederation,* 14ff.
4. Hartz, *Economic Policy,* 7-9.
5. Labaree, *Patriots and Partisans,* 42-43.
6. *The Essex Result,* 370-376, quoted in Labaree, *Patriots and Partisans,* 45-46.
7. Nevins, *American States,* 119.
8. Craven in Higham, *American History,* 57-59; see also Benson, *Turner and Beard.* For summary of property holdings, see McDonald, *We the People,* 88-92, 358ff.
9. J. E. A. Smith, *Pittsfield, 1734-1800,* 343, quoted in Handlin and Handlin, *Commonwealth,* 12.
10. See Rogers, *Evolution of a Federalist,* 112.
11. The first *Reports* appeared in 1789. See Flaherty, *Essays,* 25.
12. See Handlin and Handlin, *Commonwealth,* 145-146.
13. Aumann, *Changing American Legal System,* 93.
14. Hurst, *American Law,* 276.
15. Aumann, *Changing American Legal System,* 141.
16. *Ibid.*, 140.
17. Hurst, *American Law,* 195.
18. Graham, *Everyman's Constitution,* 517.
19. See Hurst, *Law and Economic Growth,* 468, 601.
20. Handlin and Handlin, *Commonwealth,* 67.
21. Hartz, *Economic Policy,* 207. Massachusetts and Pennsylvania politico-economic policies have been studied in detail from 1775 to 1860 by Oscar and Mary Handlin and Louis Hartz. Some phases on New York policy are covered in Miller, *Enterprise of a Free People* and in an unpublished Columbia University thesis by Elizabeth Reuben. Cadman in *The Corporation in New Jersey* discusses this type of policy from 1790 to 1860, Coleman, *The Transformation of Rhode Island* deals more with economic history than state political policies. Other Northern state policies before 1820 have not yet received monographic treatment.
22. Miller, *Enterprise of a Free People,* 10; for some details see Cochran, *Confederation* 31-32, 36-37, 51-52, 64, 165n, 167.
23. Handlin and Handlin, *Commonwealth,* 64.
24. Hartz, *Economic Policy,* 204ff.; Handlin and Handlin, *Commonwealth,* 67ff., 218ff.; Miller, *Enterprise of a Free People,* 10ff.; Coleman, *Transformation of Rhode Island,* 73ff.
25. Handlin and Handlin, *Commonwealth,* 72ff.

26. *Reports of Committees* (Nineteenth Congress, Second Session, vol. 2, no. 99), 2.

27. Warren, *Bankruptcy*, 6ff.

28. Hartz, *Economic Policy*, 237.

29. Warren, *Bankruptcy*, 7.

30. *Ibid.*, 19-20.

31. *Ibid.*, 24, 51.

32. Hartz, *Economic Policy*, 228, 229. Handlin and Handlin, *Commonwealth*, 219-220. The Rhode Island Assembly exercised many judicial duties, including granting petitions of debtors for stays of execution. In 1827 this power was turned over to the courts. See Coleman *Transformation of Rhode Island*, 252-253.

33. Warren, *Bankruptcy* 56ff.

34. *Ibid.*; also Hartz, *Economic Policy*, 227-229.

35. Warren, *Bankruptcy*, 81.

36. *Ibid.*, 87-88; Hartz, *Economic Policy*, 229-235.

37. Handlin and Handlin, *Commonwealth*, 116, 139-142. For discussion of the use of corporations in the South, see Heath, *Constructive Liberalism*, 310ff.

38. Hammond, *Banks and Politics*, 186.

39. *Ibid.*, 195.

40. Handlin and Handlin, *Commonwealth*, 129.

41. Hammond, *Banks and Politics*, 172-197.

42. *Ibid.*, 605. Minnesota and Oregon were Territories.

43. Miller, *Enterprise of a Free People*, 32.

44. Handlin and Handlin, *Commonwealth*, 186-187. For New York and Pennsylvania see Miller, *Enterpriise of a Free People* and Hartz, *Economic Policy*; for the Middle West, McGrane, *Foreign Bondholders*.

45. *Dartmouth College* v. *Woodward*, 4 Wheaton 518.

46. See for example, Heath, *Constructive Liberalism*, 314-315.

47. *Charles River Bridge* v. *Warren Bridge* 11 Peters 420.

48. Warren, *The Supreme Court*, II, 21ff.

49. *Ibid.*, 11, 50.

50. *Ibid.*, 53.

51. *Bank of Augusta* v. *Earle*, 13 Peters 519 (1839).

52. Hunt, *Law and the Locomotive*, 171.

53. Handlin and Handlin, *Commonwealth*, 149.

54. Kirkland, *Men, Cities and Transportation*, I, 274-275.

55. See Benson, *Merchants, Farmers and Railroads*, 2; Cadman, *Corporation in New Jersey* 222-224; Hartz, *Economic Policy*, 69ff; Coleman, *Transformation of Rhode Island*, 179-180.

56. Kirkland, *Men, Cities and Transportation*, II, 234.

57. *Ibid.*

58. *Ibid.*

59. For more discussion see Cochran, "The Social Impact of the Railroad," in Mazlish, *The Railroad and the Space Program*, 171-177.

60. See Clement Eaton, *Old South*, 223, 241-242.

61. See Lewis Atherton, *Main Street*, and Primm, *Missouri*.

62. Primm, *Missouri*, 124.

63. See McGrane, *Foreign Bondholders*, 102ff.

64. Primm, *Missouri*, 126.

65. See Hawk, *South*, 310-314, 316-340; and Heath, *Constructive Liberalism*, chap. XI.

66. Heath, *Constructive Liberalism*, 249ff.

67. Primm, *Missouri*, 114-120.

68. Miller, *Enterprise of a Free People*, 12-14, 137ff.

69. Hartz, *Economic Policy*, 290.

70. *Ibid.*, 310.

71. *Congressional Globe* (Twenty-ninth Congress, First Session, appendix), 1006.

72. See Wilkinson, "Land Policy and Speculation in Pennsylvania" for detailed discussion of the policy of one of the states with vast tracts of land for sale between the Eastern seacoast and the Ohio Valley.

73. John Murray Forbes to Paul Forbes, November 28, 1848: "John Murray Forbes Letters 1843-1867" (Manuscript, Baker Library, Harvard University).

74. Porter, *John Jacob Astor*, II, 966.

75. Josephson, *Golden Threads*, 29.

76. Cole, *American Wool Manufacture*, I, 162.

77. Taussig, *Tariff History*, 70.

78. Rezneck, "Industrial Consciousness," 800ff.

79. Dorfman, *Economic Mind*, II, 526, and Cole, *American Wool Manufacture*, I, 168.

80. Dorfman, *Economic Mind*, II, 576-577.

81. *Ibid.*, 166-173.

82. For votes in the House on tariff changes in the 1820s, see Carman, *Social and*

Economic History, II, 31.

83. See Lee Benson, *Jacksonian Democracy* 139-142.

84. *Ibid.*, 272-73.

85. For a careful economic analysis of federal promotional expenditures see Henry W. Broude, "The Role of the State in American Economic Development, 1820-1890" in Aitken, *The State and Economic Growth*, 4-25.

86. Harts, *Economic Policy*, 11.

87. Review of James J. Hopkins, *The Papers of Henry Clay*, vol. I, by Charles M. Wiltse, *American Historical Review*, 66 (Oct., 1960), 173.

CHAPTER 8

1. In this period there are many accounts by foreign travelers, including the famous Alexis de Tocqueville. In recent years many books of excerpts have appeared, such as Handlin, *This Was America*; Still, *Mirror for Gotham*; and Nevins, *America Through British Eyes*.

2. Quoted in Carpenter, *American Schoolbooks*, 251.

3. Wade, *The Urban Frontier*, 339-340. See also Atherton, *Main Street* and Vidich and Bensman, *Small Town* for the enduring character of this situation.

4. Wecter, *American Society*, 205.

5. Quoted in Dorfman, *Economic Mind*, II, 705.

6. The reference is specifically to Cincinnati as a representative Western city, Green *American Cities*, II, 50.

7. As quoted in Wyllie, *Self-Made Man*, 9.

8. R. Richard Wohl, "Henry Noble Day," in Miller, *Men in Business*, 172.

9. Mazlish, *The Railroad and the Space Program*, 163-165.

10. Goldstein, *Patterns of Mobility*.

11. See Green, *American Cities*, 9, 17, 31, 49-53.

12. Wade, *The Urban Frontier*, 78.

13. Goodman, "Ethics and Enterprise," 437-451, and Jaher, *Industrialism*, 188ff.

14. Wade, *The Urban Frontier*, 73.

15. Green, *American Cities*, 31.

16. Wade, *The Urban Frontier*, 80.

17. *Ibid.*

18. See for example, R. Richard Wohl, "Henry Noble Day," in Miller, *Men in Business.*

19. Reed, "The Vision Spurned," 12. (In 1970 Mr. Reed was curator of parks in New York City.)

20. Warner, *The Private City*, 49.

21. Green, *American Cities*, 53.

22. Paul Goodman, "Ethics and Enterprise," 438.

23. Quoted in Frederic Cople Jaher, "The Boston Brahmins in the Age of Industrial Capitalism," in Jaher, *Industrialism*, 196.

24. *Ibid.*

25. Goodman, "Ethics and Enterprise," 437-438; Jaher, *Industrialism*, 190.

26. Wade, *The Urban Frontier*, 185.

27. Goodman, "Ethics and Enterprise," 442.

28. Curti, *American Thought*, 155.

29. As quoted in Curti and Karsten, "Man and Businessman," 5.

30. *Ibid.*

31. Wade, *The Urban Frontier*, 106.

32. Scharf and Westcott, *History of Philadelphia*, II, 1449-1491.

33. Curti, *American Thought*, 291. See also Wade, *The Urban Frontier*, 209.

34. Gusfield, *Symbolic Crusade*, 41.

35. Lyman Beecher, *Six Sermons on Intemperance*, 58-59, quoted in Gusfield, *Symbolic Crusade*, 43. See also Timberlake, *Prohibition*, 4-14.

36. For the continuing connection of business leaders with the temperance movement see Rumbarger, "Political Temperance Movement."

37. Cochran, *Pabst Brewing Company*, 37-40.

38. Dulles, *America Learns to Play*, 90.

39. Williams, *American Society*, 415-469. For further discussion, see Williams, *Military Operations*, 90-120.

40. Sutton, et al., *American Business Creed*, 251.

41. See Cochran, *The Puerto Rican Businessman*, 122ff., and Cochran and Reina, *Entrepreneurship in Argentine Culture*, 262ff. American definitions are based on the work of the two Williams, already cited, Clyde Klukhohn, and a number of years of unpublished seminar investigations at the University of Pennsylvania.

42. See Fayerweather, *The Executive Overseas.*

43. See Cochran, *Railroad Leaders*, 113-117, 214-216.

44. Sawyer, "American System of Manufacturing," 367-368.

45. Curti, *American Thought*, 292.
46. *Ibid*, 295.
47. Elkins and McKittrick, "A Meaning for Turner's Frontier," 341.
48. Wyllie, *Self-Made Man*, 17.
49. See Sutton, et al., *American Business Creed*, 256-257; Williams, *Human Factors in Military Operations*, 111; DuBois, "American Culture," 123ff.
50. Dulles, *America Learns to Play*, 76-77.
51. *Ibid*., 209.
52. Vol. 15 (1846), 348. The article was reprinted from Macgregor, *Statistical Account*.
53. Hirschman, *Economic Development*, 17.
54. Cochran, *Railroad Leaders*, 110-115, 134-136.
55. See Strassman, *Risk and Technological Innovatiion, passim*.
56. Barnett, *Innovation*, 249.
57. See *Ibid*., 87-88, 93.

CHAPTER 9

1. "Statistics and Geography in the Production of Iron, 1856," in Nevins, *Abram S. Hewitt*, 95.
2. Oberholtzer, *Jay Cooke*, I, 58.
3. Cochran, *Railroad Leaders*.
4. *Historical Statistics*, 570.
5. Curti, and associates, *American Community*, 223.
6. *Ibid*., 227.
7. Leslie E. Decker, "The Great Speculation: An Interpretation of Mid-Continent Pioneering," in Ellis, *Paul Wallace Gates*, 365.
8. *Ibid*., p. 367. See also Glaab, *Kansas City and the Railroads*, 36-47.
9. *Ibid*., 210ff.
10. Swierenga, *Pioneers and Profits*, 101. The tract analyzed was known as Royce Session, 262, and included the major part of central Iowa. A history of the land, or real estate business, toward which this book is an important contribution, is a major need.
11. *Ibid*., 210ff.
12. Danhof, *Change in Agriculture*, 81.
13. Bogue, *Prairie to Corn Belt*, 176.
14. Graham, *Everyman's Constitution*, 499n.
15. See for example Klein, *The Great Richmond Terminal*.
16. Oak, *Negro's Adventure*, 41-44.
17. *Literary Digest*, 31, no. 9 (Aug. 26, 1905), 266.
18. Oak, *Negro's Adventure*, 44.

19. Pease, *American Advertising*, 13.
20. Curti, " 'Human Nature' in the Literature of American Advertising," 338-339.
21. See Raucher, *Public Relations and Business*. Westinghouse hired a "press agent" in 1889, *Ibid*., 10.
22. See for example Cochran, and others, "Historical Aspects of Imperfect Competition," 27-50; and Veblen, *Theory of Business Enterprise*, 54.
23. For examples of opposite attitudes, see Cochran, *The Puerto Rican Businessman*; and Cochran and Reina, *Entrepreneurship in Argentine Culture*.
24. Lloyd, *Wealth Against Commonwealth*, 3.
25. Thorelli, *Federal Antitrust Policy*, 77-80. Seager and Gulick, *Trust and Corporation Problems*, 51.
26. Wiebe, *Search for Order*, 45-46.
27. For condensed texts of the Sherman and Clayton Acts see Hacker, *Documents in American Economic History*, I, 124 and II, 41, respectively.
28. Quoted in Josephson, *Robber Barons*, 309.
29. Keller, *The Life Insurance Enterprise*, 158-161. By 1905 premium income was nearly $250 million a year.
30. Edwards, *Finance Capitalism*, 167.
31. Sullivan, *Our Times*, 318.
32. *Historical Statistics of the United States* lumps trade, finance, and real estate together through 1900, and real estate and finance thereafter; see 74.
33. Carnegie, *Autobiography*, 182.
34. Bradlee, *Eastern Railroad*, 83.
35. A. H. Cole to T. C. Cochran, November 27, 1966, Cochran Correspondence, Archives, University of Pennsylvania.
36. Mimeographed letter by Frank W. Johnson, July 8, 1908, Western Historical Collection, University of Missouri, Columbia Missouri

CHAPTER 10

1. For a more detailed discussion of the early executive role, see Thomas C. Cochran, "Business in Veblen's America," Qualey, *Thorstein Veblen*, 63-71. The basic data comes largely from *Railroad Leaders*, and essays in Miller, *Men in Business*.
2. Cochran, *Railroad Leaders*, 117.
3. *Ibid*., 211.

4. Elson, *Guardians of Tradition*, 248-249, 251.
5. See Herbert G. Gutman, "Class, Status, and Community Power in Nineteenth-Century American Industrial Cities—Paterson. New Jersey: A Case Study," in Jaher, *Industrialism*, 263-288.
6. Wiebe, *Businessmen and Reform*, 25, 33.
7. Steigerwalt, *National Association of Manufacturers*, 122. See also Bonnett, *Employers' Associations*, and Senate Committee on Education and Labor, *Report*, Seventh-fourth Congress, *Labor Policies of Employers' Associations* (Washington, D.C.: Government Printing Office, 1939). The local branches of the organization were called Citizen's Industrial Alliances.
8. Steigerwalt, *National Association of Manufacturers*, 124-128.
9. Quoted in Bonnett, *Employers' Associations*, 312.
10. *Ibid.*, 313.
11. *Loewe* v. *Lawlor*, 208 U.S. 274.
12. *Industrial Commission*, N, 291ff. and *passim*; Cochran, *Railroad Leaders*, 179.
13. Cochran, *Railroad Leaders*, 175.
14. See Cochran, *The Pabst Brewing Company*, 203-204, 250-251; and *Railroad Leaders*, 177.
15. *Historical Statistics*, 91.
16. *Industrial Commission*, IV, 290.
17. *Ibid.*, 20, 32-33, 308.
18. Cochran, *Pabst Brewing Company*, 253.
19. *Industrial Commission*, IV, 3, 22, 26, and *passim*; Cochran, *Railroad Leaders*, 179.
20. Cochran, *Pabst Brewing Company*, 253.
21. See Shaw Co., *Handling Men*, 47-52.
22. Nadworny, *Scientific Management*, 9.

CHAPTER 11

1. See for example DuBois, "The Dominant Value Profile of American Culture," L, 1233-1234; Greenstein, "Changing American Values," 441-450; and Lipset, *The New Nation*, 120ff.
2. Lerner, *America as a Civilization*, 626.
3. Wyllie, *Self-Made Man*, 14ff.; Elson, *Guardians of Tradition*, 252-254.
4. Bryce, *The American Commonwealth*, Hacker, ed., II, 457.
5. As quoted in Handlin, *This Was America*, 236.

6. *Ibid.*, 417.
7. As quoted in Wyllie, *Self-Made Man*, 90.
8. See Thernstrom, *Poverty and Progress*, for a view that there was less upward social mobility in nineteenth- than in twentieth-century America.
9. Wyllie, *Self-Made Man*, 116ff. and *passim*. See also Cawelti, *Self-Made Man*, 62, for the emphasis on luck rather than hard work in popular novels.
10. Calhoun, *American Family*, III, 166.
11. *Ibid.*, 145.
12. Smith, "socialization for Competence," 20.
13. Good, *The Family*, 77-78.
14. Quoted from Smith, "Socialization for Competence," 20. See also Whiting and Child, *Child Training*, 210; and Brim, "Socialization Through the Life Cycle," 1-5.
15. Abbott, *Gentle Measures*, 28, 268.
16. Trumbell, *Child Training*, 38.
17. Abbott, *Gentle Measures*, 271.
18. Kirkpatrick, *Use of Money*, 16, 69-70.
19. Stead, "Queen of American Democracy," 435.
20. Burrell, *Mother's Book*, 30.
21. See Hall, *Youth, passim*, and *Adolescence*, 406-407.
22. Paper on Boy Scouts of America by Jay Mechling, at University of Pennsylvania.
23. Birney, *Childhood*, 1. This book has an introduction by the famous psychologist, G. Stanley Hall.
24. Quoted from Cochran, *Inner Revolution*, 11.
25. Winterburn, *Nursery Ethics*, 151.
26. Jacoby, *Child Training*.
27. Perry, *Henry Lee Higginson*, 329.
28. See Tyack, "Bureaucracy and the Common School," 489.
29. See Cremin, *Ellwood Patterson Cubberley*, 38.
30. Kirkland, *Thought and Dream*, 53.
31. *Ibid.*, 70.
32. Cubberley, *Public Education*, 469.
33. Tyack, "Bureaucracy and the Common School," 489.
34. Solomon, *Cost of Schooling*, 63; and Fishlow, "American Investment in Education," 426.
35. Fishlow, "American Investment in Education," 432-433.
36. Cremin, *Ellwood Patterson Cubberley*, 38.
37. De Charms and Gerald B. Moeller,

"American Children's Readers," 136-142; see also Elson, *Guardians of Tradition.*

38. Elson, *Guardians of Tradition*, 246ff.
39. Curti, *Social Ideas*, 218.
40. *Ibid.*, 219-220.
41. Curti, *Social Ideas*, 220-221. See Kirkland, *Thought and Dream*, 69ff. for business review.
42. Tyack, "Bureaucracy and the Common School," 478.
43. Elson, *Guardians of Tradition*, 248-251.
44. Cubberley, *Public Education*, 410-415.
45. Haynes and Jackson, *Business Education*, 105.
46. Cubberley, *Public Education*, 416.
47. Haynes and Jackson, *Business Education*, 29-30.
48. Quoted from Lyon, *Education for Business*, 273.
49. U.S. Commissioner of Education, *Report*, II, 1443.
50. Kirkland, *Thought and Dream*, 78.
51. See Davis, "Business in High Schools," 804-808.
52. Bossard and Dewhurst, *University Education for Business*, 250.
53. Annual Report, 1894 in *Public School Journal*, 43 (Pennsylvania, 1894-95), 286. For the Pennsylvania history see microfilm thesis by William Issel, University of Pennsylvania (1969).
54. Wesley, *NEA*, 60.
55. Dewey, *Experience and Education*, 6, 87.
56. Hofstadter, *Anti-Intellectualism in American Life*, 377, 385. It is interesting to note that Dewey, like the rest of his generation, took an overly simply view of the decisive effect of conditioning on personality.
57. Callahan, *Cult of Efficiency*, 6-7.
58. Wesley, *NEA*, 240-241.
59. Callahan, *Cult of Efficiency*, 7-10.
60. NEA, *Proceedings, 1911*, 559-561. See also the discussion in Hofstadter, *Anti-Intellectualism in American Life*, 333-334.
61. Ellwood P. Cubberley, *Public School Administration*, 338, as quoted in Tyack, "Bureaucracy and the Common School," 496.
62. Cubberley, *Public Education*, 410.
63. Bossard and Dewhurst, *University Education for Business*, 248.
64. Lyon, *Education for Business*, 283.

65. U.S. Statutes at Large, XII, 503.
66. Boorstin, *National Experience*, 163.
67. Carnegie, *Empire of Business*, 80.
68. Goodstein, *Henry W. Sage*, 223.
69. Quoted from Cochran, *Railroad Leaders*, 211.
70. Canby, *Alma Mater*, 37-38.
71. DeVane, William C., "Higher Education," in Abrams and Levine, *Twentieth Century America*, 23.
72. As quoted in Cochran, *Railroad Leaders*, 81.
73. Cheyney, *University of Pennsylvania*, 294-295.
74. Bossard and Dewhurst, *Education for Business*, 252-257.
75. Goodstein, *Henry W. Sage*, 227.
76. DeVane, *Higher Education*, 31.
77. Goodstein, *Henry W. Sage*, 224
78. *Ibid.*, 225.
79. DeVane, *Higher Education*, 37 and 35.
80. Curti and Nash, *Philanthropy*, 215-217.
81. Lee, *The Daily Newspaper*, 166.
82. Peter A. Demens, "Sketches of the North American United States," in Handlin, *This Was America*, 351.
83. Lee, *The Daily Newspaper*, 528.
84. May, *Protestant Churches*, 86.
85. Quoted from Wyllie, *Self-Made Man*, 61.
86. *Ibid.*, 55.
87. Cawelti, *Self-Made Man*, 5.
88. McLoughlin, *Modern Revivalism*, 291.
89. Still, *Mirror for Gotham*, 223.
90. Kirkland, *Dream and Thought*, 11-12.
91. May, *Protestant Churches*, 44, 54.
92. *Ibid.*, 86.
93. *Ibid.*, 55n.
94. Henry Ward Beecher, "Liberty in the Churches," *Plymouth Pulpit*, II (March-September, 1874) (New York, 1896), 209. Quoted in Mead, "American Protestantism since the Civil War."
95. McLoughlin, *Modern Revivalism*, 301, 269n.
96. Quoted in May, *Protestant Churches*, 96. See also Cashdollar, "Religion and the Panic of 1872."
97. May, *Protestant Churches*, 111.
98. May, *Protestant Churches*, 106. See also Gutman, "Protestantism and the American Labor Movement," 74-101.
99. Hopkins, *Social Gospel*, 209.
100. *Ibid.*, 211.
101. Strong, *Our Country.*
102. Berghorn and Steere, "American Values," 52-62.

CHAPTER 12

1. Hurst, *Law and Social Progress*, 5.
2. John P. Roche, "Entrepreneurial Liberty and the Fourteenth Amendment," *Labor History*, IV (Winter, 1963), 3-31, reprinted in Abrams and Levine, *Twentieth Century America*, 125-153.
3. Hurst, *American Law*, 371.
4. *Ibid.*, 347.
5. See Friedman, *Contract Law*, 18ff, for the close relations, however, between "pure" contract law and laissez-faire economic principles.
6. Pound, *Legal History*, 111.
7. Hurst, *American Law*, 289.
8. Curti and associates, *American Community*, 249; and Hurst, *American Law*, 314.
9. Ari Hoogenboom, "Industrialism and Political Leadership," in Jaher, *Industrialism*, 54.
10. Graham, *Everyman's Constitution*, 497.
11. Hurst, *American Law*, 314.
12. Bryce, *The American Commonwealth*, II, 504, 508.
13. See Hofstadter, *Age of Reform*, 148-163 for a discussion of the legal profession at the turn of the century; and Warner, *The Private City*, for the general upper and middle-class attitudes.
14. Friedman, *Contract Law*, 209.
15. Cochran, *Railroad Leaders*, 193.
16. *Ibid.*, 190.
17. Hunt, *Law and the Locomotive*, 34.
18. See Pierce, *Railroads of New York*, 97-104.
19. *Ward* v. *Maryland*. For more examples, see Woolfolk, *The Cotton Regency*, 186-190.
20. Quoted in Graham, *Everyman's Constitution*, 530.
21. Hurst, *Law and Economic Growth*, 290, 344.
22. In Abrams and Levine, *Twentieth Century America*, 129.
23. Hurst, *Law and Economic Growth*, 468. See also Friedman, *Contract Law*, 184.
24. *Translation of the Code of Commerce*, Division of Customs and Insular Affairs, War Department (Washington, D.C.: Government Printing Office, 1899), Title III, Art. 33, 17; Art 48, 21-22.
25. Graham, *Everyman's Constitution*, 121.
26. 94 U.S. 113.
27. Cochran, *Railroad Leaders*, 191.
28. 134 U.S. 418. See Paul, *Conservative Crisis*, 39-44.
29. 169 U.S. 466, and 212 U.S. 19, respectively.
30. Roche, in Abrams and Levine, *Twentieth Century America*, 144.
31. See Warren, *The Supreme Court*, II, 626.
32. *Wabash, St. Louis and Pacific Railroad* v. *Illinois*, 118 U.S. 557.
33. *Leisey* v. *Hardin*, 135 U.S. 100.
34. Warren, *The Supreme Court*, II, 731ff.
35. Paul, *Conservative Crisis*, holds the count from 1886 to 1892 to be two to one against the validity of the legislative acts; see 45.
36. 113 Pa. St. 431, quoted from Paul, *Conservative Crisis*, 13-14.
37. Tiedeman, *Police Power*, 10.
38. 169 U.S. 366.
39. 198 U.S. 45.
40. 208 U.S. 412.
41. Abrams and Levine, *Twentieth Century America*, 125.
42. *New York Central Rail Co.* v. *White*, 243 U.S. 188; *Mountain Timber Co.* v. *State of Washington*, 243 U.S. 219; *Hawkins* v. *Bleakly*, 243 U.S. 210.
43. 156 U.S. 12.
44. *Trans Missouri Freight Association*, 166 U.S. 290; *Joint Traffic Association*, 171 U.S. 505; and *U.S.* v. *Addystone Pipe and Steel Co., et al.*, 175 U.S. 211.
45. 157 U.S. 429. See the excellent chapter on this case in Paul, *Conservative Crisis*, 185-220.
46. Paul, "Legal Progressivism," 507.
47. *Corrington Drawbridge Co.* v. *Shepard*, 21 How. 112.
48. *Fosdick* v. *Schall*, 99 U.S. 235.
49. Hurst, *Law and Economic Growth*, 121.
50. *Ibid.*, 416-421.

51. Abrams and Levine, *Twentieth Century America*, 125.
52. Friedman, *Contract Law*, 211.

CHAPTER 13

1. Stampp, *And the War Came*, 9-10; and Woolfolk, *The Cotton Regency*, 13.
2. Foner, *Business and Slavery*, 238.
3. Fish, *Civil War*, 104.
4. See Callender, "Early Transportation and Banking Enterprises," 111-162.
5. Hurst, *Law and Economic Growth*, 518.

6. Quoted in Mandelbaum, *Boss Tweed's New York*, 77.

7. Bryce, *The American Commonwealth*, II, 509.

8. Steffens, *Autobiography*, II, 465.

9. Bremner, *American Philanthropy*, 97-98.

10. Hartz, *Liberal Tradition*, chap. VIII.

11. Sturges, *American Chambers of Commerce*, 31, 41.

12. McKelvey, *Urbanization*, 43; Wade, *The Urban Frontier*, 205; Belcher, *St. Louis and Chicago*, 63-64, 69.

13. *Congressional Record*, 46th Congress, 392, 515, 516, 517, 749, 909, 932, 934.

14. See Nash, *California*, 26 and *passim*.

15. Benson, *Merchants, Farmers, and Railroads*, 25-27, 78-79, 119-124, 143-147, 220-221.

16. *Ibid.*, 188.

17. Sturges, *American Chambers of Commerce*, 45.

18. *Proceedings of the Adjourned Meeting of the National Board of Trade* (Chicago: Knight and Leonard, 1874).

19. See *Proceedings*, of the Annual Meetings of the National Board of Trade, 1873-1885.

20. See Hill, "Government Engineering Aid," 235-266.

21. Henry W. Broude, "The Role of the State in American Economic Development, 1820-1890," in Aitken, *The State and Economic Growth*, 24.

22. Hibbard, *Public Land Policies*, 235.

23. *Ibid.*, 236.

24. *Ibid.*, 239, 241.

25. Fogel, *The Union Pacific Railroad*, 49.

26. *Ibid.*, 103-110. Cochran, *Railroad Leaders*, 223. 223.

27. See Decker, "The Railroads and the Land Office," 679-699.

28. See for example Shannon, *The Farmer's Last Frontier*, chap. III.

29. Hamilton, *Men and Manners in America*, 278, 286.

30. Rothman, *Politics and Power*, 201.

31. Katz, *August Belmont*, 269.

32. See Coben, "Northeastern Business," 67-90.

33. *Ibid.*, 89.

34. Quoted from Gabriel Kolko, *Railroads and Regulation* 13.

35. See Josephson, *The Politicos*, 322-323.

36. Latham, *Communist Conspiracy*, 461.

CHAPTER 14

1. For business, see Hidy and Hidy, *Pioneering in Big Business*, 40-74; for political impact, see Hays, "Reform in Municipal Government," 164ff.

2. Haber, *Efficiency and Uplift*, 85, 113-114.

3. Sturges, *American Chambers of Commerce*, 169-189.

4. Hays, "Reform in Municipal Government," 168.

5. Bannister, *Ray Stannard Baker*, 146.

6. Steffens, *Shame of the Cities*, 3.

7. Hays, "Reform in Municipal Government," 164ff.

8. See Mandelbaum, *Boss Tweed's New York*, 130.

9. Bannister, *Ray Stannard Baker*, 55-56.

10. Sturges, *American Chambers of Commerce*, 137ff.

11. McKelvey, *Rochester*, 92-98.

12. Steffens, *Autobiography*, II, 598ff.

13. See for example, Ryan, *History of Ohio*, IV, 408-409.

14. Hays, "Social Analysis," 382.

15. Ellis, et al., *New York State*, 375.

16. Hurst, *Law and Economic Growth*, 139-140.

17. Atherton, *Main Street*, 333.

18. *Ibid.*, 339-340.

19. Sturges, *American Chambers of Commerce*, 45.

20. Steigerwalt, *National Association of Manufacturers*, 152-153.

21. Wiebe, *Businessmen and Reform*, 49.

22. *Ibid.*, 35-36.

23. *Ibid.*, 38.

24. Abrams, *Conservatism*, 65.

25. Cochran, *Railroad Leaders*, 170; Kolko, *Railroads and Regulation*, 15ff.

26. Cochran, *Railroad Leaders*, 197; Kirkland, *Thought and Dream*, 115ff.

27. Kolko, *Railroads and Regulation*, 39.

28. Cochran, *Railroad Leaders*, 198.

29. Ripley, *Railroads*, 463.

30. Kolko, *Railroads and Regulation*, 53.

31. *Report of the Industrial Commission*, vol. IV, Transportation (Washington, D.C.: Government Printing Office, 1900), 300 and *passim*.

32. *Ibid.*, 103.

33. Kerr, *Railroad Politics*, 11.

34. *Ibid.*, 134-135.

35. *Ibid.*, 186.

36. Wiebe, *Businessmen and Reform*, 86-87.

37. Raucher, *Public Relations and Business*, 21.
38. Kolko, *Conservatism*, 98-102.
39. *Adulturation of Food Products*, Senate Committee on Manufactures, Senate Report no. 516, Fifty-sixth Congress, first session (1900), 311-312.
40. See Kolko, *Conservatism*, 217-254.
41. Wiebe, *Businessmen and Reform*, 132.
42. Kolko, *Conservatism*, 264.
43. Davis, "Federal Trade Commission," 439.
44. Everett E. Edwards, "American Agriculture—The First 300 Years," in U.S. Department of Agriculture, *Farmers in a Changing World*, 245; and Wayne D. Rasmussen and Gladys L. Baker, "The Department is Built," in U.S. Department of Agriculture, *After One Hundred Years*, 9.
45. Wiebe, *Search for Order*, 178, 205.
46. U.S. Department of Agriculture, *Farmers in a Changing World*, 279. See also McConnell, *Agrarian Democracy*.
47. Turner, "The Problem of the West," 289-297.
48. Edwards, *Finance Capitalism*, 188.
49. Williams, *American Diplomacy*, 26. See also La Feber, *The New Empire*.
50. Steigerwalt, *National Association of Manufacturers*, 19.
51. *Ibid.*, 26.
52. May, *Imperial Democracy*, 26.
53. *New York Times*, January 1, 1900.
54. May, *Imperial Democracy*, 57-58, 63.
55. Williams, *American Diplomacy*, 33-34.
56. May, *Imperial Democracy*, 144.
57. Steigerwalt, *National Association of Manufacturers*, 55.
58. *Ibid.*
59. May, *Imperial Democracy*, 257.
60. See Keller, *The Life Insurance Enterprise*, 81-123, for insurance activities.
61. *Ibid.*, 154, 156.
62. Joseph, *Jewish Immigration*, 179-180.
63. For a discussion of business views on immigration restriction, see Wiebe, *Businessmen and Reform*, 182-185.

CHAPTER 15

1. See Lewis H. Blair, Woodward, *A Southern Prophecy*, xix-xxiii.
2. Grady McWhiney, "Reconstruction: Index of Americanism," in Sellers, *The Southerner*, 101.
3. *Historical Statistics*, 624.
4. *Ibid.*, 208, 75. Physicians numbered about 150,000 in 1915.
5. Atherton, *Main Street*, 148-170.
6. See, for example, Barclay, *Ducktown*.
7. Heald, *Social Responsibilities*, 6.
8. Still, *Mirror for Gotham*, 262.
9. Frances W. Gregory and Irene D. Neu, "The American Industrial Elite of the 1870's," in Miller, *Men in Business*, 195ff.
10. See Jaher, *Industrialism*, 188-262, and Kolko, in Wolff and Moore, *The Critical Spirit*, 343-363.
11. Bryce, *The American Commonwealth*, I, 174.
12. Miller, *Men in Business*, 286ff.
13. *Ibid.*, 289.
14. Miller, "American Historians and the Business Elite," 204.
15. *Ibid.*, 206.
16. Baltzell, *Protestant Establishment*.
17. Still, *Milwaukee*, passim. See also McKelvey, *Urbanization*.
18. See Baltzell, *Protestant Establishment*, 127-135.
19. For the later period, see Ratner, *Great American Fortunes*.
20. Bryce, *The American Commonwealth*, Hacker, ed., II, 452.
21. For example, see Presthus, *Men at the Top*, based on two small New York cities.
22. *Review of Reviews*, 25 (April, 1901), 432.
23. For all these figures, see *Historical Statistics*, 570-572; and Lee, et al., *Population Redistribution*, 519.
24. Diamond, *American Businessman*, 62.
25. *Ibid.*
26. Bremner, *American Philanthropy*, 97.
27. Scharf and Westcott, *History of Philadelphia*, II, 1449-1491.
28. Rosenberg and Rosenberg, "Pietism," 27ff.
29. *Ibid.*, 29
30. See Bremner, *American Philanthropy*, 108ff. for more discussion.
31. *Ibid.*, 109.
32. Hower, *History of Macy's*, 178.
33. For more on the business connections with architecture in this period, see Tunnard and Reed, *American Skyline*.
34. *American Art Annual*, 1-3 (1897-1899), passim.
35. See Haber, *Efficiency and Uplift*.

CHAPTER 16

1. Bendix, *Work and Authority in Industry*, 216.
2. See Cyert and March, *The Firm.*
3. *Statistical Abstract, 1967*, 484-491.
4. Worcester, *Monopoly*, 66.
5. *Historical Statistics*, 570. Unfortunately this table has not been continued in the annual *Statistical Abstracts.*
6. Quoted in Heald, *Social Responsibilities* 92.
7. *Ibid.*, 93.
8. *Ibid.*, 94, 107.
9. Harris, et al., *American Business Creed*, is largely based on the opinions of trade association and other professional spokesmen for business.
10. Silberman, *Automation*, 2.
11. *Ibid.*, 14.
12. See Chandler, *Giant Enterprise* for evolving forms of management; and Chandler, *Strategy and Structure* for the problems of diversification.
13. *Statistical Abstract, 1967*, 490. The figures are taken from *Fortune Magazine*'s annual supplement.
14. Heald, *Social Responsibilities*, 97.
15. See Raucher, *Public Relations and Business.*
16. Bernays, *Memoirs*, 288.
17. *Ibid.*, 384.
18. Long, "The Corporation and the Local Community," 123.
19. "The Changing Concept of 'Human Nature' in the Literature of American Advertising," Curti, 353.
20. Ferry, "Forms of Responsibility," 68.
21. Warner and Abbeglan, *Occupational Mobility*, 108.
22. *Fortune* (June, 1964), 184.
23. Warner and Abegglen, *Occupational Mobility* 55. See also tables in Heald, *Social Responsibilities*, 68-70.
24. Whyte, *Is Anybody Listening*, 180.
25. Guzzardi, "The Young Executives," 2.
26. *Fortune* (Aug., 1960), 108.
27. Mann, "Corporate Responsibility," 58.
28. Miller, "Business Morality," 99-100.
29. See "The Incredible Electrical Conspiracy," *Fortune*, (April, May, 1960) and Cochran, *Railroad Leaders*, 190ff.
30. Moore, *Corporation*, 186.
31. *Ibid.*, 24-25. For some examples of decisions in which profit considerations triumphed over social policy, see Miller, "Business Morality," 100.
32. *Fortune* (Aug., 1969), 92.
33. *Ibid.*, 164.
34. Leonard, "Towards a New Policy on Mergers," 33.
35. *Fortune* (Aug. l960), 109.
36. Cole, "Study of Entrepreneurship," 12.
37. Cawelti, *Self-Made Man*, 202.
38. Sutton, et al., *American Business Creed*, 251-262.

CHAPTER 17

1. Commons and associates, *History of Labor*, III, 30.
2. *Ibid.*, 31.
3. See Domhoff, *Who Rules America*, 138ff., for a recent discussion of "class" as used by social scientists.
4. *Industrial Relations: Final Report and Testimony*, vol. 8, 7795.
5. *Ibid.*, vol. 5, 4863.
6. *Ibid.*, vol. 3, 2385.
7. *Ibid.*, vol. 3, 2670.
8. *Ibid.*, vol. 1, 314.
9. *Ibid.*, vol. 3, 2709.
10. *Ibid.*, vol. 8, 7461.
11. Interchurch World Movement, *Steel Strike of 1919*, 179.
12. Perlman and Taft, *History of Labor*, IV, 491.
13. *Ibid.*, 494.
14. *Ibid.*, 494.
15 Prothero, *Dollar Decade*, 147-156.
16. Bonnett, *Employers Associations*, 509, 550.
17. Lester, *Economics of Labor*, 642.
18. U.S. Statutes at Large, (Seventy-third Congress, Second Session, vol. 48, Ch. 474), 945.
19. *Historical Statistics*, 98, and Bernheim and others, *Labor and Government*, 79.
20. *Report of the Committee on Education and Labor* (1939), 3, 48.
21. *Ibid.*, 116ff.
22. For the details of this history, see the four volumes of the *Report of the Committee on Education and Labor* (1939) already referred to.
23. For a detailed, scholarly discussion, see Fine, *Sit-Down.*
24. *Report of the Committee on Education and Labor* Part III, 110.
25. Mills, *New Men of Power*, 143.
26. *Ibid.*, 135.
27. McAdams, *Power and Politics*, 3.
28. *Ibid.*, 176ff.
29. *Ibid.*, 192.

30. Heald, *Social Responsibilities*, 290.
31. Rayback, *American Labor*, 454-455.
32. See Vidich and Bensman, *Small Town*, for a study of a township of 3,000 people in 1952.

CHAPTER 18

1. Heidbreder, *Seven Psychologies*, 198.
2. Warner and Abegglen, *Occupational Mobility*, 40, for family origins.
3. Watson, "Psychology as the Behaviorist Views it," 158-177. His most influential book was *Psychology from the Standpoint of a Behaviorist*.
4. Watson, *Infant and Child*, 12.
5. Leuchtenburg, *Perils of Prosperity*, 163.
6. Abbott, *Parents*, 123.
7. Steere, "Child Socialization."
8. *Ibid.*, Chap. IV.
9. O'Shea, *Child Training*, 28-29.
10. *Ibid.*, 28.
11. *Ibid.*, 128-129.
12. Potter, *People of Plenty*, 194, 208.
13. *Ibid.*, 193.
14. Lerner, *America as a Civilization*, 568.
15. Greenstein, "Changing American Values," 445.
16. Williams, "Individual and Group Values," 35.
17. Clyde Kluckhohn, "Have There Been Discernible Shifts in American Values During The Last Generation," in Morison, *The American Style*, 171-72. In this long essay Kluckhohn assembled a large amount of additional material measuring change, 145-217.
18. Cawelti, *Self-Made Man*, 208.
19. Beale, *Freedom of Teaching*, 256.
20. *National Education Association Proceedings* (1911), 559-561.
21. Hofstadter, *Anti-Intellectualism*, 336.
22. *Ibid.*, 264.
23. See Cochran, *Railroad Leaders*, 80-90, for earlier period; Cochran, *American Business System*, 70ff. for later period.
24. Curti, *Social Ideas*, 560.
25. Ford, *My Life and Work*, 212.
26. Dudden, "The Organization Man as Student," 286.
27. Quoted in Lyon, *Education for Business*, 104.
28. See Callahan, *Cult of Efficiency*, passim.
29. Dr. V. T. Thayer, quoted in Curti, *Social Ideas*, 564.
30. *The Schools and Business* (Washington,

D.C., n.d.) 23, quoted in Curti, *Social Ideas*, 563.
31. *Historical Statistics*, 209.
32. Lyon, *Education for Business*, 237.
33. *Journal of the NEA* (Jan., 1933), 1-2.
34. *School and Society* (Oct., 6, 1934), 440.
35. *Historical Statistics*, 208.
36. Cubberley, *Public Education*, 469 (quoted in Chap. XI).
37. Hofstadter, *Anti-Intellectualism*, 346.
38. *Ibid.*, 341.
39. "The Changing Business Education Curriculum," *American Business Education Yearbook* (1947), 108.
40. Hanna, *Education*, 77.
41. Beckman, "Failure of Education," 83-84.
42. *Life* (March 24, 1958), 25, 37.
43. Lynd and Lynd, *Middletown in Transition*, 218.
44. Curti and Nash, *Philanthropy*, 253.
45. United States Office of Education, *Bulletin #5-18=25* (1964), 85, 93.
46. Marshall and others, *Collegiate School of Business*, 5-9.
47. Bossard and Dewhurst, *University Education for Business*, 254, and Federal Bureau of Education, *Bulletin*, no. 26 (1929), 3.
48. *American Business Education Yearbook*, XIV (2957), 33.
49. Isaiah Bowman, "The Graduate School in American Democracy," United States Office of Education, *Bulletin*, no. 10 (1939), 6.
50. *American Business Education Yearbook*, XIV (1957), 46.
51. Hanna, *Education*, 22.
52. Clyde Kluckhohn, "Have There Been Discernible Shifts in American Values During the Last Generation?", in Morison, *The American Style*, 177.
53. *Ibid.*, 185.
54. Greenstein, "Changing American Values," 443.
55. Kluckhohn, "Discernible Shifts in American Values," in Morison, *The American Style*, 185.

CHAPTER 19

1. Lee, *The Daily Newspaper*, 537.
2. Banfield and Wilson, *City Politics*, 321.
3. Goldstein, *The Norristown Study*, 232-233.

4. Beard and Beard, *America in Mid-Passage*, 594.

5. Steinman, *Film and Society*, 51.

6. Potter, *People of Plenty*, 167ff.

7. *Ibid.*, 177.

8. *Ibid.*, 182.

9. McLuhan, *Understanding Media*, 64ff.

10. Banning, *Commercial Broadcasting Pioneer*, 132-133.

11. Dunlap, *Radio and Television Almanac*, 83ff.

12. Hoover, *Memoirs, 1920-1933*, 140.

13. Rothafel and Yates, *Broadcasting*, 88.

14. Ernst, *The First Freedom*, 159.

15. See Chappell and Hooper, *Radio Audience Measuremennt.* The effectiveness of magazine and newspaper advertising was also measured by these agencies.

16. Bogart, *The Age of Television*, 67.

17. Figures from McCann-Erickson, Inc., quoted in Bogart, *Age of Television*, 178-183.

18. Williams, *Listening*, 75.

19. Seldes, *The Public Arts*, 200.

20. Bogart, *Age of Television*, 67.

21. Glick, and Levy, *Living With Television*, 75ff. See also Bogart, *Age of Television*, and Skornia, *Television and Society*, 268.

22. Barnouw, *The Golden Web*, 264.

23. *Ibid.*.

24. *Ibid.*, 275, and Cogley, *Report on Blacklisting*, II, 248-249.

25. Muelder, *Religion and Economic Responsibility*, 20.

26. Bellah, "Civil Religion in America," 5.

27. Lynd and Lynd, *Middletown in Transition*, 374.

28. Callahan, *The New Church*, 154.

29. Ellis, *American Catholicism*, 142-143.

30. Carter, *Social Gospel*, 63.

31. Lynd and Lynd, *Middletown in Transition*, 350-351

32. *Ibid.*, 347-348.

33. *Ibid.*, 405.

34. See Gilkey, "Sources of Protestant Theology," 81.

35. Mathews, "Business, Maker of Morals," 398.

36. Purrington, "Big Ideas from Big Business," 395ff. Quoted from Huthmacher, *Twentieth Century America*, 170.

37. Barton, *The Man Nobody Knows.*

38. *Literary Digest* (Sept., 17, 1927), 30.

39. Carter, *Social Gospel*, 72.

40. *Ibid.*, 70.

41. *American Magazine* (March, 1926), 14-15, 208.

42. *Literary Digest* (June 11, 1927), 34.

43. Lynd and Lynd, *Middletown in Transition*, 347.

44. Meyer, *Political Realism*, 171-172.

45. Miller, *American Protestantism*, 121.

46. *Ibid.*, 77.

47. Meyer, *Political Realism*, 174.

48. Miller, *American Protestantism*, 122.

49. *Commonweal* (July 28, 1933), 320.

50. Ellis, *Documents*, 647.

51. Abell, *American Catholicism and Social Action*, 261-262.

52. *Historical Statistics*, 228.

53. Quoted in Herberg, *Protestant, Catholic, Jews*, 64-65.

54. *Ibid.*, 86.

55. See for example Forna and Miller, *Industry, Labor and Community*, 521.

56. *Time* (Feb., 23, 1962), 77.

57. Herberg, *Protestant, Catholic, Jew*, 88.

58. Forna and Miller, *Industry, Labor and Community*, 358-359.

59. Harrison, "Church and Laity Among Protestants," 47.

60. *Ibid.*

61. Forna and Miller, *Industry, Labor and Community*, 364.

62. Greenwalt, *The Uncommon Man*, 51.

63. See Hauser and Schnore, *The Study of Urbanization, passim,* and particularly "The Folk-Urban Ideal Types" by Oscar Lewis and Philip N. Hauser, 491-518.

64. McLuhan, *Understanding Media*, 2nd ed., first page (unnumbered).

CHAPTER 20

1. Siegfried, *America at Mid-Century*, 226.

2. Friedman, *Contract Law*, 183.

3. *Ibid.*, 188.

4. See Hurst, *Law and Social Progress*, 327-330.

5. Smith and Butters, *Taxable and Business Income*, xviii.

6. See Boudin, *Government by Judiciary*, II, 475-502.

7. See Vatter, *The U.S. Economy*, 210-216.

8. See Syrett, "Business Press," 226, for 1914-1917; and Adler, *The Isolationist Impulse*, 272ff., for 1940-1941.

9. Syrett, "Business Press," 219.

10. *Ibid.*, 224.

11. "Second Executive Forum," *Fortune* (Oct., 1940), 74-75.

12. "The Fortune Survey," *Fortune*, 22

(Nov., 1940), 77.

13. Lynd and Lynd, *Middletown in Transition*, 421.

14. Hero, *Opinion Leaders*, 7.

15. Banfield and Wilson, *City Politics*, 276.

16. Atherton, *Main Street*, 28ff; Curti and associates, American Community, 418-424.

17. Vidich and Bensman, *Small Town*, 101.

18. *Ibid.*, 100.

19. *Fortune*, 118.

20. Hero, *Opinion Leaders*, 3ff.

21. Hunter, *Community Power Structure*, 75.

22. See Banfield and Wilson, *City Politics*, 328-346.

23. Dahl, *Who Governs*. See also Banfield and Wilson, *City Politics*, 244; and Greer, *The Emerging City*, (1962).

24. Scott Greer, "Metropolitan Anomie and the Crisis in Leadership," in Baltzell, *Search for Community*, 153.

25. Lynd and Lynd, *Middletown in Transition*, 88.

26. See Presthus, *Men at the Top*, 410ff, for a summary discussion of local elites.

27. Banfield and Wilson, *City Politics*, 269.

28. See Scott Greer, "Metropolitan Anomie and The Crisis in Leadership," in Baltzell, *Search for Community*, 168.

29. For general discussion, see Banfield and Wilson, *City Politics*, 261-276.

30. Hero, *Opinion Leaders*, 8.

31. For the 1920s, see Gruening, *The Public Pays*; and Danielian, *A.T. & T.*; for similar nineteenth-century activities, see Cochran, *Railroad Leaders*.

32. Hunter, *Community Power Structure*, 150.

33. *Ibid.*, 155.

34. Walt W. Rostow, "The National Style," in Morison, *The American Style*, 284.

35. *American Magazine* (Feb., 1921), 16.

36. See Prothero, *Dollar Decade*.

37. Gabler, "The Advance and Equalization."

38. See Kerr, *Railroad Politics*, 101-127.

39. Davis, "Federal Trade Commission," 441-442.

40. Huthmacher, *Massachusetts People and Politics*, 59.

41. Nash, *United States Oil Policy*, 71-91.

42. See Kirkendall, "The New Deal as a Watershed," 839-852.

43. *Christian Century* (Sept. 24, 1932), 1096.

44. For cotton textiles that welcomed regulation, see Galambos, *Competition and Cooperation*, 173-202; for automobiles that opposed much of NIRA, see Fine, *The Automobile*, 44-74.

45. Galambos, *Competition and Cooperation*, 269.

46. See Brown, "The Rise of Business Opposition to Roosevelt."

47. Cleveland, "N.A.M.," 357.

48. Hoover, *Memoirs, 1929-1941*, 97.

49. Copeland, *It Takes Two*.

50. DiBacco, "American Business and Foreign Aid," 25.

51. *Ibid.*, 32.

52. For an analysis of the opinions in thirty-three business magazines from August 1964 to October 1967, see DiBacco, "The Business Press and Vietnam," 426-435.

53. *Time* (July 27, 1970), 67.

54. Zeigler, *Interest Groups*, 125. See also Cherington and Gillen, "The Company Representative in Washington," 113.

55. Kolko, *American Foreign Policy*, 46.

56. Lane, "Law and Opinion in the Business Community," 241.

57. Quoted from DiBacco, "The Political Ideas of American Business," 52.

58. Domhoff, *Who Rules America*, 153.

59. "Regulation by Elephant, Rabbit and Lark," *Fortune* (June, 1961), 137-139.

60. *Ibid.*, 237. See also *Business Week* (Aug. 3, 1968), 64, on shortage of top-level federal personnel.

61. "The Root of FTS's Confusion," *Fortune* (Aug., 1963), 156.

62. Zeigler, *Interest Groups*, 282.

63. See Cater, *Power in Washington*, 7 and *passim*.

64. Sherrill, "We Can't Depend on Congress," 6, 7.

65. Hunter, *Top Leadership*, 160.

66. See for example Mills, *The Power Elite*, 271-274.

67. *Ibid.*, 168, 232.

68. Zeigler, *Interest Groups*, 290, for change from the earlier period.

69. Hunter, *Top Leadership*, 256.

70. See Domhoff, *Who Rules America*, 138ff.; and Baltzell, *Protestant Establishment*, 277ff.

CHAPTER 21

1. Purington, "Big Ideas From Big Business," 395.

2. Friedgood, "Life in Buckhead," 109-111. 109-111.
3. *Ibid.*, 114-115.
4. See Cochran, *American Business System*, 177-178, but the complete results of this research have never been published.
5. Warner and Abegglen, *Occupational Mobility*.
6. Whyte, *The Organization Man*, 298.
7. Bendix, *Work and Authority in Industry*, table 214. In 1923 administrative employees were 15.6 percent of the total in industry; in 1947 the figure was 21.6 percent.
8. Andrews, *Corporation Giving*, 26-32.
9. Heald, *Social Responsibilities*, 117ff.
10. Lynd and Lyn., *Middletown in Transition*, 462-465.
11. Heald, *Social Responsibilities*, 161, 162.
12. *A. P. Smith Manufacturing Company v. Barlow et al.*, 13 N.J. 145, 98 A. 2d 551 (1953).
13. Heald, *Social Responsibilities*, 175.
14. *Ibid.*, 203.
15. *Statistical Abstract, 1967*, 311.
16. James, *Metropolitan Life*, 226-231.

17. Commons and associates, *History of Labor*, III, 385.
18. Latimer, *Industrial Pensions Systems*, I, 26-57, 474-477.
19. *Ibid.*, 843-847.
20. *Ibid.*, 296.
21. Heald, *Social Responsibilities*, 103, 105.
22. *Ibid.*, 260-263.
23. Fund-Raising Counsel, *Giving USA*, 22.
24. *Ibid.*, 18.
25. Kahn prepared a little booklet *Art and the People* for the New York Shakespeare Tercentenary. This is quoted from in an article in *Current Opinion*, January and February, 1917. Above statement, February, 139.
26. *Statistical Abstract, 1967*, 314.
27. Chamberlin, "Mind of the Firm," 145.
28. Williams, "Individual and Group Values," 36.
29. Silk, "Business Power, Today and Tomorrow," 188.
30. *Ibid.*, *passim*, and also 157, 187.
31. *Ibid.*, 174.
32. *Ibid.*, 179-180.
33. *Ibid.*, 183.
34. *Ibid.*, 167ff.

Index

It is the author's feeling that a topical index dealing with those aspects of our history which influenced and were influenced by business in America will be of more value to the reader of this work than the familiar factual presentation of names, dates, and places. The detailed Table of Contents and the chronological presentation within the work will readily allow one to locate specific historical periods and events. The index is intended to serve as an aid in tracing important factors in the development of business in the context of our national history.

overseers, 18
paternalistic, 84
pension plans, 168
power of, 85
problems, 84
as a profession, 251
profit sharing, 168
rise of, 245ff.
small, 82
specialization, 79
stock purchase plans, 168
and stockholders, 78
structure of, 81
supervision, 17
and technology, 81
as trustees, 85
unions, to check, 168
worker fear of company "welfare," 168
Managers, 161
Managerial enterprise, 75, 85, 141, 146, 160, 161
beginning of, 84
defined, 84
not fully aware, 168′
Markets, 22, 23, 26, 32, 63, 69,, 72, 90-91, 141, 152, 156
adjustments, 152
city, 133-134
competitive, 147
expanding, 146
immediate gains, 86
laws of, 99
for manufacturers, 74
mistakes, 134
national, 120, 145, 157
pressures, 153
regulation of, 133
security, 157
towns, 131
type of, 87
Marketing, 69-70, 81
branches, 150
expediters, 150
importance of, 150
mail-order catalogues, 150
new ways of, 150
securities, 155-156
television and radio advertising, 294
traveling salesman, 150
Mass Media
advertising, electronic, 291
and business upper class, 185
culture, uniform national, 287
education by, 184
"electronic revolution," 292
elite, opinions of, 185
magazines, 71, 288-289
role in business, 289
moving pictures, 289-291
and a national community, 287
newspapers, 71, 184, 288
as agency for new business, 185
as big business, 185
editorial grants, 185

one-cent, 185
role in community, 288-289
Outlines of Political Economy, 128
Patron of Industry, 128
patronage, 185
press associations, 186
radio, 288
censorship, 293
market value of time, 293
small business, means for cultural re-enforcement, 185
Merchants, 19, 20-25, 32, 36, 37, 38, 40, 47, 49, 50, 53, 56-57, 61-62, 80, 82
acquisitiveness of, 136
appreciation of the arts, 135
banking, 131
and British imperial system, 51
business roles, luxurious character of, 54
chief businessmen, 62
check democracy, 112
in colonial period paintings, 55
conservative leaders, 65
control of cities, 132
and education, 99
failure, 66
influence, 48-49
influence, 65
and law, 114
in the majority, 48
patronage of arts, 135
power of, 48
protected by England, 52
Quaker, 40
real estate, 24
redefinition of term, 65
religion, *see* Religion, merchants
resistance to regulations, 52
set standards of living, 135
and social reform, 137
social responsibilities of, 136
Migration, 18-19, 56, 65, 77, 86, 88, 109, 133, 138, 141, 158
business, 147
of business elite, 330
colonial, 10-14
conformity, 330
and dishonesty, 158
effects of, 230, 233, 287
emigration of skilled workers, 75
from England, 13
from failure, 91
immigrants, 83
immigration, 28
control of, 228
national origins, 228
restrictions, 228-229
impersonality, 158
inland, 29
missionaries, 110
of Negroes, 262
from New England, 110
opportunities, 132
of service, 249
sound business, 110

Catalog

If you are interested in a list of fine Paperback
books, covering a wide range of subjects
and interests, send your name and address,
requesting your free catalog, to:

McGraw-Hill Paperbacks
1221 Avenue of Americas
New York, N.Y. 10020